In Part I of this posthumous collection of essays, Marshall G. S. Hodgson examines the place both of Europe and of modernity in world history. The result is a challenging contribution to the current debate on Eurocentrism and multiculturalism. In Part II Hodgson seeks to locate Islamic civilization in a world historical framework. Finally in Part III, he argues that in the end there is but one history – global history – and that all partial or privileged accounts must necessarily be resituated in a world historical context. The book also includes an introduction and a conclusion by the editor, Edmund Burke, III, contextualizing Hodgson's contribution to world history and Islamic history.

Rethinking world history

Studies in Comparative World History

Editors

Michael Adas, Rutgers University
Edmund Burke, III, University of California, Santa Cruz
Philip D. Curtin, The Johns Hopkins University

Other books in the series

Michael Adas, *Prophets of Rebellion: Millenarian Protest Movements against the European Colonial Order* (1979)
Philip D. Curtin, *Cross-Cultural Trade in World History* (1984)
Leo Spitzer, *Lives in Between: Assimilation and Marginality in Austria, Brazil, West Africa, 1780–1945* (1989)
Philip D. Curtin, *The Rise and Fall of the Plantation Complex: Essays in Atlantic History* (1990)
John Thornton, *Africa and Africans in the Formation of the Atlantic World, 1400–1680* (1992)

Rethinking world history

ESSAYS ON EUROPE, ISLAM, AND WORLD HISTORY

MARSHALL G. S. HODGSON

Edited, with an Introduction and Conclusion by
EDMUND BURKE, III

Published by the Press Syndicate of the University of Cambridge
The Pitt Building, Trumpington Street, Cambridge CB2 1RP
40 West 20th Street, New York, NY 10011-4211, USA
10 Stamford Road, Oakleigh, Victoria 3166, Australia

First published 1993

Printed in the United States of America

Library of Congress Cataloging-in-Publication Data

Hodgson, Marshall G. S.

Rethinking world history : essays on Europe, Islam, and world history / Marshall G.S. Hodgson ; edited, with an introduction and conclusion by Edmund Burke, III.

p. cm. – (Studies in comparative world history)

ISBN 0-521-43253-7. – ISBN 0-521-43844-6 (pbk.)

1. World history. 2. Europe – Civilization – Islamic influences. 3. Civilization, Islamic – Western influences. 4. History – Philosophy. I. Burke, Edmund, 1940– . II. Title. III. Series.

D21.3.H63 1993

909 – dc20 92–32575

CIP

A catalog record for this book is available from the British Library.

ISBN 0-521-43253-7 hardback
ISBN 0-521-43844-6 paperback

Contents

Editor's preface

Marshall G. S. Hodgson is known primarily as the author of the masterful three-volume *The Venture of Islam: Conscience and History in a World Civilization* (Chicago: The University of Chicago Press, 1974). That he was also a world historian who in addition to a number of seminal articles left a posthumous work, "The Unity of World History," is known to few. Hodgson died in 1968 at the age of 46, leaving this work unfinished.

Although I was never privileged to know Marshall Hodgson, I have been continually nourished by his thoughts about world history. For some time, I have felt that a collection of the best of Hodgson's writings on world history could provide an important contribution to current discussions about world history and the place of Europe in it. Many of the essays included here were published previously, although only a few have received anything like the audience they deserve. They date from the 1940s to the 1960s;[1] however, their conceptual brillance and methodological rigor are still relevent today.

The essays in Part I of this book explore the place of Europe in world history, challenging adherents of both Eurocentrism and multiculturalism. The Part II essays are concerned with Hodgson's parallel effort to locate the history of Islamic civilization in a world historical framework. The essays in Part III argue that in the end there is but one history – global history – and that all partial or privileged accounts must necessarily be resituated in a world historical context. My retrospective appreciation of Hodgson's three-volume *Venture of Islam* as a work of world history concludes this book.

Hodgson's spelling, use of neologisms, and transliteration of Middle Eastern terms deserve comment. As with everything else, Hodgson's

[1] I discuss the provenance of the essays included in this book in the introduction which follows.

prose was an expression of his methodological self-consciousness and dissatisfaction with conventional terminology. (In Chapter 5, "Historical Method in Civilizational Studies," he argues for the necessity of devising new terms, and of self-consciousness in the use of language by historians.)

I have sought to remain faithful to the original spelling employed by Hodgson insofar as possible. His transliteration of Arabic and other Middle Eastern languages has been simplified, however, in the interests of presenting a more readable text. The specialist will know the appropriate transliteration to insert, and the general reader will not be inconvenienced. A glossary of Islamic terms has been appended at the end of this volume. While many of the essays included here were published previously in a variety of different venues, in the interests of consistency, spelling has been conformed throughout.

At the suggestion of Professor Eugene Gendlin of The University of Chicago, Hodgson's literary executor, I came to see the possibility of publishing the best of Hodgson's writings on world history. The encouragement from his widow, Mrs. Phyllis Hodgson, helped me see this project through to completion. Support for the editing of this volume came primarily from research funds of the Division of Humanities, University of California at Santa Cruz. I wish here to record my debt to Michael Cowan, former Dean of Humanities. Finally, I am especially grateful to Helen Wheatley (who input the text) and to Zoe Sodja (who prepared the final manuscript) of the U.C.S.C. Word Processing Center. My thanks to them both.

Introduction: Marshall G.S. Hodgson and world history

Edmund Burke III

Something important has been happening to the writing of world history in the past two decades. A scholarly tradition that was rooted in the paradigm of civilizational studies has been challenged from both within and without. As a result of the collapse of the sense of moral exceptionalism which had privileged the West above the rest of humanity as well as a new sense of global interdependency, historians have expanded their focus. As a consequence, comparative history has had an increasing impact even on the writing of American history. Neither the history of slavery in the Old South nor that of Reconstruction will ever again be the same. The contribution of Marxism to this new awareness of the ways in which the different societies are linked to one another in time and space is evident. Immanuel Wallerstein, Eric Hobsbawm, Eric Wolf – but also Andre Gunder Frank and Samir Amin – have developed historical accounts of the rise of capitalism that stress the shaping impact of the world economy.[1] In so doing they have devised new conceptual tools for discussing the history of humanity, and a new terrain on which to situate it. The social and economic interactions of peoples, rather than the cultural interchanges of civilizations, constitute the basic building blocks of this new perspective.

Important though the contributions of those working within the Marxist tradition have been, the remaking of world history owes perhaps more to the work of William McNeill, whose *The Rise of the West* has provided students with a comprehensive account of the history of the

[1] Immanuel Wallerstein, *The Modern World System*, 2 vols. (New York: Academic Press, 1974, 1977); Eric Hobsbawm, *The Age of Revolution, 1789–1848* and *The Age of Reform, 1848–1875* (New York: New American Library 1962, 1975); Eric Wolf, *Europe and the People Without History* (Berkeley: University of California Press, 1982); Andre Gunder Frank, *World Accumulation, 1492–1789* (New York: Monthly Review Press 1978); Samir Amin, *Unequal Development* (New York: Frank 1976).

world within the tradition of civilizational studies.[2] McNeill's innovation was to unhook the study of civilizations from the Procrustean bed of metaphysics – whether it be the pessimism of Spengler or the cyclicalism of Toynbee. Borrowing the concept of cultural diffusion from anthropology, McNeill's world history is one in which what goes around comes around – but where inexplicably the West is the principal beneficiary. As opposed to those working in the Marxist tradition, whose concern with the development of capitalism has led them to focus almost exclusively upon the post-1500 period, McNeill situates the emergence of modernity in the context of all of human history. This permits a less presentist and less Eurocentric discussion of the shape of the human past – though as the title of his book suggests, some difficulties remain. Indeed, for both Marxists and followers of McNeill the place of Europe in the history of humankind and of modernity in global time perspective continues to be problematic. It is here that the contribution of Marshall G. S. Hodgson may be relevant.

While McNeill was writing his magnum opus at The University of Chicago during the 1950s, his colleague and friend Marshall Hodgson was simultaneously at work on his three-volume *The Venture of Islam: Conscience and History in a World Civilization*.[3] An Islamicist and Quaker, Hodgson operated in the tradition of textual analysis called orientalism, and utilized the civilizations approach to the history of Islamic peoples. However, unlike standard orientalist accounts, *The Venture of Islam* situates the history of Islamic civilization in the context of world history, and not just that of the Middle East. It is this dual aspect of Hodgson's work, together with his methodological self-consciousness and moral sensitivity, that constitutes his chief claim upon our attention. As the chair of the interdisciplinary Committee on Social Thought at Chicago (which has rather different emphases in its current incarnation) until his death in 1968, Hodgson was deeply engaged in an effort to rethink the philosophical and historical traditions of Western civilization. With his vast erudition and enormous self-confidence, Hodgson was a formidable figure. (I'll have more to say about the Chicago environment in my concluding essay.)

It is not generally known that Marshall Hodgson was also a world historian of unusual rigor and commitment.[4] As a world historian, Hodg-

[2] *The Rise of The West: A History of the Human Community* (Chicago: The University of Chicago Press, 1963).

[3] Chicago: The University of Chicago Press, 1974.

[4] For example, Hodgson does not figure in Gilbert Allardyce's otherwise thorough and insightful survey, "Toward World History: American Historians and the Coming of the

son was concerned with locating the history of the civilization he called Islamic in the context both of West Asian history and of all of prior human history. "Mankind is the only ultimately tenable field of discourse of all human inquiry and consideration of meaningfulness," he remarks at one point. Anything less might permit Eurocentric and presentist biases to distort the basis of the inquiry. For this reason as well, he compared the development of Islamic civilization at particular points in its history with the history of Western European civilization the better to defuse the incipient European exceptionalism which has marked most orientalist writings about Islam.

Among Hodgson's earliest writings (1941) is an essay (written at the age of 19) outlining a new conceptual approach to world history. For the next 25 years he continually reworked this early piece, which went through a number of different forms, always changing, always deepening.[5] Over the years that followed, Hodgson's thoughts on how to reconceptualize world history and the place of Europe in it were published in a number of seminal articles. Others were included in *The Venture of Islam.* Versions of these essays and others that he did not live to complete were to be included in his unpublished manuscript, "The Unity of World History."

Because of the way Hodgson worked, his unpublished book-length work, "The Unity of World History," has not yet found a publisher. (He constantly revised this manuscript, publishing parts in articles or borrowing them for *The Venture.*) Much of what he has to say on the shape of

World History Course," *Journal of World History* I, 1 (1990), 23–76, which includes some important pages on what might be called the "Chicago school" of world historians: Louis Gottschalk, L. S. Stravrianos, and William McNeill (though in fact much separates the approaches of the three men).

5 The Hodgson papers at the Department of Special Collections of the Joseph Regenstein Library at The University of Chicago allow us to follow this evolution in detail. The essay published here as Chapter 3, "World History and a World Outlook," which dates from 1944, was the first published expression of his distinctive approach to world history. In 1945, inspired by the title of an article by Margaret Cameron, he planned to call his world history "There Is No Orient." Its purpose was to be "to combat western provincialism." Later, in 1955, he spoke of what he called My Epic History: "I have in mind something on the order of the *Divina Commedia,* an imaged world-view like Milton or Ibn Arabi, i.e., epic or occult with the hope it might displace works such a Toynbee's." In October 1960 he referred to the book as "The Structure of World History: an Essay on Medieval and Modern Eurasia." By 1962, the chapter outline resembled the table of contents of his eventual "Unity of World History" unpublished manuscript (the last three chapters of which are reprinted in the present volume). World federalism, for which he had a youthful affection, gradually dropped by the wayside, as did the romantic enthusiasm of casting it in the form of an epic. By examining the gradual transformtions of the project over the period from its inception, we see the maturing of a young scholar into an established professional.

world history in the "Unity" manuscript, for example, exists in a more finished form in his world history articles or as sections in *The Venture of Islam*. Finally, it should be noted that since Hodgson began working on the manuscript in the 1950s, portions of it are simply obsolete. (World historians such as Alfred Toynbee and Harry Elmer Barnes are no longer widely read, their insights long bypassed by the development of the field.)

As an anoynmous reader of "The Unity of World History" manuscript a decade ago, I was much struck both by its enormous potential importance to world historians, and by the unlikelihood a publisher would be willing to undertake it. If "The Unity of World History" was unlikely to be published, I began to wonder, might it be possible to make a book of the published articles and some of the selected chapters of the "Unity" manuscript? I decided to try. Research in the Hodgson papers on deposit in the Department of Special Collections of The Joseph Regenstein Library of The University of Chicago in June 1987 turned up a few additional essays that might be included. I also found a note in Hodgson's hand (undated, *c.* 1962) suggesting that he had thought of collecting his essays on world history, including sections of *The Venture of Islam*, into a book. The selection of chapters for this book has been guided by this list.

Because of my conviction that Hodgson's conceptual approach and methodological rigor have an important contribution to make to current efforts to develop global history, I decided to gather the best of Hodgson's scattered writings on Islam and world history into this volume. I have grouped the essays included here in three sections.

A central focus of Hodgson's writings on world history was to resituate the history of the West in a global context, and in the process unhook it from Eurocentric teleologies (or what we might call, post-Foucault, the European master discourse on itself). The essays in Part I, "Europe in a Global Context," group together some of Hodgson's most important work on this topic. His article, "The Interrelations of Societies in History," which first appeared in 1963 is probably best known among them.[6] The early essays "In the Center of the Map" and "World History and a World Outlook" provide an accessible introduction to his conceptual

[6] "The Interrelations of Societies in History," *Comparative Studies in Societies and History*, V (1963), 227–250. An earlier version of this article was published in *Cahiers d'histoire mondiale/Journal of World History* I (1954), 715–723. (Both articles are themselves reworkings of Hodgson's 1941 unpublished letter, written while he was an undergraduate at The University of Chicago.) His unpublished "Unity of World History" manuscript from which we have excerpted chapters 11–13, included in this volume) itself derives from this precocious piece.

approach to world history.[7] The problem of modernity, and how one may situate it historically – as a global process rooted in Europe or as a specifically European manifestation – is broached in "The Great Western Transmutation."[8] The chapter "Historical Method in Civilizational Studies" presents Hodgson's views on the perils and pitfalls of doing world history without first thinking through some of the major epistemological and conceptual issues.[9] It is Hodgson at his teacherly best. Finally, the fragment "On Doing World History" presents in brief compass one of the most lucid brief presentations of the main points of Hodgson's approach to world history, in which he develops a brief critique of William McNeill's book, *The Rise of the West.* (It is an excerpt from a letter to John Voll of the University of New Hampshire dated December 16, 1966.) Hodgson was an inveterate letter-writer, and some of his best ideas first appeared in letter form, including the germ from which "The Unity of World History" eventually emerged – it first appeared in a letter in 1941.

In Part II, "Islam in a Global Context," one can find some of Hodgson's main statements on Islam and world history. "The Role of Islam in World History" is a tour de force overview of the history of Islamic civilization.[10] The essay "Cultural Patterning in Islamdom and the Occident" first appeared in *The Venture of Islam.*[11] It presents a remarkable sustained comparison of Islamic civilization and Western European civilization. The writing is dense but the ideas enormously stimulating. "The Unity of Later Islamic History" argues that there was an underlying unity to post-Mongol Islamic history – against what was then the established scholarly orthodoxy.[12] In the chapter "Modernity and the Islamic Heritage," Hodgson reflects on the situation of modern Muslims. Here, as so often, he anticipated events.[13]

Part III of this book, "The Discipline of World History," brings together

[7] "In the Center of the Map," *UNESCO Courier* (May 1956), 16–18; "World History and a World Outlook," *The Social Studies* 35 (1944), 297–301. The latter essay bears the dateline: Camp Elkton, Elkton, Oregon. It may be helpful to know that Hodgson was a Quaker pacifist who was interned during World War II for his views. Camp Elkton was established to house Quaker conscientious objectors. (On the intellectual importance of Hodgson's Quakerism, see my essay at the end of this text, *passim.* The influence of ideas of world federalism on this essay is striking. This theme, so strong in his early conceptualizations of global history, gradually diminished over time.)

[8] Originally published in *Chicago Today* (1967). The reworked version included here was originally published in *The Venture of Islam,* Vol. 3, Book 6, Chap. 1, pp. 176–200.

[9] It was first published as the prologue to *The Venture of Islam* (Chicago: The University of Chicago Press, 1974), Vol. 1, 22–74.

[10] *International Journal of Middle East Studies,* I (1970), 99–123.

[11] *The Venture of Islam,* Vol. 2 (1974), 329–368.

[12] *Journal of World History,* 5 (1960), 879–914.

[13] *Islamic Studies,* I (1962), 89–129.

the last three chapters of Hodgson's unpublished work. "The Unity of World History." Here Hodgson discusses the question of objectivity in world history, presents his reflections on historical comparison, and argues for world history as *the* master discipline which alone can give sense to historical inquiry at lesser levels of generalization. Many of his thoughts continue to have relevance to current discussions about world history as a scholarly endeavor.

The book concludes with my essay, "Islamic History as World History: Marshall G. S. Hodgson and *The Venture of Islam*," which provides a series of reflections on the ways these two themes continually interacted in Hodgson's thought.

Islam and the West: Resituating Western civilization

The recent debate provoked by Edward Said's *Orientalism*[14] is a strategic place to begin a reassessment of the relationship of the history of the West to that of rest of the world. Said stresses the putative role of orientalism as a discipline in the extension of European hegemony over the Middle East, and more generally the ways orientalism as a discourse of power was predicated upon the domination of the West over the non-West. On a deeper level, however, Said's approach implicitly questions the validity of civilizational studies, in particular the view that a civilization's Great Books provide the key to its special character. If orientalism is the discourse on the Other, as Said asserts, then it might be argued that Western civilization is the discourse on ourselves. It is here (despite evident differences) that Said's critique joins that of Hodgson, for whom essentialism is a central trait of civilizational studies. At the same time it is important to note that despite Hodgson's awareness of the limitations of the civilizational approach to the study of world history, he remained committed to it.

For Hodgson, before one could engage in the critique of Western civilization, there was an epistemologically prior step: it lay in recognizing that all works are the products of their author's *precommitments*, which fundamentally shape their understanding of the phenomenon in question. For Hodgson, these include not only religious affiliations, but also Marxism and (more surprisingly) what he calls *Westernism*. More clearly than many

[14] Edward Said, *Orientalism* (New York: Pantheon, 1978). See also Hichem Djait, *Europe and Islam* (Berkeley: University of California Press, 1985); Malcolm Kerr (ed.), *Islamic Studies: A Tradition and Its Problems* (Santa Monica: Undena Publications, 1980); Bryan S. Turner, *Marx and the End of Orientalism* (London: Allen & Unwin, 1978); and Jean-Claude Vatin, *Connaissances du Maghreb: Sciences sociales et colonisation* (Paris: C.N.R.S., 1984).

more recent authors, Hodgson does not presume to be speaking from some epistemologically sanitized space, in which one is liberated from having one or more precommitments; rather, he assumes we all have precommitments which both enable and constrain our understanding in various ways. (See Chapter 5 for a more complete elaboration.)

For both Hodgson and Said, Western civilization as a discourse is predicated upon a deeply rooted sense of the moral as well as cultural superiority of Western Europe to the rest of humanity. Both orientalism and Western civilization begin in the textualist position that civilizations have essences, and that these essences are best seen in the Great Books they have produced. (Who decides what's a Great Book, or what connection it might have to the lived lives of men and women in particular places and times is never satisfactorily explained.) The textualist position foreshortens history, annihilates change, and levels difference the better to represent an image of the past in dramatic form – either as tragedy, as in the case of Islamic civilization, or as triumph, as in the case of the rise of the West. In either case, it is a story whose rhythms are guided by the ineluctable working out of civilizational essences allegedly encoded in foundation texts. Thus we get the history of the West as the story of freedom and rationality, or the history of the East (pick an East, any East) as the story of despotism and cultural stasis. While the concept of discourse was unavailable to Hodgson, his understanding of the essentializing tendency in Westernist scholarly precommitments anticipates in important ways the work of Foucault, Said, and others.

Marshall Hodgson clearly saw that Islamic history was a strategic point from which to undertake a critique of the discourse on Western civilization. (Though the nature of that critique was always blunted by his commmitment to the civilizations as a unit of analysis.) As he notes, Islamic civilization is the sister of our own. Its roots lie in the same basic Irano-Semitic religious and cultural values, crossed with the ambiguous legacy of West Asian imperium. Islam was the vastly richer and more successful Other against which the West defined itself. Seen in perspective, the history of the Occident and of Islamdom makes a fascinating study in the emergence of two distinctively different yet suggestively similar societies, both of which traffic in blends of Hellenistic learning, West Asian prophetic monotheism, and agrarian-based bureaucratic empires. The study of Islamic civilization thus almost by necessity invites a reexamination of European history in which its development can be placed in world historical context, and in the process, de-exceptionalized.

Moreover, the fact of Islam's spread from the Middle East throughout the rest of Afro-Eurasia further undermines the dominant paradigm of the Great Books variety of civilizational studies. The global reach of Islam as a religion spawned a host of Islamic societies, and in the process broke down the walls between the regional civilizations of Afro-Eurasia. The interaction between local societies and the formative ideals of the religion necessarily led to the proliferation of myriad new social and cultural hybrid forms, which while undeniably Islamic, were also patently Chinese, African, Turkish. Thus for example, we get distinctive regional styles of mosque architecture – pagoda-like in Peking, mud brick in Timbuctu, or the needle minarets and vaulting domes of Istanbul mosques. Islamic civilization, by the messy way it spills over the conventional regional boundaries between world civilizations to assert its presence throughout Afro-Eurasia, points toward a more global, pluralistic, and interactional image of the history of world societies. At the same time, it subverts the dominant idea of world history as the story of static civilizational essences in which the couplets East and West, traditional and modern, constitute the conceptual underpinnings. As a world historian, Marshall Hodgson instinctively grasped the subversive potential of Islam's ubiquity for the study of civilizations. (At the same time, his Toynbeean commitment to the civilization as a unit of analysis undermined some of the salience of his insights.)

In his seminal article "The Interrelations of Societies in History,"[15] Hodgson made a key conceptual breakthrough which enabled him to situate both Islamic and European civilization in the context of world history. In it, he argued that from a world historical point of view the history of civilization is necessarily an Asia-centered history. He notes that the interconnecting band of agrarian citied societies which spanned the entire Afro-Eurasian landmass from China to Western Europe (an ensemble of civilizations which he calls, after Toynbee, the Oikoumene)[16] is predominantly Asian. (Four of the five major civilizations are Asian.) It followed, for him, that an interregional hemispheric approach to history was logically superior to approaches which placed the West at the center of history. Moreover, he observed, not until around 1500 did Western Europe reach the cultural level of the other major civilizations of Afro-Eurasia.

In his approach to world history, Hodgson took nothing for granted. He even questioned the validity of our images of the world, notably the venerable Mercator projection map. In his article "In the Center of the Map" (Chapter 2 in this volume), he points out how the Mercator projec-

[15] *Comparative Studies in Society and History*, 5 (1963), 227–250.
[16] Which McNeill renders as *ecumene*.

tion, because it is centered upon Western Europe, systematically distorts our image of the southern hemisphere, whose actual land area is substantially larger than the map indicates. For this reason, Hodgson referred to it as "the Jim Crow projection." Although Europe has approximately the square mile area of the other two peninsulas of Asia, India and Southeast Asia, he notes, Europe is called a continent, while India is but a subcontinent, and Southeast Asia has not even that status. Each has approximately the same number of major river systems, language groups, etc. The size of Africa is even more drastically reduced in the Mercator projection.

One of the most important conceptual moves that Hodgson made in *The Venture of Islam* was to focus on what he called "the Middle Periods" (pointedly not the Middle Ages) of Islamic history. (See Chapter 9.) By this he meant the period from the decline of the Abbasid caliphate as a centralized bureaucratic empire (*c.* A.D. 945) until the rise of the gunpowder empires in the sixteenth century. This focus was important for several reasons. First, although conventional scholarship emphasized that after A.D. 945 Islamic societies entered into a long period of decline from which they allegedly emerged only in the nineteenth century, Hodgson noted that the most celebrated cultural, scientific, and artistic figures of Islamic civilization (including among others, Ibn Sina, al-Ghazali, al-Biruni, and al-Firdawsi) lived after this date, and that this alone would call for a searching reevaluation. Hodgson's emphasis on the Middle Periods enabled him to argue that Arabic was not the only Islamic language of culture. Rather, from A.D. 945 Persian and Turkish played major roles in the elaboration of a cosmopolitan Islamic culture. It is this which provides a key to grasping the hemisphere-wide role of Islam in China, India, South and Southeast Asia, as well as the Balkans and the Maghrib. The Middle Periods were times of the greatest advances of Islamic civilization. Thus Hodgson's reexamination of the traditional periodization led to a remarkably fruitful reinvention of how Islamic civilization might be conceived, this time not as a truncated version of Europe, but in a world historical context and on its own terms.

By giving equal time to the Middle Periods, Hodgson was able to reassess the impact of the Mongol invasions on West Asia. As he shows, it was catastrophic, leading to the depopulation of much of the countryside, the destruction of many cities, and the collapse of the political and cultural infrastructure. Moreover, the Mongols did not depart, as barbarian hordes generally did. They remained in place, and Mongol successor states ruled western Asia until the end of the fifteenth century. The gunpowder empires which emerged from the rubble were profoundly marked by the experience, their possibilities of action sharply constrained by the heavy adverse impact of two centuries of pastoralist occupation. While Islamdom was enduring two centuries of decline and cultural turmoil under the Mongol yoke, Western Europe was undergoing the series of transformations which were to give rise to modernity. If we are to understand the rise of the West, Hodgson cautions us, we must first grasp the meaning of this parallel history.

Islam and the problem of modernity

One of Hodgson's most important contributions was his reevaluation of modern (i.e., post-1500) history and the place of Europe in it. The fact that Marshall Hodgson was a student of Islamic history helped him to attain a different view of modernity, one at least partly shorn of the Western exceptionalism which was a major feature of the modernization theory of his day. As the author of an unpublished world history, his approach to Islamic history was less influenced by culturalist views of all kinds. This comes out clearly in his article "The Great Western Transmutation,"[17] in which he outlines the global dimensions of the complex process of change which, from the eighteenth century on, progressively transformed first the West and then other regions. We are still working to assimilate his re-vision of the roots of modernity.

Hodgson's world historian's eye enabled him at least partially to transcend the Eurocentrism of modernization theory. Modernity, which has generally been confused with Westernization by historians, was for Hodgson a global process. Although the West happened to be the first society to transcend the constraints of agrarian civilization, Hodgson insisted that this development must be placed in world historical context. Given the rough parity among Afro-Eurasian citied societies and the tendency for cultural innovations to pyramid, he argues, it was inevitable that a radical break with agrarian conditions would have occurred somewhere on the planet sooner or later. Had it not been the West, Hodgson sugggests, it could plausibly have taken place in either Sung China or the Islamic world. Before it was overrun by pastoral nomads, Sung Chinese society had pioneered patterns of large-scale social and technical investment which allowed it for a time to transcend the limits of agrarian conditions. While this first Chinese "industrial revolution" did not ultimately succeed, it is interesting to speculate on

[17] *Chicago Today* (1967), 40–50. It is included here as Chapter 4 in its final version, that found in *The Venture of Islam* (Book 6, Chap. 1).

what might have happened had it done so. Similarly, if modernity had first emerged in Islamdom, Hodgson suggests, the egalitarian and cosmopolitan tendencies of modern society would have been heightened. But instead of occurring within the chrysallis of the nation-state (a form tied to the Western experience), the modern world would be characterized by an egalitarian universal state under the aegis of a super-ulama and a super-shariah.

The fact that the Industrial Revolution occurred in Western Europe was, to be sure, freighted with consequences for the future. New patterns of social investment and a new mentality (which he calls *technicalism*) led to a breakthrough to fundamentally new levels of social power. By the end of the sixteenth century, these changes had so far altered Western European society as to move it to a new level – though what this might mean in actuality was only gradually to be worked out.

Hodgson broke with the modernization paradigm in seeing that modernity was from the outset a global process. While the West was the epicenter of these changes, once having occurred somewhere, conditions for development were fundamentally transformed everywhere. Even states like Afghanistan, Thailand, and Morocco, which fell under the looming shadow of the West only late in the game, were in important ways affected by these changes beginning in the sixteenth century. (Here Hodgson anticipates Eric Wolf's observation that the isolated peasant village so dear to anthropologists was in fact a trope. Wolf argues that upon investigation, even the most remote village was affected by the emerging world economy and Western-dominated system of states.)

An important aspect of Hodgson's reevaluation of modernity is his insistence that in historical time it is the discontinuities and not the continuities of Western history which are most striking. He notes that the ascending curve which runs from ancient Greece, to the Renaissance, to modern times is an optical illusion. In fact, he argues, for most of history Europe was an insignificant outlier of mainland Asia. Furthermore, he notes, the Renaissance did not inaugurate modernity. Instead, it brought Europe up to the cultural level of the other major civilizations of the Oikoumene. It did so in some measure by assimilating the advances of the other Asian civilizations. The list of inventions which developed elsewhere and diffused subsequently to Europe is a long one. It includes gunpowder firearms, the compass, the sternpost rudder, decimal notation, and the university, among others. Seen in this light, the European experience looks much less original. This is not to deny that there were original European developments. But in the context of three millennia of agrarianate citied life in the Afro-Eurasian Oikoumene, there was a tendency for civilizations to achieve a rough parity with one another as cultural innovations diffused throughout the Oikoumene.

There is a deep tension in Hodgson's thought between his tendency to view modernity as a world historical process and as linked to particular cultural trends deeply rooted in the West. "Just as an understanding of the history of Europe cannot be reduced to that of the history of England because industrialization first developed there, so the history of the world cannot be reduced to the history of the West, because industrialism first spread there." This tension may be seen best in his concepts of the *Great Western Transmutation* and *technicalism*. In his theory, these concepts distinguish the agrarian age from the modern age. They are what characterizes our time from all that came before it. Modernity, for Hodgson, was linked to the increasing spread of technical specialization across the entire band of citied societies from the sixteenth-century emergence of gunpowder firearm weapons. As innovations accumulated, especially in the West, the result was a qualitative change in the level and kind of human social organization. This shift he likens to that which civilization underwent at Sumer in the emergence of agrarianate citied life. It was this new cultural attitude, and not industrialization, which was the hallmark of the modern age. (Denmark, he explains, is indubitably modern, yet predominantly agricultural.)

Hodgson's emphasis upon the formative role of culture – and his commitment to the civilizational approach – is apparent in his use of the concept of technicalism. Technicalism is "a condition of calculative . . . technical specialization in which the several specialties are interdependent on a large enough scale to determine patterns of expectation in the key sectors of society." While this cultural tendency may be found elsewhere, only in the West did the effort to maximize technical efficiency become exalted above other values. When Hodgson developed this idea in the 1950s, it seemed a helpful gloss on Weber's rationalization. In the 1980s, its defects are apparent. By turns overly abstract, single-mindedly culturalist, and Eurocentric, technicalism seems to us a conceptual tool of rather limited utility. In the wake of recent work emphasizing the broad patterns in global social and economic change over what the French call *la longue durée,* the limitations of Hodgson's thought are apparent. Because it focuses upon culture, the civilizational approach favored by Hodgson has only a tenuous grasp on the crucially important long-range demographic, economic, and social transformations which accompanied (perhaps even preceded) the onset of the modern age.

In sum, Hodgson's effort to situate the rise of the West in a global context had a rather mixed result. In some respects, his conceptual insights have yet to be surpassed. Yet in others, his view of modernity remains bound to the old problematic of Western exceptionalism. Here, it must be admitted, Hodgson is in good company. Neither McNeill nor the Marxists have been able to place the momentous changes that ensued first in Europe before spreading around the globe in an authentically world historical framework. Flawed though Hodgson's views were, they constitute a permanent claim on the attention of all who would seek to measure their work by the highest standards of rigor and epistemological seriousness. If world history is to have a more significant place in our consciousness (as the need to produce citizens fully able to operate in the coming century insists that it should), we should listen to his voice.

I

Europe in a global context

1

The interrelations of societies in history

It has been long pointed out that the destinies of the various sections of mankind began to be interrelated long before the twentieth century, with its global wars and cold wars; or even the nineteenth century, the century of European world hegemony. Here we will study certain of the historical ways in which these destinies were intertwined; in this way we may distinguish more valid modes of tracing large-scale history and of comparing the societies involved in it, from a number of popular but unsound modes of trying to do so. I shall speak mostly of the ages before modern times, noting only briefly at the end of the paper certain crucial ways in which modern interrelations among human societies have been different from earlier ones.

The geographical world-image of the West

It would be a significant story in itself to trace how modern Westerners have managed to preserve some of the most characteristic features of their ethnocentric medieval image of the world. Recast in modern scientific and scholarly language, the image is still with us; indeed, all sorts of scholarly arguments are used to bolster it against occasional doubts. The point of any ethnocentric world image is to divide the world into moieties, ourselves and the others, ourselves forming the more important of the two. To be fully satisfying, such an image must be at once historical and geographical. As in the Chinese image of the "Middle Kingdom" and the Islamic image of the central climes, so also in the Western image,

This paper was delivered originally as a lecture at the downtown College of the University of Chicago in a series on "The Idea of Mankind," sponsored by the Committee for the Study of Mankind. It contains a sketch of ideas which the writer hopes to substantiate more fully; meanwhile, it constitutes an advance over the writer's "Hemispheric Interregional History as an Approach to World History," in *Cahiers d'histoire mondiale,* Vol. I (1954), pp. 715–723.

most of this sleight of hand is performed through appropriate historical maneuvers. Western Europe may be admitted to be small geographically, but all history is made to focus there.

But we must begin with the map. A concern with maps may seem trivial; but it offers a paradigm of more fundamental cases. For even in maps we have found ways of expressing our feelings. We divide the world into what we call "continents." In the eastern hemisphere, where more than four-fifths of mankind still live, there are still the same divisions as were used by medieval Westerners – Europe, Asia, and Africa. As we know, Europe west of the Russias has about the same population as historical India, now India and Pakistan; about the same geographical, linguistic, and cultural diversity; and about the same area. Why is Europe one of the continents but not India? Not because of any geographical features, nor even because of any marked cultural breach at the limits we have chosen. The two sides of the Aegean Sea have almost always had practically the same culture, and usually the same language or languages and even the same government. Much the same is true of the Black Sea and the Ural Mountains.

Europe is still ranked as one of the "continents" because our cultural ancestors lived there. By making it a "continent," we give it a rank disproportionate to its natural size, as a subordinate part of no larger unit, but in itself one of the major component parts of the world. Incidentally, we thus also justify ourselves in evaluating it on a far more detailed scale than other areas. I believe it was the *New Yorker* magazine that published the "New Yorker's map of the United States," in which New York City, New England, Florida, and the West appeared as roughly comparable subdivisions. With our division of the world by continents, we allow ourselves a similar projection of our own interests. Italy is a country in the south of the "continent" Europe; India is a country (naturally "vast" and "mysterious") in the south of the "continent" Asia.

The *New Yorker* map of the United States went on to reflect the New Yorker's notions in the very sizes the several areas appeared to have on the map. Our Mercator world maps have done much the same thing for our Western world image. Some say the Mercator world map is so popular because it shows the correct angles essential for navigation (even though its shapes are almost as badly distorted as its areas). But if you use a map not for navigating but for placing and comparing at a glance different parts of the world, shapes and areas are more important than angles. Moreover, areas are more important than shapes, because they have cultural implications. What is objectionable about the Mercator world map in fact is not that it distorts the shape of North America, nor even that it shows Greenland so large – our conception of Greenland makes little difference. Rather, it is that it shows India so small, and Indonesia, and all Africa. (I call such a world map the "Jim Crow projection" because it shows Europe as larger than Africa.)

The interrelations of societies in history

The point is not, of course, simply that we make Europe big or put it in the upper center. Such matters in themselves might be as irrelevant as the fact that we put the prime meridian at Greenwich. What matters is the peculiar way our perceptions get distorted by the map projection (as they are by no prime meridian). The fortieth parallel north has a curious significance for our world image. Historically, almost all the great centers of civilization have lain south of the fortieth parallel; all, that is, save Europe. Most of Europe lies north of that parallel. But it is precisely at about the fortieth parallel that the Mercator projection begins to exaggerate areas unconscionably. In consequence, that projection and others like it show Europe on a far larger scale than the Middle East, or India, or China. India does appear to the eye on that projection, as a "country in Asia" on the order of, say, Sweden in Europe. And it is possible to show on such a world map numerous details in Europe, towns and rivers that are famous among us, while India or Indonesia, say, are quickly filled up with only the most essential features – which, indeed, are all we have usually heard of.

No wonder, then, that despite all our awareness that Mercator distorts, and that many better projections are available, Mercator remains the most common form of world map outside geographers' classrooms. It confirms our predispositions. It flatters our egos. If we decide we must abandon Mercator because of its notoriety, we adopt a projection which may reduce the size of Greenland, but leaves India as diminutive as ever, compared to Europe; for instance, Van der Grinten, used by the National Geographic Society. Yet what we really want is to face the world as it actually is, not as our Western self-esteem would like to picture it. We may study our own Europe in more detail than other areas – on appropriate separate pages of the atlas. But when we look at the world as a whole – when we look at mankind as a whole – we want our own parts of it to fall into place so that we can see ourselves in true proportion. We need an equal-area world map for any purposes for which we need a world map at all.

The historical world-image of the West

So much for our geographical paradigm. An idea of world history is much less tangible than a map of the world. But much the same points can be made about the Western image of world history. Here too the very terms we allow ourselves to use foster distortion. We aim to overcome any parochial outlook, but so long as we do not radically overhaul our historical categories and our notions of the structure of the historical world, we find ourselves dragged back by older preconceptions the moment the center of our attention shifts to other concerns.

We know how the traditional story runs; history began in the "East" – in Mesopotamia and Egypt (but not in Paradise, still further east, as the medieval Westerners had said); the torch was then passed successively to Greece and Rome and finally to the Christians of northwestern Europe, where medieval and modern life developed. During the Middle Ages, Islam temporarily was permitted to hold the torch of science, which properly belonged to the West, until the West was ready to take it over and carry it forward. India, China, and Japan also had ancient civilizations but were isolated from the mainstream of history and "contributed" still less to it (that is to Western Europe). In modern times Western Europe expanded over the rest of the world, so that Islam and India and China have ceased to be isolated, and have entered the orbit of the ongoing Western Civilization, now becoming a world civilization.

In this story, there are two key notions. There is a "mainstream" of history, which consists of our own direct antecedents. This includes all West-European history since it became civilized, of course; and, before that time, selected periods from areas to the southeast: Greek history 'till the time of the Roman empire (but not since – the Byzantines do not count as mainstream); and the Near East till the rise of the Greeks, but not since. Note that this conception of "mainstream" is not identifiable with the history of lands of cultural creativity, or times of intensity of historical change. The "mainstream" of history, in the traditional image, runs through northwestern Europe in the Dark Ages of the Merovingians – although everyone knows that the Byzantines and the Muslims (and the Indians and the Chinese) were far more civilized then. The "mainstream" of history is simply our own closest historical antecedents.

In fact, all the lands of the "mainstream" are sometimes identified with the "West." Classical Greece is called "Western," though Byzantine Greece is often included in the "East." This brings us to the second key notion which allows us to construct a world history in which our own cultural ancestors hold most of the attention. All the other civilizations of the Eastern Hemisphere are lumped together under the heading "East," "Orient." This concept in history is the equivalent of the concept "Asia" in geography. It enables us to set up our West as conceptually equivalent to all the other civilized regions taken together – "Asia." Apart from Eurasia and the northern part of Africa (the latter is, of course, included in the "East," though Morocco is west of Spain), the more distant parts of the world were relatively sparsely inhabited and for the most part not highly civilized; their history does not force itself on our attention. Hence such a conception of Eurasia allows us to erect a classic ethnocentric dichotomy in the main part of the world – ourselves and the others, Jews and Gentiles, Greeks and Barbarians, "West" and "East." Since by definition the "mainstream" of history runs through the "West," by the same definition the "East" is isolated and static; hence the West, already appearing as one half of mankind, is made the more important half also.

One of the most curious features of this modern Western ethnocentrism has been its superimposition on all the other ethnocentrisms of the world, generally compounding the confusion. Muslims or Hindus have tended to accept modern Western conceptions as indiscriminately scientific; they have commonly accepted their geographical and historical terms from the West, and the implications that follow from them. Sometimes the Western conceptions prove convenient, as when an Egyptian, identifying himself as "Oriental," claims spiritual superiority to the West on the ground that Jesus, Buddha, and Confucius were also all "Orientals"; or, accepting the Western conception of "Africa" as a continent, finds an excellent excuse, as an "African," to meddle in sub-Saharan politics without looking imperialistic. Sometimes the Western conceptions proved less convenient. I found displayed on the wall of an ardent Muslim in a government office in Cairo a map of the Muslim world, showing how widespread is Islam. But the map was a French one, drawn on the Mercator projection, and consequently drastically minimized the area of Islam as compared with Europe. The official was so used to the Mercator projection that he had not noticed this case of what might be called official imperialism.

Now just as the Mercator projection has been criticized so much that everyone is aware that it distorts, so the Western historical world image has been criticized; most of us are uneasily aware that "the East" is more important than we had thought. But just as most people think of Greenland as the best example of Mercator's distortion, failing to see just where the distortion is most misleading, and why certain related projections are just as bad, so it is rare for one to see the full implications of the distortions in the Western picture of world history, and to judge soundly of the various attempts to improve on them. Jim-Crow world maps continue to be the usual map in newspapers, magazines, and general books; and few protest. Similarly, one or another modification of the Western world-historical image still underlie most discussions of mankind. This is true, unfortunately, even on the scholarly level, for some of the presentations of world history that try hardest to escape the traditional pattern still show its distortive influence.

The Continuity among the regions of the Eurasian historical complex in pre-modern times

I must limit myself here to discussing the major civilized regions of the Eastern Hemisphere. The overwhelming majority of mankind – until the last two centuries – lived within the region I am including. It was in a zone of Afro-Eurasian lands extending from Atlantic to Pacific, but chiefly north of the equator, that most of those societies were to be found, before modern times, which had the developed agricultural and urban life which carried with them density of population. It is becoming conventional to articulate this Afro-Eurasian zone of civilization into four main nuclear regions, which we may call Europe, the Middle East, India, and the Far East of China and Japan. Such a division makes a good deal of sense from about 1000 B.C. on, at least down to about 1800 of our era. Each of these regions presents a considerable continuity over some three thousand years of cultural development. More precisely, in each of these regions there was a core-area with reasonably persistent traditions, from which the cultural influences have radiated more or less continuously into a wide surrounding region.

We must place these areas with greater precision, as we will have much to say of them. The core-area of what may be called Europe was the northern shores of the Mediterranean, from Anatolia to Italy especially. It had a Greek (and, later, Greco-Latin) culture which pervaded increasingly the lands to the north; but the Mediterranean lands remained economically and culturally over the more northern ones, on the whole, from the time of the Minoans to the end of the Middle Ages. The core of the Middle East was the Fertile Crescent and the Iranian Plateau, to which lands north and south from Central Eurasia to Yemen and East Africa looked for cultural leadership, as did increasingly even Egypt, despite its distinct roots in its own past, and North Africa, and eventually all of Sudan. The great cultural languages of the Middle East were of the Semitic and Iranian families; though the particular Semitic and Iranian languages changed, much cultural lore was carried over from one period to the next. In the vast domain of Indic tradition east and south from the Hindu-Kush range, the Indus and Ganges valleys formed a somewhat similar core; there the Sanskrit and Pali languages developed, which became classical as far away as Cambodia and Java. Finally, the Hoang-Ho and Yangtze valleys in China formed a fourth creative core-area, from which cultural influences spread to an ever-increasing distance in all directions, within a constantly expanding China and beyond it to such lands as Japan and Vietnam.

Western scholars, at least since the nineteenth century, have tried to find ways of seeing this Afro-Eurasian zone of civilization as composed of distinct historical worlds, which can be fully understood in themselves, apart from all others. Their motives for this have been complex, but one convenient result of such a division would be to leave Europe, or even Western Europe, an independent division of the whole world, with a history that need not be integrated with that of the rest of mankind save on the terms posed by European history itself. But such attempts, if pressed consistently, leave us with a false notion of both world history and even European history. For even among the four great nuclear regions, the cleavages were not decisive enough to sustain such an interpretation. A brief survey of some of the more obvious cleavages will enable us to assess their significance.

If one tried to group these great cultural regions so as to divide the whole of the Afro-Eurasian historical complex into two portions (which is not often seriously attempted), the least useful division would be one in which Europe formed one portion, the "West," and the other three formed a second portion, the "East"; for the cleavage between Europe and its nearest neighbors was unusually slight. The lands north of the Mediterranean were always very closely linked with those of the Fertile Crescent and Iran. I have listed the Anatolian peninsula (the western half of the present Turkish Republic) as part of Europe, since it was one of the chief formative centers of Greek culture, and has always shared the fortunes of the Balkan peninsula; but it is commonly listed as part of the Middle East, and not entirely without reason. The Mediterranean Basin formed a historical whole not only under the Roman empire but before and since; even at the height of the Middle Ages a land like Sicily brought together creatively Greek, Arab, and Latin. Greek thought became an integral element in the Middle Eastern tradition, while Middle Eastern religion had a central place in European life.

A somewhat sharper division existed before Europe and the Middle East on the one hand and the Indic lands on the other. Greeks and Arabs,

Latins and Persians, have had much the same reaction to India, in medieval times, finding it alien to a degree that they have not found each other alien. The Hindu-Kush and the Baluchistan desert formed a more serious barrier than the Taurus. Yet even so the constant thriving trade between the Middle East and India was reflected in important cultural exchanges, which reinforced the fact of a partly common background. For, long before the coming of the Indo-Europeans assured a common origin to the languages and myths of India, Iran, and Greece, the Indus Valley civilization had been closely linked with that of Mesopotamia.

The greatest breach in continuity was between China on the one hand and the Indian, Middle Eastern, and Mediterranean lands on the other. The Himalayas were more effective even than the Hindu-Kush. Until modern times, direct contact was usually limited to mercantile expeditions. Alexander invaded both Greece and the Punjab; the Turk, Timur, campaigned in Russia and on the Gangetic plain; but though Timur dreamed of China, he could scarcely have reached it. Yet the Mongol armies at one point mastered much of China and at the same time won victories in Germany, in Iran, and on the Indus. As we know, Buddhism, originating in India, colored deeply the life of China and Japan; while numerous important inventions, among them gunpowder, the compass, paper, and printing, apparently came at various times from China to the Middle East and so to India and Europe.

As Eurasian history is studied, it becomes clear that these interrelations were not purely external, accidental cultural borrowings and influences among independent societies. They reflect sequences of events and cultural patterns shading into each other on all cultural levels. The four nuclear regions are imperfect historical abstractions. All regions formed together a single great historical complex of cultural developments.

'Till modern times, the four core-areas were the most creative centers; but there were always lesser creative centers beyond them, such as Tibet; and the core-areas themselves cannot always be taken as units. Very early the cultural traditions of the western and eastern Mediterranean regions began to be distinguished, 'till finally Greek and Latin, Orthodox and Catholic, developed relatively independently of each other. Iran and Central Eurasia often seemed to have had their own history apart from the Fertile Crescent and Egypt. Northern and southern India presented a major contrast to each other. Finally, there is no point where the sort of differences that existed between the great regions could be decisively distinguished from the sort of differences that existed between particular nations. Yet all our modern serious attempts at understanding world history are based on all the assumptions of a series of distinct societies, distinct culture worlds, each with its own inner unity and with only external relations to the others. Universalizing efforts, such as that of Ranke, are only seeming exceptions, based on optical illusions which made Europe seem the world, and all other regions isolated and parochial.

As we consider the origins of the great civilizations, it will become evident both why it is impossible to draw any sharp lines within the Afro-Eurasian historical complex, and why none the less historians constantly try to draw such sharp lines. As we know, literary culture arose very nearly at the same time, but in different (though usually urban) forms, in the Indus, the Tigris-Euphrates, and the Nile valleys and probably somewhat later in the Hoang-Ho and other less independent places such as Crete. This process seems to have had a common, interdependent development at least from the Indus to the Aegean; that is, in the areas which became the subsequent cores of the Indian, Middle Eastern, and European traditions. Some sort of Neolithic life had been widespread for some time; when it once crystallized into urban, literate forms in one place, it did so in many; and then rapidly spread over wide regions. It was only when developing civilization had come to a certain point – at about the same time in the main centers of the Afro-Eurasian zone – that the great regional traditions can come to be distinguished. They grew out of a relative breakdown of the local cultural traditions in a more cosmopolitan setting, into which many local strains had intermingled, from the Aegean to the Indus valley. The distinction among the different great regions was secondary, and based largely on accidents not only of geography but of history, even from the start.

This point is supported by the fact that in the marginal areas, such as Central Eurasia, where influences from the several core-areas overlapped, the culture cannot be reduced to a mixture of those of the main cultural regions. Commonly, all areas had their own traditions reaching back into Neolithic times, and forming directly an integral part of the broader Eurasian cultural whole. The French have emphasized this in the case of ancient Gaul; it is equally true of Malaysia or of Central Eurasia. In the Oxus-Jaxartes valleys, no doubt Semitic-Iranian influences had the greatest sway of any from outside; the writing systems came from the Fertile Crescent, for instance. For long periods, again, the Oxus-Jaxartes region was linked with northern India both politically and to a large degree in religion, literature, and the arts. Buddhism flourished there (it was from there that it came most readily to China). Chinese influence was strong recurrently, not only when the area was under Chinese political domination. Even Hellenism flourished there for a period. Yet the history of the Oxus-Jaxartes basin possesses its own continuity over time; it cannot be read simply as a function of the history of the several great cultural regions. Moreover, the historical context in which its history makes sense can be nothing less than the whole Eurasian civilized zone.

The place of supra-national societies in the Afro-Eurasian complex

Hence the more sophisticated have tried to make not permanent regions as such, but supra-national societies, defined purely historically and so limited in time as well as in space, the desired independent historical worlds. It is in this sense that the phrase, "the Western world," has meaning, if it has any serious meaning at all. This attempt has its own limitations. Such societies are conceived as held together by some element of conscious solidarity, perhaps through spiritual presuppositions or through creative style. They are distinct "worlds" in the sense of realms of communication on the highest cultural level. Spengler's is the most famous of the many attempts at distinguishing such societies. Toynbee made a rather half-hearted attempt to do the same, with his doctrine of separate "intelligible fields"; but the weight of his material forced him to go beyond the usual limits, and in effect he abandons the attempt. If we examine Toynbee's work more closely we find that his alleged "intelligible fields" are not really independent intelligible fields, nor even the most important intelligible fields of his own historical study. In the end what is most important in this system comes to be the development of the religions, and he shows the religions developing right across the lines of his nineteen civilizations, which he began by supposing to be independently intelligible fields. In the end most of his work makes no sense except in terms of one large intelligible field – the whole Afro-Eurasian historical complex, in which the several generations of his "societies" are variously related to each other.

This is necessarily so; for important as the various supra-national societies were as frameworks of historical life, they overlapped each other, and even so they did not exhaust the field among them. They were superimposed on a continuum of historical life which recognized no insuperable geographical boundary anywhere between the two oceans. Commercial life, the patterns of urban and rural relations, and the spread of technology, particularly military technology, commonly evolved in relative disregard of the boundaries of religious or literary traditions; such matters were often determined more by local conditions on the one hand and by the general cultural level of the civilized zone on the other.

When historians speak of civilizations or societies, in such connections, they are usually referring primarily to certain limited, if very important, aspects of civilized life. Normally, before modern times, a given area was indeed associated, at any given time, much more closely with some neighboring areas than with others. These associations have been of three main types, political, literary, and religious. The political associations have usually been relatively transient, and only rarely come into consideration here except as reinforced by literary and religious associations.

In the early days of civilization, each language area seems to have developed with relative autonomy from every other; but fairly early certain languages came to be recognized as unusually rich in cultural values, and were cultivated as cultural languages even by peoples which did not use them as the vernacular. Thus Sumerian and Babylonian came to be classical languages for the Fertile Crescent and to some degree of deference to that classical tradition formed in some sense a single civilization. They possessed common terms of reference and common standards; and sometimes the recognition of a classical literary tradition carried with it varying degrees of common legal forms, common political ideas, common artistic patterns. This became especially true by the end of the first millennium B.C., when local cultural traditions within the main geographical regions had been largely submerged.

But by the Middle Ages, the rise of the religions of salvation had established bonds which were as strong as, or even stronger than, those of literary tradition; such bonds sometimes cut right across the lines of literary association. In the regions from Europe to India, religious affiliation became more important than literary, and peoples came to be linked together as Christian or Zoroastrian or Buddhist, rather than as using Greek or Cuneiform or Sanskrit. In China and the Far East, religious affiliation was eventually outbalanced by literary affiliation, and Chinese society was ruled in the end in the name of the Confucian classics rather than of Buddhist or Taoist faith. In any case, on the "high cultural" level most educated men found themselves associated with a given lettered tradition, "literary" or religious, normally to the exclusion of any others.

The importance of such groupings for the development of human life can hardly be overestimated, particularly for that of the ideal and the imaginative life, religion, art, belles-lettres, and even law and political and social institutions. To some degree even the life of the peasant was molded by the ideals set forth in the lettered tradition cultivated by the educated elite of his area. But it is not because of any implications for peasant life, but because of literary and philological implications, that historians have concentrated attention on them. They are indeed the central concern of a humanistic historian. But in the course of giving them almost exclusive attention, many historians have misinterpreted them; they have absolutized these lettered traditions into "historical worlds" to an illegitimate degree.

Such societies were never closed wholes; there were always fields of activity, even important fields, that were but superficially molded by the central tradition in question. As in the case of the geographical regions on which they were often based, there were always territories where two or more traditions competed, and actual life, even on the high cultural level, was a synthesis of diverse elements. These were not anomalies, as our theorists have tended to count them. Indeed, different sorts of lettered tradition mingled in different degrees in given societies. Thus it is possible to regard Byzantine life on the one hand as a continuation of the ancient Greek culture and on the other hand as part of a Christian complex, wider in area, but more restricted in time. Revealingly, there existed lesser lettered traditions of the same basic sort, which had less extensive effects, but cut across other lines. Thus the society formed by the Platonic-Aristotelian philosophers, clinging to a particular strand of the Greek literary tradition, cut across the lines formed by Christianity, Islam, and Judaism; these philosophers lived lives largely molded by their common philosophical heritage, and often had more in common with each other than with any of their respective religious groups. More tenuous, but perhaps even more important, was the interregional tradition of natural science, originating in Babylonian and Greek writing, taken up in Sanskrit and later in Arabic, and transmitted still later to Chinese and Latin – a vigorous tradition of wide implications, which cut across all the main cultural lines of the Afro-Eurasian zone.

Islam was the community which succeeded perhaps most strongly in building for itself a total society, demarcated sharply from all culture before and beyond its limits. Though it appeared relatively late in Eurasian history, as the religions go, it developed its own system of comprehensive law – where the Christian communities took over pagan Roman law. It created its own classical literatures, with only a limited reminiscence of earlier Middle Eastern traditions. Social organization, economic patterns, the arts, all carried an unmistakable Islamic coloring. Moreover, though the Islamic society was far the most widespread among its contemporary medieval societies, yet an unusually strong social solidarity prevailed among Muslims, from Morocco to Java and from Kazan to Zanzibar.

Yet even so, on investigation, it is clear that Islam as a lettered tradition cannot be treated as a distinct historical world, an exclusive intelligible field. The Middle Eastern beginnings of the Islamic society are relatively obscure; we know too little about life in the Fertile Crescent and Iran in the immediately preceding centuries. But it seems likely that one central phenomenon of early Islam had gotten well under way in the last generations of Sasani rule: the centering of power in urban mercantile communities, under the lead of an absolute monarch who could override and break down the locally rooted power of the landed nobility and gentry. The rise of the late Sasani sects and that of the classical Muslim sects both seem to be closely related to this situation. We are learning that we cannot really make out what was going on in early Islamic political and religious life without a much fuller understanding of the Sasani life which preceded it. Moreover, the orthodox faith of Islam itself, as it was created in the course of the first two or three Muslim centuries, cannot be understood simply as a fulfillment of the vision of Muhammad; that vision could have been fulfilled in innumerable other ways, or indeed (as might have seemed most likely), reduced to a merely political ideology, to wither away as the Arab ruling class became assimilated. The being of Islam must be explained in terms of the aspirations of Syrian Christian monks and Mesopotamian Jewish zealots – aspirations which gave to early Muslim converts their very notion of what a religion ought to be, and which they fulfilled in an unprecedented way.

When later the Islamic society expanded over half the Afro-Eurasian civilized zone, the persisting regional configuration of that zone reasserted itself despite all Muslim solidarity. By the sixteenth century, at the latest, Islam in eastern Europe, Islam in the Middle East proper, and Islam in India were clearly pursuing their separate paths. Already when Babur, founder of the Mogul empire, entered India, he seems to have found the local Muslims as alien to him as their Hindu friends; and, despite the continued reliance of his descendants on Middle Eastern and Central Eurasian personnel, and despite a strong puritanical force within Indian Islam which rejected its Indian-ness and eventually won over the Mogul emperor himself, Islamic society in India under the Moguls increasingly developed its own Indian institutional framework and cultural patterns, and formed a relatively independent society. East-European Islam, under the Ottoman empire in Anatolia and the Balkans, evolved in a like direction. The Ottoman empire, like the Mogul, reversed in its own area the long-standing trend of Islam towards decentralization and toward reduction of the social role of political authority; it built up enduring central institutions, religious, legal, and political, though quite different ones from those of the Moguls. But the heart of Ottoman life remained its European center – the formerly Greek lands of Anatolia and the Balkans. The Arab areas south of the Taurus remained only half-subdued dominions, sharing relatively little in the creative sides of Ottoman life; Iraq, at least, tied its sympathies to the third great Muslim empire of the time, the Safavi empire of Iran.

Indeed, not only in these three empires, expressing the traditions of the three core-areas of previous millenniums, but throughout the Afro-Eurasian zone, Islam was a microcosm of interregional civilization, containing within its society all the types of relationships which had formerly been carried on as between the several regions into which it had spread. In Malaysia, Islam had powerful effects; it overlay the earlier Indic traditions with the hemisphere-wide Muslim allegiance, and replaced the earlier Indic-type literary inspiration with a new inspiration expressed in a new alphabet, if not a new tongue. Yet even in their new faith, the Malaysians were inspired largely by Indian Islam as they had been by Indian Hinduism; and their new literary traditions, so far as these did break with the old (which was not entirely), derived also from the mixture of Persian and Arabic heritage which prevailed in southern India. More important, Islam in Malaysia (sometimes a bit to the scandal of orthodox Muslims there and elsewhere) rarely took on, before quite modern times, the rigorous severity which from time to time purged Islamic life in its more central regions; Islam for Malaysia was a new and more universal mysticism, and was taught as such by the heirs of the Indic gurus. In fact, Islam for Malaysia was the natural consequence of its position in the Afro-Eurasian zone as a whole. Malaysia lay at the crossroads of the Southern Seas. Its higher cultural life, from the time when civilization first came there, was ultimately adopted from the life of its ports. Yet these on the one hand remained somewhat apart from the life of the interior – never deeply rooted in local traditions, and on the other hand naturally remained open to the broad currents of culture from throughout the Southern Seas. When the dominant culture of merchants in those waters was Hindu or Buddhist, the port cities became Hindu and Buddhist, and eventually the hinterland followed them. As interregional trade gradually increased in volume and range, the Middle Eastern ports came to have a more pivotal role in the trade of all the Southern Seas; it was then the Middle Eastern culture which increasingly prevailed in the ports of those seas – especially in Malaysia. By the later Middle Ages this meant Islam. But the fundamental pattern of

Malaysian life persisted; and it can be understood only in the context of the Afro-Eurasian civilized zone as a whole.

It has become clear that historical life, from early times at least till two or three centuries ago, was continuous across the Afro-Eurasian zone of civilization; that zone was ultimately indivisible. The various regions had their own traditions; important social bodies arose, sometimes within a regional framework, sometimes cutting across regional life, which molded much of the cultural life of their constituents. But all these lesser historical wholes were imperfect wholes. They were secondary groupings. Local civilized life could go on without full participation in any of them; some of the most creative of historical activities, such as that of natural science, cut right across their boundaries. The whole of the Afro-Eurasian zone is the only context large enough to provide a framework for answering the more general and more basic historical questions that can arise.

The Afro-Eurasian complex as a context of interregional change

At the same time it will have been increasingly clear that the Afro-Eurasian civilized zone was not a static historical context. It had its own characteristics as a set of interrelations. The several civilized regions formed a persistent historical configuration, in which each region had its typical place, its repeatedly typical relationships to the others. This interregional configuration, then, even while maintaining its key characteristics, constantly changed as to the detailed manner of its interrelationships. The civilized zone as a whole had its own history.

Throughout the millennia, resources of information and technique accumulated in each region and sooner or later found their way throughout the Afro-Eurasian zone. The sources of wealth available for interregional trade constantly increased as new areas were drawn in. Such cumulative growth meant that possibilities open to later generations were markedly different from those open to earlier ones. This accumulation was especially important in the case of the techniuqe of travel and of warfare. The invention of the horse-chariot changed, in the immediate event, the relationship of people to people; more importantly, it seems to have changed the nature of distance itself; and launched the first empires. A like result came from the advent of the armed and mounted horseman, in whose presence – and notably in Central Eurasia – distance shrank still further. Related to these changes, of course, was the rise of nomadic herding as an ever dangerous complement and challenge to agriculture. A constantly more effective use of gunpowder brought further decisive changes in warfare which men had to adapt to in most Afro-Eurasian regions within centuries after its primitive beginnings in China, and which almost everywhere seem to have had effects on the concentration of political power. There was a gradual improvement of shipbuilding and of marine charting in both major sections of the Afro-Eurasian chain of seas which led from the northwest Atlantic and the Mediterranean through the Indian Ocean to the South China Sea. The invention of the compass in China and its dramatic use in Western Europe for ocean travel formed only the most striking of the changes in navigation. Not merely in war and commerce, but in every field the constant piling up of changes petty in themselves broadened the range of cultural activity, and so the number of points at which various cultures could be important to each other; Chinese art fashions could not have been so important to Persian and Indian painters as they were, had there not been the discovery of numerous subtle pigments and of the technique of book illumination, to say nothing of paper itself.

Even in the realm of the mind, interregional conditions altered significantly. Certainly the technical invention of paper in China and its transmission to the other regions had important intellectual results. Less "technical" was the invention of the monastic life – of an order of men detached from normal social connections, eminently mobile, and yet specialized in the highest intellectual or spiritual discoveries of their society. Such men made perfect long-range missionaries; when the Afro-Eurasian zone came to be permeated with them, there could arise a level of interregional contact never possible when the chief agents of intercultural contact were tired businessmen. Buddhism, Christianity, and Manicheanism all took full advantage of this mobility of their religious specialists. But perhaps more important than the invention of monasticism – though not unrelated to it – was the general development of large-scale systems of personal orientation, the historic religions, which with or without monks had an almost universal tendency to proselytize. Particularly in the case of Islam, at last, such religion transcended the purely personal level and carried with it direct social initiative, moving toward the establishment of a total society on an unprecedented, hemisphere-wide basis.

One sort of cumulative trend, to which most of the tendencies already mentioned contributed, was of singular importance: that is, of the area in which urban-dominated civilization was able to spread its commercial and political domination. Of special importance in this process were innovations such as the invention of the mold-board plow in northern Europe or the adaptation of the camel to the Sahara. These helped to expand the area of effective agricultural exploitation of major commercial intercourse, and not only helped to change the internal balance of population and economic power within a given region but eventually changed the role of particular regions in the Afro-Eurasian configuration as a whole. Many at least minor adaptations in agricultural technique had to be made wherever agriculture and cities were to find new terrain; and these were in fact repeatedly made.

Both through such inventions and in many other ways that led to expansion, all the regions contributed to the continuous extension of civilization, and this expansion became a basic determinant in the fate of them all by shaping the sort of world they were to exist in. Sheer size of the interconnected zone was important in itself, determining the availability of total human resources at any given time; but still more important was the multiplying of the historical components in Afro-Eurasian development; for one thing, the variety in the regions contributing to it. The historical significance of the unbroken chain of trade that passed through the Afro-Eurasian chain of seas from Atlantic to Pacific was very different in different times according to the area of urbanization achieved. Access to the sea routes had a higher value, for instance, when Malaysia had become itself an active commercial area, and not a mere way station. The significance of the Central Eurasian steppe changed likewise. The constant expansion not only brought in new peoples, widening the scope of Afro-Eurasian commerce, but by altering the proportion of the urbanized area to the rest of the hemisphere, it changed the position of the remaining more distant peoples vis-à-vis the civilizations. In particular this was the case with the Central Eurasian nomads and other unsettled peoples, increasingly limited in their range (though this fluctuated) and in their independence from urban influences. Owen Lattimore, in the *Inner Asian Frontiers of China,* has indicated how parallel were the nomadic and the agricultural evolutions, and how in time the latter impinged ever more on the former. Thus in numberless ways the cultural and economic possibilities in each era depended on the extension of the Afro-Eurasian civilized zone in the whole eastern hemisphere. The whole of that expansion had effects greater than any of its parts.

Outline history of the Afro-Eurasian zone

The changes effected in the interregional configuration of historical relationships in these various ways not only were large; they interlocked. Since the elements of the configuration were interdependent, any given changes were likely to lead to new ones, and the total course of all these changes forms a single story. In the sketch that follows, we can see some of the main lines of development of interregional relations, and its most important turning points. These are matters of the development of interregional relations, and so not necessarily the main events of human history as such, but in fact the development of the Afro-Eurasian interregional configuration involved directly some of the most significant aspects of the history of its various regions; hence the sketch is rather like a brief world history. At any rate, it is closer to a true world history than is the traditional historical image of the West, with which it may be mentally compared.

Very early the expansion of the area of civilization took on a fundamental importance. The early isolated river-valley civilizations, islands in a sea of barbarians, were in touch with each other at best through tenuous, long-distance trading; yet if it is true that one important feature they had in common was certain processes of working metals, and if in the very search for those rare metals their traders and rulers forced an expansion of the civilized patterns into their hinterlands, then it is this requirement common to them all that led in turn to a new condition which determined the fate of them all. For in time this came to depend on the fate of larger regions of civilization. Only in such regions was the cosmopolitanism of the Amarna age possible, such as prevailed at least in the Middle East, when diverse literate nations found themselves for the first time neighbors. Thus one large-scale situation led to developments which produced a new large-scale situation. But even the larger regions of the Amarna age were still surrounded by yet larger areas scarcely touched by urban culture. From these wider regions, borne by the improved military horsemanship developed in the presence of and in response to the civilizations themselves, came the several waves of great invasions, especially at the end of the second millennium B.C. These invasions, largely led by Indo-Europeans, could almost swamp and eventually transform the developed regions of the Middle East, of northern India and possibly also of northern China. So ended the period of the bronze-age cultures, with their recondite, basically pictographic scripts – though the already typical relative isolation of China may have permitted the survival of such a script there.

A world of Greeks, Hebrews, Persians, Indo-Aryans, and Chou Chinese emerged from those invasions in the first millennium B.C. Among these there prevailed a new historical climate, that of the iron age – in which the zone of civilization expanded to hemispheric dimensions, and some of the main constant elements of the Afro-Eurasian interregional configuration were already visible. Despite the distances involved, there was already clearly a degree of community of destiny, though whether it was more by parallelism of separate developments or by active interrelation among regions is not always clear at this early period. Interregional trade was beginning to make use of coinage, almost simultaneously in Europe and in China though independently as to detail; and from the Mediterranean to India there was a new alphabetic – and so relatively accessible – type of writing, which gradually prevailed as the remnants of the old local valley traditions disappeared.

We now come to an age everywhere great, and at the same time important for the changes it wrought in the Afro-Eurasian historical configuration. Everywhere the secular expansion was continuing – the more rapidly perhaps for the seeming interruption of the great invasions. Urban control spread in the Mediterranean westward; in Iran and Central Eurasia; in India southward; in China. The sheer spatial vision of a Macedonian Alexander, fighting in the Punjab, eager to sail down the Ganges, and trying to grasp with his mind the Afro-Eurasian zone as a geographically realizable whole, witnesses to a breadth of horizons impossible a thousand years before; a breadth which left its mark in what followed – that is, in the great philosophical outbursts from Thales and Isaiah to Mencius. For as has often been pointed out, in the latter half of the first millennium B.C. we have unparalleled creative flowerings in all the four great Afro-Eurasian core-areas.

Indeed, the core-areas were in some measure constituted precisely by these flowerings. It is over against both the area which ultimately accepted a Greek tradition, and that which ultimately accepted a Sanskrit tradition, as formulated in this period, that the Middle East set itself off by clinging to contrasting ideals. The intellectual life of this time remained ever after classical for Europe and China. Even for India it was of more significance than might appear on the surface; for this was the age of philosophy par excellence behind the India of Shankara. For the Middle East, this was the age of prophecy – Iranian and Hebrew – which credited norms contrasting sharply with those of more ancient lettered traditions, and were presupposed in the later work of Muhammad and his followers in reconstructing the Middle East. Jaspers has with reason called this the "Axial Age." It was an age which differentiated cultures, but it also led to a deeper interregional interchange. Whatever may have been the initial role of interconnections in the intellectual atmosphere of the time in fostering these simultaneous wonders, they resulted in the presence everywhere of selective intellectual standards which permitted intercultural influences to proceed on the level of abstract thought – a fact above all important for the course of science.

The world was at any rate now ready for the pervasive spread of Hellenism – aspects of which traveled from the Atlantic to the Ganges, with repercussions also in the Far East. Then Hellenism itself – perhaps even in India, where the imperial impulse came from the northwest – helped to make the world ready also for the age of the great regional empires, that of Rome in the Mediterranean, of the Mauryas and their successors in India, of the Han in China. For these empires reflected in some degree, all of them (even that of the Hellenophile Parthians, the most obscure of them), the work of the classical sages, Stoic or Buddhist or Confucian, in human integration. The relatively stable and widespread order brought about by this handful of empires in turn affected interregional relations. The Romans soon complained of the loss of gold to distant India. This was surely a symptom of a wider movement of the same sort as Hellenism. As the direct force of Hellenism receded, what may be called Indicism, in varied forms, spread equally widely – in the Far South East, in the Middle East (especially Iran and Central Eurasia), in China itself; and it had repercussions even in Europe. Indicism involved no spectacular conquests such as that of Alexander, but it is possible that its effects went deeper in a wider area. But the most important result of the empires was, as the early Christians themselves saw in the case of the Roman Empire, that each of them cleared the way for one, or more than one, of the great universal religions. The most prominent fact about the interregional as about the regional aspects of the following period was the towering position of the religions.

For meanwhile, in the wake of the sages had arisen (out of more local antecedents) the great universal religions, with their scriptures, their exclusive moral and cosmological creeds, their hope for the ordinary individual beyond death, and their demand for his personal commitment now.

These appeared now either in the form of faiths like Christianity and Mahayana Buddhism, created in this mold from their inception, or of old faiths made over like Rabbinical Judaism and (apparently) the Hindu Shaivism and Vaishnavism. From the cities as centers, everywhere they moved out to prevail over the population; early in the first millennium C.E., throughout the Afro-Eurasian zone one or another of them achieved political power and attempted to gain an exclusive recognition for itself. They left practically no gaps, though they were some areas where none was fully successful in its rivalry against the others; among them, they practically stamped out the old paganisms or else subordinated them to the new spirit. Simultaneously with the drive of the religions for power arose – with or without the inspiration of the almost universally present Indian influences, the ascetic and monastic tendencies which came to dominate one aspect of Afro-Eurasian life for more than a thousand years. With the advent of the universal religions, region was linked with region as fellow-worshippers believed one creed across the most distant frontiers; but at the same time barriers were raised between many regions as the new orthodoxies, on a higher level than any more primitive ones, developed their own self-contained intolerance, with which they tried to dominate the life of one region or another.

In the course of all this – and partly as a fruit of the activity of the empires – whole provinces were being opened up to the latest forms of urban life, for instance Gaul or Szechuan; hence by the time of Attila the urban-dominated areas of greater Eurasia had come to present a solid belt of territories across the hemisphere equivalent in mass to the remaining areas to the north. The new invasions (nomadic or simply barbarous) might overcome outlying areas like Western Europe or even the specially exposed north of China, but they no longer overwhelmed the whole of the continuing cultural and commercial nexus. Till the beginning of fully modern times there was no general breach in the literate traditions such as that which so sharply reduced the role of the bronze-age cultures. This was, to be sure, only in part the result of sheer size; in part it was a matter of wider participation in the higher traditions within the several regions – a result to which both the structures of commerce and the character of the religions had contributed. Indeed, the religions undertook a new sort of cultural offensive in their missionary activities – particularly those of Christianity, Judaism, Maincheanism, and Buddhism, but also Hinduism – which extended beyond the old centers to marginal areas such as northern Europe, Central Eurasia, the Far South East, or northeast Africa.

There prevailed in the middle of the first millennium C.E. a radically different temper from that of the age in which Hellenism had spread. Everywhere now the idea of a universal religion as commanding the allegiance of a population was taken for granted. It was into this cultural setting that Islam erupted, claiming to be the culmination of universal religion, and immediately transforming the balance of political power in the Mediterranean, the Indian Ocean, and the Eurasian steppe, where it sets bounds to Chinese influence. It created a powerful social and spiritual ideal which within not many centuries began to penetrate into almost every part of the hemisphere, and which presented, to a greater or lesser degree, a permanent cultural and political challenge to each of the great civilizations which it did not actually absorb. For centuries the regional imagination, in both India and Europe, was dominated by the Muslim peril and given its unity by it. The unifying effect of Islam in the Middle East itself soon had far-reaching results. Islamic scholars gathered up the scattered scientific traditions of Greece and Iran and India and, using them, spread them from China to Western Europe. Islamic merchants carried widely some technological discoveries of China; most notably paper. At the same time that Islam was thus changing interregional conditions, other Afro-Eurasian developments gave Islam itself new directions. New regions, such as the Far South East, were being more fully developed; there Islam made rapid headway, so outflanking the older centers. Islam promised itself, not without reason, that it would soon be absorbing the whole world.

During these centuries of the appearance and the later expansion of Islam, there was taking place at least the usual cumulative improvement in technique, notably in military and even financial techniques; the range of commerce expanded, as in sub-Saharan Africa, which now effectively entered the Afro-Eurasian arena of civilization with the advent above all of the camel in the Sahara; or as in the far north-west (where a subarctic link to North America aborted). The diverse strains of learning were being integrated in scholastic-type syntheses of the old philosophical traditions with the dominant religions, from Shankara, who in ninth-century India finally disposed philosophically of Buddhism, to Chu Hsi and Aquinas in the thirteenth century. Practically as widespread as scholasticism was a marked institutional cultivation of love-mysticism (in the form of bhakti in Hinduism, Sufism in Islam, and the mystical traditions in eastern and western Christianity) – a mysticism which was often associated with the rise of numerous vernacular languages alongside the handful of classical ones dating chiefly from the Axial Age.

Here again it is hard to know what extent the parallel developments in learning and religion were purely parallelisms, resulting from a common set of historical problems without much actual interaction in any form. Certainly to a degree it was simply that common problems were being met, and sometimes they were answered differently – thus, in contrast to all other regions, in China in this period there was a clear decline of the universal religions, Buddhism and Taoism, to the profit of what was essentially a philosophical system of the "Axial Age," Confucianism. Nevertheless, by this time the interactions among regions – as a result of Islam, or of the Mongols, or of scientific or artistic borrowing, and the like – were so frequent, and involved even the isolated China and the distant Western Europe so freely, that these developments cannot be fully disengaged from each other. Whether merely parallel growths from the past, or the fruit of a contemporary climate of needs, they formed the inescapable context of interregional contacts, which commonly assumed a religious guise.

In the midst of this period occurred an event which was unusually conducive to bringing all cultures of the Afro-Eurasian zone together on a common level. The variegated richness of the urban cultural traditions was matched by their tendency now to dominate increasingly even the remoter parts of the Afro-Eurasian land mass. Muslims, Chinese, and, later, Russians continued to converge in their Central Eurasian expansion, so that by the thirteenth century a tribe in remote Mongolia might find itself cramped by the overweening demands and overwhelming prestige of the urban powers. The young Chingiz Khan, at the farthest edge of the steppe, was outraged, it is said, by imperial agents. Once it was the river-valley civilizations that were surrounded; later, in Han-Roman times, the civilizations were merely equivalent in combined mass to the barbarian ranges on their margins, and able to absorb their attacks. But now it was the turn of the barbarians, of the nomads, to feel themselves surrounded. Their desperate last massed fury under Chingiz Khan perhaps reflects the advance of urbanism as much as does their unprecedented use of urban skills in all their regional forms. This unexpected product of the joint efforts of the Afro-Eurasian peoples in turn devastated the greater part of the Afro-Eurasian zone, and permanently deflected its cultural and political history.

But the Mongols' fury, under the interregional circumstances, only speeded the day when the urban tradition would penetrate far into the greater part of Central Eurasia, the nomads themselves turning Buddhist and Muslim and becoming increasingly abject in subjection to imperially oriented khans. Despite what seems to have been an Afro-Eurasian zone-wide depression of urban prosperity in the fourteenth century – under the Yuan, under the later Delhi Sultanate, in the Middle East that failed to repair ports and irrigation canals, in the slowed growth of West-European towns; despite the vast interregional sweep of the Black Death (with its uncalculated effects on the continuity of culture in marginal areas like North Africa, and generally on the interregional balance of power), the economic stage was being set for the world-wide exploitation of the "riches of the East" by upstarts of the far West. The range of commercially developed areas had come to cover the larger part of the hemisphere, and the techniques of travel and trade, as well as the varieties of luxury and of specialized use, were innumerable. The far West had been stimulated by religiously-inspired wars in the Middle East, but insulated from most of the Mongol torrent (in contrast to the time of Attila) by newly urbanized territories in eastern Europe.

We have been seeing that the Afro-Eurasian historical complex was not merely a framework for mutual borrowings and influences among organically independent civilizations; it was a positive factor with its own proper development. This is visible even in the diffusion of inventions. At this point, after the Mongol turmoil, the most recent Chinese inventions evidently found a faster diffusion than ever; their historical effects are not however reducible to sheer diffusion, but reflected the complex pattern then attained by the interregional configuration. They had very different effects as developed in different areas. Notable among these inventions were gunpowder weapons, the sea compass, and printing (including most recently moveable print). Some of these might have been independently invented in Europe or elsewhere, inspired by a common background won through the then relatively direct made relations; all of them could well have been inspired from the Far East by "Stimulus Diffusion" (that is, by suggestion through mere general awareness that they existed), or even have been direct imports from the Far East. In any case, all of them came to be known, and most of them to be used in some degree, almost everywhere in the main centers at about the same time. Everywhere (save in China itself) the rise of gunpowder seems to then have passed gradually from its first use as a minor auxiliary "fire-works" weapon, to more efficient and at last decisive uses. But these uses differed in different areas, according to regional social conditions and according to the position of the region in the wider context, and so had strongly diverse consequences. These inventions helped send the fresh Occident out into the oceans, most importantly, at first (because of the pattern of interregional trade), the Indian Ocean. Yet a similar gunpowder artillery seems to have helped create, likewise at the start of the sixteenth century, the three great Muslim land empires (Ottoman, Safavi, and Mogul) which, all three being oriented away from the Indian Ocean, failed to regain control of the long-distance trade in that ocean for Muslims after it had been lost to the first rush of Occidentals.

Western Europe as an Afro-Eurasian frontier

As we have come to realize, within this vast historical complex, Western Europe played a peripheral and 'till well into the Middle Ages a backward role. The Carthaginians and Etruscans were remarkable peoples, but they added few basic improvements to the cultural patterns which came to them from the eastern Mediterranean. The same was true of the Romans. Though they won political supremacy over the Hellenistic eastern Mediterranean, on the northwestern fringe of which their city was located, they always themselves looked to the east for cultural guidance. Even their most treasured creation, the Roman law, was rather a Mediterranean creation than an Italic one, though its language was for a long time Latin. Only in the High Middle Ages did Western Europeans begin truly to rise to the creative level of the core-areas of civilization. At the start of the Crusades they were still crude and ignorant as compared with either Greeks or Arabs in fields like medicine and chemical technology; they were not up to the "Greek fire" of the Arabs; by the end of the Crusades the Latins had for the first time become more or less their equals.

The famed Westward march of empire, as we have seen, dissolves into a general expansion of civilization in all directions of the compass. Western Europe was a frontier region rather in the same sense as the Sudan or Malaysia, though it began to develop urban, literate culture earlier than either of those areas. It shared with them a dependent relation to the older cultural centers. As in those areas, the flow of cultural learning was quite one-sided – from China, India, the Middle East, and (above all) the eastern Mediterranean to the Occident, with little going in the opposite direction. For a long time this was reflected even in interregional trade. The Occident, like other frontier areas to the south or the east, had primarily natural resources, including slaves, to offer, rather than perfected finished goods. Accordingly, local Occidental events – the ups and downs of local urbanization and learning – were of relatively little importance to the world at large. Medieval Islamic writers were strongly aware of Byzantium and India and China, but except at moments and places of direct contact had little more interest in the far Occident than in Tibet or East Africa. The main features of the Afro-Eurasian historical context, the "mainstream" if there was one, were little affected by events in such far corners.

Perhaps the Occident had advantages in its frontier position, somewhat similar to those which Korea and Japan seem to have had in roughly the same period, being equally removed from the main lines of interregional intercourse. In virgin soil, as it were, the Occidentals were able to develop independent cultural variants upon older themes, relatively undisturbed by the cultural and military turmoil which often prevailed from the Aegean to Bengal. Moreover, till the later Middle Ages the West Europeans always had attractive space beyond the current limits of civilization in which to expand their sphere of activity (something which was largely denied to the Japanese). The clue to much of the Occident's character may lie in its long being a frontier region. In any case, comparisons between the Occident and other peripheral regions, which stood in other relations to the core culture areas, might be more fruitful than between the Occident and those centers themselves; for instance, as regards the relation between local creativity and receptivity to outside influences.

When we look at human historical life as a whole, it will not do simply to give more attention to "Eastern" societies – either for their own interest or as influencing or contributing to Europe. We must learn to recognize the Occident as one of a number of societies involved in wider historical processes to some degree transcending or even independent of any given society. Though the Occident was relatively isolated, the effect even on the Occident of its involvement in these wider processes can be reduced to the sum of influences or borrowings from this or that other society. It cannot be reduced even to more general effects, positive or negative, resulting from the powerful presence of its neighbors to the south or east. Through them, the wider interregional pattern ultimately sets limits at any given time to what alternatives were open to the Occident or any other society within it. The expansion of the area of civilization, the accumulation of technique, the steady rise in the level of social power everywhere, as well as many more particular sequences of events, took the forms they did on an interregional basis. The evolution of Western Europe depended, in some of its first presuppositions, on the course of development of the Afro-Eurasian historical life as a whole.[1]

[1] What has been said so far has serious implications for the way in which we must view the relation of Modernity to the older Occidental culture. I have developed some of these implications in an article to appear in the *Journal of the Central Institute of Islamic Research* (Karachi). Briefly, the most popular views of world Modernization have seen it either as a shift from essentially unchanging tradition into repetition, at an altered pace, of Modern Western sequences (cf. J. M. Romein, "The Common Human Pattern," in *Cahiers d'histoire mondiale,* Vol. IV, 1958); or as an expansion of the historical Occidental society which may be either adopted in various degrees or resisted by other societies. Both views are inadequate. They must be supplemented by understanding Modernity as the outcome of the breakdown of the common historical conditions on which rested the pre-Modern Afro-Eurasian historical complex as a whole. A degree of deliberate innovation was always present in the Afro-Eurasian civilized societies as compared with tribal societies; even major florescences such as those of classical Greece or classical Islam, which sometimes led to serious changes in the historical configuration, could be consistent with its continuity. The Renaissance and the early Occidental expansion in the oceans, in fact, did not in themselves escape the presuppositions of the pre-modern historical pattern in any crucial way. In the sixteenth century the level of cultural and social power of the several Afro-Eurasian civilizations was still essentially on a common level (everywhere far higher than so many millenia earlier). Between 1600 and 1800, developments within the Occident finally destroyed these common historical presuppositions; but as soon as they were fully destroyed for the Occident itself (that is, by the generation of 1800) they were effectively destroyed for all the other civilized societies also, as a result of the already existing solidarity of Afro-Eurasian history. Since 1800 the results of that event in most other societies have been very different from those in the Occident, but equally "modern" in an important sense. Modernity is not to be compared with the spread of Hellenism, nor to be reduced to the stages of internal Occidental experience. Though its initiation within the Occident has certain crucial consequences. Modernity is simply "Western" neither in its origins, nor in its impact as a world event, nor even as an expression of regional cultural continuity; above all, not in the nature of the cultural problems it raises for us all.

2

In the center of the map

Nations see themselves as the hub of history

In the sixteenth century the Italian missionary, Matteo Ricci, brought to China a European map of the world showing the new discoveries in America. The Chinese were glad to learn about America, but one point in the map offended them. Since it split the earth's surface down the Pacific, China appeared off at the right-hand edge; whereas the Chinese thought of themselves as literally the "Middle Kingdom," which should be in the center of the map. Ricci pacified them by drawing another map, splitting the Atlantic instead, so that China appeared more central; and maps are still commonly drawn that way in that part of the world.

Europeans of course have clung to the first type of map, showing Europe in the upper center; while the commonest maps in North America show the U.S.A. in that post of honor, even at the cost of splitting a continent in two. The temptation not only to put one's own land in the center of the map, but one's own people in the center of history, seems to be universal.

The most famous case of this is indeed that of the "Middle Kingdom." Many Chinese used to suppose that the Temple of Heaven at the Emperor's capital, Peking, marked the exact center of the earth's surface. To be sure, Chinese scholars even in the Middle Ages were aware that China could not be said to be mathematically central; they knew the general lay of Europe and Africa and the Indian Ocean, and a writer could remark that the "center" of the earth was along the equator. Nevertheless, even for sober historians, the pivotal fact of human history was the condition of the great Chinese empire, in which was concentrated all the splendor of polished civilization.

At times that empire was strong. Then (as they told it) the Emperor was able to command peace among the fair lands stretching out around its capital; the choicest products of the mountains on the one hand and the sea on the other poured in to enrich the vast fertile plains of the empire; and the barbarians of the less favored lands beyond – deserts, mountains, and remote islands – divided and weakened by the Emperor's wise policies, came to bring humble tribute and to learn what they could of the arts of civilization.

Thus came the Koreans, the Japanese, the Tibetans; thus came also the English from their distant islands, seeking Chinese luxuries and offering little in return the Emperor could approve – such as opium. Even the English envoys were graciously received, but when they showed want of proper respect for the Emperor they were dismissed with contempt.

At other times the imperial power grew feeble, local rulers seized power and tyrannized the people, prosperity faded. It was then (as they told it) that the barbarians came as insulting conquerors, and civilization was eclipsed in the world. Thus came the Central Asian Turks, thus came the Mongols under Kublai Khan; and thus came the English when the Manchu dynasty was declining, invading the Middle Kingdom (whose wealth attracted every barbarous nation), and forcing their crude ways upon the people.

It could in fact be claimed that for a time China was the wealthiest and most populous, the most esthetically cultivated and even the most powerful state on the earth; but when this fact was made the basis for the Chinese picture of the world, the result was tragic miscalculation.

For the medieval Hindu the world was a place for the purification of souls. Kings and their empires came and went, the gods themselves arose and perished – time was infinite, space immense, with unlimited opportunity for every soul to reap in birth after rebirth what it had sown. In much of the universe, indeed, souls dwelt in untroubled bliss; it was the distinction of our own toiling, earthy regions that here men could choose responsibly between good and evil and their consequences. Here life was arranged for the exercise of virtue, each caste of men having its own function in society; if a man fulfilled one role well, in another life he would have a higher role to play, and might eventually rise beyond the transient vicissitudes of existence altogether.

Accordingly, so far as history was significant, it was as ages varied in the degree to which society was well enough ordered to give virtue its due place. As a given cosmic cycle wore on, disorder increased and justice faded. Our own age (they explained) was in the latter part of such a cycle; only in the central parts of the earthy regions – in India, that is – was society still well ordered: there Brahmins still offered sacrifices and the other castes ruled or served according to their status.

In the benighted lands to the east and west so tainted already with decline that pious Brahmins dared not set foot there – souls were doomed to be born as barbarous Mlecchas; there they lived unhallowed lives till they should earn the right to be born in India. As our degenerate age drew on, even in India itself the social order was upset, rulers rose from the basest castes, and finally even Mlecchas entered as conquerors – Muslims from the west, and even the remotest Europeans. Through all this outward humiliation, however, the Hindu could know that there in the central lands where the sacred Ganges flowed he could still live the way of truth and holiness – inaccessible to lesser breeds of men – and aspire to the highest degrees of rebirth.

To the medieval Muslim the world looked very different from what it did to his Chinese or to his Hindu contemporaries. History was not a matter of the varying strength and weakness of an imperial center of authority and civilization, nor was it a passing incident in an infinite succession of worlds. Rather it was the story of a single species created just some 5,000 years ago by God to do His will once for all. From Adam on, God had sent thousands of prophets to the various peoples, bringing to each its laws and sciences; at last he sent Mohammed, proclaiming the final law in which all earlier truth was perfected and which was gradually to prevail over the whole world, replacing all former laws.

Many Muslims believed that Mohammed's birthplace, Mecca, was the center of the earth's surface. To Mecca, men pilgrimaged yearly from the farthest parts of the earth, and it was supposed that in the heavens above it the angels themselves performed worship; here was the very throne of God, where heaven and earth were nearest. To be sure, scholars knew that the earth was a sphere, and God equally present everywhere in the hearts of the believers. But their more sober picture of the world was equally effective in supporting the eminence of Islam. They thought of the inhabited quarter of the globe as a land mass lying between the equator and the North Pole, and between the oceans to the west and to the east – roughly Eurasia and northern Africa.

This was divided into seven "climes" from south to north, and from extreme heat to cold. Muslims writing in the latitude of Syria or Iran explained that in the hot south men grew lazy and so remained backward in civilization; and likewise in the far north where it was too cold – in northern Europe, for instance – men's skins were pallid and their minds sluggish. Hence it was that only in the central, moderate climes, like the Mediterranean lands or Iran, were minds most active and civilization most advanced; from there the blessings of Islam were gradually being brought even to the remotest areas, among the Negroes in the hot south and the white men in the cold north.

World histories written by medieval Muslims might, therefore, have a preliminary section on the older Persians, Hebrews, and Romans; but, from the time of Mohammed, the modern part of the history dealt almost exclusively with the Islamic peoples. Other peoples might be curious in their quaint ways; the Chinese might be clever at gadgets, and the Greeks at philosophy; but now the only peoples whose story really counted were those who had abandoned their old local creeds with their many idols or their many saints' images and joined in the imageless worship of the One God, in the international brotherhood of Islam which, advancing farther every year, already stretched from the straits of Gibraltar to those of Malacca.

The West Europeans of the same age had many of the same ideas of history and geography as the Muslims, getting them from the same Greek and Hebrew sources; but their interpretation was very different. For them history was the story of God's progressive dispensations of law or of grace to his favored people. Out of the descendants of Adam, God has first chosen the Hebrews, but with the coming of Christ it was a "new Israel," the Christians, that received His favors.

Even among the Christians God had made a further selection – casting aside those of the Levant and Greece as heretics or schismatics in favor of the West Europeans under the Pope at Rome. The favored people of each age lived under a succession of great monarchies; in earlier times Chaldean, Persian, and Greek, which all conquered the Hebrews; but last and greatest, under which Christ Himself was born, the empire of Rome in the west, which should endure 'till Judgment Day.

The West Europeans allowed that the center of the world's surface was Jerusalem (by exaggerating the length of the Mediterranean, their maps could show Spain and China as equally distant from it); but they assured themselves that, just as at the beginning of history Paradise was in the east where the sun rises, so in these latter days the center of God's vicarship on earth was in the west, where the sun sets; henceforth Rome was the center of all authority, spiritual and temporal.

In modern times all these medieval pictures of the world have vanished, or been modified. With the discovery of America and the circumnavigation of the globe, the discovery that Earth is a tiny planet in an immensity of space, that mankind has been upon it hundreds of thousands of years and is still a newcomer, we have had to rethink our situation. The great ideals of faith and of culture have to be seen in spiritual terms rather than as reflected in the very map of the universe.

The West Europeans were the first to be really faced with the new discoveries and have consequently led the way toward creating a new picture of the world. But they have not yet escaped the temptation to make geography and history center upon themselves. One need only examine the table of contents of any proper Western "world history." Civilization began in Mesopotamia and Egypt (with perhaps some local variants in India and China); but (it would seem) soon history was almost a monopoly of the Greeks; and though other peoples might still be curious, in their quaint ways, hereafter it was really only Europe they counted – and after the rise of Rome only Western Europe; here was the home of truth and liberty.

If during long centuries it was hard to find either truth or liberty in Western Europe, this period was regretfully labelled the Dark Ages of mankind; but in modern times the West Europeans have duly gone forth to enlighten (and subdue) the world – so that the history of a henceforth "Westernized" world may be safely reduced almost to that of the West itself.

The map of the world is constructed accordingly. Westerners distinguish five or six "continents": Africa, Asia, North and South America – and Europe. It is sometimes ingenuously remarked how much smaller Europe is than the "other continents" – yet in political discussions, in grouping statistics, or in historical comparisons these divisions repeatedly recur as if fixed by nature.

In European "world atlases" each European country has its own map, with the rest of the world in a few pages at the end. The map ordinarily selected to show the world as a whole is ideally suited to reinforce this way of seeing mankind. On the Mercator world map not only is Europe in the upper center: it is represented as a good deal larger than the other great culture areas. Most of these lie south of the fortieth parallel, while Europe is almost wholly north of it, where Mercator's projection begins to exaggerate the size of things enormously.

Accordingly even on the world map, which ought to provide a sense of proportion, there is space to name a great many places in Europe, while in other populous centers like India or China, shown on a much smaller scale, only a few chief places need be indicated. Although equal-area projections of the world have long been available, in which shapes as well as sizes are much less distorted. Westerners understandably cling to a projection which so markedly flatters them. They explain (as if they were engaged in nothing but sailing) that the true angles on the Mercator map are of convenience to navigators; and in atlases and wall-maps, in books of reference and in newspapers, when Westerners turn to see what the world looks like as a whole their preconceptions are authoritatively gratified.

The story is often told of a small tribe whose word for "mankind" was the name for the tribe itself. Other tribes were merely incidental in their picture of the world – perhaps not even fully human. Chinese, Hindus, Muslims, and Westerners alike have smiled perhaps too quickly at the rather perilous naïvete of that small tribe.

3
World history and a world outlook

As nearly as anyone can tell, there are as many people in China as in mainland Europe; and more people in China and Japan together than in Europe with Great Britain. Furthermore, that situation has probably existed for a very long time, since all will admit that China was a civilized land even before Europe. Surely China's fate, then, purely from the point of view of human beings, is in general just as important as is Europe's.

Yet, there is an incongruous situation in our social sciences, and most particularly in our history writing, which has sometimes been noted, but about which nothing to my knowledge has ever been effectively done. The up-to-date general histories mention China in one or two chapters, whereas they spend all of the rest of their time on Europe. Is this because only Europe has changed, only Europe has had things happen? Anyone who has studied the history of China will tell you this is not true. Is this because most of mankind now lives in a European culture, and the Chinese culture patterns have been ended?

Is it true that Europe has colonized vast areas; but the only dense population resulting has been in the United States. With all her colonies, Europe still has not a great deal more population than China and Japan, whose past culture certainly has not ended. The history of Chinese culture, then, is very nearly as important, from an international point of view, to modern world humanity as is the history of Europe. Yet when we read "world history" we read chiefly of Europe.

Why is this? There seem to me to be three chief reasons. The first one will be evident when one remembers that the historians of the "Middle Kingdom" considered *China* as very nearly the only actor in world history. The reason for both the Chinese and the European exclusiveness is the same: snobbish misunderstanding.

The second reason is rather more defensible: Europe has had more influence on China since the Industrial Revolution than China has had on Europe. Granted! But will we get a true picture of the world, if we study only the dominating power, and not the dominated? After all, until extremely recently – as the history of civilization goes – there was probably more influence in the other direction; and we are beginning to realize that that may well be the case again.

The third reason goes to the heart of the matter: our civilization is European, therefore we are interested only in that history which can tell us how we got this way. In this case let us be frank about it, and stop talking about *world* history, or *general* history, when we really mean the history of European countries and their colonies (with a few remarks about the rest of the world thrown in). Some modern historians do this, indeed; but not the average person. However, I think that it is by no means true that *world* history has no great importance for us.

What are the purposes of history? They are many. Certainly a primary purpose of general history, either of all Europe, or of the civilization of the world, is to help us to understand the civilization of today, and to put it in its historic setting – just as a social worker, when taking up a case, first makes as all-inclusive a case history as he can in order to guide him.

But surely now we must realize, even if never before, that we Europeans are not alone in the world: China, Japan, India, Egypt, Iran – these lands are playing important parts in the lives of Europeans and Americans now, and may play a still more important part in our children's time. If we are to treat the ills of one country, we have learned we must take the whole world into consideration. Are we not rather foolish when we say that we have no use for a history of the world as a whole?

A particularly pressing need for world history is presented now by the crisis in the European empires. A certain popular writer analyzes the causes of European imperialism solely in terms of internal European factors. But can we understand why Europe could rule, without finding out why the rest of the world could be ruled? How successful will the writer now be in understanding the general but varying resurgences of the dominated lands, if he has only European background for his analysis?

And further, is it true that we can understand even our own history of Europe and Europeans without understanding its setting in the world as a whole? No matter how much the Chinese studied the history of China, could they really understand it before they realized that it was not the central point of the earth? Could not the same thing be said of us?

We have known a long time that "the Crusades brought Europe knowledge of a more advanced culture" than her own. Is it enough to point out the specific items Europe learned, without attempting to set the European and Near Eastern cultures objectively side by side in a single history, where we could see not only what details Europe got, but also what she failed to accept; and more important, in what ways both developed in common? There is danger, in studying one country, that one may analyze all its events in terms of that country alone, whereas if one looks around he sees evidently related events elsewhere, that shows causes and development cannot be purely national but must be international. Likewise in studying Europe, should we assume that we are safe in looking for the causes of European developments within Europe alone?

I would go so far as to believe that if we began to study the history of the world as a whole, and not in the unbalanced way we have pretended to study it, we would discover the European history – in all its phases, social, economic, artistic, religious – has in the main, at least until recently, been a *dependent* part of the general development of civilization. Studying it in that light we will receive a new understanding both of Europe and of the human race. It will not do categorically to deny this surmise; the only way to show its falsehood is to study world history from this point of view, and see.

There is a further reason for studying world history as such, even apart from its value as history: its value in breaking down our ethnocentrism. What I have here to say could be said for most of the social sciences, but a world history is a particularly suitable way to meet the problem. We Americans need almost as much as anything else these days to acquire a healthy realization of the position we hold in the modern world. It is strong, to be sure, but precarious. We have only about 6 percent of the world's population. [Ed. note – current when published in 1944]. So far, we have been more highly industrialized than most of the rest of the world. But India and China are becoming industrialized, and we have learned to our sorrow that Japan already is.

Consider that the population of the world can be divided into four roughly equal parts: 554,000,000 in China and Japan; 526,000,000 in Hither and Further India; 534,000,000 in Europe with Britain; and 556,000,000 in all the rest of the world.[1] Even all Europeans and their descendants overseas make up at most about a third of the world population. We Europeans have been lording it over the rest of the earth; the other nations are already objecting, and their objections seem likely to increase. Is it not time that we wake up to the fact that we are not the only people in the world that matter?

Teachers and writers of the social sciences, and especially historians,

[1] League of Nations statistics for 1941. [Editor's note: current when published in 1944].

can do much to bring us to the world outlook that is necessary. And now is the time to bend every effort toward that aim. There is a map published I expect by the *New Yorker* showing that United States as seen from that city. On that map Manhattan becomes bigger than Illinois. Chicagoans laugh at that; but Chiang Kai-shek [President of Republic of China in 1944 – Ed. note] does not laugh when he sees that we Americans have just this kind of a view of the world: America and Europe are very big, the rest is insignificant. We must change that map!

I do not suggest, of course, that America and Europe be given no more attention in our schools and libraries than China and India. Particular histories of phases especially important to the reader are very important. But just as we don't write histories of the modern Occident three-fourths of whose content deals with the United States, but rather have special books and courses meeting our special need for American history, so we should not allow our special need for Occidental history to destroy our chance to learn world history. A general history – whether a thin volume for the public, or a quarter or a semester course for the student – is also needed, to supply an undistorted framework into which a particular history can be set as an elaboration of one or another part of the general history.

Now if it is of the utmost importance that our historians and social scientists in general build a "global," world outlook, then there are many things we can do about it. Specifically, we should do two types of things: first, encourage the writing of *world* history. I believe I am safe in saying that there is not a single history book in existence which attempts to present as *one* picture, with no undue prominence for Europe, the development of civilization all over the Old World.[2] Second, even if that cannot be done just now, we should not sabotage the possibility of people thinking in terms of a "global" world, by continuing to talk in terms which give the lay mind a distorted picture of the world, and so help to maintain the already disastrously provincial ideas which we have.

The things I shall mention in this respect may seem minor; and they would not be important if it were not that the prejudice which they confirm is already with us. But unfortunately it is, and it is surely unwise to pamper and feed it, even in little things.

For instance, the Mercator's projection map of the world literally does

[2] Perhaps the informal letters of Nehru should be considered a regular history, and hence a rather inadequate exception. Toynbee's work is, of course, a study, not a narrative history.

for our distorted world-view very nearly what the *New Yorker* map does for New Yorkers. On Mercator's projection, England, actually smaller than the Indian state of Hyderabad, appears nearly three times the size of that region. This is because Mercator exaggerates the north – North America, Europe, Russia – at the expense of areas farther south, like India or the Near East. And it is our own already exaggerated countries that tend to be in the north. When other maps of the world, based on better scales, and serving every purpose the Mercator can, are available, it seems serious negligence to go on using so distorted a map, in classrooms or elsewhere.

There are, then, three general types of phrases which I urge to avoid. First come those about the geographical nature of Europe, which elevate that peninsula to the status of a continent. Geologically speaking, to divide Eurasia into two continents at the Urals is silly. The peninsula of India is only a little smaller than Europe, and has a much more real division from the rest of the continent. If there is any historic division between Europe and the rest of Eurasia, it is the line the Greeks used, about in the middle of "European Russia," where the peninsula ceases to be peninsular: for there has been found if anywhere the dividing line between Slav and "Central Asian." But this is no continental division.

The reason I urge that this elevation of Europe to continental status be abandoned should be evident. An amusing instance of how it misled an intelligent author will help to make it clear. Van Loon (after noting the absurdity of calling Europe a continent, but not wanting to add to the confusion by denying it that status) tries to compare the historical positions of "Asia" and of Europe.[3] He says that while "Asia's" rivers ran "in any old direction," Europe's all flowed straight to the sea – hence Europe expanded and "Asia" didn't. The statement might have made sense if it had compared comparable areas and populations – Europe with India or China, for instance; but in that case, the whole point about the rivers would have been gone. Van Loon might be commended for not wanting to "add to the existing confusion" if the existing confusion were not already so great that it could hardly be added to.

Therefore, in order to avoid encouraging the idea that Europe is a continent on a par with the rest of Eurasia, we should: (1) not refer to "the whole continent" of Europe, but rather to "the mainland," or "the whole peninsula" of Europe; (2) avoid that use of maps which carry a pointless line through the middle of Russia; (3) not speak of "Asiatic" as if it characterized anything specially concrete as does "European" or

[3] Hendrik W. Van Loon, *Geography*, p. 78.

"American"; (4) scrutinize everything we say about "Asia" or its subdivisions to make sure we are not making inapplicable comparisons with Europe or its subdivisions.

The second type of phrase to avoid is that which speaks of "East" and "West" as complementary *halves* of world civilization. Is there anything more absurd than our use of the word "Eastern" or "Oriental"? We cover everything with them, from Algeria and Russia to Java and Japan – that is, almost everything non-European. Yet it is clear that we are not dealing with a single civilization here similar to the single "Occidental" one.

A brief survey will show at least three great civilizations in the "East," as different from each other as each is from Europe. For instance, whereas Europe uses the Greek (and Roman) alphabets, the Near East uses the Arabic script, the Indias use distinctively Hindu types of letters, and the Far East uses the Chinese characters. Europe is Christian, the Near East Moslem, the Indias Hindu and Hinayana Buddhist, the Far East Mahayana Buddhist. In other things the underlying cultures are equally diverse. The equation of "East" and "West" not only implies that *our* culture is the equal of the sum of the others, but ignores the very important fact that all non-Europeans are by no means alike. It would probably be a great deal more reasonable to divide the world into Celestial and Barbarian civilizations, as the Chinese did; for the Chinese is probably the most distinctive of all the cultures.

Of course, certain things can be predicated of Europe which cannot be of the other lands; but likewise certain things can be predicated of Iceland that cannot be of any other place. This does not make it reasonable to divide world culture into the two branches Icelandic and non-Icelandic; Norway's culture, for instance, is much closer to Iceland's than it is to Brazil's. It is similarly unreasonable to create a dichotomy between Occidental and non-Occidental; Egypt's culture, for instance, has much greater affinities with Poland's than with Japan's. Such a dichotomy may be useful for some few purposes; but its oversimplification is tremendously dangerous if one is trying to build a world outlook.

Almost any example of the use of the words "Eastern" and "Oriental" will illustrate the dangers involved, whether it be, as in a recently popular book on strategy, in an argument for ignoring Japan; or in general characterizations such as "Oriental seclusion of women" (does that apply to China more than to Europe?); "Oriental weariness of life" (has no one ever heard of Mohammed?); or any other "Oriental" traits. It is amazing to note how many people really believe that "East is East and West is West," and that they'll never meet. General Gordon and C. F. Andrews were not miracle men when they adapted themselves to China or India; they were just carrying on a little further the process by which an American artist can become "more Parisian than Paris." The difficulty of an American or Frenchman understanding India is only in degree greater than that of an American understanding France.

Therefore, the need is not just to point out that "the East is just as good as we are"; it is to get rid of the idea that the "East" is one cultural entity complementary to that of Europe at all. Hence we should among other things: (1) refuse to refer to this or that characteristic as "Eastern" – even when a careful study has shown this to be true of all "Eastern" lands and of no "Western" lands (a rare situation) – because of the danger of supporting the idea that the Occident is coordinate with the sum of all the "East"; (2) avoid all use of the terms "Eastern" and "Orient" as ambiguous, and use instead Far Eastern, Indian, Near Eastern, African, Chinese, etc.; (3) be exceedingly careful in the use of the terms "Western," "Occidental," etc.; (4) stop talking about the "incomprehensibility of the East," and refer if necessary instead to the "incomprehensibility of cultures other than one's own."

The third type of phrase which I hope we will avoid is that which speaks of Europe – or of the most direct predecessors of European culture – as always being "in the center of the stage of world history." Thus, I have seen a chart of history, with dates across the top; bars in the space below running parallel to the dates, arranged to show "the length of time a people is important in history"; and dots preceding and following the bars "to remind us that these lands were still inhabited before and after they were the center of the stage." Egypt and Babylonia start out in the upper left-hand corner, become after 500 B.C. rows of dots extending to the present. Further down and to the right come the Hebrew and the Greeks, then Rome, then still further down and to the right, a double bar of the Moslem and medieval European cultures, and in the lower right hand corner the modern West. Since the lands east of the Indus form more than half of the Old World's population, if the "center of the stage" is to be placed with any one group, how does it manage to be west of the Indus at all? It is more reasonable to say that *Europe* "was isolated from the main stream of history" than to say that *India* was.

Actually, of course, the chart is deliberately invented to illustrate what the author thinks is the "slow march westward of civilization" – a fiction which has proved useful to some American nationalists. The unsoundness of the impression it makes can be shown by pointing out that the Moslem civilization which it graciously ranks coordinate with the medieval European is really found in the same lands as the Babylonian and ancient Egyptian (still shown as dots on this chart) and therefore does not, as the chart tries to imply, continue the "march to the west."

The impudence of such a chart is amazing. Except for Greece, which on the map looks more Near Eastern than European, and whose ties have always until the last century been eastward rather than westward, Europe can be said to have produced very little of world importance before the late Middle Ages; until then there is not the slightest trace of civilization's moving west. Even vaunted Rome depended on Egypt and the eastern Mediterranean not only for her wheat, but for her teachers and models. The largest and richest cities of the Empire were in the east, where civilization had always been, and it was there that the bulk of science and culture continued to be produced.

The reason for this chart, however, is easier to understand than its impudence. When we have studied history, we have always studied whatever culture was farthest west – nearest to our northwestern Europe. Thus when Greece comes into the light, we switch our whole attention to Greece – and then are surprised when, under Hellenism, lands other than Greece have a great deal to contribute. Meanwhile Italy having begun to be civilized, we switch our attention thither, never returning east of the Adriatic again, but rather turning as fast as possible to the forests of Britain, Gaul, and Germany (and are again amazed at the time of the Crusades to find that the east is better developed than they).

When Christian culture west of the Adriatic shows itself to be slow in getting started in spite of its bit of brilliance at the beginning, we decide that a dark age has fallen over the whole world! We even develop the crust to claim that a chieftain who tries to overcome local difficulties is the chief character in the world, in the age of Geber at Baghdad, and the T'ang dynasty in China! Charlemagne himself knew better.

In order to avoid encouraging the idea that "Babylon, then Greece, then Rome, then northwestern Europe have occupied the center of the stage of history," historians should, among other things: (1) stop talking about the "known world," as that expression is usually used – known to provincial Europe; (2) stop talking about Rome's being "mistress of the civilized world" – or of "her world," since the ordinary person will not get the difference subtly admitted between these phrases; (3) stop talking about the fall of the Roman Empire, when only the loss of three or four western provinces is meant – remember that Rome was in the hands of the Empire centuries after the traditional A.D. 476, as was most of the west Mediterranean coast up to the Moslem invasion; and (4) stop talking about the Dark Ages as if they were a period of history.

There are many other points at which we must avoid encouraging our provincialism, but I hope we will note at least these in writing or in teaching. My fundamental hope remains that someone will undertake to write a real world history, giving us a perspective view of ourselves, an undistorted framework into which to fit our own civilization and times.

4

The great Western Transmutation

The Western Transmutation as a world event

Between about 1600 and about 1800 there took place in Western Europe a general cultural transformation. This transformation culminated in two more or less simultaneous events: the Industrial Revolution, when specialized technical development decisively transformed the presuppositions of human production, and the French Revolution, when a kindred spirit established likewise unprecedented norms in human social relations. These events did not constitute the transformation I am speaking of: they were its most obvious early consequences. But the transformation had far-reaching effects not only among Europeans but also in the world at large. Its long-run implications for us all have not yet become entirely manifest. We will take some of them up later. From the point of view of the world at large, however, and particularly of the Muslim peoples, there was a more immediate consequence which will concern us here. This was that, by about 1800, the Occidental peoples (together with the Russians) found themselves in a position to dominate overwhelmingly most of the rest of the world – and, in particular, to dominate the lands of Islamdom. The same generation that saw the Industrial and French Revolutions saw a third and almost equally unprecedented event: the establishment of European world hegemony.

It was not merely, or perhaps even primarily, that the Europeans (and their overseas settlers) found themselves in a position to defeat militarily any powers they came in contact with. Their merchants were able to outproduce, outtravel, and outsell anyone, their physicians were able to heal better than others, their scientists were able to put all others to shame. Only a limited part of the world's surface was actually occupied by European troops, at least at first. European hegemony did not mean direct European world rule. What mattered was that both occupied ("colonial" or "settled") areas and unoccupied ("independent") areas were fairly rapidly caught up in a worldwide political and commercial system the rules of which were made by, and for the advantage of, Europeans and their overseas settlers. Even "independent" areas could retain their local autonomy, in the end, only to the extent that they provided European merchants, European missionaries, even European tourists, with a certain minimum of that type of international "law and order" to which they had become accustomed in Europe, so that the Europeans remained free to vaunt a privileged position and to display among all peoples the unexampled new physical and intellectual luxuries of Europe. (For otherwise, the European powers would feel forced to intervene; and wherever one of them concentrated its efforts it would almost infallibly succeed.) Thus all peoples had to adjust their governments to a modern European international political order; but also to adjust their economies – a harder task – to the competition of technically industrialized Europe; and finally to adjust their mental outlook to the challenge of modern science as studied in Europe. The mere presence of the Europeans was enough for their new power to be felt.

We may summarize this by saying that the Europeans (including, of course, their overseas descendants) had by 1800 reached a decisively higher level of *social power* than was to be found elsewhere. (The exceptional position of Europeans in the eighteenth century, with their institutionalized capital accumulation, already reflected an advanced stage of this process.) Individual Europeans might still be less intelligent, less courageous, less loyal than individuals elsewhere; but when educated and organized in society the Europeans were able to think and to act far more effectively, as members of a group, than could members of any other societies. European enterprises, such as firms or churches or, of course, governments, could muster a degree of power, intellectual, economic, and social, which was of a different order from what could be mustered among even the most wealthy or vigorous peoples in the rest of the world. It is perhaps premature to refer to what had happened in Europe simply under the heading of "progress." This word implies a moral judgment – "progress," as against regress or mere digression, implies movement toward a goal, or at least in a good direction. It can be disputed what aspects of our modern life have meant change for the better and what have meant change for the worse. What concerns us just here is not any general "progress" that may have occurred, but the immediately decisive rise in the level of social power, whether for better or for worse. We will find this point important when we come to try to understand the responses of the Muslim peoples to what had happened in the West.[1]

At least till very recently, there was a tendency among Europeans (including, of course, Americans) to take this remarkable fact for granted. (In the same way many Muslims, before the Western Transmutation interrupted, assumed a natural superiority in Islamicate institutions which would make them prevail over all unbelievers sooner or later.) Such Europeans have wondered why in recent years, after many centuries (so they suppose) of static quiescence, the various "backward" peoples now are stirring. They have overlooked the wonder of how it could be that, for what is in fact rather a brief period of little more than one century, Europeans could have held so unique a position in the world.[2] The real question, from the standpoint of the world at large, is just that: what gave the Europeans such overwhelming power for a time?

I have styled the cultural changes in Europe between 1600 and 1800 which led to this increase in social power a "transmutation." I intend no close biological analogy. Yet the changes, insofar as they led to this rise in social power, formed a markedly interrelated unity, which can, with proper caution, be discussed as a single, though vast and complex, event. This event was relatively sudden, as human history has gone. Moreover, the essential changes were constitutive: they altered not merely particular social and cultural traits but some of the most elementary presuppositions of any subsequent human social and cultural development. Henceforth, historical events, as such, took place in certain respects in a radically new way.

What happened can be compared to the first advent several thousand years B.C. of that combination, among the dominant elements of certain societies, of urban living, literacy, and generally complex social and cultural organization, which we call "civilization." The "civilized," that is, cited agrarianate communities – starting probably with Sumer – found themselves on a much higher level of social power than the other agricultural groupings, to say nothing of food-gathering tribes; it was not long before an urban type of life came to have a decisive role in wider and wider circles, both politically and, in the end, culturally. What had hap-

[1] For my usage of the terms "West," "Occident," and "Europe," see Chapter 5, "Historical Method in Civilizational Studies," below.

[2] The notion of the "millenial torpor" of "the East" remains so widespread partly because of touristic misimpressions but also because it has been subsumed in the approach of two sorts of scholars: the Westernists, who downgrade all alien societies, and the area students, who suppose all pre-Moderns were overwhelmed by tradition. Cf. "On determinancy in traditions" in Chapter 5, "Historical Method in Civilizational Studies."

pened in Sumer soon (as ancient time-spans go) determined the fate of much of the Eastern hemisphere. Among these societies on an agrarianate level, the character of historical change was so altered that what had come before we sometimes call "pre-history": for instance, its pace was immensely speeded up, so that a degree of change which before consumed thousands of years now consumed merely centuries. Similarly, after the Western Transmutation the kind of changes that earlier, in agrarianate times, had required hundreds of years now required, at most, decades.

Moreover, just as civilization on an agrarianate level had appeared in one or at most a very few spots and spread from there to the greater part of the globe, so the new modern type of life did not appear everywhere among all citied peoples at the same moment, but first in one restricted area, Western Europe, from which it has spread everywhere else. It was not that the new ways resulted from conditions that were limited entirely to the Occident. Just as the first urban, literate life would have been impossible without the accumulation among a great many peoples of innumerable social habits and inventions, major and minor, so the great modern cultural mutation presupposed the contributions of all the several citied peoples of the eastern hemisphere. Not only were the numerous inventions and discoveries of many peoples necessary – for most of the earlier basic ones were not made in Europe. It was also necessary that there exist large areas of relatively dense, urban-dominated populations, tied together in a great interregional commercial network, to form the vast world market which had gradually come into being in the eastern hemisphere, and in which European fortunes could be made and European imaginations exercised.

Technicalism and society: The decisive institutional traits of the Transmutation

At this point, we must consider just what happened in the Occident itself. For though these events have been analyzed innumerable times, the analysis has not normally been made from a genuinely world-historical viewpoint, but virtually always from the standpoint of the local Occidental past. The Western Transmutation can be described, for our world-historical purposes, as consisting primarily in transformations of culture in three main fields: the economic, the intellectual, and the social. In economic life there took place that great increase in productivity – due to a sequence of new techniques, and carried out through a concentrated control of production based on capital accumulation and mass markets – which led up to and culminated in the "Industrial Revolution" and the accompanying "Agricultural Revolution." In intellectual life there came the new experimental science, from Kepler and Galileo on, and more generally the philosophical exploratory independence made widely popular in the Englightenment. In social life there came the breakdown of old landed privileges and supremacies and their replacement with a bourgeois bureaucratic or mercantile power which ushered in the American and French revolutions, with their repercussions throughout Europe.

In all these fields the changes which in retrospect can be seen as decisive, from the viewpoint of the Occident's level of social power in the world as a whole, can be dated to a period of not much more than two centuries. In the sixteenth century on the whole, as we have seen, the parity of the citied societies of the Oikoumene still prevailed: despite the general Occidental florescence associated with the Renaissance, politically the West-Europeans were even receding before the Ottoman empire, and commercially the Muslims were still at least their equals in most parts of the Oikoumene. Culturally too, the Muslims were in one of their most brilliant periods. This fact of world history reflects the fact of European history that the Renaissance florescence did not yet, in itself, transcend the limitations of agrarianate-level society. But the crucial changes were clearly under way by the end of the sixteenth century. By the end of the eighteenth century already, they were all of them completed at least as regards some particular field in some particular place, e.g., as regards astronomical physics throughout the Occident, or cotton cloth production in England. Correspondingly, Islamicate society was routed in a land like Bengal.

Just as to include the Renaissance within the actual transition to Modernity, rather than among its prior conditions, is to falsify the picture from a world-historical viewpoint, so also to extend the critical period beyond the eighteenth century is to confuse arbitrarily one or more phases of the unfolding consequences of the decisive event with the world-historical event itself. Subsequent changes have been of enormous importance; for instance, the later introduction of electricity as a basic form of industrial energy, or the theory of relativity in physics. But as regards the nature of the historical change involved, they merely carried further the Modern pattern of development already established *in nucleo* about the year 1800. In any case, it was transformations of the seventeenth and eighteenth centuries that served to set off decisively the Westerners from the rest of mankind.

What was the relation among all these changes, that they should all happen at once? What was it that made for such a relatively sudden and comprehensive transformation of the society, with such far-reaching effects? It is clear that the changes were closely interrelated and, indeed, interdependent. However, this was not always in the sense that particular changes in one field depended on particular changes in another (thus scientific and industrial developments long went parallel, with only relatively superficial contacts); rather, all the changes presupposed common social resources and even common psychological patterns of expectation.[3]

For historical purposes, one ought to analyze the Great Transmutation as a historical *event* or process, not merely as the presence of a new *state* or age of human culture; but such attempts have been infrequent. Schumpeter, however, successfully transforms what even for the Marxists is a relatively static capitalist "stage" of society into a complex and real equilibrium, and a foreseeable end. In such a perspective, the analyses of the capitalist market by the conventional bourgeois economists as if it were a condition essentially based on an approximated equilibrium, take on an unreal air: at most, they are analyzing short-term equilibriums in a process which itself is creating and modifying the market which they purpose.

In this perspective my own study is doubly lacking. I have treated the Transmutation primarily as a shift from one state to another, as being completed with the generation of 1789, when it was achieved *in nucleo* in certain fields in certain places. In the long run, it must probably be treated as a completed process only from the perspective of the day when all relevant fields of social life and all parts of the world will have been technicalized, if such a day comes. From such a vantage point, the seventeenth and eighteenth centuries will seem merely preliminary, though they will still retain their special status. At present, however, I cannot venture to assume such a perspective.

Hence many have seen the Transmutation as the expression in many fields of a single overall basic change: a change from what is called a "traditional" to what is called a "rational" society. In a "rational" society, choices can be determined less by the dictates of ancestral custom and

[3] From the time of Burckhardt, we have had many perceptive attempts to analyze just what "modern man," that is a European of the Technical Age, really "is." However, apart from some distorted information on what is called "Oriental," these attempts have usually made use only of data from within west European and ancient Greek history. Hence they have blurred the difference between local stages within the Occidental evolution, and changes more universally relevant. Area-studies men, on the other hand, rarely know anything about *any* part of the world before the nineteenth century. Hence I have had to develop my own analysis.

more by practical calculation of immediate advantage. Persons, then, will be granted status and authority less on the basis of their birth and family connections, and more on the basis of their effective competence as individuals. Efficient, predictable organization will prevail over familial, patriarchal arrangements and social relations will be determined less by private personal commitments and more by impersonal legal status. Immediate efficiency will be valued more highly than continuity with the past, and people will be less hesitant about change lest it prove degeneration, and instead continuous practical improvement, even at the expense of what has been valued before, will be not only welcomed as "progress," but expected as a natural social condition. Once "rationality" was established and innovation was accepted as normal, all the economic, social, and intellectual improvements followed naturally.

Some such shift did occur in the Transmutation. But this change was by no means so sharp a change as is often assumed, for in fact the standard picture of a "traditional" society is rather a fiction. As we have seen in discussing the nature of a cultural tradition, even in a very "primitive" society, cultural traditions must be in constant development to remain viable, for they must always effectively meet some current need or no amount of ancestral privilege can save them. Moreover, the rationality referred to, that is, the impersonal and innovative private calculation called "rationalization" in industry, is a relative manner. Most agrarianate-level societies could even be evaluated as relatively "rational," indeed, as against even the relative "traditionality" of most pre-literate societies. In respect simply of "rationalization," the sort of shift that occurred in the Transmutation was one that had occurred, on one level or another, time and again in history – not only at the advent of cities, but in every great cultural florescence and even, on a lesser scale, whenever a new religious or political tradition was being initiated. At all such times, independent, innovative calculation (but not necessarily human rationality as such) has been more emphasized and traditional custom less. Moreover, some residue of such attitudes had commonly been institutionalized in subsequent social life, especially in the more cosmopolitan societies.

Thus Islamdom, being more cosmopolitan in the Mid-Islamic periods than was the Occident, embodied more provision for rational calculation and personal initiative in its institutions. Indeed, much of the shift from "traditional" to "rational" which in Europe was a part of the Mutation's "modernization" has the air of bringing the Occident closer to what was already well-established in the Islamicate tradition. (This is especially true of those "Modern" developments which were beginning already in the Renaissance and are often cited to show that "Modernity" had already begun then.) The depreciation of aristocratic birth in favor of greater social mobility did not go so far in the Occident as it had in Islamdom. The inclination to allow a primary role to freely made individual contracts as against the authority of guilds and estates was in accord with the principles of sharia law.

The shift from reliance on custom and continuity to reliance on reason and innovation, although it occurred only in a limited measure, was not in itself what was specific to the Modern Western Transmutation. It was not this that set the Westerners apart from both their ancestors and the rest of the world. It merely accompanied and facilitated a change in the patterns of investment of time and money. This, as we shall see, occurred only in a special form, one that I shall call *technicalistic,* so that *specialized technical considerations tended to take precedence* over all others. Indeed, in that special form – rather than in other forms – the shift went to unprecedented lengths, so that the results set new conditions for all historical life. It was not that the human mind as such was suddenly emancipated, as if by some mutation, and could therefore begin freely to explore all calculable possibilities where, before, new paths could be opened only by chance and despite the weight of customary bias. Rather new concrete sorts of opportunity for social investment, hitherto impractical even for the most emancipated mind, became praticable, attracting even minds that still, by and large, resisted any deviation from intellectual habit. And then the resistance was gradually reduced.

To begin with, we must identify what was distinctive in the new forms of investments, as such. The calculative innovation in the Renaissance still presented a degree of initiative and creativity "normal" for great florescences in the Agrarian Age. But in time such a florescence would normally taper off. Usually such activities had found sooner or later a point at which further cultural complexity was so subject to interruptions by historical accidents that it did not repay the risks it incurred.

What made the difference was that the tendency toward rational innovation, always present in the very nature of tradition, was permitted – in certain forms (and only in those forms) – to be carried to unprecedented lengths, and to set the conditions for all historical life. In sum a critical point of social development was reached, at which types of investment (material and mental) which had before been sporadic and precarious were occurring on a sufficiently large scale so that they could be institutionalized and built on further – and finally be made socially irreversible. This new situation offered new opportunities to human enterprise, new occasions for cultural creativity of many sorts. The new opportunities were rapidly taken up. On the basis of the new creativity, new and rapidly developing traditions proliferated, and the new patterns were established as rapidly as the process of evolution in cultural traditions could carry them. When the inner dialogue in a tradition is unhampered and its field of action is unexploited, this can be very fast. The historical conditions which allowed this at all, allowed it in many fields of endeavor at once. The precariousness of cultural complexity beyond the agrarianate base level of the urban-rural symbiosis was at last overcome, and a new, higher base level was presumably established.

The rational innovation in the Renaissance still presented a degree of initiative and creativity "normal" for great florescences in the Agrarian Age. Usually, such activities had found sooner or later a point at which further cultural complexity was so subject to interruptions by historical accidents that it did not repay the risks it incurred. This was especially true in any field that required large-scale social investment of time or money, and hence freedom from such disorganization or arbitrary intervention as would disrupt the peace and social orderliness which such investment presupposed. This was a far more pressing danger than the oppressiveness of too grand an internal balance which might trap men's minds in some form of style cycle. By the end of the sixteenth century, just those kinds of calculative, innovative investment that were most dependent on freedom from social disruption were reaching levels rarely reached before: that is, improvements in technical methods of achieving concrete, material ends by way of multiple, interdependent specialization. And, despite such disasters as the Thirty Years' War and the English Civil War, nothing happened to stop the process as a whole, especially in northwest Europe. A very similar process had been stopped in later Sung China under the nomad dynasties.

The Occidental florescence did not taper off. Rather, innovative investment persisted till a critical point of social development was reached by about 1600. By then, certain types of investment (material and mental) which all through the Agrarian Age had been sporadic and precarious, even during florescences (and during the Renaissance), were now occurring on a sufficiently large scale so that they could be institutionalized, built on further, and finally be made socially irreversible. This new situation offered a new set of opportunities to human enterprise, new occasions for cultural creativity of many sorts. The new opportunities were swiftly taken up. On the basis of the new creativity, new and rapidly developing "technicalistic" traditions proliferated, and the new patterns were established as rapidly as the process of evolution in cultural traditions could carry them. When the inner dialogue in a tradition is unhampered and its field of action is as yet unexploited, this can be very fast.

The historical conditions that allowed this at all, allowed it in many fields of endeavor at once. As a result, the previous precariousness of any cultural complexity beyond the agrarianate base-level of the rural-urban symbiosis was at last overcome. A new higher base-level was presumably established.

These new impulses carried everything with them, including old institutions. Existing institutions had, to be sure, proved sufficiently open to make such an advance possible. (Probably any set of mature institutions can provide a great deal more flexibility than is at first apparent.) But such institutions were hardly well adapted to it, surely no more so than, say, the Islamicate institutions. Yet they were pressed into serving the new possibilities, or were superceded. A good deal of institutional rigidity was implicit in the Occidental corporative expectations, and some of this rigidity acted as an obstacle to the new impulses. (For instance, the church Inquisition was more oppressive to the ordinary thinking citizen that anything found in Islamdom.) Nonetheless, this very corporative structure – when the occasion was ripe – did act to protect individual innovation at least as effectively as might the social mobility and the sharia autonomy of Islamdom.

At the core of the new innovation was the pattern of multiple technical specialization. Such technical specialization was not altogether new: since the introduction of gunpowder weapons, that aspect of military practice had represented a microcosm of the innovative technical specialization which was to be the hallmark of the Transmutation. But now it reached a breadth of scale, a "critical mass," which allowed much more extensive institutionalizing of such innovation than before, an institutionalizing which was to embrace and finally dominate all the key sectors of the whole society. Economically, it appeared in forms of industrial and commercial investment in the seventeenth century in northwest Europe during the seventeenth century: capital was systematically reinvested and multiplied on the basis of continuing technical innovation and of anticipated expansion in market patterns. Intellectually, it appeared in the work of such associations as the Royal Society: in many cultures there had been associations for cultivating existing scholarly learning, which might welcome the occasional piece of new information. In the seventeenth century the Royal Society aimed explicitly at gathering and disseminating that new knowledge which would replace the old, and did so largely in expectation of the continual new inventions of the by then professionalized instrument-makers and the new observations they would make possible.

One must suppose that the intellectual side of the movement was dependent on the economic side, but not in the sense that the natural sciences benefitted directly from the inventiveness of industry. Rather, the expansion of industrial investment released more resources to the whole economy. These were then made use of, among scholars, in a manner consonant with the expansive mood of which the pace was surely set by the exhilaration associated with the new mercantile and industrial ventures. The intellectual development was apparently quite autonomous. After a certain point is reached in the development of natural sciences, at any rate, it cannot advance further without a disproportionate amount of human investment on all fronts at once: i.e., increasing specialization in many different fields. Whether or not we suppose that a lull in scientific work in the Occident after 1300 resulted from the difficulty of proceeding further with the then available level of human resources, it nevertheless seems that the science had reached the point where the sudden increase of such resources could have great liberating effects – and precisely in those aspects of knowledge that were most dependent on multiple specialization. To the extent that industrial experience entered into scientific advantage, it was mostly by way of the increasing skills and technical resources of the instrument-makers, whose specialized innovations surely confirmed the technicalistic tendency in science.

In both scientific and economic life, the scale of increasing technical specialization brought with it qualitative changes. Perhaps most obviously it reached a level on which it paid to invest the requisite time, funds, and concern into institutions that embodied and further confirmed the technical specialization. These very institutions, then, helped to hasten the process. Gradually, in the seventeenth and eighteenth centuries, it became so well-rooted and widely ramified in Occidental society that no social process or historical event originating outside the process could reverse it or seriously slow it down.

This institutionalization presupposed further a close interrelation among specializations. There was no mere conglomeration of individual technical advances. As isolated technical specialization, the techniques of mechanized cotton spinning, for instance, could be reckoned equivalent to the highly specialized and relatively efficient ancient techniques of the Coptic land surveyors in Egypt. Especially within the main fields in which the process occurred, all depended on the growth of an increasingly inclusive and interdependent nexus of technical specialism, such that the technical efficiency of any particular activity was increased by its use of the fruits of other specialties, and it in turn served to increase their efficiency. For such a process to be carried far, a major part of all the activities of a society must become involved. Once this process was well-established, new discoveries and inventions, along with the human and financial investment needed to realize them, grew at a geometric rate of progression. Each new round of inventions, once exploited, cleared the way for yet another.

It will readily be seen that such a technicalistic process left behind most basic presuppositions of all agrarianate society. Even those agrarianate-level societies that were not themselves immediately agrarian – being, say, pastoralist or mercantile – had depended for their existence on the social relations prevailing in their agrarian hinterland, in which the agrarian surplus provided the chief income on which the carriers of the high culture, the chief market of the mercantile cities, depended. The growth of inter-dependent technical specializations freed the income structure of the privileged classes in large areas from primary dependence on agrarian exploitation of the agriculturalists.

It did so, of course, not because industrial production could take the place of agricultural in providing the common necessities of life, such as food. Rather, what the non-agricultural sectors of the economy could support now was the special income of the privileged, the carriers of the high culture; and this was not only in a few immediate urban situations, as before, but in the overall economic nexus. Even with no increase in the agricultural surplus, that is, with no increase in the number of non-agricultural laborers that could be fed, technical specialization could vastly increase productivity, and hence total production, till so much of it was nonagricultural that a correspondingly large proportion of income in the society need not be determined by agrarian relationships. If the technicalistic process was to progress far (and if the proportion of the privileged in the society was ultimately to expand) not only greater productivity per laborer was required, but also more laborers (and also more agricultural raw materials). Hence even the limitations on agricultural production, imposed by localized manual and animal methods, must be escaped by extending the new social process to agriculture itself (though a partial alternative could be to import agricultural products from distant lands not yet undergoing the technicalistic process – which could mean exporting manufacturers thither, displacing the local craftsmen, and turning those lands more solidly to agriculture than before). All phases of the new roles of agriculture and agrarian relations were to become significant in the future of Islamdom.

This overall process, and then the condition of society in which it has resulted, I call *technicalization*, which I will define as *a condition of rationally calculative (and hence innovative) technical specialization, in which the several specialties are interdependent on a large enough scale to determine patterns of expectation in the key sectors of a society.* I choose the word "technicalization" in contradistinction to "industrialization," which is only one aspect of the whole process. The Industrial Revolution at the end of the eighteenth century was constituted by the joining of specialized machines, adapted to an expanding "mass" market, to the indefinitely expandable resources of steam power. "Industrialization" has meant the prevalence of such power-mechanized industry in a country's economy. (When steam power is replaced by electric power or by atomic power, or when the efficiency of any source of power is multiplied by the use of assembly lines or of automation, the human consequences may be important but the basic equation established at the end of the eighteenth century, marking the contrast to the role of industry in agrarianate-level society, remains essentially unchanged.) This was certainly the culmination of the seventeenth and eighteenth century economic transformations, and in recent times the preponderance in a country's economy of power-mechanized industry has been taken as the essential mark of Modernity. For a country to be Modern has meant for it to be industrialized. But this is as yet only a token.

For our purposes we need a far broader conception. "Industrialization" may not exclude a highly technicalized modern land like Denmark for, though Denmark is primarily agricultural, the prevalence of power-mechanization in agriculture itself, and especially in the processing subsidiary to agriculture, may be included by extension under "industrialization." But the whole process of technicalization is far more inclusive. Even in the economy proper, there could be a high degree of technicalization without power-mechanization – at a time before power-mechanization had imposed itself (as it did once it became available at all) thenceforth on any participants in innovative technicalization. Thus the pre-power-mechanized industries of France in the eighteenth century already displayed many of the traits of technicalization in their internal evolution and in their consequences in world trade. The process of technicalistic specialization in the sciences and in social organization and even in other aspects of society was equally important with that in economic production. A term like "technicalization" will neutrally cover all aspects of the process, without assigning primacy to any given aspect.

Moral dimensions of technicalism

Now we must look to the indispensable psychological side of such investment patterns. Reliance on multiple technical specialization was correlated with a pattern of what we may call technicalistic expectations. Some such expectations in a certain sector of the population had been necessary to get technicalization launched, but then the process itself evoked them in others and intensified them.

Central to the technicalistic spirit was the expectation of impersonal efficiency through technical precision. There had in all times been concern with efficiency, especially military efficiency, in limited ways. There had also been a certain amount of technical specialization and precision, for instance in fine craft work. Even technical inventiveness had held a respected place within a more rounded economic pattern. But now in western Europe technical efficiency was increasingly given a primary role, such that all other considerations of a less universally or obviously objective sort – aesthetic, traditional, interpersonal – were increasingly made to yield to this, and it was relied on as the most important basis for excelling in constructive activities. On this psychological level, to say that all aspects of social organization were being technicalized means that they were organized primarily in terms of specialized procedures calculated to yield maximum efficiency for the limited ends immediately in objective view. It is in this form that technicalization meant institutionalizing a major shift from authoritative custom toward independent calculation.

It is on the psychological level, then, that we come to the contrast that has been expressed by the words "traditional-rational." Despite a general awareness among us that much in Modern life is less than humanly rational, the current literature of economic and social development gives evidence that there is still need to warn the reader against identifying the technicalistic spirit with human rationality as such. The exercise of human reason cannot be identified with the calculative pursuit of any given sort of goals alone. Sometimes even a narrowly practical innovation, however shrewd, may be so risky (in its disregard of immemorial experience) as to be positively irrational. But in any case, to subordinate all considerations of ethics or beauty or human commitments to maximizing technical efficiency, however successfully, is quite likely to prove an irrational nightmare.

It may be said that "rational" and "traditional," as differentiating Modern from pre-Modern, bear technical meanings: "rational" means "calculative with regard to specialized technical aims," and "traditional" means "authoritative by way of custom." But the terms have in fact been understood, both by readers and by the writers themselves, in a more general way. It is quite natural, if a bit arrogant, for a modern Westerner to see his own technicalistic ways as rational and to condemn the ways of agrarianate societies as the effects of blind tradition set in contrast to rationality.

The scholarly use of the terms, however well-intentioned, merely reinforces this bias. All too often it is necessary to demonstrate what should have been obvious: that the "Modern," i.e., technicalistic, sector of an economy often proves less than rational in the ordinary human sense so long as other than technical considerations are ignored, or that "traditional" institutions may be undeniably rational in the ordinary human sense, and even contribute to technicalistic development. It will be wise to reserve the terms *rational* and *traditional* for their more normal usage. In this usage, every society is traditional in that it operates through cultural traditions – however rapidly those traditions may evolve in some cases, notably under technicalism. And every society is rational in that its institutions will long survive only as they are pragmatically functional. This, because the personal decisions of its more intelligent members reflect rational calculations so far as serious alternatives are envisageable and actually practicable – however narrow the range of practicable alternatives may be in some cases. It can be argued, indeed, that the greatest advantage of the highly technicalized lands has been the continuity and effectiveness of their *traditions,* which have served to channel individual rationality; while the greatest problem of less technicalized lands has been ungoverned opportunistic *rationality* among them, which has been loosed by the severe breaches in high-cultural tradition they have suffered.

In economic production, the technicalistic spirit emerged in an increased dependence on such things as even more clever inventions, and statistical analysis of output and market. These and other expressions of a demand for technical efficiency increased throughout the two centuries till there resulted new presuppositions for any economic activity. Instead of considerations of craft family continuity, of personal status, of mercantile solidarity, the weight shifted more to considerations of productively reinvesting returns on capital, of external economies in location, of keeping ahead in technique. The family trade secret was replaced with the public patent office.

In scientific work a similar spirit appeared. Even in astronomy (like military practice, a field where an element of "technicalization" had already prevailed) the new spirit took noticeable effect. Starting with Brahe and Kepler (in contrast to Copernicus), infinitesimal precision of measurement, with the aid of highly specialized technical instruments, was the keynote of the new type of investigation. I doubt that Kepler would have conceded priority to the ellipse over the geometrically "purer" circle, despite his metaphysical justifications of it, if he were not, unawares, coming to assign priority to technical precision and manipulation over philosophical elegance. The result was to place in jeopardy any sense of a cosmic whole. The natural science traditions had maintained also in the Occident that degree of intellectual autonomy they had early won from commitment to the intellectual predispositions of overall life-orientational traditions. This autonomy had made itself apparent on occasion among both Muslims and Christians in a relative empiricism, bound to but not overwhelmed by philosophic notions of the teleological and hierarchical nature of entities. Now, with intensive specialization, the autonomy of the natural-science traditions was pushed much further, and the accompanying empiricism became almost routine. Every major scientist found himself forced to try to work out for himself (if he cared) his own sense of the cosmic whole, and alert laymen were left with "all coherence gone." By 1800 the technicalist spirit had spread from astronomy and physics to chemistry, geology, and biology. From Descartes to its culmination in Kant, the new epistemological philosophy was inspired by the new technicalistic science and by its very disengagement from ultimate questions.

Finally, in social life, administration came to reflect a like technicalistic tendency, though at first with traits less unprecedented from a world point of view. The new absolute and "enlightened" monarchies (inspired in part by older Chinese precedents) were still at first bringing Occidental administration up to an effectiveness already achieved in some parts, some time earlier, for instance in the Ottoman empire. But by the time of the French Revolution, the increase in the efficiency of legally operated social control, the technical precision of its files and its reports, and (more important) the implementing of the whole conception of government as a public service to be judged by its usefulness, had gone beyond even Sung China and had made obsolete every earlier governmental tradition in Europe. In the following decades they all found it necessary to reconstitute themselves, or be reconstituted, on a new basis.

As the interdependent range of technical specialties widened, the new standards of efficiency necessarily came to hold not only for a small circle of learned men or experts, but for a large section of the west European population. It was only because British clerks and factory hands had gradually grown accustomed to working on the new basis that it was possible for those who introduced power machinery at the end of the eighteenth century to find workers to make the delicately adjusted machines and workers to run them without catastrophe. (It was only later, after the power-machinery was well-established, that relatively raw recruits could be trained in large numbers.) Increasingly large proportions of the population were involved in even the intellectual innovations, as the use of printed books spread amongst Protestant and also Catholic townsmen. Almost any major undertaking came to depend on the fairly immediate contributions of a great variety of specializations, each increasingly technical and difficult for an outsider to penetrate without disproportionate training. In some degree, practically the whole population, and certainly all the more ambitious elements in it, came under pressure to cultivate a technicalistic viewpoint and technicalistic expectations.

Indeed, from the viewpoint of the moral qualities involved, it may be said that technicalization has proceeded far enough to characterize social organization generally at the point when technical specialization is sufficiently diverse and intricate so that it has become the socially determinative situation that a given worker or scholar is no longer able to follow in detail the whole of the process of which his own work forms a fragment. Goethe, the greatest writer of the generation in which the Transmutation culminated, has suitably been called the "last of the universal men"; yet even he cannot have hoped to follow minutely all the technical processes in which the tools were cast which made the machines to service his theatrical innovations. Either Ibn Khaldun or Leonardo could still have done the equivalent in their time.

There was, thus, something of a dehumanizing implication in technicalism. At the same time, the Transmutation also saw important moral changes of a creatively human kind. A distinctive ideal human image (or, rather, a complex of such human images), new equally to the Occident and to the rest of the world, was becoming increasingly attractive in wide circles. Closely related to the growth of technicalism was the spread of the image of the man who would undertake new and imaginative efforts with resourcefulness and dedication – no longer merely as a private adventurer, but as representatives of hopes for new patterns of life in a wider public. This "projector," satirized from the time of Ben Johnson and immortalized by Swift in *Gulliver's Travels* (and given more level-headed advice in Kipling's *If*), became increasingly a recognizably effective type among the proliferating business classes as investment increased – active not only in business affairs but in science, administration, and even religion.

Seemingly in contrast to the image of the "projector," but not unrelated to it, was the image of the man of humane "civilization." Indeed, the time of the Transmutation saw new moral standards of an explicitly humane bent which had little to do directly with the technicalistic spirit. Notable was what may be called a "gentling of manners," based on the active expectation that much of what had always been acknowledged as an ideal might be realized in practice. The manners of the better classes were being softened and "civilized." Consistently with the new gentler tastes, heretics were being left alone and even torture was being dispensed with, both as punishment and as means of extorting information. The idea was arising that with more "philosophical" or else "natural" education, and freer laws, human minds and spirits generally might be enlightened and "perfected."

Much in the newer human images recalls earlier similar images: for instance, the glorification of individual effort found in different forms in the Iranian heroic tradition of Firdawsi or Rumi, and in still different forms in the chivalric tradition of the Occident satirized by Cervantes. But the tone now was the reverse of aristocratic. Indeed some strands, conservatives found disquietingly vulgar. It was surely one of the contributions of the Renaissance (though it might have come from some other florescences almost as readily) to glorify a human image of boundless individual initiative on a quite mundane and pragmatic level. Such an image is crucial in defining the possibilities open to a society, and, in this way, in keeping them open.

It was doubtless the optimistic spirit, as well as the economic expansiveness, produced by the progress of technicalization in its proper spheres that made such idealism suddenly appear practical. Yet the idealism does seem to have helped mitigate the arbitrariness of state officials and especially the destructiveness of warfare, which after 1648 became increasingly limited in aims and disciplined in conduct. It is quite possible that without such mitigation, governments might (as had happened before) have killed the goose that laid the golden egg. They might have allowed the work of scientists and investors to be disrupted, thus showing that further technical specialization would not, in fact, pay.[4] By the generation of 1789, the new moral outlook burst out in the most diverse directions and contributed importantly to the psychological gap between the West and the other societies. By then, as we shall note, it was carrying a considerable element of the expressly technicalistic mood.

The "gentling of manners" initially, at least, largely took the form of a religious and aesthetic development, by no means so epoch-making (especially as compared with what had happened in some other florescences in agrarianate times) as the scientific and economic developments, yet not to be overlooked. Particularly in religion, partly under the impact of the new philosophy, the evolution marked by several figures

[4] John U. Nef, the same man who has brought to our attention the basic role of the "earlier industrial revolution" in England, has brought out this point also in several works and notably in *Cultural Foundations of Industrial Civilization* (Cambridge: Cambridge University Press, 1958).

from Pascal to Schleiermacher was laying the groundwork for a religious consciousness grounded in direct human spiritual experience and not requiring an elite mysticism to free it – or cut it loose – from communal dogma; so that dogma itself had therefore, in the end, to be rethought on a more universal basis. (The advent of Protestantism as such marked no step outside the religious presuppositions prevalent in agrarianate times – some of its key traits can be found equally in agrarianate Islam, for instance – though it may have facilitated the subsequent religious development.)

Nevertheless, there seems to have been some degree of narrowing in the range of reality that Occidentals were prepared to invest greatly in exploring. Even other technical ends than those to which an investment in interdependent specializations could contribute, at least under the circumstances of the time, were not taken up or much cultivated (as if the keenest minds were too busy exploiting the new specializations opened up). Notable especially are areas that can mean much to an individual person. In the field of health, personal human regimen in its various aspects received little more attention – perhaps sometimes less – than physicians had given it for millennia, while a technical means of curing ills (once they had been allowed to happen) multiplied. The intense muscular training for dance or fight, which developed (sometimes fairly late) in several high cultural traditions, received no real Western equivalent.

Perhaps most notably, Westerners did not much explore some areas that could not be formulated in concrete, material terms. For instance, the sort of specialized mystical techniques represented in certain forms of Yoga and also of Sufism were almost ignored, despite promising beginnings earlier even in Christian Europe. Or they were severely curbed within communal religious assumptions, though elsewhere they often have carried pragmatic rational calculation and personal initiative to an extreme, and have called for, or seemed to call for, a ceaseless attempt to improve on predecessors, often by discovering new techniques.

To a large degree, then, the main changes in patterns of expectation which accompanied the process of technicalization did reflect not merely a generalized mood of rational optimism but a selective and recognizably technicalistic spirit, which both Westerners and Muslims were to call "materialistic."

The accompaniments of technicalism

The primacy of technical efficiency implied several correlative tendencies, which can be included within the technicalistic spirit. Like the emphasis on rationalized technique, they can be subsumed under a shift from authoritative custom towards independent calculation. They were, however, orientated to the needs of multiple technical specialization, not to rationality of every possible sort, and were, moreover, cultivated on such a scale as to institutionalize not merely occasional expressions of the shift but its most basic traits directly. A rationalizing calculativeness, crucial to technical specialization, depended, especially at first, on an *expectation of continuous innovation;* on encouraging an attitude of willingness to experiment, taking as little as possible for granted what had already been thought and done, rejecting established authority of every sort, and running the inherent risks of error that such rejection entails. At the beginning of the period, even though the full sway of the conservative spirit was to some extent subsiding during the Renaissance, the dominant institutions, in the Occident as elsewhere, represented agrarianate conservation: the maximum retention of established patterns holding out for order against the chaos which the natural flux of life's instability must tend towards. (Indeed, the very definition of culture is still the transmission of ways of doing from one generation to the next, so that each individual need not start out from scratch.) By the end of the eighteenth century, however, some of the most important institutions in the Occident had come to embody frankly and zealously the very principle of change, of innovation. Scientific journals, like the scientific societies, existed not primarily to preserve old knowledge but to seek out new. Legal protection of rights to inventions by patent recognized what had become a commonplace in industry: success went to whoever innovated most effectively most quickly. In the new social organization, innovation was institutionalized.

At last, government itself embodied this principle. The very institution of a legislature – an assembly whose explicit task it was not simply to grant taxes, nor even just to appoint administrators and decide on current policy in wars and crises, but to meet regularly to *change* the *laws* – reflected the degree to which conscious innovation lay at the heart of the new social order. Thinkers since the Axial Age – of whatever civilization – had granted that administrators must change and even current policies must change with circumstances. But the laws, if nothing else, ought so far as possible to be eternal. The laws were in fact sometimes changed in all societies at all times. Some provision was generally made for this, for instance (in the Ottoman case) in the regularizing of *qanun* law decrees. The whole purpose of social institutions was to obviate or at least minimize such change. Yet the very name of "legislature" suggested an opposite conception.

It was inevitable in such an atmosphere that the notion of "progress" became for the first time the dominant theme of serious thinking about historical change. Not merely perpetual variation but constant improvement of all kinds became a routine expectation. The normal "old man's" assumption that the younger generation was going to the dogs was at least counterbalanced by the youthful hope that every new generation could build bigger and better.

Somewhat slower to appear, but perhaps eventually even more essential a corollary to technicalism, was the *mass participant society:* one in which as many as possible are drawn into the nexus of multiple technical specialism in all its aspects. The new economic order depended on a large and mobile supply of skilled labor, and particularly on a mass market of persons living above subsistence levels to absorb the steadily increasing product of what was becoming mass production. With mass production and mass consumption, the lower classes, even the peasantry, had to share in the refinements associated with urban living at levels previously reserved to an elite: eventually it became clear that mass literacy was required if a technicalized society were to function well. Inevitably such masses became a political force. (In the end it proved that even those technicalized societies in which power was in fact most systematically reserved for a few, were not merely to tolerate a political role for the masses. They were even to require the active loyalty and participation of the masses in a "totalitarian" political process, so that the pervasive machinery of the state would be able to run more smoothly.)

In fact, the enormously extended role of the state, which entered every home in unprecedented detail and with inescapable efficiency, was as characteristic of technicalized society as was the notion of progress. Intervening groups based on personal contacts, such as had stood between the individual and the ultimate government in most agrarianate-level societies, were reduced to relative impotence or replaced by functional groupings based on specialized roles in the new technicalism, and not humanly integral. The state dealt, to a degree unprecedented in large territorial societies, directly with the individual. Only the impersonal power of the state, to which everyone was compelled equally to submit, seemed adequate to controlling so vast an interlocking network of technical specialties as emerged in the mass society.

Finally, technicalization carried with it an important moral discipline of its own, which merged with and reinforced the gentling of manners we have noted. It presupposed not only a mass society but, as its complement, an *individual at once privately isolated and yet highly cultivated and cooperative.* Only an independent, self-reliant individual, not tied to guild rules or tribal loyalties or communal religious conventions, could innovate with the freedom required or even cultivate second-hand the ever-new specializations demanded for technical efficiency. This made for an increasingly high valuation of individual freedom from controls by other individuals. It also meant ultimately a tendency toward anonymity and impersonalization as all intermediaries between the individual and the mass were attenuated (till finally the individuality was to seem distilled into a filing card number). Yet as important as independence and private isolation were private integrity and personal growth and cultivation, which were to develop in conjunction with the spirit of teamwork and willing co-operation. Hence, at the same time, technicalism meant an expectation of high personal moral standards and respect for the individual's special gifts.

Accompanying the British Industrial Revolution itself was, in fact, a special moral revolution in which "bourgeois morality" asserted the primacy of its own norms. By the next generation it had gone far towards doing away with not only the grosser forms of dissipation and display in personal life, but even with graft and bribery in politics. More than ever, more even than in Islamdom, equality of rights was required.

The specialist, by technicalistic standards, was respected not for any arbitrary status he might have by ancestry or other connections but for his individual achievement as it contributed to the common development. The only ascriptive status still accorded unquestioned recognition was that of a human being. To this human status was transferred the personal inviolability which hitherto had been the preserve of various personally-linked in-groups protected by their power or their sanctity. This fact contributed to the great achievement of the eighteenth-century Enlightenment in mitigating public cruelty. Hand in hand with respect for innovation and for technical efficiency went an increase in opportunities – for ordinary persons to find a career suited to their talents; for the exceptional, sometimes, to express their unique visions.

All these changes, especially for those who made their way to the centers of social control, made for an enormous increase in physical power available, and hence in material wealth; an enormous increase in positive knowledge, and hence in imaginative possibilities; a great multiplication of channels of opportunity for accomplishment, and hence of the basis for constructive personal freedom. Wealth, knowledge, and freedom further reinforced the direct effects of technicalized organization in making for a high and constantly increasing level of social power: power to produce goods, to discover facts, to organize human life to whatever ends presented themselves.

For Muslims all this had a special moral significance. At least in some measure, the Occidentals had managed to solve the moral dilemmas of citied society as they had confronted the human conscience since the beginning of civilization, and especially as they had been articulated in the Irano-Semitic spiritual tradition, in which, indeed, the Occidentals shared. They had developed institutions which seemed to assure at least personal legal security and a sustained high level of social order and prosperity in which even the least advantaged increasingly began to share. Moreover, even on the level of individual purity they had established standards of individual honesty, industry, loyalty, and modesty, and a capacity to rise above personal competitiveness, which, while far from assuring moral perfection in Europe, yet were increasingly visible in the more responsible classes.

For an unbiased devotee of sharia Islam there was much to admire. Taking its cue from Muhammad himself, the sharia had posited egalitarian justice and had presupposed a degree of social mobility, stressing individual responsibility and the nuclear family. More than any other great religious tradition it had catered to bourgeois and mercantile values. It had struggled persistently against any merely customary authority and usage in the name of universal law and the dignity of the individual, and had borne, sometimes vocally and sometimes more silently, a witness to the crucial place jointly of good government and of personal morality in human prosperity, which it acknowledged as a divinely sanctioned good which it was a human responsibility to guard. In all these matters, the Christian European peoples following the Great Transmutation went far in translating ideal into reality. From fairly early in the nineteenth century, in fact, there were to be alert and respected Muslims to declare that the Europeans were leading a better life by Islamic standards than were the Muslim societies themselves.

In fact, to be sure, the basic moral problems of society were not yet fully solved. Such progress as had been made had been by way of altering the very terms in which such problems had been posed since Sumer, and this has been done at a cost which no one could yet be prepared to evaluate. Some Muslims were sceptical, from the start, of the value of the power and prosperity of the new Europe, and eventually many were to be disillusioned when the solutions proved imperfect.

Why only the Occident?

It is perhaps not to be expected that we can find any absolute standard for judging the excellence of a society and of its achievements in any given period. We have learned to beware measuring even prosperity and decline simply by the power a society can exert and the resources it can command at a particular moment. We are quick to look for signs of inner decay, and this is what some scholars think they find in Islamdom as a basis for contemning its apparent greatness in the later periods. It seems safer to measure a society's progress by its development in technology and especially in natural science, regarded as indicative at once of its rationality and of its inner freedom. But science and technology are not the only possible indicators of truth and freedom; rather, they afford an almost expressly technicalistic criterion, well-tailored to justify the superiority of the Modern West. In our day, we are increasingly aware that (as it has been put), though our natural science can claim to be *useful,* it is more doubtful that it is *good,* and in the ultimate sense it cannot claim to be *valid* and true. Indeed, generally we have reason to doubt most of the criteria that have made us proud of the Modern Western achievements.

Nevertheless, even if we can no longer ascribe absolute or exclusive value to the sort of "progress" the West has represented in the last three hundred years, it remains true that technicalization and all that accompanied it was a tremendous human achievement in its own way. It was an immense triumph, to the credit (whatever its ultimate outcome) of the Occidental peoples and of the strength of their local institutions, the vigor of their spiritual and intellectual life, the prosperity of a large part of their population. The Transmutation grew largely out of the remarkable cultural florescence of the Occidental Renaissance, which had already carried the Occident in some ways beyond the cultural equality with Islamdom which it had achieved in the High Medieval period. In effect, the Transmutation resulted from the zeal and intelligence that succeeded in making permanent certain aspects of the innovative vigor of the Renaissance. The question then arises, what was so special about the Occident that it, and not other societies, achieved this?

First, we must recall that, in any case, it had to happen, if at all, in some one place rather than in others. Just as civilization on the agrarianate level had appeared in one or, at most, a very few spots and spread from there to the greater part of the globe, so the new technicalistic type of life could not appear everywhere among all citied peoples at the same moment; it too appeared first in one restricted area, western Europe, from which it has spread everywhere else.

It was not that the new ways resulted from conditions that were limited entirely to one area. Just as the first urban, literate life would have been impossible without the accumulation among a great many peoples of innumerable social habits and inventions, major and minor, so the great modern cultural Transmutation presupposed numerous inventions and discoveries originating in all the several citied peoples of the Eastern Hemisphere, discoveries of which many of the earlier basic ones were not made in Europe. In particular, most of the more immediately formative elements that led to the Transmutation, both material and moral, had come to the Occident, earlier or later, from other regions. Some of the crucial inventions (notably the famous early trio: gunpowder, the compass, and printing) which had prepared the way for the subsequent Occidental development had come ultimately from China, as did apparently, the idea of a civil service examination system, introduced in the eighteenth century. In such ways the Occident seems to have been the unconscious heir of the abortive industrial revolution of Sung China. More pervasive, if less specifically spectacular, had been, of course, the elements coming from the other Mediterranean societies, particularly the Islamicate, with its incalculable impulse to science and philosophy in the Occident as early as the High Medieval period.

At least as important was the very existence of the vast world market, constituted by the Afro-Eurasian commercial network, which had cumulatively come into being, largely under Muslim auspices, by the middle of the second millennium. The vigorous internal evolution of the Occident was completed by its access to the large areas of relatively dense, urban-dominated populations that formed the world market, in all its rich variety. There European fortunes could be made and European imaginations exercised. In particular it was the mercantile expansion which followed the Iberian oceanic ventures of the fifteenth and sixteenth centuries, that initiated the financial growth which became the immediate occasion of the earlier period of major capital accumulation. Without the cumulative history of the whole Afro-Eurasian Oikoumene, of which the Occident had been an integral part, the Western Transmutation would be almost unthinkable.

Nevertheless, it could not actually happen in the whole Oikoumene at once. All cultural developments, in any part of the Oikoumene, had begun in terms of a local cultural context and had been borrowed only slowly elsewhere. The same was true of the changes that made up the Great Transmutation. When the time was ripe for it, the actual cultural transformations could take place only within a given culture and in terms of the background of that culture – as it happened, the Occident.

It is not yet established what determined that the Transmutation should occur just there and then. In a general way it could hardly have happened before the second millennium C.E. Only then, presumably, would the expansion and intensification of the hemispheric commercial nexus, and in particular the accumulation of inventions, have reached an adequate level from which to begin. Then it would be a matter of which area would first combine a sufficient number of favorable local conditions. Presumably several different combinations might have been effective in producing some such transmutation. One cannot simply look at the combination that happened to occur in western Europe and assert that only this could have led to any sort of major acceleration of productivity and innovation such as occurred.

We may suppose, however, that a social tradition and economic resources favoring specifically industrial investment will have been essential: we have seen that the role of such investment had increased among both the Chinese and the Occidentals and apparently contributed to giving them an increasing interregional role already in the Mid-Islamic periods. But surely other conditions would have been required, if only to reinforce the effects of a shift toward such investment, and to prevent its disruption. We may conjecture what some of those that happened to be effective in the Occident were.

For the Occidentals did have special advantages. First was the relative virginity and extensiveness of their own soil: the largest continuous well-watered region that still lay adjacent to the old citied regions, not having proved amenable to earlier forms of exploitation because of its northern cold. Once they had learned to farm it well, it offered much room for expansion and hence for the patterns of an expanding economy, all this at a juncture in world history when much was to prove possible that would surely have been impossible much earlier, had the north European forests been cleared much earlier. (The stimulus provided by new agricultural methods in south China, which strengthened the Sung Chinese economy, affected a far smaller area than the vast north European plain, and was presumably far more vulnerable to local setbacks.) No doubt almost equally important were subtler things, such as the stimulus to the imagination provided both by ready access to other citied societies (Europe was barred by no Himalayas) and by the crossing of the Atlantic (which would have occurred by way of the northern islands or of Brazil, surely, even if Columbus had not ventured on the long middle route; whereas no Chinese venture into the Pacific could have had such success). We must add, perhaps (but this is less clear), a relative freedom from universal massive destruction and especially from alien conquest (notably at the hands of the Mongols) for a relatively long time.

Perhaps, given time (that is, some interruption of the Occidental development), we might have found similar transmutations taking place independently in other agrarianate-level societies, some sooner and some later, each with its own forms in terms of its own background. It cannot be ruled out that the Chinese might later have repeated more successfully their achievements of the Sung period, with its enormous and sudden expansion of iron and steel production, its proliferation of new technical advances, and its general cultural effervescence. Although this was cut short and China re-agrarianized under the Mongol conquest, cultural patterns cannot be fixed forever by such events, as organisms may be. One can also imagine conditions that could eventually have given great impetus to an Islamicate India. But once one such transmutation had been completed in one place, there was no time to wait for the like to happen elsewhere. In its very nature, such a cultural change, once completed, soon involved the whole globe, and the fact of its occurrence in one particular place, foreclosed the possibility of its happening so anywhere else.

To understand this consequence, we must recur to the parity that had been maintained among the agrarianate societies. Within the Afro-Eurasian historical complex, the overall rise in the level of social power that had everywhere taken pace was cumulatively very marked. In the sixteenth century, the Spanish, the Ottoman, the Indian, or the Chinese empires could, any of them, have easily crushed the ancient Sumerians at their strongest – as one of them did crush the Aztecs, who were on a comparable level. But the rise was very gradual. In any given era, each society within the Oikoumene had to reckon with the others essentially as equals, whatever temporary superiority one of them might gain. For instance, the superiority of the Arabs over the Portuguese in the eighth and ninth centuries and the briefer superiority of the Portuguese over the Arabs in the sixteenth century were both based on relatively superficial local advantages, neither people going beyond the limitations implicit in agrarianate-level society. In each case, the superiority was soon reversed, not by a radical transformation of the hard bested people but by a general shift of circumstances. In various periods Greeks, Indians, and Muslims each had their days of splendor, but in the long run all remained roughly at parity. This was because over the millennia any really basic new developments had been gradually adopted everywhere within the space of four or five centuries – or even more rapidly in such a case as gunpowder weapons.

But it was part of the transmutational character of the new transformation that it broke down the very historical presuppositions in terms of which such gradual diffusions had maintained parity among Afro-Eurasian citied societies. In the new pace of historical change, when decades sufficed to produce what centuries had produced before, a lag of four or five centuries was no longer safe. The old gradual diffusion and adjustment was no longer possible. Very shortly – at the latest by the end of the seventeenth century – all non-Western peoples were faced with the problem of coping as outsiders with the new order of civilized life as it was emerging in the Occident. Unless, by the oddest of chances, they happened to have started a comparable transmutation of their own at precisely the same moment as the Occident, there was no time for them to follow their own independent developments, however promising. Yet, still moving, culturally at an agrarianate pace, they could also not simply adopt the Western development for themselves year by year as it proceeded (as would have been required for such adoption to be effective). Those untransmutated agrarianate-level societies that did not share the Western cultural presuppositions had perforce to continue developing in their own traditions at their own pace, adopting from alien traditions only what could be assimilated on that basis. Hence the Western Transmutation, once it got well under way, could neither be paralleled independently nor be borrowed wholesale. Yet it could not, in most cases, be escaped. The millennial parity of social power broke down, with results that were disastrous almost everywhere.

5
Historical method in civilization studies

Historical humanism

Unless a scholar is content to accept his categories (and hence the questions he can ask and hence the answers he can arrive at) as given by the accidents of current predispositions, he cannot escape the obligation of justifying his selection of units for study, which means justifying his point of view. Such a justification, in turn, must imply an explicit stand on his role as a scholar. If there were unanimity in these matters, they might be left tacit – at least, if the given scholar were in accord with the rest. Fortunately, several quite different viewpoints guide historical studies generally, and Islamic studies in particular, in our present world.

Historical studies have been called "idiographic" as describing dated and placed particulars, as do many phases of geology or astronomy, in contrast to "nomothetic" studies such as physics and chemistry, which are supposed to lay down rules to hold regardless of date. This distinction has its usefulness so long as one bears in mind certain consideration sometimes forgotten. Firstly, whether the objects of the questions are dated or dateless, the questions themselves (as befits a cumulative public discipline) ought to be, in some degree, of timeless significance to human beings: sometimes perhaps leading to manipulative power, but always leading to better understanding of things that matter to us humanly.[1] Moreover, any discipline, ideally, should not be defined exactly by the category of the objects it studies nor even by the methods it uses, and still less by the form of its results – though empirically these may be

[1] Increased predictability through the "lessons" of history, and hence increased power of manipulation, may sometimes supervene through historical study; but it is surely not its true purpose. On the other hand, prediction as a *means of verification* sometimes plays an essential role in historical inquiry. This is not, of course, prediction of "the future" – that is not the proper purpose of any scholarly or scientific discipline – but prediction of future evidence, which may come in the form of laboratory experiments, of field surveys, or (in the case of history) of newly found documents.

useful indices, especially in interpreting the various academically recognized fields of inquiry which have grown up largely by historical accident. Ideally, a discipline needs to be set off just to the degree that there is a body of interdependent questions that can be discussed in relative autonomy from other bodies of questions, at least according to some one perspective. In a discipline so set off, it cannot necessarily be decided in advance just what forms of questions will prove to be required or what sorts of methods will prove necessary to answer them effectively. From this point of view, if there is a field of historical studies (as I believe) and not merely a group of several fields, it can be nothing less than the whole body of questions about human cultural development, about human culture in its continuity over time; and here we cannot rule out a potential need to develop relatively dateless generalizations, for instance about what may be possible in cultural change, such generalizations are not simply derivable from any other discipline as such, yet they are necessary for studying what is timelessly important about the dated and placed events of human culture.

These considerations being understood, then it can be said that historical studies of human culture are preponderantly "idiographic" in the sense that even their broader generalizations are usually not dateless, in contrast to certain kinds of nature study, and perhaps in contrast also to certain kinds of social studies of human culture, designed to refine analysis of any given society at any given time. Moreover, in any case, historians' questions are concerned ultimately with the dated and placed, and when (as they must) they ask questions they are undatable within the historical context, it is for the sake of elucidating particulars which *are* dated and placed, however broad in scope, and not vice versa. The dated and placed events are not mere examples, not mere raw material for dateless generalizations.

But I am concerned here with a further distinction. Within the body of questions about culture in its continuity over time, even when the focus of interest is admittedly on the dated and placed as such, one can still distinguish historical viewpoints further in terms of what sort of datebound questions are regarded as primary, the answer to which is the goal of the inquiry; and what sort are regarded as subordinate, yielding information which will help in answering the primary questions. On this basis we may distinguish two sorts of historian, "typicalizers" and "exceptionalizers." In practice, the distinction is one of emphasis: the "exceptionalizer" is concerned with all that concerns the "typicalizer," or he ought to be; and despite his principles, the "typicalizer" generally finds himself involved in points he might feel should concern the "exceptionalizer" alone. Nonetheless, the two viewpoints can issue in the use of differing units and categories in defining the field of study. I believe that in pre-Modern civilization studies, at any rate, the more inclusive view that I am labeling "exceptionalizing" cannot be left out of account if the humanly most significant questions are to be got at. It is on this principle that I have constructed this work.

Some historians, relatively "typicalizing" in viewpoint, intend primarily to articulate intelligibly their chosen portion of the total cultural environment as it impinges by way of interacting events on the present human inquirer. They intend to present that environment as it is structured in space and time (asking, in effect, how things came to be as they are now) much as an astronomer studies the particular structure, in space and time, of the solar system. Some may even hope that their work may ultimately serve chiefly to elucidate dateless regularities of culture change, not tied to any dating or placing (at least within the particular span of time and place which human culture as a whole presupposes). Such historians, if fully consistent, must be concerned first with the typical, and then with the exceptional only as it serves to make clear (or perhaps account for) what is or has been typical. If they study a state, or a novel, or a sect, they will study it primarily as typifying, or at least causing, general political or esthetic or religious patterns – at least the patterns of the time, and perhaps preferably those of all time.

On the other hand, from what may be called a more humanistic viewpoint, the reason for studying the typical is rather that thereby we may be better able to appreciate the exceptional, seeing more fully in just what way it is exceptional. We need to know works of artists or acts of statesmanship which are typical of a period just so that we may the better place the excellent, the outstanding.[2] We study Islamdom as a whole, as a great complex historic event, as well as the various less extensive events that compose it, not primarily as examples of something more general but as something unrecurrent and unrepeatable, and as having importance precisely for that reason. In consequence, we can be as concerned with the great failures as with the great successes, and as concerned with the potential moral implications of an act as with its immediate outcome.

Such inquiry remains legitimate public inquiry, and not just private

[2] This is not reducible to esthetic criticism, of course, let alone to straight moral judgment. The difference between the art historian and the art critic – and the corresponding difference in other fields than art – is a matter of the historian's concern with culture as such in its dimension of continuity over time. But such a concern cannot do away with the sense of greatness; it rather puts it in perspective.

antiquarianism, to the extent that the exceptional events were in some sense or other outstanding in the context of mankind generally, and not just for private individuals or groups. Events evidently meet this test when they have altered the context of routine human life in their time, insofar as no region or period of human life has, in the long run, been so isolated that it has not had its effects in turn on the rest of us. On this level, the "exceptionalizer" is at one with the "typicalizer." But he wants to add a further dimension.

It is not merely as events have altered the natural or the socio-cultural context that they can have exceptional significance. So far as there is moral or spiritual solidarity among human beings, apart from physical confrontations at any given time, the fate of each people is relevant to all human beings whether or not it had permanent external consequences otherwise. It is, then, also, and perhaps above all, as events and acts have altered the moral context of human life that they are of universal significance, for they have set irreplaceable standards and norms, and they have posed distinctive challenges and established moral claims which as human beings we dare not ignore. Herodotus wrote his history, he said, to preserve the memory of the great deeds done by the Greeks and the Persians: unrepeatable deeds that have an enduring claim to our respect. Those deeds cannot be imitated, though they may be emulated and in some sense perhaps surpassed. But even now we dare call no man great whose deeds cannot somehow measure up to theirs. Once having known those deeds, the world can never be quite the same for us again: not because of what they may tell us of *what* we are, may tell us statistically about the potentialities of our hominid species; but because they add to our understanding of *who* we are, of what we are committed to, as human beings, what is worthy of our wonder and our tears.

We are speaking here of such events and acts as form human cultural institutions on the level of public action. We are dealing with peoples – or, more accurately, with groups of men and women at least relatively autonomous in culture. Purely individual exploits may have something of the same quality, but they are meaningful on a different level and their student is the biographer, not the historian. Yet it is especially in this "exceptionalizing" perspective that persons' ideal norms and expectations and even the special visions of individuals can be crucial. For they prove to be the mainsprings of creativity at the interstices of routine patterns, when exceptional circumstances arise and something new must be found to do. This is how, in fact, the would-be "typicalizer" finds himself dragged into matters more suited to the program of the "exceptionalizer."

Clearly, the serious "exceptionalizer" – despite the doubtful example of some scholarly story-tellers – necessarily needs to understand all that the most "social-scientific" of the "typicalizers" will want to be studying. Always, of course, visions and ideals can come into play only within the leeway allowed by the human interests (material and imaginative) of those less concerned with ideas. Ultimately all historical "why's" must be driven back (often in the form of "how could that have become effective?") to circumstances of hominid natural and cultural ecology – the circumstances which determine that what would otherwise be the individual random "accidents" that shape history will not simply cancel each other out but will be reinforced and cumulatively lead in a single direction.[3] However irrational human beings may be, in the long run their irrationalities are mostly random. It is their rational calculations that can be reinforced in continuing human groups and can show persisting orientation and development – even when they are calculations on misconceived presuppositions.[4] Hence group interests have a way of asserting themselves. Group interests seem ultimately based in ecological circumstances in general and, more particularly, in that cumulative development of cultural resources which the essential internal instability of cultural traditions assures will be likely, in the long run, to be ever more elaborated and so to require ever new adjustments.

But such ecological circumstances merely set the limits of what is possible. Within those limits, the personal vision has its opportunity. For when habitual, routine thinking will no longer work, it is the man or woman with imagination who will produce the new alternatives. At this point, the concerned conscience can come into play. It may or may not prove adequate to the challenge. But in either case, it is such personal vision that is the most human part of human history.

Hence the humanistic historian must concern himself with the great commitments and loyalties that human beings have borne, within which every sort of norm and ideal has been made explicit; and he must concern himself with the interactions and dialogues in which these commitments have been expressed. Hence, for an "exceptionalizing" historian with such intentions, it is Islamdom as a morally, humanly relevant complex of traditions, unique and irreversible, that can form his canvas.

[3] It is for this reason that every "why this?" presupposes at least one "why not that?" "Might-have-beens" are built into the inquiry of any historian, whether explicit or not, just as they are built into that of any other scholar or scientist.

[4] On the self-determination of each new generation – as against "blind tradition" – compare the section on determinacy in traditions, below.

Whether it "led to" anything evident in Modern times must be less important than the quality of its excellence as a vital human response and an irreplaceable human endeavor. In this capacity, it would challenge our human respect and recognition even if it had played a far less great role than, in fact, it did play in articulating the human cultural nexus in time and space and in producing the world as we find it now.

On scholarly precommitments

Because of the central role, in historical studies, of human loyalties and commitments, the personal commitments of scholars play an even greater role in historical studies than in other studies, a role that stands out in special relief in Islamic studies.

On the most serious levels of historical scholarship – where the human relevance of major cultural traditions is at issue, such as that of religious or artistic or legal or governmental traditions, or even that of whole civilizations – historical judgment cannot be entirely disengaged from the basic precommitments of inquirers. Indeed, it is not necessarily desirable that it should be: the very issues can arise only as we are humanly deeply engaged. Inquiries by pure specialists, seeking only to straighten out this or that detail brought up by some greater scholar who *was* humanly engaged and had discussed the great issues, may bring useful clarifications but often miss the main points. Precommitment can lead the unwary – and often even the most cautious scholar – to biased judgment. Bias comes especially in the questions he poses and in the type of category he uses, where, indeed bias is especially hard to track down because it is hard to suspect the very terms one uses, which seem so innocently neutral. Nevertheless, the bias produced by precommitment can be guarded against, the answer to it cannot finally be to divest ourselves of all commitments, but to learn to profit by the concern and insight they permit, while avoiding their pitfalls.

Such basic precommitments are always to a degree idiosyncratic in really serious scholars; yet the deeper they are, the more fully they are likely to be rooted in one of the major cultural traditions of ultimate overall commitment. In fact, certain of these traditions have loomed especially large in determining the viewpoints of the masters of Islamic studies, who have done the most to set the problems and the framework within which other Islamicists have worked. I shall mention five, three old and two new. The Christian tradition – in Catholic or in Protestant form – has been deeply determinative for many Western scholars, as has Judaism for still others. More recently, increasing numbers of scholars committed to the Islamic tradition – sharia-minded or Sufism – are making their contributions to scholarship in the field. The pitfalls that await scholars committed to any of these traditions are evident enough in such scholars' work, at least to any scholar of a rival commitment. It is no guarantee of balanced insight, to be a Muslim, nor of impartiality, to be a non-Muslim. Alongside these older traditions, and representing precommitments leading to the same sorts of pitfalls as lurk in commitment to Christianity or Islam, we find Marxists on the one hand and dedicated Westernists on the other. I call "Westernists" those whose highest allegiance is to what they call Western culture, as the unique or at least the most adequate embodiment of transcendent ideals of liberty and truth. They usually share, to some degree, a Christian viewpoint on Islam, insofar as the Christian tradition has been so central to Western culture, however much personally they may reject the claims to allegiance of Christianity in itself. Not all Islamicists are consciously committed to one of these major allegiances; but for many who are not, the alternative is not genuine independence and objectivity. Commonly the alternative, rather, is more limited horizons and shallower awareness, together with unconscious and hence unanalyzed piecemeal commitment to partisan viewpoints which, in those consciously committed, are subject to conscious review and control.

Accordingly, the problem of how one may legitimately go about studying Islam from within a commitment to another great tradition – and in particular how to go about studying it from within a Christian commitment – is no by-problem of interest only to a few scholars who by exception are religiously inclined. It is central to the whole scholarly problem. Jean-Jacques Waardenburg, in *L'Islam dans le miroir de l'Occident: comment quelques orientalistes occidentaux se sont penchés sur l'Islam et se sont formés une image de cette religion* (The Hague: Brill, 1963), has demonstrated how the work of the formative Islamicists Ignaz Goldziher, Christiaan Snouck Hurgronje, Carl Becker, Duncan MacDonald, and Louis Massignon was in each case intimately and pervasively marked by the basic precommitments of these men (though he does not use the concept "Westernist"). The cultural allegiance of the serious scholar is crucial in his work. This is not to say that it is impossible to study fairly one religious tradition from within another, as has sometimes been suggested. Ultimately all faith is private, and it is often far easier for congenial temperaments to understand each other across the lines of religious or cultural tradition than it is for contrasting temperaments to make sense of each other's faith even when they follow the same cult and utter the same creed. We are primarily human beings and only secondarily participants in this or that tradition. Nevertheless, not only the scholars' cultural environment at large but their explicit precommitments, which brought the greater of the scholars to their inquiry in the first place, have determined the categories with which they have undertaken their studies. Only by a conscious and well-examined understanding of the limits of these precommitments and of what is possible within and beyond them can we hope to take advantage of our immediate humaneness to reach any direct appreciation of major cultural traditions we do not share – and perhaps even of traditions we do share.

When we compare the Occident and Islamdom in general, and Christianity and Islam in particular, such awareness is especially essential. There has been a tendency, among those Christians who have been willing to concede spiritual validity to Islam at all, to see Islam as, in one way or other, a truncated version of Christian truth: all or virtually all the truth to be found in Islam is to be found in Christianity, but Christianity leads beyond that truth to a crowning essential truth that eludes the Muslim's grasp. Correspondingly, Muslims have historically seen Christianity as a truncated or perverted Islam. But such a comparison is, on the face of it, unsound at least for historical purposes. It can hardly be intelligible, to those Christians or Muslims having such views, how it can be that intelligent, sensitive, and upright persons can prefer Islam to Christianity, or vice versa, once they have been exposed to the appeal of both.

In sensitive hands, some such approach can have suggestive results, indeed. The most attractive such interpretation of Islam from the Christian side is surely that of Louis Massignon, set forth allusively in a number of his articles, such as "Salman Pak et les prémices spirituelles de l'Islam iranien," *Societé des Etudes Iraniennes*, vol. 7 (1934), and in his several articles on the Seven Sleepers; he saw Islam as a community in spiritual exile, veiled from the divine presence, yet through that very exile charged with a special witness to bear. (Giulio Basetti-Sani, *Mohammed et Saint François* [Commissariat de Terre-Sainte, Ottawa, 1959], has developed part of Massignon's idea in his beautiful and knowledgeable, if not very scholarly, book, which forms a suggestive contribution to a modern mythology.) A less poetic, though still sensitive, approach to Islam in Christian terms is offered by Eric Bethmann's *Bridge to Islam* (Nashville, Tenn., 1950) and by the works of Kenneth Cragg. Yet it remains true that the ultimate judgments such approaches presuppose are suspect. A serious exploration of any one religious tradition in its several dimensions could consume more than one lifetime, and it is not to be expected that many persons can genuinely explore two. If this fact helps account for so many intelligent persons not seeing the truth as the apologist sees it, it also suggests that the apologist too is deceiving himself if he thinks he is qualified to judge the rival tradition. A view of Islam as a Christianity manqué, or the reverse, however elegantly formulated, must be received with great scepticism.

But the readiest alternatives, among those willing to concede some truth to a rival tradition, are equally unsatisfactory for making a comparison. One may resort to syncretistic assimilation, as if superficially similar elements in the two traditions could be identified; but this is bound to falsify one tradition or both – if only by not recognizing the genuineness of the demand, at the heart of each, for exclusive historical commitment. For instance, in both traditions there is a demand for moral behavior on the basis not of arbitrary human custom but of divine revelation; and at least in broad areas, the moral norms implied in the two revelations are much alike. Yet for Christians, being based in revelation means being in response to redemptive love as it is confronted through the presence of a divine-human life and the sacramental fellowship of which that is the source. For Muslims, being based in revelation means being in response to total moral challenge as it is confronted in an explicit divine message handed on through a loyal human community. The two senses of revelation not only contrast to one another: they exclude one another categorically. Yet to abstract from them is to make pointless both the Christian and the Muslim demand for a revealed morality over against human custom.

To avoid the over-explicit identifications of syncretism, one may resort frankly to reducing both traditions to some lowest common denominator – a formless mysticism or a vague appeal to the common goodwill of mankind. But in practice this means appealing to the prestige carried by the great traditions, on behalf of something that can rise above the level of impotent platitudes only as the quite private viewpoint of an individual.

The two traditions, as such, must be recognized as incompatible in their demands, short of some genuinely higher synthesis presumably not yet available to us. And we must retain this sense of tension between them without interpreting the one by the standards of the other. This may be accomplished in some degree, through a comparison of the two structures, of what sorts of elements tend to get subordinated and what tend to get highlighted. In such a perception, those committed and those with no commitment can join, provided each maintains a sensitive human awareness of what can be humanly at stake at every point. But this is possible only so far as the elements chosen can be evaluated in some independence. This is an ideal only approximable at best. Hence even the best comparison cannot be regarded as providing an objective basis for ultimate judging between traditions. Yet it may make more understandable the special strengths of Islam – and its weaknesses – in the given historical circumstances.

I have developed this point about the irreducible incompatibility of any two traditions of faith somewhat more in detail in my "A Comparison of Islam and Christianity as Frameworks for Religious Life"; but there I did not develop adequately what I feel must be the basis for mutual comprehension among religious traditions: growth within tension, through persistent dialogue.

On defining civilizations

In civilization studies – the study of the great cultural heritages (especially those dating from the pre-Modern citied ages) – what may be called a "civilization" forms a primary unit of reference. Yet the specification of such units is only partly given by the data itself. In part, it is a function of the inquirer's purposes.

Once society has become fairly complex, every people, even each sector of the population within what can be called a people, has had a degree of cultural self-sufficiency. At the same time, even the largest identifiable group of peoples has never been totally self-sufficient. Even the cultural patterns so large a group have in common will show interrelations with those of yet more distant peoples. Social groupings have intergraded or overlapped almost indefinitely throughout the Eastern Hemisphere since long before Islamic times. If we arrange societies merely according to their stock of cultural notions, institutions, and techniques, then a great many dividing lines among pre-Modern civilized societies make some sense, and no dividing line with the Eastern Hemisphere makes final sense. It has been effectively argued, on the basis of the cultural techniques and resources to be found there, that all the lands from Gaul to Iran, from at least ancient classical times onward, have formed but a single cultural world. But the same sort of arguments would lead us on to perceive a still wider Indo-Mediterranean unity, or even (in lesser degree) the unity of the whole Afro-Eurasian citied zone. In these circumstances, any attempt to characterize a less extensive "civilization" requires adopting an explicit basis on which to set off one body of peoples from another as a civilization; but too often such groupings have been taken as a given, on extraneous grounds, and characterizations have then been attempted without regard to the basis on which the grouping was made.

We have yet to develop an adequate analysis of cultural forms for studying the pre-Modern citied societies. Anthropologists have acquired some sophistication in dealing with non-citied societies, and some of them have extrapolated their methods into citied societies. Sociologists have learned to study Modern Technical society, and generally societies of the Technical Age in the light of it. But far too few since Max Weber have systematically explored the periods and areas between – that is, from Sumer to the French Revolution. This is partly because the lack of a tenable framework of world history, which would supply an elementary sense of the proportions and interrelations of the field, has hampered any comparative studies there. Anything may be compared with anything else, but fruitful comparisons require relevantly comparable units of comparison, which can be assured only through a sound sense of overall context. In consequence, the questions posed about the pre-Modern civilizations, and in particular about the Islamicate, have often been irrelevant or misleading, and the answers they yield have been beside the point of positively false.

It may be noted here that this lack of a proper world-historical framework has probably arisen at least in part for want of a proper framework for scholarly co-operation. What are commonly called "Oriental studies" from the larger part of what are better called "civilization studies," including the European heritage along with the others, since fundamentally the same methods are involved in all cases, and the historical problems are all interrelated. It is absurd for scholars in Islamic studies to be sharing conferences with those in Chinese studies more readily than with those in Medieval European studies.

It has largely been philogians who have – by default – determined our category of "civilizations": a civilization is what is carried in the literature of a single language, or of a single group of culturally related languages. This notion has been presupposed by Carl Becker, Gustave von Grunebaum, and Jörg Kraemer, for instance. It is not, in fact, a bad notion, to the extent that my definition of a civilization in terms of lettered traditions is sound. But it is not the same as what I am suggesting; it needs to be refined. In crude form it has led, for instance (as we shall be noting), to an approach in which everything carried in Arabic, including pre-Islamic pagan Bedouin customs, is regarded as native and ancestral to the civilization that later expressed itself largely in Arabic; while materials in Syria, for instance, produced in the mainstream of cultural development under the earlier Muslim rulers and leading directly to central features in the urban life of the civilization, as regarded as "foreign" to it, and as "influencing" it when their ideas were "borrowed" into it at the point when their exponents began to use Arabic. The resulting picture of cultural development is, I believe, erroneous. In principle, a field of study such as "whatever culture happens to be attested in Arabic documents" can be legitimate; but its relevance is limited. If, for instance, we deal not with Islam but with Arabic as our point of departure, so regarding Iranians as outsiders, we think of Bedouin notions as "surviving" while Iranian ones "influence" the later culture from outside. The Arabic culture of the High Caliphate then takes on two traits: (*a*) suddenness; (*b*) a derivative character, as largely "borrowed." What a difference in tone, if rather we should look at the problems posed by an overlay of Arabic "borrowing" upon Iranian and Syriac "survivals"! Accordingly, we must respect the challenge presented by men like Toynbee, who defines his civilizations according to criteria based on inner cultural development. When he divides what has been called "Islamic" civilization among three different civilizations, I believe he is in error, but he reminds us that if we make it a single civilization we must give some reason why.

The reason for distinguishing a "civilization" cannot be a single, universal one, however; it must almost be special to each case. For no more than language does any other one criterion necessarily determine a grouping that will be worth studying as a major large-scale culture. Even a localized culture, at least on the level of citied and lettered life, cannot be defined simply in terms either of component traits or of participant families. In cross-section, a culture appears as a pattern of lifeways received among mutually recognized family groups. Over time, it may be more fully defined as a relatively autonomous complex of interdependent cumulative traditions, in which an unpredictable range of family groups may take part. It forms an overall setting within which each particular tradition develops. But even within one relatively local culture, some traditions – a given school of painting, say, or a particular cult – may come to an end, and new ones may take their places. It is not possible to distinguish, in any absolute sense, authentic or viable from unauthentic or unviable traits in a culture, or even authentic from unauthentic traditions. Yet a culture does have a certain integrality. The consequences and the meaning of any given trait, inherited or newly introduced, will depend at any given time on what implications it has for the ongoing interaction, the dialogue or dialogues into which it fits (or which it confuses). The consequences and ultimate meaning of any given particular tradition will in turn depend on its implications for the cultural setting as a whole. These implications will be more decisive, the more they touch the most persistent and widely ramified features of the culture. Over time, then, what sets off a culture as an integral unity in some degree is whatever makes for cultural continuity in that particular culture.

On the wider and more rarefied level of what may be called a "civilization," cultural identity is even more problematic and what will make for continuity is even less predictably formulable. We may indeed describe the most likely situations in general terms which may seem to settle the matter. If we may call a "civilization" any wider grouping of cultures in so far as they share consciously in interdependent cumulative traditions (presumably on the level of "high culture" – of the relatively widely shared cultural forms at the urban, literate level of complexity and sophistication), then the shared traditions will be likely to center in some range of "high" cultural experience to which the cultures are committed in common. This may be a matter of literary and philosophical as well as political and legal values carried in lettered tradition, with or without explicit allegiance to a given religious community. (Usually, lettered tradition is indissociable from the continuity of written language; yet there need not be cultural identity except marginally between two groups, especially in different periods, using the same language. Many would refuse to put ancient Attica and Christian Byzantium in the same civilization just because both used Greek and even read Homer. What matters is the dominant lettered traditions, with their attendant commitments, in whatever language.) When such major lettered traditions, then, are carried in common, often there will be continuity likewise in social and economic institutions generally. All cultural traditions tend to be closely interdependent. Often the integration within one area has been so marked and the contrasts between that area and others so strong that at any given time a demarcation line has been quite clear, and that line has tended to perpetuate itself. Thus we get, especially in cross-section, the impression of clearly marked civilizations parceling out among themselves the Eastern Hemisphere.

But this apparent clarity should not persuade the historian to take his categories for granted. There will always be "borderline" and "anomalous" cases which are quite as normal as the major groupings. It would be hard to place such peoples as Georgians and Armenians unequivocally within any one major "civilization." In any case, it cannot be clear in advance what sorts of life patterns will in fact be found to be shared among the peoples forming what can be called a "civilization." Each civilization defines its own scope, just as does each religion. There may even be several sorts of basic continuity which may overlap in range. Thus, depending on one's viewpoint, Byzantine culture may be seen as continuing the ancient Hellenic tradition, or as part of a Christendom briefer in time but wider in area; and in each case there is a genuine and effective continuity on the level of "high culture" and its commitments. Hence over a time span it often becomes a matter of choice – depending on what sort of lettered traditions one specially wants to inquire into – which among several possible delimitations will prove most suitable. Then the scholarly treatment of the "civilization" must differ with the grounds for singling it out.

On determinacy in traditions

However a civilization be defined, it must not be hypostatized, as if it had a life independent of its human carriers. The inherited cultural expectations at any given time form part of the realities that members of a given society must reckon with. They even put limits on what the most alert of those members can see in their environment. But they have no effect except as they interact with the actual environment and the immediate interests of all concerned. The determinacy of tradition is limited, in the long run, by the requirement that it be continuingly relevant in current circumstances.

Continuing relevancy is crucial to recall especially when cross-cultural comparisons are being made. For instance, in an attempt to understand why it was in the Occident that, eventually, technicalized society arose, scholars have looked to the state of the Occident in the centuries preceding the transformations. This can be done along two lines: by studying the special circumstances of the time when the transformations began and the special opportunities open to Occidentals at that time; or by studying inherent differences between Occidental culture and other cultures. In the latter case, a comparative study of the High Medieval Occident with its contemporaries is fundamental.

It is this latter case that has seemed the easier in the past. An adequate framework of overall world history was lacking as a basis for studying the special characteristics of the time of the transformation itself, whereas the chief other societies were just well enough known as isolated entities to allow specious global generalizations to be made about their cultural traits, traits which could be contrasted to subtle traits traceable in the more intimately understood Occident. Moreover, studying inherent traits in the Occident did have undeniable relevance to a related question, often confused with the question why it was the Occident that launched Modernity. The special form that modern technicalization took, coming where it did, certainly owes much to special traits of the

Occident in which it arose. Since without adequate world-historical inquiries it is hard to sort out what has been essential and what accidental in technical Modernity, studies of what was special to Occidental culture as such, which were assured at least some success in accounting for the shape of Modernity as it actually arose, were mistakenly supposed to have succeeded in accounting for where and when it arose. Accordingly, scholars have been tempted to invoke, in accounting for the advent of Modernity, the determinant effect of a fortunate traditional attitude or combination of attitudes in the pre-Modern Occident. Complementarily to that, often enough, they have invoked the "dead hand of tradition" to explain the "failure" of other societies such as the Islamicate, which are then compared, to their disadvantage, with the pre-Modern Occident. The circumstances of the time when Modernity was launched have been relatively neglected.

All attempts that I have yet seen to invoke pre-Modern seminal traits in the Occident can be shown to fail under close historical analysis, once other societies begin to be known as intimately as the Occident. This applies also to the great master, Max Weber, who tried to show that the Occident inherited a unique combination of rationality and activism. As can be seen here and there in this work, most of the traits, rational or activist, by which he sought to set off the Occident either are found in strength elsewhere also; or else, so far as they are unique (and all cultural traits are unique to a degree), they do not bear the weight of being denominated as so uniquely "rational" as he would make them. This applies to both Occidental law and Occidental theology, for instance, where he partly mistook certain sorts of formalism for rationality, and partly simply did not know the extent among Muslims, for instance, of a probing rational drive. But when the several traits prove not to be so exceptional, the special combination of them that he invoked as decisive loses its cogency.

It must also be noted that his method, as such, sometimes did not push quite far enough. He sometimes depicted the attitudes he found as if they were standing facts with automatic consequences, rather than processes that never remain quite the same and have regularly to be renewed. Accordingly, he could neglect the historical question of what it was that *kept* the attitude in being once it had arisen; and so he failed to see the full range of its interaction with other things, including with its own consequences.

The question of the relation of pre-Modern Occidental culture to Modernity is a specially intriguing case of a much wider problem: the relative role in historical development of traditional culture and of the current play of interests. When it becomes clear that long-range historical change cannot be adequately interpreted in terms of the initiative of great men or of direct geographical or racial causation; and when interpretation through the evident moral level of the leading classes or even through immediate economic interests proves to require explanation in turn of why the moral level or the economic interests were as they were; then recourse can be had to explanation by unevident but seminal cultural traits. These seminal traits are supposed to have latent implications, not visible in the earlier course of the society, the consequences of which unfold at a later state of the society's development – if it may be assumed that the society has a determinate course of development. Of the several sorts of seminal traits invoked, the most commonly appealed to are inherited attitudes of mind, evaluations of what is good and what bad. Thus in contrast to an Occidental inclination to rationalize and to reinvest is posited in an eternal Chinese inclination to tao-ize and to become gentry; whereupon the failure of the Chinese to carry through an industrial revolution is ascribed to their successful families' not persisting in industry, but turning to other, more honored, careers. (If the Chinese *had* been the first to fully industrialize, they might have accounted for this also by their wealthy families' tendency to become gentry – and so to sell their industries to ever new blood, willing to innovate.)

I am sure that seminal traits may exist, though it is hard to pin them down. But any evaluation of their historical effects must take into account the full ecological setting of a given generation – that is, all the conditions (including both geographically and socially given resources as well as current interrelations with other groups) that would determine the effective advantage of various possible lines of action and hence of attitudes that might be adopted. Ideally, one should determine the points at which, under the given conditions, additional investment of money, time, intellectual effort, etc., would yield diminishing returns. Such calculations would have to take into account natural, man-made, and demographic resources, technical and scientific alternatives available, and social institutions as given to that generation, including patterns of expectation, and what *at that time* these expectations depended (that is, what it was that, at that time, might have altered them). Such a listing would have to include the *consequences* of ancestors' attitudes; but under the circumstances facing any given generation, the consequences of those attitudes need not come to the same thing as the attitudes themselves. Even the outcome, in a given setting, of child-raising techniques – the area where an unconscious past seems likely to weigh heaviest – can vary strongly.

Attitudes like "individualism," "sense of personal vocation," or "world-negation" are hard to define closely enough for such purposes. It is easier to trace the particular tokens of such attitudes; and these can come to take on quite opposite implications in a new setting. Thus the expectation in the U.S.A., that each nuclear family should have its own lawn-surrounded house, which originally was doubtless a bulwark of certain aspects of individual independence, can lead, in certain sorts of "organization-man" suburbia, to bolstering social involvement and conformity. Or the exclusivity of the Quran, with its rejection of the reliability of Jewish and Christian religious witness, could contribute (by way of the self-containedness of the Quranic exegesis) to the special universalism and tolerance of divergent traditions (and not only of those of the People of the Book), which characterize some strains of Sufism.

Indeed, whatever the situation may be in non-lettered societies, in every complex society most relevant attitudes are to be found either among the multiplicity of variant and practical traditions, or within that lettered tradition that has maximum prestige. Most temperaments and most possible facets of experience that are to be found in any major tradition can be found in corresponding traditions elsewhere. Accordingly, tradition can account for almost anything. Thus for a time it was sought to prove that basic familistic attitudes would prevent the Chinese from turning Communist; now the Chinese bureaucratic heritage is shown to have made the Chinese peculiarly susceptible to Communism.

Accordingly, it is wise to posit as a basic principle, and any deviation from which must bear the burden of proof, that *every generation makes its own decisions.* (This is perhaps a partial application of Ranke's principle that all generations are morally equidistant from God.) A generation is not bound by the attitudes of its ancestors, as such, though it must reckon with their consequences and may indeed find itself severely limited by those consequences in the range of choices among which it can decide.

The difference between major traditions lies not so much in the particular elements present within them, but in the relative weighting of them and the structuring of their interplay within the total context. If this structuring remains relatively constant (in the very nature of tradition, it cannot remain absolutely so), it will be because the predisposing conditions remain relatively constant, and because they are further reinforced by the institutionalizing of attitudes appropriate to them. Such institutionalizing can indeed be crucial in making the predisposing conditions fully effective: e.g., the mercantile bias of the Irano-Semitic cultural traditions, already so visible in the development of the monotheisms, was given fully free play only under the auspices of Islam. The triumph of Islam was made possible by its special adaptation to that bias, but its triumph in turn allowed that bias to determine the subsequent course of Irano-Semitic history. Nevertheless, the consequences of such institutionalization cannot reach very far in independence of the predisposing conditions. They can allow a tendency already the strongest in that field to become fully effective, and they can then reduce fluctuations that might result from variations in the underlying conditions, so that a temporary or a local deviation from the general norm will not produce a total cultural disruption. But if altered basic conditions long persist, the corresponding attitudes and their institutionalization will soon be changed to match.

Historical change is continuous and all traditions are open and in motion, by the very necessity of the fact that they are always in internal imbalance. Minds are always probing the edges of what is currently possible. But even apart from this, we are primarily human beings with our personal interests to pursue, and only secondarily participants in this or that tradition. Any tradition must be regularly reinforced by current conditions so that it answers to current interests or it will perish by drying up – or be transformed into something relevant. Whatever unity of patterning we may be able to discover, as to primacy of orientations or as to validation of norms of organization – whatever sense of common style we may find in the culture, that is – may be very pervasive and persistent and yet be essentially fragile. As soon as new positive possibilities open up, the unity of patterning is quickly vulnerable. To the extent that a homogeneous and compelling style is attained, in fact, it must be regarded as a delicate flower, not a tap root; it is not something imposed by cultural necessity, though the range of potentialities may be given so, but something achieved by creative effort.

A special word has to be said about one of the crudest, yet remarkably pervasive forms of hypostatizing a cultural tradition – or, in this case, a whole series of them. The misimpression that "the East" has latterly been awaking from a "millennial torpor" is still remarkably widespread. It results, of course (like the term "East" itself), from the profound ignorance of world history not only among modern Westerners but among others as well, whose eager vaunting of the antiquity of their institutions was taken at face value by Westerners.

We may single out two types of scholar who have reinforced the misimpression. Western tourists, whose moods played a large role even in scholarship, easily mistook the exotic for the immemorial, and were necessarily blind to subtler institutional changes. Their impressions, then, were dignified into learned theses, sometimes of a racialist hue, by scholars bemused by the spectacular progressiveness of their own West, and ready to write off other societies as irrelevant. Reading back the recent Western pace of activity into the earlier Occidental past by a foreshortening of time-spans in the distance, and unaware that in other parts of the world there was a comparably active past, Western scholars assumed that the comparatively slow pace of technical and intellectual development which they could perceive in the nineteenth-century world abroad amounted to no development at all, and marked a difference of race and place rather than one of age.

But other Western scholars – well represented in "area studies" – have confirmed the misimpression by an opposite error. While more or less recognizing the comparability of pre-Modern Western and non-Western societies as to degree of cultural activity, they have blanketed all pre-Modern areas under the common term "traditional," the misleading tendency of which we have already seen, as if all had been asleep together (save in certain periods of undeniable florescence) – rather than all awake together. As we have noted, the degree to which pre-technicalized and even pre-literate peoples have been bound by the "dead hand of tradition" has been greatly exaggerated. Among Muslims, at any rate, the major institutions of each age can be shown to have their own functional justification in their own time: Muslim social decisions, even under the conservative spirit, were made not primarily out of deference to the past but as meeting concrete practical interests of dominant social groups. Whether it is the "East" or the "pre-Modern" that is being misperceived, the postulate of essential changelessness obscures the important question of how the particular posture in which various peoples happened to be at the moment of the Transmutation affected their destiny under its impact. There is too ready an answer to the question of why "reform" efforts so often failed: the "tradition-bound" lands were ruled by blind conservatives. Some are thus spared the trouble of discovering what very practical and alert statesmen those "tradition-bound" men often were . . . except in the case of the Japanese, who are gratuitously labelled "good imitators."

6

On doing world history

My concerns with world history are several. Perhaps I can outline some of the points at which I think world history is important, and this will be more useful than anything else, for it leads to everything else. In the first place, while all historical study results from the fact that people already have some sort of sense or image of history, which it is desirable to refine and correct, this is especially true in the case of world history. Our image of the physical and temporal pattern of the human world as a whole, is fundamental to our sense of who we are. No one is without some image of the sort, however crude. The problem of the person who would present world history is to move from whatever images his students have, to a more satisfactory image. Of course, this does not mean that he will first take a survey of what images are present and then proceed to correct each one. Pedagogically, this would be too clumsy. Yet one of his most important functions is to do something like this in effect.

There are several images of the world likely especially to appear among the American public. One is a Christian or "Judeo-Christian" image. This is almost always far more refined in college students than it is on the Sunday-school level, but it has far more profound effects on the world-historical image than merely the establishment of the dividing point between B.C. and A.D. A second image that will occur occasionally, and is more significant generally than might be expected from its explicit occurrences, is the Marxist image of world history. This, too, comes in several different forms – for instance, according to what is made of that "Asiatic system of production." The most important basis for an image of world history present among us is the Westernist image. This is very subtle and very persuasive, and goes back directly at least to Hegel. It divides world history into three categories: the Primitive, the Oriental,

Extracts from a letter of Marshall Hodgson to John Voll, December 19, 1966. Used with permission.

and the Western. The Primitive is not really historical at all and is human only in a curiously ambivalent sense. The Oriental is either a preliminary stage, as with Hegel himself, or a complement in certain ways to the Western. In any case rationality, liberty, and progress are characteristics of the Western. Sometimes the "Oriental" is "one-sidedly" spiritual; sometimes it is given credit for still more; but always its patterns were essentially formed in some sort of antiquity and it has been degenerating since.

The Westernist image of world history, which as you know is reinforced by our usual maps of the world, which put the Western countries on a much larger scale than the others, is reinforced in a thousand subtle ways, intentional and unintentional, by historical scholarship. If one reads a "history of technology" it is a history of Western technology, and inventions within the West and introduction from beyond the West are treated as exactly the same sort of "progress," and little effort is made to distinguish time or place outside of the limited Western area. The result, in our sense of what humanity is, is obvious. I have just been reading some materials on ancient Greek religion, especially Orphism. What is astounding and persistent is the trichotomy between Primitive, Western, and Oriental. In this case "Greek" is only what is not "Primitive" or "Oriental"; what is Greek is whatever is limpidly rational; whatever is not is assumed to be non-Greek, and the history is oddly managed to fit this categorization. The Orphic material is compared to the Mazdean of any age, and the fact that giving high rank to the concept of Time appears in the Mazdean tradition is used as evidence that it is not a philosophical concept, but an "Oriental" one. No consideration is given to the possibility that the abstract Mazdean concepts cited must have arisen at a particular time and possibly in a process analogous to what was going on in Greece. Indeed, it is taken for granted that anything "Persian" must be static and pre-Greek and even pre-Orphic. Even though something of this outlook is being overcome in some cases now, the outlook is extremely pervasive and underlies the majority of the work in Islamic studies. Institutional liberty and legality, rationality and pure morality, literary and artistic form, are all identified with certain segments of what is called "Western" and other experiences are judged in terms of the resultant norms. Moreover historical relevance is judged in terms of impact on Western Europe, and the significance of Islamdom recedes as it recedes from the Mediterranean.

Now lately we have been seeing a new kind of attempt at world history, which may be called the four-region pattern. It has been brought to its first fulfillment (in the first genuine world history ever written) in

Bill McNeill's "Rise of the West." This orientation was developed essentially among anthropologists or, more precisely, pre-historians. It has begun to shake up the Westernist approach rather seriously on some levels, especially in the form given it by Toynbee. (In this respect, Toynbee represents a very different sense of world history from Spengler, who was still operating in a Hegelian framework.) The four-region pattern, however, is far from adequately developed as yet. From its anthropological ancestry it inherits a strong emphasis on diffusionism. Moreover, it has not had the same basic philosophical underpinning that either Christian, Marxist or Westernist images have had. It has been rooted in merely empirical observation and has not yet been guided by a fundamental sense of what happens historically. Consequently, it is not immune to being taken over by an essentially Westernist approach. Both the diffusionism and the Westernism are highly displayed in McNeill's book.

I find that book is unpalatable partly because I disagree with his analysis of most of the particular civilizations he presents, such as the Hellenic and the Islamicate; but even more because of its unphilosophical structure. The diffusionism of culture traits cannot be properly understood without a very great stress on the total context which determines the nature of any diffusion which took place within it. McNeill is not at all adequate in tracing the development of an overall world-historical configuration as context for particular events. Then McNeill displays a persistent Western bias, despite his very sincere attempts to get beyond it, which obviously results from the Westernist ideology and its philosophic pre-suppositions which he has not yet sufficiently analyzed in order to emancipate himself from them. This lack is reflected not only in the weird notion of Greek science and of the eternal European belligerence and the like, but most significantly in his choice of the time for demarcating modern from pre-modern. The choice of 1500 instead of 1600 as the round number here, is disastrous. It causes him, for instance, to treat Portuguese expeditions not as one more venture within an essentially agrarianate-level historical complex, which was rather readily contained in the course of the 16th century by the other peoples in the Indian Ocean, but rather as a part of the modern technicalistic advance. This necessarily obscures the nature of the modern advance, making it simply continuous with the Renaissance, and disguising its very innovative relation both to the West and to the rest of the citied historical complex of which the West was a part. In short, an adequate basis for world-historical studies, beyond the older bases grounded in certain ideological pre-commitments, has not yet developed.

To me, one of the main reasons for studying world history is to discipline the several communal allegiances such as the Judeo-Christian and the Westernist. I do not hope to see those allegiances undermined, still less destroyed. But I would like to see a basis for conversation and dialog among them. A Westernist image of world history, if not disciplined by a more adequate perspective, can do untold harm; in fact it is now doing untold harm. That is why I lay so much stress on not assuming "decadence" in the Islamic society before the 18th century unless one has really good evidence. As long as no one has studied natural science being produced in Islamdom after the Latins stopped translating from Arabic, we have no right to say that it declined, on the basis of very occasional peeps at its quality. With every decade the time at which the so-called decline is supposed to begin gets pushed farther forward toward modern times. Since the scholars work primarily with older material – have to do so in fact – it is not surprising that they have not gotten to the more recent works yet; but we must not assume what they will find. But in any case, natural science is not the proper basis on which to measure even the rationality of a civilization. This is why the work of such men as Henry Corbin, reminding us of the great importance of philosophical figures in the 16th and 17th centuries, is so important. Indeed I have been increasingly realizing that without a study of the later philosophical tradition and in particular of that tradition in the central areas of Islamdom (i.e., not Egypt which never was very important, but Iraq and Iran which were in recent times largely Shi'i), much of the 19th-century development of modernism in Islamdom is unintelligible. For instance, I think it very significant that al-Afghani has been found to have been trained at Najaf, and to have evoked some of his most important response (perhaps more important than in Egypt) in Iran. Again, it is for this same reason that I find so appalling the reduction of the Islamic area, in our manners of thinking, to the boundary lines of the British Middle East Command in the Second World War; in particular the eternalizing of the British boundary down the middle of Iran splitting Khurasan in two. To make use of current political boundaries in our discussion of historical materials turns out, with remarkable frequency, to be another means of reinforcing Westernist biases. One of the most important tasks of world history, as I see it, is to give people a sense of the pattern of time periods and geographical areas which is free of the multifarious Westernist presuppositions.

II

Islam in a global context

7

The role of Islam in world history

Until the seventeenth century of our era, the Islamicate society that was associated with the Islamic religion was the most expansive society in the Afro-Eurasian hemisphere and had the most influence on other societies. This was in part because of its central location, but also because in it were expressed effectively certain cultural pressures – cosmopolitan and egalitarian (and anti-traditional) – generated in the older and more central lands of this society. The culture of Islamdom offered a norm of international sophistication to many peoples as they were being integrated into the hemispheric commercial nexus. It also offered a flexible political framework for increasing numbers of long-civilized peoples. In this world role, the Islamicate society and culture demonstrated persistent creativity and growth, though some periods were more creative than others, until quite modern times; then the development was disrupted, not by internal decadence but by unprecedented external events. These are viewpoints that I have been forced to develop in the course of attempting a general history of Islamicate civilization, viewpoints that seem to emerge cumulatively from recent studies in several particular fields as well as from the synoptic approach I have adopted. I think they are important for historians, even those outside of Islamic studies, to take cognizance of, though neither the full grounds for them nor their precise implications or limitations can be presented completely here.

In the sixteenth century of our era, a visitor from Mars might well have supposed that the human world was on the verge of becoming Muslim. He would have based his judgment partly on the strategic and political advantages of the Muslims, but partly also on the vitality of their general culture.

Their social and political eminence leaps to the eye. In the eastern hemisphere, where lived nine-tenths of mankind, allegiance to Islam was far more widespread than any other allegiance. Muslims, that is persons committed to worshipping God according to the teaching of

Muhammad of Arabia and of the Quran which he brought, formed the majority of the population in areas as far apart as Morocco and Sumatra, as the port cities of the Swahili coast of east Africa and the agricultural plains around Kazan on the Volga, in the latitude of Moscow. In many of the lands between, even where they did not form the majority, Muslims were socially and politically dominant. The eastern Christian and the Hindu and southern Buddhist lands, even when not ruled outright by Muslims (as in most of India and in southeast Europe) were most subject to the cultural and even political attraction of surrounding Muslim states; in most cases, Muslim traders, or other traders from Muslim-ruled states, formed their most active and continuous link with the outside world. In particular, the greater part of the key historic lands of citied culture in the hemisphere, from Athens to Benares, were under Muslim rule. In all the citied regions of the Afro-Eurasian land mass and its dependent islands, only two culture blocs seriously resisted a potential Muslim hegemony: the Chinese and Japanese Far East and the Christian far Northwest.

Some Westerners have thought of Muslims as reaching the peak of their power in 732, when a minor raiding party was turned back by Franks in Northern Gaul. But this is a parochial illusion. On the world scale, the Muslim peoples reached the height of their political power in the sixteenth century, when a large part of Islamdom was ruled under three large empires, whose good organization and prosperity aroused the admiration of Occidentals: the Ottoman, centered in Anatolia and the Balkans; the Safavi, in the Fertile Crescent and the Iranian highlands; and the Mughal or Timuri, in northern India. Westerners have focused on the empire nearest them, the Ottoman; but though it may sometimes have been slightly the strongest of the three, it was not geographically central to Islamdom, nor was it significant culturally as the central empire, the Safavi, or even the Indic empire. The three empires treated each other diplomatically as equals. One of them singlehanded, the Ottoman empire, was able to defeat the allied forces of Christian Europe, and during the sixteenth century it steadily advanced to the northwest.

But Muslim power was not limited to these major empires. In the Indian Ocean, the many little Muslim states faced a serious challenge early in the century. We all know the glory of the Portuguese. When they rounded the Cape, they were fortunate to find in East Africa a Muslim pilot who was no ordinary sailor: he was advocating among Muslims the publication of the trade secrets of navigation in the Indian Ocean, and himself wrote a book on the subject. True to his principles, he guided the Christian newcomers across to India. His principle of the open door was not reciprocated. The Portuguese, who had navigated the stormier Atlantic, had gained a certain degree of technical superiority over the Muslims. Only the Chinese shipping from the Pacific was larger and stronger. The Portuguese also had bases in West Africa inaccessible to the Muslims, which gave them a political advantage. They proceeded to attempt to monopolize certain parts of the Indian Ocean spice trade, trying especially to cut off the limited portion of that trade which went up the Red Sea and the Persian Gulf to the Mediterranean, serving as source of supply for their own European rivals, the Venetians.

It is only now coming to be realized how far the Portuguese were from marking the start of a European hegemony. At first they had some success, partly by taking advantage of rivalries among the Muslim powers. Neither the Ottoman nor the Timuri Mughal power, oriented away from the Southern Seas, proved of much help against them, though the Ottomans sent one expedition as far as Sumatra (and at one time planned to cut a ship canal between the Red Sea and the Mediterranean). But by the later part of the century, the Muslims of the Indian Ocean had themselves matched the Portuguese technical advantages and had succeeded in containing them, reducing them to one element among others in the multinational trading world of the Southern Seas. Muslim political power continued to spread in the Malay Archipelago, and the spice trade up the Red Sea and the Persian Gulf seems to have been as great as ever.[1]

In the far north, Muslims were also facing a challenge from Christian Europeans. The Muscovites, who had become independent of Muslim rule in the preceding century, were building up a vast and powerful domain, and actually succeeded during the century in overpowering the Muslim states on the Volga. The Ottomans attempted to turn the tide by cutting a ship canal between the Don and the Volga (at Stalingrad, where, finally, the Soviet Union has in fact cut a canal), so as to ensure regular communications between the Black Sea and the Caspian. They failed, partly through the jealousy of the other northern Muslim powers. But the northern powers themselves actively staved off the Russian advance for a time. The Özbegs of Bukhara helped by sending peasant colonists north to the Irtysh basin (the original "Siberia") so as to stiffen

[1] The man who has done most to revise older ideas on the sixteenth century in the Indian Ocean is Jacob C. van Leur, *Indonesian Trade and Society* (The Hague: van Hoeve, 1955). The modifications of his thesis by M. A. P. Meilink-Roelofsz, *Asian Trade and European Influence in the Indonesian Archipelago between 1500 and about 1630* (The Hague: Nijhoff, 1962), have not reversed his conclusions.

the Muslim khanate there, which was based on a rather sparse population, against the steady influx of the Russians.[2]

The Europe of the Renaissance was not yet able to do more than dent the vast mass of Muslim power, and indeed the Christian Europeans themselves (as we know) lived in some dread that "the Turk" might overrun them all. When the French temporarily gave the Ottomans a naval base on the southern coast of France, they were regarded as traitors to the most pressing of common European causes. But, at least late in the century, an extraordinary perceptive visitor from Mars might have been able to foresee a change. Already by the end of the sixteenth century, basic transformations were beginning in Occidental economic and scientific life, transformations that were to result, within two centuries, in the unquestionable supremacy of the Christian European powers throughout the world. During these two centuries, largely as a result of changes in the Occident, the economic and cultural life of Muslim peoples was to be denatured and undermined.

But meanwhile, in the sixteenth century and well into the seventeenth, the Muslims found themselves at a peak point not only of political power but also of cultural creativity. This was especially the case in the old core area of Muslim culture, the Fertile Crescent and the Iranian highlands; but the Muslims of India took a great part and also, to some degree, those of the Ottoman empire. The subsequent time of decline has cast a shadow over the greatness of the age, which by no means leaps to the eye any more; yet it was quite as much Muslim cultural splendor as Muslim political power that might have persuaded the Martian visitor that Islam was about to prevail among mankind, and some of the monuments of that splendor are known even to the relatively casual modern Westerner.

In the visual arts, a new tradition of painting (what we usually call the "Persian miniatures"); beginning in the fourteenth century, came to a first climax at the end of the fifteenth century with Behzad, and in the sixteenth century was further developed in several directions – including not only formal illustration but pen-and-ink genre scenes and fine portraiture. At the same time, an architectural tradition was developing whose most famous point of culmination was the Taj Mahal in India, completed in 1653. In the field of letters, the three great Muslim languages were Persian, Arabic, and Turkish, though numerous lesser languages also

[2] On Ottoman and other Muslim political and economic activity in the sixteenth century, an illuminating recent survey is W. E. D. Allen, *Problems of Turkish Power in the Sixteenth Century.* (London: Central Asian Research Centre, 1963.)

were developing literary forms in that period. Poetry remained the pre-eminent form of expression: the sixteenth century was the age of the "Indian style," later rejected by Persian critics as too *recherché* in the unpoetic days of the eighteenth century, but recently being recognized again for its subtle and creative command of all the resources of allusion that rich Persian poetic tradition has built up in the preceding five centuries. In Turkish and Persian prose, especially, the old solid tradition of historical, geographical, and biographical literature was supplemented with a new vogue for revealing autobiographies which matched the portraiture of the time in its interest in the private and personal: notably the Turkish memoirs of Babur, Timurid conqueror of north India.[3]

We have little idea what was being done in the natural sciences. In the time of the great observatory at Samarqand, in the fifteenth century, Muslim astronomers certainly were abreast and possibly still ahead of those in China and the Occident, where, after a peak in the thirteenth century under Muslim influence, scientific studies had become less active in the fourteenth century. But the rows and rows of Arabic and Persian scientific works of all sorts that survive have scarcely been catalogued and still less read since the end of the eighteenth century.[4] In philosophy, however, the sixteenth and early seventeenth centuries saw much vigorous new inquiry, the most prominent figure being Molla Sadra, whose doctrine of the mutability of essences inspired a series of philosophic movements still having repercussions among twentieth-century Muslims.[5]

It is conventional for modern scholars to assume that Islamicate culture underwent a decline or decadence after the collapse of the High Caliphate or, at latest, by the time of the Mongol conquest in the thir-

[3] The master study on Persian literature now is that of Alessandro Bausani, in A. Pagliaro and A. Bausani, *Storia della letteratura persiana* (Milan: Nuova Academia Editrice, 1960), which pinpoints the newer insights into sixteenth-century poetry. I might add that Martin Dickson of Princeton University, though he has not yet published much, has helped those who know him perceive the cultural vigor and variety of this period.

[4] C. A. Storey, *Persian Literature: a bio-bibliographical survey* (London: Luzac, 1927–1984), the volumes of which are still appearing, suggests in its sections on the sciences the wealth waiting to be investigated.

[5] The most important recent writer to bring out the importance of Islamic philosophy in the sixteenth and seventeenth centuries is Henry Corbin: perhaps even more revealing than his works dealing directly with Molla Sadra is volume I of his *Histoire de la philosophie islamique* (Paris: Gallimard, 1964). But already the Indian poet and inspirer of Pakistan, Muhammad Iqbal, in the last pages of his *The Development of Metaphysics in Persia* (London: Luzac, 1908), had indicated to the perceptive reader what active seeds lay in Molla Sadra especially.

teenth century; and therefore to regard any evidence of vitality or greatness in the later periods, notably in the sixteenth century, as somehow exceptional, as if it were no part of Islamicate culture proper but only a series of unrelated accidents. I believe this is a misconception, partly due to the want, hitherto, of any real overview of Islamicate culture as a whole. In any case, the notion of Muslim decadence cannot be seriously maintained until the effect is eliminated of a variety of preconditions and unbalanced procedures of inquiry that would be bound to produce the illusion of a relatively early decadence, whether there was decadence or not. I cannot here do more than mention a few of these cases; a comprehensive analysis would have to deal with certain prevalent misconceptions of Western history itself and with the relevance to Islamic studies of certain problems inherent in any historical comparisons as well as with the peculiar ways in which the study of Islamicate history as such has been approached.

One natural but unfortunate tendency that has effectively molded our conceptions of Islamdom has been our concentration on the Mediterranean Muslim lands, since they were nearest to the Occident. Once this meant focusing on the Ottomans as they entered European diplomatic history; more recently, it has highlighted the peoples now using the Arabic language, in part because of a philological interest in the language and in classical "origins." A popular identification of Muslims with Arabs has resulted in an especially pervasive series of misperceptions. In fact, the most creative centers of Islamdom were, in all periods, mostly eastward from the Mediterranean – from Syria to the Oxus basin (and largely in non-Arab territory). It is in these areas that most men of all-Islamic influence were born, whereas exceedingly few were born in Egypt, for instance. Many basic institutions seem to have originated in the farther east of this zone – in Khurasan (the northeast Iranian highlands): *Madrasah* schools, *Sufi* brotherhood organizations, the acceptance of *Kalam* theology as integral to Islam, and so on. Another source of misconceptions has been the tendency of Muslims themselves, since the nineteenth century, to reject the immediate past as a failure and look to certain earlier "classical" strands in their heritage that seem to offer resources against modern Western encroachments; a tendency that Westerners have often encouraged for their own reasons. Thus, Western scholars discuss cultural decline in Islam, attempting to pinpoint the time and manner of decadence in the arts, religion, philosophy, and science, without really proving that such decadence really existed, and without evaluating the great works of later periods; the criteria for such cursory evaluation as is made tend to be very subjective.[6] The esthetic and philosophic criteria used are now being challenged in the light of recent Western changes in taste.

Only in the study of the Islamicate economy and of natural science do we have much hope of reasonably detached inquiry. It seems clear that there was a contraction in the economy of most of the central Muslim lands between the ninth and the seventeenth centuries; yet even so we have no real knowledge of the overall picture. In some cases, we know that the contraction was due at least in part to conditions beyond human control at the time; thus, in parts of the Iraq, remarkable feats of engineering were undertaken, but failed to reverse a deterioration in the irrigation system which in part was the result of geological changes.[7] The decline cannot be written off as due simply to a reduction of cultural vigor. Then, even within areas where an economic contraction can be identified in one sense or another, little distinction has been made between the cultural effects of contraction as a process at a given time and those of a lower but stabilized level of economic resources after the contraction has long since happened; or between limitation of resources available for patronage of non-economic cultural activities, which might decline as a result, and an actual reduction in the level of economic technique and sophistication, which in any case would be hard to demonstrate (before the eighteenth century). In short, even to the extent that we can speak of economic contraction, we cannot yet identify surely any cultural correlatives of it, economic or otherwise.

Natural science also is discussed by Westerners, who suggest that though the quality of the best of it remained unsurpassed through the fifteenth and possibly the sixteenth centuries, there was less great work after 1300, and the level of popular manuals declined after 1500. But on investigation, one finds that the data such studies are based on are mostly from the Mediterranean area rather than the more central Islamicate areas; that is, they are largely representative of relatively marginal lands. One may assume that there may have been a relatively less creative period in Islamdom between, say, 1300 and 1450 (as in some other parts of the world at the time – in some respects, even in Western Europe), and yet we find that the crucial blocking of creativity in the overall tradition came only after 1650 or 1700 as a result of competition

[6] R. Brunschvig and G. F. von Grunebaum, *Classicisme et declin culturel dans l'histoire de l'Islam* (Paris: G. P. Maisonneuve, 1957).

[7] Robert McC. Adams, *Land Behind Baghdad* (Chicago: University of Chicago Press, 1965), has shown what was happening in at least one small area.

with a newly transformed West. In this case, one would expect that the greater figures in the centuries just before 1700 would remain unappreciated; for when modern investigation began, to suggest what of the later work was worth reading would be second-rate epigones. Such men would indeed be aware of the famous earlier names, but would incapable of judging among more recent figures, not yet fully winnowed by fame when the best men's attentions were diverted. A picture such as is reported would naturally result, especially in the less central lands. Such evidence as there is would be consistent with this hypothesis. We must await further investigations before we can decide whether, even in the special field of natural science, there was any actual decadence.

One reason for the assumption of an earlier and ingrained decadence is a question that naturally arises, given the usual notions of world history, in a modern perspective. Westerners often ask what it was that went wrong, that the Muslim lands, once powerful, did not go on to share in the great Western transformations of the seventeenth and eighteenth centuries and enter modern times on a par with the Occident. We shall deal very briefly with that question later. The answer does not lie, I am sure, primarily in any prior internal failure of Muslim society; and certainly not in any special obscurantism of Islamic religion. On the contrary, before we can properly pose the question of what happened in the eighteenth century, we must first understand how Islam came to have so great a success for a thousand years. This will require that we turn back to the origins of Islam and its history – and this, in turn, will require us to understand the yet earlier Irano-Semitic cultural traditions of which the Muslims were the heirs. And then we will find our way forward to the sixteenth century.

The immediate background of Islam in the Arabian Hijaz, like that of Christianity in Palestine, is significant; but in both cases, the actual formation of the religion took place in a wider setting, which was at least as important as the local milieu of the founder. Islam was first established, as the allegiance of a major community, in the extensive zone of Semitic and Iranian lands between the Nile and the Oxus rivers. Islam has often been interpreted chiefly in terms of its Arabian environment, and elements identifiable as tracing back to sources outside Arabia have been envisaged as borrowings; but it is truer to the dynamic of events to recognize that, from the beginning, its development presupposed and built upon the cultural resources of the whole wider region.

Mecca depended for its existence on commercial ties with the Fertile Crescent and was keenly aware of the shifting political forces in the region as a whole. Muhammad's political policy seems increasingly to have taken into account the regional balance of power.[8] Though the majority of the local population was pagan, several Arab groups had adopted Jewish or Christian allegiance; Muhammad's preaching in Mecca presupposed a general acquaintance with the monotheistic traditions, which Muhammad claimed he was sent to confirm – and to correct. Jews were especially strong in Medina, where Muhammad went in 622 to lead an independent community that would put his ideals into practice. Many of the religious disputes that were agitated among Christians and Jews in the region at large found an echo at Mecca and Medina. It is possible to interpret much of the Quran as an attempt to get behind those disputes to common basic essentials, to the faith of Abraham who was before Jews and Christians. Almost immediately after Muhammad's death in 632, his community made itself master of the whole region from Nile to Oxus. In doing so, it did not enter essentially alien territory. When Islam was announced there, the new doctrine did not seem strange, and indeed increasing numbers found it quite a logical further step in their own religious development.

The conquered peoples were expected, in principle, to carry on essentially in their old ways, maintaining their old religious allegiances. But it was not many generations before the majority of the urban population insisted on adopting Islam, and even those who did not do so tended to use Arabic as a common medium of culture. The Muslim empire had been based on a pastoralist military force, but that force had been led by urban merchants whose outlook was not incompatible with that of the mercantile elements in the conquered lands. In any case, in marked contrast to other pastoralist empires, the one created by the Arabs stayed in one piece and endured; and, as the Arabs were assimilated into the regional population, they did not adopt the local languages and religious systems but instead were able to impose their own language and allegiance on the various peoples they had conquered.

After a century, the empire ceased to be a strictly Arab state; it came to be dominated by the converted peoples in the name of a supranational Islam, though for some time the common language of culture was Arabic. The religion, at first scarcely more than a ruling-class code and a powerful but ill-defined spiritual impetus, was deepened and broadened by the contributions of the various peoples from Nile to Oxus; these included many of the presuppositions of the *sharia* law

[8] The implications of Muhammad's campaigns toward Syria, in the light of Byzantine-Sasani vicissitudes at the time and of earlier Meccan history, have not yet been fully explored; Wm. Montgomery Watt, *Muhammad at Medina* (Oxford: Clarendon Press, 1956), has gathered much suggestive material.

itself, sometimes thought of as the heart of Islam, which was effectively tied to the Quran only by a relatively late stroke of genius (that of al-Shafi, d. 820).[9] The institutions that the ruling Arabs had begun to build around the religion served to recast all the older Irano-Semitic cultural traditions on a new and more integrated basis. Thus developed a flourishing international Perso-Arabic civilization with its distinctive arts and letters, science and traditions, and manners and mores, which one can call Islamicate culture. As we have seen, this civilization, including its religious core, later spread far beyond the original centers from Nile to Oxus and proved to have so great an appeal that it was accepted even in the heartlands of the Hellenic and Sanskritic cultures. It has continued to follow in the wake of the Muslim trader and missionary ever since, throughout the globe, somewhat as Western ways have followed the modern Christian missionary.

What was it that Islam contributed to the Irano-Semitic heritage to make of it so potent a force? It was partly religion in the stricter sense: a specially satisfying sense of the human relationship to the divine. But associated with this was an unusually flexible social order, which gave anyone who became a Muslim an opportunity to develop his talents on a scale that was relatively unfettered by pre-Modern standards. I believe this social order was rooted in the special geographical and cultural circumstances of the region from Nile to Oxus, but it was reinforced and brought to flower under the aegis of Islam. I have discussed the religious appeal of Islam elsewhere[10]; here I want to discuss more the social side of its power.

For this purpose, I shall be stressing the role of mercantile elements; but it must not be assumed that Islam was essentially a merchants' religion. Other classes played equally important formative roles. Even the strength of the sort of institution associated with mercantile interest was often made possible, indirectly and even directly, only by the special

[9] The work of Joseph Schacht, *The Origins of Muhammadan Jurisprudence* (Oxford: Oxford University Press, 1950), brings out the remarkable role of al-Shafi, but we have yet to pin down how it was that the basic expectations about religion that governed the formation of the *sharia* came to be so close to those governing the Jewish *Halakha* law; studies of correspondences in detail between *sharia* and *Halakha* scarcely touch this deeper question. The parallelism cannot simply be derived from primitive Islamic principles, for quite diverse consequences could be and were drawn from those.

[10] Particularly "A Comparison of Islam and Christianity as Frameworks for Religious Life," *Diogenes* (1960), pp. 49–74 (badly mangled in editing); also "Islam and Image," *History of Religions*, vol. 3 (1964), pp. 220–60, where I also develop in more detail some of the argument here presented.

role of pastoralist groups. And such central phenomena as popular *Sufi* mysticism and the men's associations that came to be allied to it must be associated more with craftsmen than with any other one class, though different forms of them appeared on several class levels. But I believe that the strategic position of the mercantile class, and even the activity of its members, accounts for much of the institutional pattern that gave Islamdom its strength. I must add that we know too little of actual social structures in various periods and areas to do more than indicate certain directions of social pressure.

Karl Jaspers has given us a name for that remarkable age from about 800 to 200 B.C., when there were formulated the greatest motifs of the major pre-modern lettered traditions that subsequently dominated all the core culture areas of the old hemisphere: that is, the Chinese tradition in the Far East; the Indic south of the Himalayas; the Hellenic or European tradition in the Anatolian, Greek, and Italian peninsulas; and the post-Cuneiform Irano-Semitic tradition between Nile and Oxus, from Syria to Khurasan (the northeast Iranian highlands). He called that age the "Axial Age," the age of Confucius, Buddha, and Socrates, and of Zoroaster and Isaiah. It is the age in which originated the prophetic tradition of moralistic monotheism which Islam later brought to a certain culmination.

From that time on until the advent of industrializing modernity, the citied zone of the eastern hemisphere continued to be articulated around the core areas that were set off by the four lettered traditions.[11] But the relations among these four traditions altered greatly. For a time, the post-Cuneiform Irano-Semitic tradition seemed to be weak relative to the other three, and it was almost submerged under the Greek and even the Indic traditions. This phenomenon must be seen not simply as an alien imposition upon the region, but as an aspect of the transformation going on within the Irano-Semitic lands themselves. Beginning at the end of the Axial Age, as the massive Cuneiform tradition was being slowly replaced between Nile and Oxus, many aspects of lettered culture were transferred not into the newer local Iranian and Semitic languages, such as Aramaic, but into Greek, a language less overshadowed by the prestige of the Cuneiform, and used for relatively cosmopolitan purposes by many persons of local, non-Greek cultural background. The shift was

[11] I have tried to pinpoint the relations among these lettered traditions as forming a world-historical phenomenon in "The Interrelations of Societies in History," *Comparative Studies in Society and History*, vol. 5 (1963), pp. 227–50.

especially notable, of course, in the tradition of natural science, which had been making important advances in the Axial Age within the Cuneiform tradition itself. Greek prevailed as the cultural language even at Iranian royal courts. Later when the Indic tradition (especially as carried by Buddhism) was proving so widely influential in the hemisphere, Sanskritic culture rivalled Greek in much of the region from Nile to Oxus.

Even under Greek domination, however, the Irano-Semitic tradition pursued a distinctive development, based on the work of the monotheistic prophets of the Axial Age. While the Greek lettered tradition had become the vehicle of many aspects of culture from Nile to Oxus, new traditions of Irano-Semitic origin, developing in diverse ways the heritage of the prophets, captured its urban conscience. Such traditions proved strong enough, especially in the form of Christianity, to mold much of the religious life of the European region itself. But within the central Iranian and Semitic lands, the monotheistic allegiances played an especially formative social role. Increasingly, the cultural life of the region was articulated in a series of autonomous religious communities, relatively independent of territorial state formations, and many of them (for instance, the more popular Christian sects) identified with the ordinary town population as against any agrarian aristocracy. We shall see that Islam maintained this communal articulation while overcoming its divisiveness.

The communal articulation affected all the lettered traditions of the region. Greek was unchallenged in its European peninsulas, from Anatolia to Italy; Latin played there for centuries a culturally secondary and imitative role. Sanskrit was unchallenged in the north Indian plains, and of its several rivals only Pali, used by some Buddhists, achieved a limitedly independent life. Chinese was unchallenged throughout the realm of the Han empire. But between Nile and Oxus, no one language gained such a position – not even Greek. Aramaic, the Semitic language of the Fertile Crescent, came to form different literary languages for Jacobite Christians, Nestorian Christians, and Jews. Parthians and Persians used different forms of Middle Iranian. Gradually, in the early centuries of our era, all aspects of the culture of the region were embodied in these several literary languages, which differed not merely in religious allegiance but in cultural orientation generally. Thus the Nestorian form of Aramaic carried one branch of the philosophical and astronomical tradition, while the Jacobite form of Aramaic carried a different branch, and in Middle Persian still a different philosophical synthesis was evidently being attempted, in association with official Zoroastrianism.[12] All these traditions had most of their cultural roots in common, but they did not "speak the same language"; the monotheistic religious allegiances, which afforded what cultural integration each had within itself, divided them implacably from one another, even within the same political comity. Such a division was not paralleled within the ordinary population of Greek and Latin peninsulas, even though they were also adopting a monotheistic religious tradition, Christianity.

At the same time, in the early centuries of our era, the role of these Iranian and Semitic populations commercially and even politically in the hemisphere was becoming more important. Not only between Nile and Oxus was Greek yielding (even as language of science) to the several communal languages. In the wider commercial network which joined India and the Mediterranean basin, Greek was losing its commercial position, and Iranian and especially Semitic groups were coming to the fore. It was in the same period when Greek was ceasing to be used in western India that the historic Jewish and Christian colonies, later to be joined by Muslims, were forming on the southwest Indian coast. In the opposite direction, though Greek was not ousted from its home soil in the Mediterranean basin, traders in the west Mediterranean lands came to be thought of as "Syrians" and as Jews. In Central Eurasia, also, Indic influence was rivalled by that of Aramaic groups. The East African trade was dominated by Semites with ties to Syria. The expansion of the Irano-Semitic culture thus began some time before Muhammad.

The communal articulation of the Irano-Semitic traditions and their simultaneous outreach into the wider Indo-Mediterranean regions are to be explained, I think, in part by two features of the region between Nile and Oxus; features that were accentuated in Islamic times. As compared with the Mediterranean peninsulas and the north Indian plains, the region was sufficiently arid to make for insecurity, as time went on, in any system of agrarian aristocracy. Marginal lands could easily pass into and out of cultivation, and desperate peasants could shop around for advantageous terms. At any rate, it was never so easy to fix the peasants to the soil in most areas between Nile and Oxus as it was in Europe or even in much of India: Irano-Semitic (and then Islamicate) society there-

[12] R. Walzer's summary of how these diverse strands were brought together in Arabic, in "Islamic Philosophy" in *History of Philosophy East and West*, ed. Sarvepalli Radhakrishnan, vol. II, pp. 120–48 (London: Allen and Unwin, 1953), has been reprinted in his *Greek into Arabic: Essays in Islamic Philosophy* (Cambridge: Harvard University Press, 1962).

fore was founded on a relatively free peasantry, bound by neither manor nor caste. (Political literature of the region is full of warnings against so abusing the peasantry that they will leave the land.) Correspondingly, the position of the agrarian gentry was necessarily more readily put in question. This became increasingly the case over the millennia, as possibilities of independent pastoral life were developed, first among the horse nomads to the north and then among the camel nomads to the south. Pastoral use of farmlands became an ever-present alternative to agricultural use; indeed, a certain proportion of the peasants themselves eventually came to be settled pastoralists, retaining their ties to nomadism, and ready to return to it at need. And eventually a pastoralist privileged class came to form a standing alternative to the established agrarian class.

While the tenure of the agrarian gentry was less secure, on the average, than in the other core regions, the position of the mercantile classes, again on average, was economically more secure, for they had special sources of strength. In no other region was there such a concentration of bottlenecks of long-distance trade in all directions with such varied and extensive areas, east and west, north and south. Through cities like Nishapur and Balkh in Khurasan (northeastern Iran) passed almost all the external land trade from the Indic region: up through the Khaibar pass and westward toward the Mediterranean, northward to the Volga and Irtysh plains, eastward to China. Through them also passed the most used land routes between China and the Mediterranean. The central cities of western Iran likewise carried the land trade between the Mediterranean on the one hand and either India or China on the other; and much of that between the Southern Seas and the Caspian land and water routes northward to the Volga-Irtysh regions. In the Fertile Crescent, finally, or next door in Egypt, converged many of the land routes mentioned above, as well as all the routes between the far-flung Southern Seas and the Mediterranean region, with its northern (European) hinterlands and also the Sudanic lands to the south. As a region, the Semitic-Iranian lands were the only one of the great core cultural areas in direct contact with each of the others, as well as with the great frontier areas – the Eurasian fluvial plains, the Sudanic lands, and the Far South East.

Long-distance trade was never the chief source of urban income; and not all of these routes were of equal importance at all times. But cumulatively over the centuries they seem to have afforded the leading mercantile classes of the principal cities in these regions a strongly cosmopolitan orientation and, frequently, the opportunity to build a relatively dependable source of wealth relatively independent of local agrarian conditions at any given time. At the same time, they were not politically independent. As in all the pre-Modern agrarian-based societies, the classes that controlled the land had a dominant position in the society as a whole over any large territorial region; though here and there, as on the coasts of the Mediterranean or of the Indian Ocean, mercantile cities would be self-governing. The relative accessibility of most cities to large-scale military campaigns from an agrarian hinterland prevented the formation of independent city states in most areas and forced each city to work out its cultural patterns in intimate union with the wider territory around it.

This tendency to a qualified independence in the mercantile classes, like that to relative insecurity in agrarian tenure, likewise increased with time. The commercial network across the Afro-Eurasian citied regions expanded fairly steadily over the millennia – steadily, if gauged at five-hundred-year intervals, that is – both as to range of relatively direct contacts and as to variety and potential importance of the trade. In Babylonian times, long-distance trade through the Fertile Crescent was scarcely to be distinguished from trade between the Iraq and Syria. Then, even after a larger commercial network had established itself, the network continued to grow. The Malaysian islands, for instance, from way stations when the southeastern sea routes were first opened up at the beginning of our era, were gradually developed into important sources of varied products and then, as citied life developed there, into complex markets. With time, the variety of goods handled in long-distance trade increased, and hence its importance in any one area; while dependence of the long-distance commercial network as a whole on any one region or trade route lessened.

Such considerations were surely marginal; the region from Nile to Oxus, like other regions, continued to support a primarily agrarian-based society, with all the limitations on historical development which this implied. Nevertheless, these conditions, tending on the average to exalt the mercantile role in the society at the expense of the agrarian, seem to have had their effects. It is surely in part because of the secular tendency toward an increased mercantile bias, as the zone of citied culture expanded over the hemisphere, that in the Indo-Mediterranean regions the early eminence of the Mediterranean commercial tongue, Greek, gave way before a greater dominance by the more centrally placed peoples.

A more interesting indicator of the mercantile bias can be traced in the history of the Irano-Semitic monotheisms. With time, the egalitarian and cosmopolitan tendencies in these traditions became more prominent:

their tendency to reject hierarchical or aristocratic ties; to devalue local nature-bound symbolisms; to stress interpersonal, moral norms at the expense of the esthetic or symbolically emotional sides of religious experience; and to exalt the saving community of the faithful over any other social structuring.

As so often, a most sensitive index of this development lay in art, where the rise of iconophobia plots out the curve. I refer not only to its development among the Jews and many Christians – especially the Monophysites – but also to the tendency among Mazdeans to use abstract symbols, like fire, and the limitation to aristocratic circles among them of the use of images, which were associated with older nature-bound cults; so that with the fall of the court such elements scarcely survived among Zoroastrians. As we shall see, cult images seem to have been associated sometimes with aristocratic luxury, sometimes with the worship of nature gods rather than the one moral God; but in any case they seem to have been increasingly rejected by the various religious communities, even those with Mazdean connections. And along with the stress on more abstract symbolization of divinity went an emphasis on the all-sufficiency of the religious community as sole legitimate channel of human social and cultural efforts; this led to the canalization of all cultural life into these communities and their communal languages, mentioned above.

In the middle of the first millennium of our era, then, the Irano-Semitic peoples between Nile and Oxus were becoming increasingly prominent in the commercial life of the expanding Afro-Eurasian citied complex; and internally their culture was developing a relevant variant on the religious orientation common to all the core areas. They were working out the prophetic impulses of the Axial Age within increasingly communal channels, with an increasingly egalitarian and cosmopolitan bias; and this bias was singularly appropriate to the relatively rootless merchant classes, with few ties to nature and to its gods, with a distrust of aristocratic excellences and subtleties and a preference for social organization autonomous from the gentry, and with a strong need for an egalitarian market morality. The chief empire in the region, the Sasanian (ruling all the Irano-Semitic core area save the Syrian end of the Fertile Crescent), was indeed founded on an aristocratic and agrarian form of the monotheistic traditions. The Zoroastrian priesthood formed a high aristocracy. But it had to allow for the existence and often the predominance in its cities of less aristocratic communities; and in its last century the empire underwent serious upheavals, both religious and political, which apparently badly undermined the position of the agrarian gentry on which it was founded.[13]

At this point Islam appeared, establishing not only a new common religious allegiance but also a new policy where the Sasanian had stood. Both the new religion and the new polity and its conquests were largely the work of merchants of a cosmpolitan outlook. Originated by a merchant in an independent mercantile town engaged in long-distance trade, it became the rallying-point of a rather complex political movement. One thread in this movement was the extension of a political and economic system which the Meccans had already established to control the routes between Syria and the Yemen.[14] The prosperity of Mecca seems to have been founded with the help of tribesmen along the route to Syria, who in Muhammed's time were within the Roman sphere of influence; but Mecca had thrived by painstakingly maintaining its neutrality between the three centers of agrarian power that surrounded Bedouin Arabia: the Iraq, Syria, and the Yemen. When Muhammad took over the Meccan system of tribal contacts, he made a special point of trying to absorb into it the tribesmen at the Syrian end of the west Arabian trade route, who incidentally had formed a military reservoir for the Romans; when his successors finally won those tribesmen over, all Syria capitulated and thenceforth cooperated faithfully – a fact that made possible the other conquests. The outcome was that the early Muslim empire was ruled, from Syria, by the leading merchant family of Mecca (the Umayyads), a family that had been engaged specifically in the Syrian trade.

I mention such points, however, chiefly to remind us that the establishment of Islam was, from its origin, not reducible to a supposedly recurrent wave of surplus and nomad population stirred to martyrdom by tales of black-eyed maidens – a conception both ecologically and psychologically most improbable. In fact, whatever the form it took at the moment of conquest, the history of the first century of the Muslim empire

[13] The most ambitious attempt to analyze these events from a world-historical viewpoint, that of Franz Altheim, *Utopie und Wirtschaft* (Frankfurt am Main: Klostermann, 1957), comes to a very different conclusion from the present essay; it suffers from a drastic schematism as well as an arbitrary interpretation of details – its analysis of Muhammad, for instance, is weirdly anachronistic; but it has suggestive data.

[14] The several works of H. Lammens, notably *La Mecque a la veille de l'hegire,* (Beirut: Imprimerie catholique, 1924), which pointed out the extensive dimensions of the Meccan system, are full of over-daring suggestions and have been justly criticized; but their main conclusions still stand and have not even been fully replaced by the several subsequent studies in a similar vein.

was the history of its gradual reconstitution as an Irano-Semitic agrarian empire such as the Sasanian had been. But the advent of Islam made several enduring differences. Because of the special circumstances of the conquest, an even greater degree of social mobility was introduced than is usual in such cases. At the same time, the area of the former Sasanian imperial structure was somewhat enlarged. Partly for this reason but partly also because of the pressure of other social elements, the old Sasanian gentry, though it was converted to Islam, lost its supremacy. Indeed, the effort to maintain an effective agrarian bureaucratic order partly foundered because it proved impossible, under the conditions of high social mobility which the Arab conquest had brought about, to exclude cosmopolitan mercantile elements from the administration. In the long run (by 945) this meant the collapse of the Irano-Semitic imperial tradition itself.

But this would probably not have ensued without reinforcement of the political fluidity by the more positive effects of Islam itself as a religious allegiance. Islam fulfilled in a remarkable way the moralistic, egalitarian, and communal tendencies that had been growing in the Irano-Semitic monotheisms. Indeed, Bedouin Arabia, as something of a mission field for the several monotheistic traditions, had displayed in a most direct way the paradoxes of the communal plurality that was fragmenting the region from Nile to Oxus into a multiplicity of lettered traditions. A sensitive observer could soon learn there how the various prophetic traditions had come to contradict one another, as we have noted, much of the Quran can be read as an exhortation to reject all the varying communal traditions and to hearken to God alone, the God of Abraham, who was a true believer before any of the communities arose. Yet Islam had its own effective communalism. Already as developed in Muhammad's time, Islam seemed to fulfill in an unparalleled way the ideal of a total egalitarian community dedicated to godly moral norms.

Under the special circumstances of the conquest, Islam was further developed as an autonomous total community. Those who were developing Islam as a set of social ideals soon found themselves in bitter opposition to those who were developing the political heritage of Muhammad in practice; and in particular to the tendency to organize the Islamic society as an agrarian absolutist empire. When the representatives of Islamic idealism found, despite an apparently successful revolution (in 749–50), that they could not guide the representatives of Islamic power into their own ways, they set about at least to make them harmless. The Islamic *sharia* law was largely an expression of the responsibility of individuals not only for their personal life but for the whole ordering of society: public offices, as such, were ruled out; everything became the responsibility of the community as a whole and therefore of the individuals who made it up. The Caliph might have a function, but it was, in principal, minimal. Wherever Muslims were found in sufficient numbers, the *sharia* law would allow them to constitute their own fully legitimate social structure in all needful respects. And the authority of the *sharia* law was such that (though several other sorts of laws were used alongside it) no alternative institutions, which might have neutralized its effect, could achieve legitimation and hence long-run durability.

Because *sharia* law was formed and maintained by the private initiative of private persons, special provision had to be made to ensure uniformity and predictability. It was widely held that a jurist must declare himself the adherent of one or another of a handful of recognized schools of law, and if a particular point had been agreed on by the majority of his school in the past, he had to follow the majority. Such requirements have been regarded as enforcing excessive rigidity. But if one looks not at the elementary textbooks but at the authoritative collections of legal decisions, it turns out that in each of the main legal schools ways were found to adapt to changing circumstances at a pace sufficient for pre-modern needs.

One consequence of this autonomy and exclusiveness in the *sharia* law was an undermining of the legitimacy of any agrarian absolutist authority, including the Caliphate itself. But another consequence rather made up for this; to give a religious community as such a viable total political role as the basis for society. This gave the Irano-Semitic populations at last a common vehicle for their traditions, representing, as their several religious communities had long begun to do, the populistic urban ideals over against any agrarian government. Into the Islamic framework and the Arabic language were transferred – and often directly translated – most of the more vital elements of the Irano-Semitic heritages: the elements of monotheistic religion, of course (the old popular lore, and much of the more élite wisdom, received an Islamic dress); but also belles-lettres, history, science, and philosophy. Nestorians and Monophysites learned Arabic to write their medical treatises even when they did not turn Muslim. At last the region from Nile to Oxus had its common literary language, like the other great regions. That language was built up precisely upon the prophetic heritage; and now its communalism, which before had fragmented the region, united it.

The Muslim *sharia* law represented the most radical of the old tendencies. It was highly egalitarian, and therefore, perhaps, what may be called contractualistic. A very wide range of relations were left to contracts between responsible individuals – including, in theory, even the whole range of politics. In principle, no man was properly a ruler till he had been accepted in covenant by the representatives of the Muslim community; and even then – again, in principle – what we would call public duties were potentially the obligation of every Muslim if no one Muslim was fulfilling them. More generally, and more effectively, the directive offices of society were never filled on the basis of fixed heredity, but normally by designation and/or consultation, even when they were filled from a given family. Remarkably little was left, in the *sharia* law, to ascribed status, which was so very important in the two great "idolatrous" regions that flanked the Nile to Oxus region, Europe and India.

Even the marriage law, in which ascribed status played a relatively large role, reflected this egalitarian contractualism. It is not just that marriage was not a sacrament, but that it was a simple contract. Muslim and Occidental law deviated from what may be called a common norm in opposite directions. In pre-Modern societies, wealthier males often maintained several women, as sex partners, one of whom commonly received special status as chief wife while the others were secondary. For Occidentals, the secondary partners (who were maintained as "mistresses" in the Occident also, of course) were held to be no different from common prostitutes; in principle (though not in practice), neither they nor their children had any rights at all; all rights were reserved to an undivorceable materfamilias and her sons – especially her eldest. For Muslims, it was the undivorceable materfamilias whose special status was ruled out. In principle, no partners were subordinated at all: all of them, with their children, were given full equality among themselves, and their treatment could legally differ only so far as varying arrangements were provided for in the marriage contract.

Such an egalitarian orientation left little to the hereditary dignity of a landed aristocracy; and one consequence, broadly speaking, was at last to throw into military hands such governmental tasks as were still recognized to require a common commander. It was long characteristic among Muslims to say: "the military hold the land"; not "the landholders form the military." But this was more than compensated for by the tremendous flexibility which was often left to the Muslim community as a whole, and particularly to the mercantile classes. Apparently it was largely merchants that drew up the *sharia* law in the first place, in the earlier Muslim centuries; and the scholars of the law, the *ulama,* were often of mercantile families or even merchants themselves. It was generally the mercantile classes that were the most faithful supporters of the law. (Indeed, they were often the only classes that were governed primarily or exclusively by it without admixture of other sorts of law.) The indefensible position of sole source of legitimacy which it long held in all Muslim lands was a triumph of mercantility. It was the Agrarian Age, and the predominant power always remained, save in a few city-states, with those who controlled the land. But these latter were forced to recognize the *sharia* law as the sole valid norm, and their own several military laws as secondary and transitory at best. In most areas, the merchant classes did not gain local independence but they did possess a certain veto power in the society as a whole.

In consequence, during the greater part of the Muslim period, the Irano-Semitic society maintained an organic unity which crossed all "political" boundary lines. By the sixteenth century, when the Muslim society extended far beyond the original Irano-Semitic limits, new sorts of institutions were arising. But at least till then no parochial corporate entity was allowed a permanent status, neither castes as in India nor estates and municipalities as in the Occident – even guilds were relatively weak. Nor was any bureaucratic state administration allowed to gain too great a predominance, as in Byzantium or in China. By way of individual ties of contract and of patronage, governed by a common universal law to which all Muslims were subject wherever they might be found, urban society proceeded on its own, with a minimum of reliance on the garrisons in which ultimate power rested but whose chief essential function was to prevent bloodshed among rival fashions within the towns.[15] Complementing the external bonds of the *sharia* law, which assured every Muslim a privileged legal status wherever he went, was the more inward bond of *Sufism:* of the spiritual discipline of the consciousness. Its exponents were not only universally respected, but worked out organizational patterns – the Sufi brotherhoods – which answered perfectly to the contractualism of the *sharia* law. Without benefit of a church or even of tightly organized monastic orders, they were capable of extending something of a sense of spiritual adventure universally to the ordinary Muslim of a pious turn of mind.

Muslim society, like all agrarian-based societies, was indeed stratified; but relatively speaking, especially before the sixteenth century, there was a high degree of social mobility and also of geographical mobility: almost every figure known in Muslim history travelled widely. Even

[15] Ira Lapidus, in *Muslim Cities in the Later Middle Ages* (Cambridge, Mass.: Harvard University Press, 1967), has studied how, in Mamluk Syria, the garrisons were in fact drawn into the urban structure of contract and patronage; so complementing the fundamental analysis of the separation of the occupying garrisons from the civilian life made by H. A. R. Gibb. (He has also noted the intershading of merchant and *ulama* families.)

military commanders, defeated in one spot, might take their troops to a distant region and establish a garrison there instead. Accordingly, wherever any Muslims settled, soon whole cadres of Muslim society and culture were set up, partly through the arrival of immigrants, partly through conversion of local people – for, on conversion to Islam, any office was open to a man. In non-Muslim territories, once such cadres were set up, ruled automatically by the *sharia* law and given inner cohesion through *Sufism*, only the right occasion had to be awaited for Muslim solidarity to make itself felt as political power. When, then, the Muslims became the dominant élite in a place, further conversion by the adventurous or the ambitious naturally followed. Conversion by violence did occur, mostly contrary to Islamic principles, but it played a very minor part in the expansion of Islam; it was not needed.

We can now see something of the role Islam played in the Afro-Eurasian historical complex at large, where even before Islam the Semitic and Iranian peoples were making themselves felt. Islam, in its religious ideals and then in its influence on social patterns, reinforced just those traits of the Irano-Semitic heritage that encouraged egalitarian contractualism and social mobility. It did so by way of the trans-territorial autonomy of the religious community as a total moral society. By denying legitimacy to alternative social norms, it encouraged the development of institutions that made it easier for the Irano-Semitic cultural traditions to be received far and wide in the hemisphere. Able to maintain local and even international solidarity independent of any particular political establishment, able to draw at once on the skills and habits of migrants from the lands from Nile to Oxus and also on the talents and local expertise of converts everywhere, the Muslims were ready to launch their great expansion just about the time when, in the tenth century, undermined by the new social patterns formed in its womb, the early Caliphate was collapsing. That expansion soon reached into almost every part of the hemisphere, far beyond the original limits of the Caliphate, and it tripled the area of Islamdom.

This social flexibility was reinforced by a sophisticated and, above all, cosmopolitan high culture. Opened up to be reconstituted creatively in the course of transference into Arabic (and later Persian), the Irano-Semitic traditions of high culture offered to the restless a rich corpus of arts and sciences. This built not only on the several Irano-Semitic heritages themselves – including their originally Greek components – but on whatever seemed most readily exportable in the Indic and even the Chinese traditions. Thus for a time Muslim astronomers, building not only on their own Babylonian and Greek heritage but also on Sanskrit developments, were teachers of astronomers everywhere from the Latin West to China; and the Muslim Sufis (or mystics) were perhaps the most sophisticated and certainly the most universal-minded of all the explorers of the place of human consciousness in the cosmos. The rich traditions of Persian poetry and of abstract art likewise proved to have a universal appeal.

None of this was tied to clerical élites or other special status groups. Uncontrolled by church or caste, the carriers of these heritages disciplined themselves in such a way that their accessibility to all did not result in intellectual anarchy. The custodians of the *sharia* law presented, along with it, official, generally accepted intellectual patterns, to which the ordinary person, brought to learning without necessarily having any preparatory family background, was directed. These were matter-of-fact, even prosaic, in tone. Whatever was subtle or paradoxical – even more closely nuanced symbolical range of thought – was kept explicitly esoteric and disguised from the public view; a person of any background could learn such lore, but only if he were accepted as competent by a master. This trait, to be sure, has not lightened the task of modern rediscovery of the culture.

There is some evidence that Islam and the social and cultural pattern associated with it not only reinforced dynamic tendencies within the Semitic and Iranian peoples, but appealed directly and selectively to certain analogous strains of culture elsewhere, which had been relatively weaker within their own original settings. Buddhism seems early to have had a populistic, egalitarian and perhaps mercantile appeal within the Indic tradition somewhat corresponding to the appeal of the less aristocratic monotheisms in the Irano-Semitic traditions. One gets the impression that in Sind, in Benghal, and probably in other places from the Oxus basin to Java, Islam inherited much of the Buddhist element in the population – possibly fulfilling their spiritual and social needs more fully than did the Buddhist tradition, often still tied, despite itself, to the more aristocratic Sanskritic nature gods and social forms.

The expansion of Islam then went into three sorts of areas. It followed most of the major long-distance trade routes – notably around the Indian Ocean basin, across Central Eurasia, and across the Sahara. Along these routes, merchants were culturally of special importance, and merchants tended to be Muslims; in this sort of area the only effective rivals proved to be West Europeans and Chinese, and they only in limited regions. Islam also tended to be adopted in frontier areas just opened to citied life, where only parochial, tribal cults had prevailed and a religious consciousness was required that could make sense of the opening wider horizons (often such areas coincided partly with the hinterlands of trade routes): in sub-Saharan Africa, in the Volga and Irtysh river basins, in the Malaysian islands, and in such marginal areas as Bengal and even Yunnan in China. Finally, Islam came to prevail politically and socially in the lands of most ancient civilization: in the old core area of Sanskrit culture, in north India; and in most of the old core area of Hellenic culture, in the Anatolian and Balkan peninsulas. Here conquest came first, and the Muslim cadres came only later to reinforce it and make it irreversible. By the sixteenth century, most of the East Christian, Hindu, and Theravada Buddhist peoples found themselves more or less enclaved in an Islamicate world where Muslim standards of taste commonly made their way even into independent kingdoms, like Hindu Vijayanagar or Norman Sicily.

Speaking very broadly, then, and referring only to certain dynamic points, we can say the role of Islam in Afro-Eurasian history was to institutionalize the more egalitarian and cosmopolitan tendencies in Irano-Semitic culture, giving to urban and communal expectations associated with mercantile prominence a key role (though, indeed, not a master role). This made possible the spread of the Irano-Semitic traditions across the hemisphere under the aegis of a single order bound together by a common allegiance. This social order, finally, formed the chief part of the wider world context impinging on the other societies of the hemisphere – which were able to offer adequate alternatives to it only in the extreme northeast and northwest of the Afro-Eurasian land mass.

We can hardly, then, look on the middle periods of Islamicate history – the centuries between about 945 (the collapse of the Caliphal state) and about 1500 (the rise of new major bureaucratic empires) – as decadent, despite their decentralization and militarization. The tremendous expansive power of Islamicate society in those centuries shows that even politically the decentralized system was extraordinarily successful; for it answered the needs of an increasingly cosmopolitan world. It was an effective development of the cultural tendencies that had produced Islam itself and its Caliphate. Given the pre-Islamic communal developments between Nile and Oxus, the High Caliphal state can (in one perspective) be regarded almost as an interlude, a transition from the agrarian monarchy of the Sasanians to a more decentralized social order long since increasingly congenial to the region, to its special expansive strength and creativity.

Culturally, likewise, we must be hesitant to write off the later forms of Islamicate art or literature (especially the Persian literature, more widely dominant then than the Arabic) or religious speculation and practice as decadent, merely because they served different needs from those we have been accustomed to honoring. It can be argued that Islamicate culture, if less excitingly innovative than in an earlier period, was more substantial and mature and perhaps enduringly valuable in those later periods.

We are coming to realize that the speculation of Ibn al-Arabi (d. 1240), for instance, which formed the starting point for so much of the thinking of the next two centuries, was not the passive monism that has been imagined, but a powerfully stimulating synthesis in which the human person, as microcosm in an infinitely meaningful cosmos, was assigned vast potentialities in every sphere of activity. It can be speculated that his expansive and optimistic mood, known in Raymond Lull, may indirectly have contributed to the expansiveness of such men as Lull's admirer Giordano Bruno and hence to Bacon and the Western moderns. Certainly it contributed to a remarkable wave of optimistic efforts at reform and revolution among the Muslim themselves in the late fourteenth and the fifteenth centuries, when the urban aristocratic elements that had found their ruthless champion in Timur (Tamerlane) and his artistically gifted descendants were pitted against revolt after bold revolt of chiliastic or antinomian idealists, not all of whom proved unpractical.[16] The brilliance of the Persianate culture of the late fifteenth century, epitomized in the famous court of Herat in present Afghanistan (which reminds one so of Florence in the contemporary Italian Renaissance), was no "last gasp" but a central expression of a culture that was vital also in other ways and that developed naturally into the greatness of the sixteenth century.

The Muslim social order that had emerged from the Caliphate was extraordinarily appropriate to a mercantile society. But like any strong system it had its chronic weakness – the precariousness of any established local corporations and of government generally, undermined by their illegitimacy in *sharia* Muslim eyes. As compared with China or Byzantium or even with Western Europe, the militarized governments tended to be arbitrary and unpredictable. The sorts of investment merchants made could survive such conditions reasonably well, if only be-

[16] On Timur, Jean Aubin, "Comment Tamerlan prenait les villes," in *Studia Islamica*, vol. 19 (1963), pp. 83–122, brings out the political alignments he depended on. One example among many of the gradual capture of organized *Sufism* in the central areas for chiliastic revolution is studied by J. Mole in "Les Kubrawiya entre Sunnisme et Shiisme aux huitieme et neuvieme siecles de l'hegire," *Revue des Etudes Islamiques* (1961), pp. 61–142.

cause their investment was commonly dispersed and movable; industrial investment, fixed in one spot and requiring continuous enlightened governmental protection, was less favored. In late Agrarian times, new conditions began to make themselves felt that made this particular weakness more significant. When the Afro-Eurasian commercial complex was reaching its maximum extent and complexity and when the steady accumulation of techniques developed all over the hemisphere, and gradually spread widely in it, had vastly altered the technical resources of all the regions as compared with Sumerian times – then (and possibly by way of consequence) began to develop, at least in Sung China and a bit later in western Europe, a new role for industrial investment. In limited areas and fields, industrial investment began to be as important an economic determinant of social patterns as commerce.[17] Both China and the Occident began to impinge unprecedentedly on the Indo-Mediterranean regions; the Occident did so with especially effective results because it was essentially a new territory (it began symbolically somewhere between Amalfi and Florence, for our purposes), never of much consequence before, and yet was at the very doorsteps of the older regions. The Franks limited Muslim commerce and naval power in the Mediterranean at a period when these were still strongly expansive almost everywhere else.

However, for a long time this had only marginal consequences. As late as the sixteenth century the Muslim peoples were still, on the whole, expanding. We may perhaps hypothesize some early effect of the new balance that was emerging when we see the tendency toward decentralization in Islamdom being reversed about 1500. Around that date, prosperous centralized bureaucratic monarchies were restored not only in the southeast European region (the Ottoman empire centered in formerly Greek Anatolia and the Balkans) and the north Indian region (the Indo-Timuri empire) but even in the Irano-Semitic heartlands (the Safavi empire, which included the Iraq at first and at some moments later). But the solidity of these empires can more immediately be accounted for by other considerations, notably the use of gunpowder weapons, which required an expensive corps of specialists and a constantly improving technique – weapons which seem to have developed *pari passu* in Islamdom and in Christendom from the thirteenth century on (the much better Occidental documentation offers instances a couple of decades

[17] Robert M. Hartwell, in a doctoral thesis at the University of Chicago in 1963, has made clear the comprehensive extent of the abortive industrial revolution in Sung China; thus throwing revealing light on the phenomenal cultural flowering in Tang and Sung China.

earlier in many cases for the Occident, but the whole development can be attested in internal Muslim materials).[18]

In any case, the empires, as we have seen, scarcely represent a decline; rather they took up the positive cultural developments of the preceding several centuries and carried them further – notably in the Isfahan of Shah Abbas the Great in Iran and the Agra of the Emperor Akbar in India. The empire of Akbar marvelously impressed Western visitors for its prosperity and urbanity even though by the end of Akbar's life the great transformations in the West were already getting under way; but its greatness cannot be ascribed simply to Akbar's eccentricities. All the notable ideas on which he built his empire and which his successors long maintained, such as the doctrines of *sulh-e kull,* universal conciliation, were foreshadowed among Muslims in the preceding two centuries, though never before so fully worked out as by men like Fayzi and Abulfazl in Akbar's time.

Yet the more industrial society of the Occident was even then beginning a further internal transformation which, by the end of the eighteenth century, had destroyed all the older bases of historical life in the Afro-Eurasian complex. Until that point, the level of social power in the Afro-Eurasian citied lands had advanced at a fairly even pace across the hemisphere. The technical resources and social complexity of the Spaniards, the Ottomans, and the Chinese in the sixteenth century were about equally removed from those of the ancient Sumerians – or of the Aztecs – and would have allowed any one of those powers to overwhelm such a less highly developed society. For though development was always very uneven, yet in the conditions of the Agrarian Age, if any given cultural bloc caught up with the others within four or five centuries, the rough balance could be maintained. But in the seventeenth and eighteenth centuries, the pace of change was enormously accelerated within one of the cultural blocs. What happened in Christian Europe in the seventeenth and eighteenth centuries doubtless emerged in part from the increased role of industrial investment there that had begun earlier; and it presupposed the special florescence of the time of Renaissance and Reformation. But even that florescence did not pass beyond the sort of agrarian-based limitations on the historical processes that had prevailed since the Axial Age, even since Sumer. It was no more innovative than like earlier florescences – those of the Axial Age every-

[18] For the development in a relatively backward part of Islamdom, Egypt, see David Ayalon, *Gunpowder and Firearms in the Mamluk Kingdom* (London: Valentine, Mitchell, 1956).

where, or those of Gupta India, of Caliphal Islamdom, and of Tang-Sung China. Correspondingly, it did not bring the Occidental peoples to a basically higher level of social power than the other culture blocs had attained, though here and there Occidentals might have temporary advantages – such as Muslims had had earlier.

But at the end of the sixteenth and the start of the seventeenth century emerges a pattern of investment (of time and of funds) in multiple, interdependent, large-scale technical specializations; a pattern that dominated, at first, crucial sectors of science and industry, but soon gave its tone to Occidental society as a whole. A technicalization of institutions that before had been sporadic (and as common elsewhere as in Europe) thereby became self-propelling and resulted in a drastically accelerated pace of social change in all fields that could profit by such interdependent large-scale technical specialization. Once this technicalization was under way, it resulted in a decisive increase in the level of social power available to Westerners; and the increase proceeded ever more rapidly.[19]

It was this phenomenon – starting not around 1500 but around 1600 – that set off the Occident from the rest of citied mankind as effectively as the citied societies had been set off from the pre-liberate tribal peoples. And as soon as it became effective in the West, it had corresponding effects on the rest of the commercial and historical complex in the Afro-Eurasian citied zone of which the Occident was an integral part. In the first instance, the effect was a matter of relative power: unless the other blocs had undergone the same transformations – by some improbable historical sleight-of-hand – at exactly the same moment, they must necessarily quickly be left hopelessly behind; for, before being transformed themselves, they could not even borrow at the requisite pace of innovation. But they were not merely left behind.

Competition with technicalistically produced goods from the West proved increasingly difficult for local craftsmen, and this by itself was ominous for a society in which mercantile interests played so crucial a role.[20] The top levels of the bourgeois classes were among the first to be ruined, and with them the balanced social structure was undermined. Intellectually, the effects were subtler but equally sure: by the eighteenth century, that handful of brightest minds on which basic advance depends were discovering that Western medicine, astronomy, and science

[19] I have discussed this technicalization in rather more detail in "The Great Western Transmutation," *Chicago Today* (Autumn, 1967), pp. 40–50.

[20] The writings of Gunner Myrdal on the contrast between "backwash" and "spread" effects of increased investment in any given area are an invaluable introduction to the plight of the non-Western societies, especially since the Industrial Revolution.

generally were already well beyond what the Islamicate tradition could yet offer; and they were discovering also that the new advances depended on a large-scale investment in multiple specializations – notably the "instrument-makers" and the technology on which they in turn depended – not available to a non-Westerner. Further advance in the old traditions was pointless, but adoption of the new traditions was impossible. Creativity, intellectual as well as economic, was almost imperceptibly strangled.

It was at this point – at the end of the sixteenth century, that the long-standing ecological and historical foundation of the greatness and creativity of the Islamicate version of Irano-Semitic culture disappeared; for now it no longer answered the social and intellectual needs of a world increasingly cosmopolitan on a mercantile basis, but rather faced a transformed world whose cosmopolitanism was on a quite new basis.

Unable to keep up or to insulate themselves, most of the non-Western societies were instead undermined and overwhelmed. In the sixteenth century, the Muslim peoples, taken collectively, were at the peak of their power, by the end of the eighteenth century they were prostrate. The Safavi empire and even the Timuri empire of India were practically destroyed, and the Ottoman empire was desperately weakened; and such weaknesses could no longer be compensated by internal developments at the old pace, but invited Occidental intervention – which occurred massively, directly and indirectly, by the beginning of the nineteenth century. If it was any consolation, even the unparalleled power, wealth, and culture of the Chinese were subjected to the same fate.[21]

The fate of the Islamicate civilization is not, then, an example of a biological law that every organism must flourish and then decay; for a civilization is not a organism. If anything, that fate exemplifies, rather, an economic principle that a successful institution may invest so heavily in one kind of excellence, adapted to one kind of opportunity, that it will be ruined when new circumstances bring other sorts of opportunity to the fore – perhaps as a result, in part, of the very excellence with which the first opportunity was exploited.

[21] I have gone into more detail on the world-historical situation of modern Muslims in "Modernity and the Islamic Heritage: Dilemmas of the Concerned Individual in the Modern Acceleration of History," *Islamic Studies*, Journal of the Central Institute of Islamic Research, Karachi, vol. I (1962), pp. 89–129.

8

Cultural patterning in Islamdom and the Occident

For Western readers, Islamicate institutions can be specially illuminated by a comparison with Occidental institutions of the same period, as well as by consideration of what the Occidentals found to learn or borrow from the Muslims. Such a comparison can suggest assessments of potentialities in the two cultural sets as well as suggest long-term directions of movement in them, which may help us understand why this or that seeming possibility was not taken into account at this or that juncture. But at this point in our studies, it is hard to sort out the properly ecological circumstances from the expressly cultural commitments that enter into such comparison. It is perhaps even harder to sort out the cultural commitments that have contributed to social patterns in particular ethnic groups – local ruling classes, relatively compact nations like Egypt, and even whole language blocs like the Iranians. Inevitably, many comparisons have been attempted by scholars as if such elements could be sorted out. Perhaps the most important function of such a comparison as we can attempt is to suggest an alternative viewpoint to complement and perhaps correct the various current comparisons, usually superficial and often invidious or self-congratulatory on one side or the other.

The Earlier Middle Period, particularly the twelfth and thirteenth centuries, roughly equivalent to High Medieval times in the Occident, is the first period during which a comparison of the Occident with Islamdom can be particularly fruitful; up till that time, the Occident had been, on the whole, too backward to compare with one of the major centers of civilization. It is not only the first but also the best period for such a comparison. A comparison drawn later, in the sixteenth century, say, would be of interest for understanding the background of Modernity, but would lose value for purposes of illuminating the two traditions *as such* because the Occident had then entered one of those periods of major florescence relatively rare in agrarianate times, while the Islamicate lands were witnessing more normal historical conditions. After about 1600, the basic conditions of agrarianate historical life itself began to be altered in the Occident, and comparisons after that date therefore introduce considerations alien to any direct comparison between two cultures as such.

Islamdom and the Occident in the thirteenth-century world

Since the rise of the confessional traditions in late Roman and Sasanian times, the Afro-Eurasian Oikoumene had not changed in the most fundamental conditions of its social life. Civilized culture was everywhere still carried primarily by privileged classes in cities, living ultimately from the labor of a great majority of chiefly illiterate peasants in the countryside. Cultural and intellectual innovation was everywhere still a secondary aspect of cultural life; the prime object of all institutions was the preservation of what had been attained rather than the development of anything new. Not only arts and crafts, but life-orientational and scientific thought, while not (as in pre-citied times) a matter of oral tribal lore, and no longer (as in citied times before the great Axial Age flowerings) the initiatory privilege of special priestly orders, nevertheless remained primarily a matter of personal apprenticeship from generation to generation on the basis of a limited number of classical texts among a small minority. Any possible historical action in any such fields could still not escape the presuppositions of society of the agrarianate level.

Yet within these limits, much that was only slightly less fundamental had changed by the thirteenth century. In these changes Muslims had played a primary role. Much change was the direct outcome of the force of Islam itself, which had had major consequences not only from Nile to Oxus but throughout the Indo-Mediterranean regions. Much change was the result of cumulative processes in which Islam and the culture associated with it were only one force among many. But even here the presence of the Muslims had often been of determinant importance. The most evident changes had been those that followed from the cumulative further development of the overall Oikoumenic complex of citied life. As compared with a thousand years before, by the year 1300 the area of civilized interaction had expanded in all directions. Cities had arisen in the Sudanic lands, in northern Europe, in the lands south of the older China, in Malaysia, and they not only traded at long distances but added their own products to the trade, and sometimes even their own ideas. In the heart of the steppe, the Mongols themselves were becoming Buddhists and were well launched on the path to abject dependence on

Chinese merchants and princes to which they had sunk by a few centuries later. In the Indian Ocean basin, trade no longer depended simply on a few northerly markets, but was active along all the shores.

In the same thousand years the technical competence of human being in the Afro-Eurasian civilized zone had markedly increased. "Greek fire" had been invented and then gunpowder; the compass had been put to work on all the seas; paper had spread from China to all regions, and printing was in use in the Far East and at least some of its elements were known elsewhere. Innumerable lesser inventions and discoveries had been made in the field of practical and of artistic technique, in the cultivation of plants and animals, in abstract scientific knowledge; some were of local application and some of general use; some of the most spectacular originated in China, but every region could be credited with some; and all (whether taken up elsewhere or merely adding to a local complexity) cumulatively contributed to a heightened level of availability of human resources everywhere in the Oikoumene. It was indeed, in part, some of the new discoveries that helped make possible, directly and indirectly, the expansion that had taken place in the area of civilized interaction; and this expansion, in turn, added to the potential sources of new discoveries. As in each millennium that had preceded, cumulatively the pace of history had quickened. (Whether mankind was *progressing* is a different question.) Here again, Islamdom shared at least as much as any other society in the overall development.

There was a third field of change during the previous millennium, less tangible than the geographical and technical accretions. This was a broadened and deepened experience with philosophical and religious life. Not only from Nile to Oxus but in all the major citied regions the rich creations of the classical Axial Age had been deeply assimilated, marvelously differentiated, a thousand and one of their possible implications worked out minutely. The labors of Ghazali and Ibn al-Arabi in appreciating and integrating the Irano-Semitic life-orientational traditions, as they had developed by their time, were matched in differing ways in the other regions by figures like Shankara and Ramanuja in India, Chu Hsi in China, Michael Psellus and Thomas Aquinas in Europe, all roughly (as world history goes) contemporaries. At least as important as any intellectual formulations was the maturing of traditions of personal experience with various aspects of the mystical life, and of institutions (usually monastic) which embodied these traditions, a maturing which had taken place likewise in all the great Oikoumenic regions.

Within this wider and more sophisticated world, Islamdom occupied an increasingly central and already almost a dominant position. The nature of this dominance has been misunderstood. The peculiar notion of some modern Western writers, that before the sixteenth century other societies, such as the Islamicate, were "isolated" and were brought into the "mainstream" of history only by such events as the Portuguese invasion of the Indian Ocean, is of course ridiculous: if there was a "mainstream," it was the Portuguese who were coming into it, not the Muslims; the Muslims were already there. But the contrary notion, also found among Western writers, that in the High Caliphal Period Arab or Islamicate culture was the greatest in the world, that Cordova or Baghdad were incomparable centers of wealth and learning, is almost as poorly founded. It springs equally from the unconsidered assumption that the Occident was the "mainstream" of world history and culture. Compared with the Occident, in the High Caliphal Period, when the Occident was still rather a backwater, Islamdom looks magnificent; but such a comparison says nothing about its relative position in the world; the Baghdad of the caliphs was merely on a plane of relative equality with Constantinople in eastern Europe and with the metropolises of India or China. (In the Earlier Middle Period, when the Occident was more developed, Islamdom looks less strikingly glorious in comparison; but most of the change in appearances is due to a change in the level of the Occident, not in that of Islamdom.) The well-known cultural superiority of Islamdom, then, was not absolute in the world at large (in the Earlier Middle Period, surely it was in China, if anywhere, that would be found the maximum economic and cultural prosperity); it was relative to the developing Occident.

Yet in certain respects, Islamdom was indeed pre-eminent in the Oikoumene. For the configuration of regional lettered traditions in the Oikoumene had, in the course of the other changes, itself subtly changed. In the Axial Age three great lettered traditions had been launched in the Indo-Mediterranean zone, the Sanskritic, the Irano-Semitic, and the Hellenic, in relatively close relations with each other but in rather tenuous relations with the fourth lettered tradition, the Chinese. The same four traditions still formed the matrix of all high culture; but their pattern had been altered now in three ways. First, the Irano-Semitic traditions had loomed much larger under Islam. In the early post-Axial centuries, the Irano-Semitic lettered traditions seemed almost ready to be submerged under waves of Hellenization and even of Indicization. By late Sasanian times, these traditions were asserting full autonomy, and under Islam the Irano-Semitic heritage was clearly established on an equal level with the others – or more than an equal level; for by 1300 already the other two heritages were being submerged, at least in their original core areas, by the Irano-Semitic in Islamicate form. Already by then the whole core area of Sanskritic culture was ruled by Muslims, and in the following centuries even independent Hindu states in the region learned more and more to live in an Islamicate world, even adopting some Islamicate patterns at least on superficial levels. By 1300 also the Anatolian peninsula was Muslim-ruled, and within a century so was the Balkan peninsula; of the homelands of Hellenic culture, only southern Italy and Sicily were not regained for Islam – and at this point, at any rate, Sicily even under its northern conquerors still retained strong traces of its earlier Muslim past and of its Islamicate surroundings. In short, by way of Islam almost the entire Indo-Mediterranean citied zone of Axial times, together with a wide hinterland, was already or was about to be united under the aegis of a single society; even though locally the Hellenic and the Sanskritic traditions maintained a certain limited vitality – a vitality visible especially in religion (and not too different from that maintained locally by the Irano-Semitic traditions at the height of the less extensive Hellenic dominance).

But there were two other events complementing this rise toward hegemony of the Irano-Semitic traditions: the potent burgeoning of China and the independent maturing of the Occident. Even at the height of Islamicate power, in the sixteenth century, when the greater part of the Oikoumene seemed to have become, if not Muslim, then at least a series of enclaved societies surrounded by Islamdom, still even then two citied societies stood out relatively impermeable to Islam: the Far East of China and its neighbors, and the Occident of Europe, part of the region grounded in Hellenic traditions. But neither of these societies played the same role as it had in Axial times. The Far East, of course, like the other societies had been doing its own expanding, and from a relatively small area along the Hoang-ho and the Yang-tze its lettered traditions had come to dominate a wide zone from Japan to Annam. But more important, in the T'ang-Sung period (from the seventh century) impulses from the Far Eastern region had impinged increasingly on the other parts of the Oikoumene; we have already noted, from the very moment of the advent of Islam down to the Mongol conquests, the relative ascendancy of Chinese art and trade between Nile and Oxus (and latterly, even some political impact); an ascendancy only limitedly attested for Sasanian times.

The Occident was at first far less wealthy or cultivated, and impressed the imagination of the Indo-Mediterranean peoples generally less than did the Chinese. But its rise represented an even greater shift in the old Oikoumenic configuration. If one can think of the Occident proper as a complex of independent Latin-using and papacy-owning peoples set off from those under Byzantine leadership, one will see that the Occidental traditions arose on essentially new ground, in lands northwest of Rome rather than southeast of it in the terrain of the old Hellenic traditions. This in itself was nothing new – throughout the hemisphere, new areas were modifying in some measure the culture of the core area from which their lettered traditions were derived; thus in further India the Indic traditions maintained in independence, in a different form, after the Ganges plain was overrun by Muslims, just as the Hellenic traditions did in northern and western Europe. But the Occident developed a much more vigorous cultural life than any other such outlying region – indeed, it came to function almost like a fifth core-area, a fifth center of persistent and comprehensive cultural innovation and radiation. After establishing its explicit independence in the eighth and ninth centuries (of course, always within the overall cultural commitments of the Christianized Hellenic tradition), by the twelfth and thirteenth centuries it was imposing its influence, economically, politically, and even culturally, on eastern Christendom, both north among the Slavs and south among the Greeks.

The Far Eastern and the Occidental traditions equally resisted the Muslim expansion – though both learned something from Islamdom as well; but the Occident was much closer to home and even, in a few isolated cases, proved strong enough to roll back Islam from territories where it had long prevailed. One may thus say that, in contrast to the situation a thousand years before, when four more or less equal core-areas had coexisted, now there was developing a three-cornered conflict among the most active cultural traditions: the Islamicate in the whole of the old Indo-Mediterranean zone; the Far Eastern, newly making itself felt abroad; and the new Occidental variant of the Hellenic tradition. The conflict rarely became explicit. The Occident made at best sporadic attempts to act together (as in the Crusades) as a joint political power in its relations with outsiders. The Chinese empire was resisted by Japanese and Annamese. In the vast middle, Muslims, for all their emotional solidarity, acted even less often in concert. But the effective course of the conflict can nonetheless be traced. At the Mongolian capital, Karakorum, representatives of all three blocs had been present and intrigued against one another; if the Tibetans or the Russians seemed for a time to form secondary but independent sources of social power or cultural influence, this soon proved to be transitory or at least closely limited in scope. The Occidental cultural complex was certainly, at first, much the weakest of the three; but it grew steadily stronger, till in the sixteenth century it was competing on a level of full equality with both the others.

In 1300, the Occident could be compared to the dark horse in a race – if it were not that there was no race, or at least no very conscious one: for world hegemony, the presumable goal of any such race, was rarely pursued consciously even on the level of religious allegiance; nor is it clear that world hegemony was a necessary or even likely unintentional outcome of the cultural conflicts I have mentioned – or of any historical forces at work before the seventeenth- and eighteenth-century transformations changed the basis of all such conflicts. The Occident, comprising the lands of Latin expression in the western part of the European peninsulas, had a very limited territory and, by its remoteness, was limited in its contacts with other cultures: it had close contacts only with its former mentors of Eastern Christendom and with the Muslims. It had done very well by itself within these limits. From the viewpoint of urban life, much of it was newly opened frontier land; much of its intellectual resources consisted of material adapted or translated from the Greek (and Hebrew) or, latterly, from the Arabic. Yet in High Medieval times high culture, as well as all aspects of economic life, came to a great flowering in the Occident: a flowering comparable to that of contemporary Islamdom in the Earlier Middle Period, and even more striking because of the much lower point from which the Occidental cultural development started. For the first time in Oikoumenic history, the culture of a great new area, not a mere minor extension of one of the older cultural core areas, had drawn abreast of the old core areas in independent fullness of cultural sophistication and originality.

Yet even so, the Occidental cultural horizons remained more limited than those of Islamdom, if only geographically. After the final defeat of the Crusades, despite occasional merchants and missionaries who traveled great distances in Mongol time (as did men from most other regions), Occidental culture was confined to its own little peninsulas. Thomas Aquinas was read from Spain to Hungary and from Sicily to Norway. Ibn al-Arabi was read from Spain to Sumatra and from the Swahili coast to Kazan on the Volga. Even so late as the sixteenth century, the central position and vast extension of Islamdom still assured it at least the apparent pre-eminence which it was beginning to acquire by 1300. In contrast to any other of the major cultural core areas, that of Islam was in direct and active contact with all the major Oikoumenic regions; and not only in the neighboring core areas but in some more outlying regions, Islam was becoming dominant politically and even culturally. If less industrially developed than the Chinese, the Muslims yet were more widely influential than any other bloc in shaping the cultural interchange and even the political life of the whole Oikoumene. But it was not merely the geographical centrality of the Muslim heartlands that put them in a pre-eminent position. It was the cultural and social mobility of the Muslims, their cosmopolitanism, that allowed them to take full advantage of their central position. Within the setting of agrarianate-level Oikoumenic society, the Islamicate culture was maximally adapted to an expansive and dominant role. It was to maintain this role, becoming steadily more dominant in the Oikoumene, until the Oikoumenic historical circumstances were totally altered – at the hands of the Occidentals.

The sources of Occidental strength and growth are the object of one of the most intriguing inquiries of world history. The sources of Islamicate strength and persistent vitality pose almost as great a world-historical problem, and one perhaps equally intriguing. To compare the two societies at their most nearly comparable stages can help to show to what degree the strength of each can be ascribed to its particular cultural composition, and to what degree to the overall circumstances in which its peoples found themselves.

Islam and Christianity as frameworks for religious life

The attractiveness of Islamicate culture and much of the potency of its institutions stemmed largely from the distinctive structure of the Islamic religious expectations as they had been developed by the Earlier Middle Period. It will be clear by now that the romantic notion that has prevailed in some circles, that Islam was the "monotheism of the desert," born of the Bedouins' awed wonder at the vast openness of sky and land and their overwhelming unpredictability, is unhistorical. Islam grew out of a long tradition of urban religion and it was as city-oriented as any variant of that tradition. Like the other confessions, Islam was practiced by many unsophisticated people and among them it could appear very unsophisticated. Even at its most sophisticated, it usually retained, like the other pre-Modern religious traditions, a number of culturally primitive traits in its cult and its myth. But it stands out among those traditions for its relative sophistication and its freedom from the age-old compounded intricacies of the nature cults.

So far as any religious structure can be called "simple," that of Islam can be. Its central formulations have been singularly stripped and direct and its essential cult has been plain to the point of austerity; the central challenge of its spiritual experience comes forth with almost blinding elemental immediacy. This is a simplicity not of naïve "primitiveness" (pre-literate and other parochially limited systems are rarely if ever simple anyway) but of single-minded sophistication which integrates all the diversity of experience through a few potent and comprehensive conceptions; and then discards all that is circuitous and irrelevant, all that hangs over from a time when perceptions were less broadly generalizable. This relative urbanity of Islam can also be interpreted as a relative rootlessness, being cut loose from any particular local setting and its local involvement with nature. It is traceable to the mercantile orientation of Islam and in turn reinforced the cosmopolitanism of the society which had produced that orientation. Along with the advantages it afforded Islam in making for social and cultural strength, it brought disadvantages too, of course. But both advantages and disadvantages, strengths and weaknesses, were proper to a highly advanced stage of agrarianate social development.

The stark simplicity of the primary Islamic affirmations was but one expression of its overall urbanity. This lay not so much in any one feature of the tradition as in the whole structure of it: that is, the mutual interrelation of the various sub-traditions that went to make up Islam as a whole. Almost every trait to be found in any one religious tradition will be found somewhere in almost any other, if not in a mainstream then in some persistent variant of it; especially where the traditions have received high development among large populations. Thus may coexist social conscience and inward cultivation, moralistic austerity and cultic splendor, stress on transcendence and stress on immanence. But traditions differ as to what form these varying experiences and perceptions are expected to take, and as to which will be granted the greatest prestige; as to what sorts of temperament will be encouraged by those who stand relatively neutral in the community, and what sorts will be, at best, tolerated. It is this, the interrelation and subordination of different elements, that forms the structure of a religious tradition and gives it its distinctive effect as a body. Though such interrelations will change during history in response to the new insights and possibilities developed in the ongoing internal dialogue, yet to a large degree the common commitment to the initial creative events and to the succeeding dialogue, as it has unfolded, assures great continuity in such structuring under even widely varying circumstances.

Since Christianity and Islam share common roots and even much common symbolism, the striking contrast between the ways in which such common elements are lined up in the two traditions can bring out the diversity of their meaning in the two contexts. In particular, comparing such structuring in Islam and in Christianity can bring out the consequences of the persistent primacy in Islam of a sense of personal moral responsibility. But at best such a comparison is full of pitfalls. To evaluate in any way a pattern of ultimate orientation seems to imply judging one ultimate standard by another – or by a standard less than ultimate. In our case, to see either religious tradition from the viewpoint of the other (the commonest procedure) amounts inevitably to showing the one as weak in the other's strong points. To judge them both by a standard alien to either (sometimes attempted in reaction) is to risk missing just those points that are most distinctive and for that reason incommensurate with any more common human norms. Yet, fortunately, human life is not divisible into watertight compartments. Apart from such explicit physiological defects as color-blindness, the sorts of experience accessible to one human being are at least in some measure generally accessible to other human beings, so that there are no ultimate barriers to mutual comprehension between different cultural frames of reference – at least so far as such frames of reference are open to diverse temperaments within their own ranks. Hence what is called a phenomenological approach – such as a comparison of the structuring of comparable elements in two traditions – allows at least an opportunity of genuine appreciation, and will guard maximally against the effects of the inevitable precommitments of the inquirer.[1]

Despite the tremendous variety of religious orientation that has arisen in different sects or orders within the Christian tradition, a central theme has retained its hold on Christian imaginations under all sorts of circumstances, a theme ever presented to them anew especially in the writings of Paul and of John: the demand for *personal responsiveness to redemptive love in a corrupted world.* An equally wide variety of religious orientation has arisen among Muslims of different allegiances and tariqas, and among them also a central theme has retained its power under the most diverse circumstances whenever the Quran has been taken seriously: the demand for *personal responsibility for the moral ordering of the natural world.*

These themes have been presented in contrasting cosmologies. Christians have seen the world as first corrupted with Adam, thenceforth to be patiently redeemed by a loving God, tirelessly forgiving His people so soon as they respond to His grace, and finally revealing Himself most

[1] This is not to say that one can actually dispense with those precommitments. On the inevitability and, indeed, the creative value of Christian, Westernistic, and other high-level precommitments, particularly in Islamic studies, see "On scholarly precommitments" in the section on historical method in Chapter 5, above.

fully among them as a perfect Life of suffering love, to which they need only respond with love, to be saved from the corruption and made whole. Muslims have seen the world as the proper sphere of Adam's viceregency; when Adam strayed into error, he turned to God for guidance and was guided; rather than a source of taint in his descendants, he is a model to them. Thenceforth, God continued the guidance through a series of prophetic summonses to a total pattern of living; finally He revealed His transcendent unity most clearly through a perfect Book; if people allow it to remind them of what they are if left to themselves, they will turn to Him and His guidance will enable them to live right and to rule the world in justice. The central event of history for Christians was Christ's crucifixion and resurrection, which most decisively evoke a sense of God's love in him who opens himself to their impact, and lead him to respond to others in the same spirit. The central event of history for Muslims was the descent and preaching of the Quran, which most decisively evokes a sense of God's majesty and his own condition in him who opens himself to its impact, and leads him to reflect and submit himself to its norms.

For Christians, the Law, the necessities imposed by social living, is transcended as people are liberated, in loving response, to act through the inward power of God's free spirit; the Sermon on the Mount provides a standard of true living. For Muslims, the laws and customs of humans are reoriented toward a universal justice; humans, stirred out of their petty neglectfulness by confrontation with God's words, are to act as the viceregents of God in the whole creation; the jihad, the struggle for social righteousness, provides a standard of true living. For Christians, the kind of religious experience most honored is the acceptance of redemptive grace, which means a process of rebirth, of inward transformation. For Muslims, the kind of religious experience most honored is the acceptance of prophetic vision, which means a process of chastening, of concentrating his attention, of inward refocusing. Christians share their experience in a redemptive fellowship, a special sacramental society, the church, which is to be in the world, redeeming the world, but is not of the world; within which, normally, some have been ordained to offer again the tokens of God's love to the rest in recurring reenactment of Christ's sacrifice. Muslims share their experience in a total society, comprehending (in principle) the whole of human life, the Ummah, built upon standards derived from the prophetic vision; comprising a homogeneous brotherhood bearing a common witness brought to mind daily in the salat worship and impressively reaffirmed en masse each year at Mecca.

It is impossible to compare directly what profundity of human awareness may be encouraged by giving primacy to one or the other of such interpretations of life. Each has encouraged its distinctive areas of intensive probing. Christian writers, facing the stark reality of evil, have found layer beneath layer of meaning in suffering and death. It is notorious that Christians have not solved the logical problem of suffering – not on the level of evident formula, that is; surely this is precisely because they have probed it too deeply to be content with a pat answer. Yet the mark of the matured Christian has undeniably been his vital joy. Muslim writers, accepting the consequences of purposefulness in the creation, have spoken on many levels to the person who finds himself facing solemn responsibilities – as father in a family or judge in a city or seer for a great community. It is likewise notorious that Muslims have not solved the logical problem of free will on the level of past formula, for all the disputes about it. Yet the mark of the matured Muslim has ever again been seen to be his human dignity.

As compared to the Christian tradition, the Islamic seems to have held closer to the central lines of the old Irano-Semitic prophetic tradition, especially as represented in the Hebrew prophets with their emphasis on direct human moral responsibility. To persons for whom the tragic sense of the classical Greek drama, focusing on irreducible evil, raises the most telling ultimate questions about human life, the Islamic tradition, where such problems have been kept to one side, may seem to lack a crucial profundity which may be found in the Christian tradition. Others distrust too encompassing a preoccupation with what is sombre or poignant or obscure as tending to tempt people to neglect what lies before them direct and clear. Such may feel the Islamic tradition to be more manly and more balanced, and even a sounder point of departure for any profundities that may be ventured on. They may agree with the Quranic description of Muslims as forming a middle community, avoiding extremes.

Enduring religious commitments in the two cultural patterns

The prime norms of a society must not be confused with the multiple actuality of the various standards and expectations actually effective in its cultural life. Peoples do not differ nearly so much in practice as may seem if one judges either by the obvious difference of symbolic detail whereby they fill the demands of daily behavior, or by the standards given primacy in their high culture, and so embodied in their literature and in the more formal events of law and social intercourse among especially the privileged classes. Any persistent cultural pattern is likely to be making sense in terms of the calculable interests of those who practice it. Hence it is doubtful if one should say of any given major society (though it is often said) that such and such practical alternatives were closed to it because of such and such unalterable culture traits. If, in the long run, a given society failed to develop along a line which might seem to us advantageous, this is generally to be explained in terms of the practical options open to members of the society at the time: one can expect to find that, in fact, given the total situation, the necessary steps were not sufficiently advantageous to sufficient numbers in any given generation to make them worthwhile. One need not invoke the dead hand of the past, supposedly exercised through traditionally imposed attitudes, religious or not. In a history such as this, therefore, the interests of particular groups and the problems of particular periods are put in relief.

Nevertheless, those norms that are given primacy in prestige, on the level of high culture among the privileged classes, have a pervasive and enduring efficacy. In a crisis, they underlie the ideals that imaginative individuals will bring to bear in working out new ways of action; they offer a guide that aspiring groups in the society can make use of as they try to approximate to the privileged classes' ways; above all, it is these norms that confer legitimacy. Other things being equal, those ideas, practices, and positions of power or authority that are recognized generally as legitimate can survive times when their current expression or implementation is temporarily weakened; for each person expects that the others will support them, and so he will be guided more by the positions' long-term prospects of strength than by a short-term weakness. A dog is obeyed in office: even a fool will be obeyed for a time if he is recognized as legitimate ruler. Hence norms given cultural primacy and legitimizing some cultural forms at the expense of others have a pervasive influence so long as the traditions that support them retain their long-term relevance. A global comparison between two cultures, as in this chapter, will necessarily bring out any more persistent constants of this sort that can be perceived.

It is not only norms in the sphere of ultimate commitment, but also in other spheres, artistic, intellectual, and socio-legal, that mold the climate of a society. The straightforward moral appeal of the Islamic religious tradition was complemented on the social level, in Islamdom in the Middle Periods, by what may be called a "contractualistic" pattern of determining legitimacy in social organization. We may subsume the whole ayan-amir system of social power under this more abstract principle. This pattern contrasted as sharply to what may be called Occidental "corporativism" as did Islam itself to Christianity. The norms of social organization cannot be derived directly in either case from the religious orientation as such, not the reverse. Yet they were not unrelated. The manner of their relationship is itself a point of contrast between the two societies.

In the case of Islam, life-orientational and societal norms were directly coordinate in our period. Both the social norms and the religious seem to have resulted from the same long-term circumstances in the Irano-Semitic core area, and the line of development taken by Islam then reinforced the corresponding social expectations. In any case, the monotheistic communal tendency in Irano-Semitic culture necessarily made for casting society into forms conceived as religious, unless religion were to be isolated and neutralized entirely. Yet Islam has proved consistent with quite different social forms and standards from those of the Irano-Semitic core area in the Middle Periods. Accordingly, we must see Islamicate contractualism not as the result of Islam but as largely a tendency parallel to that of Islamic moralism itself, though perhaps unrealizable without the support of Islam.

As to Christianity, the social pattern and the basic thrust of religious ideals were less closely interdependent. The Occident was obviously only one society among several in which the Christian tradition formed the spiritual and intellectual foundation, and the other societies were very differently organized from the Occidental. Early Christianity, in any case, gave no such primacy as did Islam to social considerations; hence it was all the more acceptable, even in a religious perspective, for each region to produce a form of Christian society congenial to itself. At the same time, the Occidental patterns of social expectation were at least consistent with a Christian approach to the world – Christian in a general sense, that is, not in a sense limited to the Occidental form of Christianity. We may probably go further and say that they cannot be fully understood without reference to the persistent Christian challenge we have outlined. Accordingly, in both Islamdom and the Occident we may identify cultural constants, even on a level where the searching conscience may rest, and see contrasts between the two traditions in respect of them; and these constants may extend broadly over many dimensions of the culture and be expressed on a highly abstract level.

A purpose of our comparison is to counteract premature assessments, if we cannot rule them out altogether. To this end, we must bear some things in mind as presuppositions of both societies. We must make our contrast against the background of any common necessities or commitments that would produce a common pattern of which the individual regions would be developing variant forms. Here this is not a matter simply of a common agrarianate substratum, but of a common dynamic situation, with an active historical dimension.

Apart from the broadest possible lines of what minimally distinguished any agrarian land tenure and any urban-based government, there were no norms of social organization evidently common to all agrarianate-level society. Yet there was one widespread tendency with its own norms which, if allowed full play, could determine legitimacy in a wide sphere: the tendency to subordinate everything to a great territorial bureaucracy. Such a tendency could be traced back at least to the great empires that arose in each of the core areas at the end of or soon following the Axial Age. Where it prevailed, agrarian relations were regulated, at last, by bureaucratic oversight from the center of imperial government, cities were administered from there, even crafts guilds or monasteries were likely to be subject to imposition of rules and even rulers from above. This was the organizational side of the absolutist ideal, invoked in the name of peace and equal justice against the tyranny of the strong. In significantly differing forms, such a pattern dominated many sectors of social organization to a great degree in the Byzantine and the Chinese societies long after the fall of the early post–Axial Age empires.

But territorial bureaucracy, though universally present in some degree, was more usually limited in its overall social effects by equally potent alternative sets of social expectations. In the Occident and in Hindu India, any tendencies toward territorial bureaucratic domination were inhibited drastically by systems of deep-rooted particularism. These two rich agricultural regions, flanking the central lands of Islamdom on either side, had in common not only the obvious reverence for images (which Muslims called idolatry) but also, less obviously, a somewhat comparable social organization. In both societies, from the time of the Rajputs and of feudalism, innumerable social bodies maintained or developed their private (caste, or corporate and estate) laws and customs, and were integrated among themselves less by any commonly recognized authorities than by an intricately hierarchical system of mutual obligations, in which every social unit retained its indefeasible autonomy.

Occidental corporativism, Islamicate contractualism

With the fall of the High Caliphate, most of such bureaucratic authority as had prevailed in Islamdom disappeared, but it was replaced not by a system of particularisms but by a unitary – or unitaristic – pattern of legitimation that made Islamdom unique among the major societies: what we shall call a "unitary contractualism." Under this head, we are to consider more formally and abstractly the open structuring of Islamic society which we analyzed more substantively in the chapter on the social order. Its implications may come clearer if we contrast them to what in the Occident may be called "hierarchical corporativism." Neither the Islamicate nor the Occidental patterns were fully elaborated in the Earlier Middle Period – rather, they were in process of formation: the most creative moves of social organization were in that direction. That is, the patterns were at the peak, at that time, not of their formal prestige but of their historical vitality.

The contrast between "contractualism" and "corporativism" will recall, in some of its aspects, the famous contrast between society and community, Gemeinschaft and Gesellschaft. Especially "contractualism" suggests status by achievement rather than status by ascription. As compared with most preliterate and even peasant life, both the "corporativism" and the "contractualism" here described are in the direction of Gesellschaft: both are subject to impersonal, formal norms, within a community impersonally and formally defined, and in both, the contractual principle plays a significant role. Yet as between them, Islamicate contractualism had many features which suggest a greater emphasis on the sort of legitimation in which personal achievement counts high and relations are fixed by contract more than by custom. But even the Islamicate pattern never escaped, historically, the presuppositions of agrarianate-level society; it never approached the level of impersonal achievement-oriented evaluations that has been associated with modern technicalized society. The contrasts between such things as Gemeinschaft and Gesellschaft, status by ascription and by achievement, decision by custom and by rational calculation, are always matters of degree; the end result of even the most drastic shift in such directions always seems to retain, in a new form, elements of ascription and custom and personal community, so that in a new historical setting it in turn can seem (to use another term in a popular but misleading way) "traditional" rather than "rational." Here what matters is less the degree of "rationality" than the distinctive functioning.

In the Occident, ultimate social legitimation and authority were conferred not on personal relationships nor on a given power structure but on *autonomous corporative offices* and their holders as such. That is, legitimate authority was ascribed primarily to such positions as kingship, vassalship, bishophood, burgherhood, electorship, membership in a guild; these offices were autonomously legitimate in that fixed rights and duties inhered (by custom or charter) in the office, in principle, without authorization or interference from any other office; and they were corporative, in that they presupposed established social bodies, limited in membership and territory, and themselves autonomous, within which the holder of an office was to exercise its duties: kingdoms, municipalities, dioceses, duchies. Such autonomous public offices have occurred everywhere, especially in ritual functions, but also otherwise, usually in more or less incipient forms: for instance, in the Muslim qadi, the village headman, the grand vizier. What was special in the Occident was that this sort of office became the leitmotif of the whole conception of social legitimacy. These offices, then, were felt to carry authority insofar as they *fitted into mutual hierarchical relations within a fixedly structured total social body:* that is, they were to be constituted and exercised in accordance with established rules of feudal tenure or ecclesiastical obedience or privileges of estates; these rules, in turn, were to be binding both on superiors and inferiors, and presupposed a closed system of mutually recognized individual rights and duties which wove together the whole of papal Christendom, under the leadership, perhaps, of pope and emperor.

The hallmark of Occidental corporativism was its legitimism. For every office there was one predetermined "legitimate" holder and any other was "illegitimate," in the eyes of legitimists, no matter how long and firmly he had been established. A monarch was "legitimate" if he came to power according to the fixed rules that applied to that particular office, however incompetent he might be – an infant, or insane; otherwise he was a "usurper," however sound or unpopular a ruler. Even a man's sons were divided into "legitimate" and "illegitimate" ones, according as their origin satisfied the rules of the system, though personally he might make no distinction in his care for them. To be sure, there were many disputes as to which claimant to an office was in fact the "legitimate" one, but that one or another was indeed "legitimate" and the others not seems never to have been doubted. At first sight this might seem a peculiarly irrational Occidental aberration, but elements of the approach, in a milder form, are to be found very widely spread in societies. But the Occidentals carried it to its logical extreme – while the Muslims systematically excluded it almost altogether.

This corporativism was an admirable way of envisaging social relations, elegantly worked out and to a remarkable degree effective in practice. It has been compared to a Gothic cathedral, the form of which was also worked out in High Medieval times. Both the "corporative" tendency in government and the art of the Gothic cathedral, as well as several other sorts of artistic and intellectual works of the time, seem to reflect a common sense of fitness as to form. Restating our description of hierarchical corporativism in slightly more general terms, we may say that those who articulated the norms of the time seem to have seen satisfying order in a pattern of *autonomous fixed units arranged in hierarchical mutual relations in a closed and fixedly structured whole.* Writers cast allegorical poems and even scholastic treatises into such a form, and something of the same feeling is traceable in the honor paid to demonstrative geometry as a model discipline and to the syllogism as a form into which to put thoughts even when they were not very syllogistic in content.

In Christian thought, in any case, the spiritually significant events of history were seen as having miraculously unique status within a total sequence of sacred dispensations, set off self-contained from ordinary history. This answered to the sacramental organization and the redemptive, supernatural, role of the church. The Occidentals now stressed even more than other Christians the autonomous corporate unity and hierarchical structure of the church and of its hisotry from the time of Adam.

Wherever a sense of fitness was called for, especially wherever validation and legitimation were consciously required, such a sense of style could come into play: in art, in theology, in government, in etiquette, even in science. It determined at least the form in which legitimation was made, if it did not always make a great difference in substance. And this sense of style could have sufficient effect upon practice to affect related activities, where there was a less conscious demand for legitimation; for certain types of expectation tend to prove mutually compatible, and so reinforce each other. Thus could be achieved, at least for a few decades in a portion of northwestern Europe, on the level of public expectations, a relatively homogeneous style ("High Gothic") in a wide range of activities. This style had been being prepared and formed, in some of its aspects, for some centuries; and elements of it, at least, proved sufficiently attractive to color a great part of Occidental culture for a long time after; but it may be regarded as peculiarly distinctive of the High Medieval Occident.

The Occidental side of the comparison just sketched will (I hope) take on substance from the reader's independent knowledge of the Occident. The Islamicate side now must presuppose all that has been said in this work. We will start by characterizing schematically an overall style answering to the "High Gothic" in which our sketch of the Occidental side culminated. Then we will go on to characterize the religious and the social order, in particular, in terms of the overall style.

In Islamdom, the elements that went to make up a corresponding style do not seem to have come to quite so sharp a focus as in the High Gothic period in northern France, but there too a distinctive style, partly prepared earlier and largely persisting in later times, was especially characteristic of the Earlier Middle Period, though (as in the Occident) never prevailing exclusively. To Islamicate "contractualism" in the social sphere, the most appropriate analogy in the visual arts is doubtless the arabesque-type patterning, including geometrical and floral interlacings as well as the arabesque proper, which came to full maturity under Seljuk rule, more or less contemporaneously with the Gothic cathedral. To put the overall style in a formula corresponding to what we use for the Occident, the sense of good order demanded a pattern of *equal and transferable units satisfying a single set of fixed standards in a field penetrable to several levels and universally extendable.* The indefinitely repeated rhythms of the arabesque, where often a bold obvious pattern was superimposed on a subtler pattern at first barely noticeable, answered to such a sense of form, as did the maqamat in prose and several genres of verse, notably the symbolic masnavi. Something of the same feeling is traceable in the honor paid to historical knowledge and the passion for hadith isnad and Sufi silsilah. Geometry, so beloved in the Occident, starts from a minimum set of premises and develops by a hierarchy of set deductions to definitive conclusions, closing the argument in autonomous self-sufficiency. In contrast, the indefinitely expandable corpus of historical reports, each documented and certified on a level with all the rest, allows the seemingly chaotic variety of life's reality to be reduced to manageable order without arbitrarily setting bounds to it either in extent or in depth of meaning.

The Islamic religious sense of the equal and coordinated responsibility of all possible individuals for the maintenance of moral standards in the natural world was probably not unrelated, from the beginning, to the orientation out of which grew this Islamicate sense of style. But it was especially after the fall of the High Caliphal state, among Jamai-Sunni

Muslims, that this atomistic dimension of Islam became most explicit. It was justified in kalam disputation and it was deepened into more inward levels by the general spread of tariqa Sufism, with its silsilahs of independent pirs bringing spiritual truth to each according to his capacities.

It was the enduring balance between sharia-mindedness and Sufism, developed in this period on this basis, that made it possible for Islam to appeal to every sort of temperament without sacrificing its egalitarianism and its moralism. One can claim that, to maintain the church and its hierarchy, Christians sacrificed both prophetic vision and mystical liberty in some measure. That is, they were limited both in any direct confrontation with the old prophetic themes, for the prophets were largely reinterpreted as mere harbingers of Christ, and in an independent growth of mystical experience, which had to be restrained within the sacramental discipline of Christ's church.[2] In contrast, Muslims had no single organizational authority over even particular sectors or local groupings of the Islamic religious establishments, unless by arbitrary and temporary superimposition. They looked, for the subtlety which sensitive persons demand, not to the guided diversity of a church but to direct personal deepening, individual by individual as he was capable of it. Hence the tacit mutual toleration of ulama and Sufis. Yet so effective was the correlative insistence on a unitary set of fixed standards, that, unlike Buddhist monks or Brahmans, say, the ulama could not develop freely independent standards, but were under effective pressure to maximize communal uniformity. The whole development of the contractualist sense of social order in this period, which expresses the same overall style, was made possible by the corresponding developments in religion. And as in religion, so in the social order the seeming simplicity required considerable social sophistication to become so effective; it was no sign of primitiveness.

The hallmark of the Islamicate social order as embodied in the ayan-amir system might seem to be – over against Occidental legitimism – what can be called its "occasionalism," the impression it can give that everything was improvised as the occasion arose, that almost no weight was given to established position and precedence once their immediate force was gone. This was the institutional expression of the general

[2] Such a contrast has been stressed by Henry Corbin in several works, including his *Histoire de la philosophie islamique* (Paris: Gallimard, 1964). It has also been hinted at in less scholarly circles, as by Aldous Huxley in *Grey Eminence* (New York and London: Chatto & Windus, 1941), and elsewhere. Such writers have taken a personal position which not all may share. But that this was a problem posed by the special structure of Christianity, and that it called for a special solution (successfully or not) will be more widely granted.

tendency to exalt individual liberty at the expense of any fixed status. As in the sphere of art, of course, such a principle was not inconsistent with an elaborate surface formalism, adaptable to any substance. If Occidental legitimism sometimes led to self-evident absurdities, this Islamicate "occasionalism" could be reduced to the arbitrary rule of violence. Yet Muslims insisted regularly that the candidate for a post be at least theoretically qualified for it – and a deposed caliph could be effectively disqualified by blinding, unlike an Occidental king. And such principles allowed Islamdom, in any case, to make good its tremendous expansive vitality – not merely to conquer but for the most part to hold what it had conquered. Here, too, there was method in the madness.

In contrast to the hierarchical corporativism of the Occident, what I have called the "unitary contractualism" of Islamdom meant that ultimate legitimacy lay not in autonomous corporative offices but in *egalitarian contractual responsibilities.* That is, legitimate authority was ascribed to actions that followed from responsibilities personally undertaken in such roles as that of amir in a town or imam in the salat or ghazi on the frontier or husband in a family. The model that defined public duties thus in the form of personal responsibilities was the ingenious sharia principle of the reduction of all social functions to either *fard ayni,* a duty incumbent on every individual, or *fard kifayah,* a duty incumbent on only so many as were required to fulfill the function – though until the function was fulfilled, potentially incumbent on anyone. Thus public duties, as a special case of personal duties, came under the same sort of rules as any others. If those who fulfilled such duties made any agreement in the course of their labors, that had the same status in sharia law as any personal contract. (We have seen an example in such arrangements for succession as that attempted by al-Rashid in dividing the caliphal state.)

This personal, contractual, principle was extreme in the opposite direction from the corresponding Occidental principle of public, corporate offices. One may say that most commonly in the great cultures some special status is allowed to acts or property and the like ascribed to a social body, such as the state, but that such status tends to be looked on as a special case of a more inclusive moral law which applies, in principle, to persons as such. The status of royalty seems to have been such among the Sasanians, where the royal *khvarnah,* as a supernatural aura, set off the monarch from other men, but only so long as he was divinely deemed fit to rule. The Occidentals tended to push the special status of public acts to an extreme point, in their emphasis on the fixed autonomy of an office; a point where there should be an unbridgeable cleavage between private and public realms, private and public law, such that the conclusion could eventually be drawn that the state had its own norms not subject to the ethical considerations applying to private actions. The Muslim principle, in contrast, denied any special status to public acts at all, stressing egalitarian and moralistic considerations to the point where it ruled out all corporate status and reduced all acts to the acts of personally responsible individuals.

It is incorrect, in this perspective, to refer to these as "private acts," since the antithesis public-private in social activity is precisely what the Muslims denied while the Occidentals carried it to an extreme. Of course, what I am speaking of here is a highly schematic perspective, of limited reach. On neither side was the contrast carried out fully in the Earlier Middle Period. Moreover, in some perspectives the difference between Occident and Islamdom dwindles to the accidental.

In both cases, one can describe what happened, when the bureaucratic absolutism disappeared, as private possession of public office. Among the Muslims, some sense of a public realm with its own norms did not disappear. For instance, the position of the caliph, as certifying agent legitimizing other rulers, retained an echo of that sense of a bureaucratic public order which had been maintained in High Caliphal times; from this centralizing perspective, the rights of an amir and of an iqta holder were public rights in private hands. In any case, it was always realistically recognized that a king, at least, must act for his own safety – for public reasons – in ways repugnant to proper ethics. Yet both iqta holder and amir were thought of as individual men in direct relations with other men – and this fact affected the manner in which they could raise revenue, their relations to other officeholders, and even the succession to their office.

Among the Occidentals, the devolution of authority to a multiplicity of autonomous offices had threatened to wipe out that very distinction between private and public which had been inherited from earlier times, and to which the eager lawyers were trying to give such a broad effect in the new setting. For a time, feudal relationships, for instance, could have been interpreted in a highly contractualistic sense. But the most characteristic drive was to reinterpret the devolution of offices and the whole feudal system in a corporative sense, in which it was the office, not the man, that was autonomous. Thus, on principles utterly alien to Islamdom, even rights to the kingship of Jerusalem could be bought and sold. However unrealistic in some ways, then, the two principles we have contrasted make explicit certain attitudes that were singularly formative in the two societies in the period.

These personal responsibilities of office in Islamdom were conceived on an egalitarian basis: in principle, they might be assumed by anyone who was qualified, once he became a Muslim, whatever his antecedents; in strict theory, they were not heritable. There were traces of inequality both in sharia and in custom. Descendents of Muhammad were given a peculiar status in certain marginal cases – they could not receive certain alms but were entitled to the special benevolence of all Muslims, and they were expected to marry among themselves. With more disruptive results, various military groups were pleased to erect themselves into closed privileged corps as long as they could. But the social pressure was such as to break open or break down such closed corps, as no other elements in society seriously acknowledged the legitimacy of their pretensions in the long run.

Above all, these personal responsibilities were, even if not exactly contracts, contractual. The sharia envisaged many relations as contractual, but the mood of the time went beyond the sharia. Whether an independent position of authority was legitimized to appeal to personal charisma or to explicit law or to custom, it was conceived as established by mutual agreement and as assuming mutual obligations between one individual and others.[3] On a relatively private level, this amounted sometimes to a relation of personal patronage – a type of relation that played a major role in such a society. Sometimes it was put into a full legal contract; notably marriage was seen not as a sacrament giving ascriptive status but as a contract subject to reversal if satisfaction was not delivered. And just such a viewpoint prevailed on the public level.

Even in the case of the caliphate, the Jamai-Sunni theory was that the next caliph, designated by the key notables of the Umma, or by the *baya*, the act of acceptance by the notaḅles generally on behalf of the whole community. That is, it was not enough simply to submit to the established ruler when occasion arose; the individual Muslim must explicitly assume his side of the relationship. (The Shi'i theory, which made the designation stem back to divine action, still demanded that the believers personally offer their act of acceptance to the imam; this is part of the meaning of the hadith report that "he who dies without knowing the imam of his time dies an unbeliever" – a report which Jamai-Sunni's also could accept.) The acceptance of an amir by his soldiers and by the community at large in the persons of its notables and the acceptance of a Sufi pir by those who sought his spiritual guidance, were on the same

[3] J. Schacht, "Notes sur la sociologie du droit musulman," *Revue africaine*, vol. 96, nos. 432–33 (1952), brings out nicely the degree to which the spirit of contract suffuses the sharia and even other sorts of Muslim law.

model; always it was a contract-type arrangement which had to be renewed personally with each new holder of authority and was properly binding only on those who had personally accepted it. (Too often Western scholars have vainly tried to reduce Islamicate transactions of this sort to Occidental legitimistic categories and found themselves baffled. The baya was analogous to the Occidental oath of allegiance but was not its equivalent either in form or in function.)

Then these responsibilities of office were exercised under *a single set of fixed legal standards, universally applicable* so soon as a minimum of Muslims were present, and, at least Sufi's would add, meaningful at once on an obvious, mechanical, level and on ever deeper levels according to the spirituality of the person concerned. Though the sharia varied in practice not only from legal madhhab to legal madhhab but from century to century, yet the constant interchange of viewpoint was bringing the madhhabs ever closer together – there was conscious pressure to avoid any really drastic discrepancies – and the gradual evolution of legal standards tended to be more or less common throughout Islamdom. As great a legal uniformity, at least on some levels, was achieved in Islamdom as ever has been in a pre-Modern society, despite its unprecedentedly widespread. The sharia law was applicable wherever Muslims were to be found in sufficient numbers, being dependent on no territorial establishment nor even on any official continuity of personnel, but only on the presence, among Muslims committed to it, of someone at least minimally versed in it to see to its application. If in a new Muslim community it was not at first very perfectly applied, every visiting sharia scholar from any other Muslim land would contribute to perfecting it, preventing it from deteriorating to a purely local customary law. Without any new enactments, the system was extendable to include ultimately the whole of mankind.

Communal moralism vs. corporative formalism in law

The contractualism of the Islamic Middle Periods presumably grew out of the mercantile-oriented communal tradition of the Nile-to-Oxus region and can be seen, from our vantage point, as its culmination. The mercantile tendency had favored, on the intellectual level, the moralistic, populistic, factualistic bent which we have already analyzed in the sharia-minded circles; on the institutional level, it favored a unitary contractualism, in the same way. In sum, what had happened was that, with the powerful crystallization in sharia-minded Islam of the most extreme populistic and moralistic tendencies of that tradition, the monotheistic religious community ceased to be a merely subordinate social form and became the major form through which social legitimation was expressed. The religious community was almost – though not quite – liberated from dependence on an agrarian-based state; so that its communal law, built on its communal presuppositions, and not that of any territorial state, assumed the persisting primacy that accrues to whatever possesses exclusive legitimacy. It was not quite liberated: the ultimate sanction of force remained critical, and was left in the hands of the state. But the role of the state was as far reduced, especially in the basic sphere of law, as it ever has been in citied high culture.

This was made possible, however, because the monotheistic tradition was gathered – at least as to the active sectors of society – into a single community allegiance. Each of the other monotheistic communities to be found within the core area of Islamdom – pursuing an evolution already begun before Islam – became juridically self-contained like the Islamic community itself. But without the overwhelmingly predominant position of the Islamic community throughout the region, the juridical autonomy of bishops or of rabbis must remain secondary. It was the universality of the Muslim community that could make it outweigh an imperial bureaucracy. Without the potent appeal of Islam with its summons to personal responsibility, the Islamicate contractualist pattern could hardly have succeeded despite the favorable conditions between Nile and Oxus.

Each of the two patterns of legitimation, the Occidental hierarchical corporativism and the Islamicate unitary contractualism, had consequences which are not immediately evident from the overall guidelines here sketched. To be sure, often Occidental and Islamicate practice were more alike than the contrast would suggest; nor was everything in which they differed attributable to this particular contrast. Yet each pattern not only facilitated some sorts of social relations but also set limits to the development of others. Normally these consequences were such as reinforced the same tendencies, arising out of the ecological setting of the core area of each culture, as had produced the pattern of legitimation in the first place. But at least in secondary details, the pattern of legitimation could itself logically entail consequences otherwise perhaps unnecessary.

The demand for a rule of law, as against arbitrary rule, took a moralistic turn in Islamdom as against the formalistic turn the same demand took in the Occident. As so often, each system pushed toward a contrasting extreme. Some formalism is found in almost all legal systems, especially those connected with cultic ritual. This was pushed in the Occident to the point of sanctioning those trials by technicality which have sometimes been the glory of its law courts, when they served to defend an unpopular position, but have more often been their shame. (Some Westerners seem to have confused a formalistic pattern in law with independent objectivity and predictability as such in law, looking to the Roman legal heritage with its formalistic bent almost as if it alone fully deserved the status of "law"; even though they would decry those excesses of formalism and literalism which even Occidentals have recognized as such.) The sharia may seem to some to have exaggerated in a contrary direction. Law is a natural field in which to emphasize moral values to the exclusion of even the most practical considerations of other sorts, but the sharia law perhaps went further in this direction than most systems. In its law of contracts, the actual intent of the parties was usually preferred (in principle) to the verbal form; perhaps the Marwani-age insistence on living witnesses as guarantors of any written contract retained its vitality in part as a means of assuring the primacy of intent. More generally, there was a tendency to insist on equity even when a person seemed willing to renounce his own rights.

The secondary institutions of law were molded to the respective legal patterns. The Occidental advocate was expected to argue the case of one party against the other in disputes, making the most of even a morally dubious case, often on the basis of his knowledge of technicalities. Such a stance might seem morally unsound, but it ensured that special circumstances in each particular case were not overlooked. The Muslim *mufti* might be as concerned as the Occidental advocate with the ambiguities of practical situations. But he was expected to give priority to eliciting and settling the decisive moral issue impersonally as it arose in such situations – advising the judge rather than either one of the parties concerned. In principle, he should not know who was on which side. The Occident saw a luxuriant growth of legal fictions – notably corporative ones, in which a corporate body was accepted as a legal entity on a par with persons, so as to exercise the autonomous rights attached to offices when such offices clearly pertained to a group as such. Such legal fictions as the sharia encouraged (especially the hila "tricks" used in commerce) were not essential to the law but incidental to its application; their function was normative, safeguarding a standard toward which the reality might, with opportunity and goodwill, be moved.

Modern Westerners have tended to see the moralism of Muslim law as a major defect. So far as, in its insistence on personal responsibilities, it denied any independent sphere to public law over against private, they feel, it had no means of legitimizing and hence taming the public reality. Because of the unconditioned universality which, at least in pre-Modern times, was ascribed to any serious moral code, a moralistic law was relatively rigid and incapable of adaptation to varying conditions of time or place. Finally, in renouncing formalism in some respects (by no means all) it lost a technique which in the Occident often proved useful in preserving the rights of the individual, whether used wisely or foolishly, from interference by public opinion or by state power, however benevolently intended.

Yet the Muslims' extensive mobility among social milieus and across geographical and political boundaries was made possible by that same sharia, and in its own way (together with the freedom of inner interpretation that went with it) ensured a wide range of personal liberty. Nor could the law have ensured this mobility without a high degree of legal fixity. This fixity was, indeed, constantly threatened by the fact that not all Muslim law in any one place was sharia law; but the sharia successfully maintained its central position and was kept adequately integrated through changing conditions by the judicious recognition of latter-day fatwas by jurists respected throughout the Dar al-Islam. Because of the independent position, then, which the relative fixity of the law gave to its interpreters, both ulama and Sufi's were in a position to hold the political powers within bounds – never in so wise a sphere as desired, yet never without substantial effect.

In Modern times, both of the legal patterns have had to be modified. Occidental formalism has latterly had to give way even to sociological considerations as to what legal concepts mean in social reality, while Muslim moralism has been forced to retreat before the new organized power of the state and the impersonal requirements of the machines.

The Occidental formalistic law was doubtless appropriate to the corporative Occident. There a person's status was determined by his position in various bodies intermediate between the individual and the total society. As a member of such bodies – municipalities or estates or the church – he enjoyed special liberties, defined historically according to the situation of the particular body; he had not so much the rights of a man, or even of an Englishman, as those of a burgher of London. Despite the attempt to invoke ancient Roman law as if it could form a universally applicable code, such particularistic rights could not in practice be defined on universal principles but depended on the historical events which gave rise to them, such as the granting of a city charter. The greater the formalism with which such rights were interpreted, the more secure they were from interference in later circumstances when the original power relations might have changed. The Muslim moralistic law was equally appropriate to Islamicate contractualism, where ascriptive status was minimized, at least in principle, and the decisive ties were those of contract and of personal patronage. What mattered to the Muslim was not particular liberties but a more generalized liberty, based on his status as a free Muslim. Such a position was best guaranteed by principles which could apply everywhere and always, without prior covenant or special historical connection.[4]

Contractual vs. formalistic status in civil and personal roles

Because the autonomous corporative office was so crucial in the Occidental system, succession to office was likewise fixed and formalistic. In the Occident, the question who would succeed to a self-perpetuating (i.e., non-appointive) office was governed by rules specific to the office and as formalistic as was the law generally. Some posts were hereditary; here normally a fixed rule of unilinear succession held, so that as soon as a baby was born in the relevant family, one could calculate under just what circumstances he would succeed: normally according to the rule of primogeniture, which during High Medieval times was being made to cover not only succession among sons but any contingency of kinship. Other posts were subject to vote; in this case, the voting was collegial, that is, a fixed body of electors was admitted to the electoral right, which in turn had to be exercised in a fixed manner to be valid. Thus succession had a formal and fixed element even when not hereditary. (It must be recalled that collegial voting was a very different sort of process from modern mass voting, which perhaps has almost as many affinities with Islamicate prestige contests). In High Medieval times the rules were still being perfected and disputes in both kinds of succession still occurred, but normally the claim of the disputants on each side was legitimistic: that is, not that their candidate was necessarily the best but that he was the legitimate one, and that the opposing candidate, however personally excellent he might or might not be, was usurping.

Westerners have been so accustomed to such a type of succession that they have expected to find similar characteristics in non-appointive offices elsewhere too. Often even scholars have read primogeniture into the fact that it was often an eldest son who proved most appropriate to take over his father's office. A certain respect for the elder brother is perhaps almost

[4] That sharia law was grounded in the principle that liberty was to be presumed as the natural human condition, and was not to be abridged without reason, has been presented effectively by David de Santillana, "Law and Society" in *The Legacy of Islam*, ed. Thomas Arnold and Alfred Guillaume (Oxford: Oxford University Press, 1931), pp. 284–310.

universal; in the Occident this was hardened into a rule, but in Islamdom, though the feeling was potent, it was not allowed any formal recognition. More sophisticatedly, some Westerners have tried to find an alternative scheme of fixed succession such as seniority, which will sometimes fit the facts a bit better. Sometimes they have labelled "usurper" a candidate who rose to power by rebellion. Then (since the exceptions to such "rules" prove disconcertingly numerous) they have complained of the irregularity of Muslim succession and its failure to follow a fixed rule which would supposedly have obviated succession disputes. But in Islamdom, formalistic succession by unilinear heredity or collegial voting was rare at best, not because Muslims were less inclined to rationalize their social arrangements but because the contractual spirit called for a different sense of legitimacy in successions. Succession was open to some choice or even negotiation: to the fixed succession of the formalistic Occident we may counterpose the succession by contest of the contractualistic Islamdom, where a personal responsibility was to be undertaken by the best man.

It did not necessarily contravene this principle when contest was forestalled by designation by the predecessor; it was as if he who was already charged with a responsibility had likewise the responsibility of seeing that his charge would be carried on by someone suitable. Otherwise, of course, contests were to be settled by consultation among the notables felt to be representative of the affected social body. It was the very point of succession by contest, to adjust various group interests according to current actualities – and this could be done only with a certain amount of bargaining. Then if formal contract was invoked it was, of course, at the final stage, in the form of a rubber stamp. Consultation should obviate an armed contest, but if not, then an armed contest seems to have been felt to be a misfortune rather than an actual breakdown in the social process.

An incidental – but essential – consequence of this approach was (on the whole) the elimination of utter incompetents. It was even a legal requirement that the candidate had to be at least minimally qualified; occasionally, at least in religious contexts, this was insisted on to the point of formal public examination by the notables. It was rare (though not unknown) for a child, a woman, or a physically incapacitated man to be accepted for long unless he had a powerful protector; for, as the political ruler was essentially an amir, a military commander, a woman was disqualified insofar as she was not qualified to a be soldier at all. Analogous considerations prevailed in other fields of action.

In the process of consultation, the Islamic principle of universality had its way. For the most part those were recognized as notables who had achieved positions of great personal responsibility and had ties of mutual obligation with a large number of people; and thus a largely common set of considerations as to what bestowed status was received throughout Islamdom and was applicable immediately wherever Islam penetrated. Since decision required not a mathematical majority as such, but a more substantial consensus, no exact lines of inclusion and exclusion had to be drawn, for no vote had to be taken. Because there was no fixed electorate, the Islamicate prestige contest had looked mysterious to some outsiders. But its chief mechanism (that of the "bandwagon") is used in many contests settled by mass voting. In Islamdom there was no set voting to cut short the contest before its natural term, so that it might take some time unless appeals were made to arms or to an amir.

Even on the level of family law, we find in the Occident the sense of fixed, autonomous status, formalistically defined. In families in which any sort of office was hereditary, of course, the status of family members had to be defined in such a way that the principles of primogeniture could hold. This already called for the special exaltation of the man's primary sex partner as his only proper wife, and her children, therefore, as sole heirs to the exclusion of his other children. As we have noted, the sharia looked to the opposite extreme from this, placing all the man's free sexual partners on the same level, as well as their children, and governing their position by contract, giving none of them an indefeasible status such as an undivorceable mater-familias could have. (As with collegial voting, so with "monogamous" marriage, the old Occidental pattern was even further, in some respects, from modern international patterns than was the Islamicate.)

But the contrast between the Islamicate and the Occidental patterns of marriage went beyond what could be deduced from the relative positions of the wives in sharia and in canon law. The contrast that springs to the eye between upper-class family life among Muslims and among Occidentals is that between the segregated slave household of the harem system, and the wife-centered servant household of the Occident. In each society the husband and father was the dominant and in theory even the despotic figure who had final power of decision; and in each society the wife in fact often ruled the husband. But the differences in norm of expectation did produce differences in practice.

In the Occident the "legitimate" wife presided; she was hostess to her husband's guests, and if he had other sex partners they had to have separate establishments as "mistresses," for she would not tolerate them in her domain. The attendants of the household were free servants at the least and, in feudal courts, often persons of high status themselves. The peasants were tied servilely to the soil and subject to the grossest indignities from their legal masters, but household slavery had practically died out. Thus the hierarchical principle prevailed even in family life: the closer to the top, the higher the rank, while even the servile mass at the bottom were governed by their own fixed rules.

In Islamdom, the egalitarian principle surely accounts in part for an opposite situation. Well-to-do men, themselves of no birth, surrounded themselves by preference with the only sort of persons whose dependence could be counted on: slaves; and where all classes mingled socially, their wives could not assert their inaccessibility by the aloofness of a hierarchical rank but preserved it rather by a rigid female segregation. If there was more than one sex partner, all shared the household alike, and none was hostess save to her own friends, who, however, might be drawn from any social level she chose. The peasants were legally and usually factually free men, while in the homes of the wealthy, slaves were preferred to free servants, though not necessarily treated any worse, and steadily emancipated. We may suggest that slavery by import (as against a more home-bred peasant serfdom) was retained in Islamdom partly because of the relative access of the wealthy Muslim cities to frontier areas of the Oikoumene where captives were available; but primarily because an egalitarian and socially mobile society seemed to require, in an agrarian age, such a class to set off those who momentarily had risen to the top.

Both in Occident and Islamdom, a correlative of the social system was a good deal of arbitrary and destructive military activity. Military power was limited in its effects in the two societies in quite different ways. In the Occident, the military were rooted in the land and their activities were increasingly being formalized, even idealized. The barons could indulge in persistent petty warfare and indiscipline, harassing peasant and townsman in a steady stream of quarrels which rules about suspending local hostilities for weekends could barely alleviate. But it was with difficulty that they could combine really massive armies under one chief for general indiscriminate slaughter, to concentrate power in one hand, the chances of fixed succession, modulated by dynastic marriages or even by purchase of succession rights, were as important as outright political and military skill. No ruler extended his sway far beyond his hereditary lands, generally rather small tracts at best. It was already a sign of new times when, in the fifteenth century, the duke of Burgundy gathered together so much arbitrary force that he could destroy the city and the entire population of Liège, pursuing those few who escaped the flames into the woods, tracing them by their tracks till they should all be killed. And even that duke found himself so bound by custom that to the end he was frustrated in his attempt to take the title of king.

In Islamdom, in contrast, the military were city men and little bound by parochial prescriptions. Nowhere was mobility more drastic than among the soldiery, whose members could rise to the highest social peaks, and could campaign for distances incredible in the Occident. Local captains seem to have been kept under some control on this basis, so that private quarrels among the military did not immediately issue in warfare; there was extensive peace on a local basis, times when the greatest alarms were raised only by bandits. (But in remoter areas, pastoral tribal chiefs could play the role of robber barons.) But aggressive concentrations of power like that of the duke of Burgundy were almost commonplace, and looting and massacring of cities took place more readily – and from the Mongol times on, in the Later Middle Period, became relatively frequent.

In religious and intellectual life, the differences between the two societies were complementary to the differences in the role of political authority. In the Occident, the noble was at once the political ruler and the focus of all social life; and the cleric was his brother or his cousin. Scholarly life was largely channelled through the church, which was highly organized along lines parallel to and interweaving with the secular establishment. In this hierarchical context, every intellectual question was likely to turn into a question of formal heresy, i.e., of institutional loyalty; heresy could be a life-or-death question in a way that was unlikely in Islamdom even if the question was formally raised here. However, at the same time, the Philosophical tradition played a more integral role in so hierarchical a structure, its more abstractly normative traditions forming the core of formal education for the clerics. This is partly because the Latin lands continued to look to the Hellenic tradition in general for their high-cultural inspiration, but surely the educational pattern was perpetuated, in part, also because it was suited to the relatively closed, fixed structure of the church, which could justify a hierarchical social structure with a hierarchical vision of the cosmos much in the manner of the Ismailis. Esoteric studies did exist, but they played a relatively marginal role. When the mystic, Eckhart, was condemned for talking too freely of subtle matters to the common people, his guilt was violation of common prudence, not of an established doctrine of concealment. Subjects like alchemy, of course, did receive a directly esoteric treatment.

In Islamdom, the ulama and the amirs stood aloof from each other. And even where learning was institutionalized in madrasahs, the ulama retained a broad independence among themselves. In both Islamdom and Occident, formal education was devoted largely to normative disciplines rather than to empirical. But the most respected Muslim education was more oriented to explicit cultural norms. This was consistent with the historical, communal emphasis of the Abrahamic tradition. But it surely reflected also the basis on which the ulama maintained their common discipline, by common legal norms rather than by any common lines of command. The Occidental sequence started with the trivium (essentially study of linguistic norms) and went directly on to the quadrivium (essentially study of mathematics), in which the content tended to refer to natural studies like astronomy and music rather than to historical studies; while law and theology came last, as specialized professions, accompanied by medicine as an integral part of the central studies. In contrast, the madrasahs stressed first what was essential for everyone – ritual, law, theology, all essentially historical subjects. Matters like literary criticism were secondary, and mathematics and logic received attention last of all. Medicine and astronomy were studied quite independently of the madrasahs, patronized by the amirs' courts, while the philosophy and psychology of the Sufis were learned at still another center, like khaniqah. And the learning of these more elite centers tended to be systematically esoteric.

Much later, traveling in the Ottoman empire, a French diplomat and scholar was impressed with the degree to which the Muslims were personally more gentle and sober than their opposite numbers in the Occident; even animals were treated with relative humanity.[5] The scholar was perhaps influenced by a desire to reform his own compatriots. In any case, it is fairly evident that by most standards, Islamicate society must be accounted more urbane and polished than the Occidental in the Earlier Middle Period, both in intellectual life and in day-to-day security. But it was also more subject to arbitrary interference and even to catastrophe.

Resources for historical action

Human excellence has been held to lie on the one hand in contemplation, in maximum awareness of reality and its meaning both in the cosmos at large and within one's self; and on the other hand in action, in free initiation of new sequences of events on the basis of a rational estimate of their consequences rather than of habit or custom. As we

[5] I refer to the well-known *Turkish Letters* of Ogier Ghiselin de Busbecq, tr. by E. S. Forster (Oxford: The Clarendon Press, 1927).

have learned to see it, our world is in fact in such continuous transformation that just as genuinely free action cannot take place without the highest contemplation, so genuinely true contemplation cannot take place without the most incisive action. If this is so, the distinction between the two forms of excellence can become artificial. Yet modern Westerners have seen, at least retrospectively, the genius of their Occidental heritage to have lain in giving maximum scope to human initiative and action, while they have often been willing to grant the palm for contemplative excellence to others. At the same time, the Islamic can seem the most activist of the great pre-Modern heritages. Even those superficial observers who have claimed that Islam led necessarily to fatalistic acceptance of whatever might happen as God's will, have also stressed the pride and fanaticism of Muslims, especially as expressed in implacable prosecution of the holy war. Both societies, then, have some repute for a bent to action. But what were the channels through which free human action could be undertaken in each society?

In some ways, freedom was greater in Islamdom than in the Occident. Islam was relatively tolerant – not so much in willingness to accept other religious bodies (in this, Islam did much better than Christianity but even so was intolerant by non-monotheistic standards) – but rather tolerant on the personal level. Diogenes and his tub would have been more readily tolerated in the Islamicate society than in the Occidental. In the latter, he would have had to show some proper status, not simply as an individual, but as member of some order or corporate body; if he had claimed a moral mission, he would have been under the jurisdiction of the ecclesiastical hierarchy; if he went naked in public, he would be duly disciplined by the church authorities. In the Islamicate society (unless he was a dhimmi unwilling to convert) he would have had but one legal status, that of a Muslim; he would, indeed, be subject to the discipline of the market overseer, the muhtasib; but if he claimed a moral mission, he would have had a good chance of passing freely as a mad dervish, to be troubled by no authority but that of his chosen pir. (As a dhimmi, of course, he might run into greater difficulties with his communal authorities.) The Occidental pattern as a whole made for great social continuity, but militated against mobility – against geographical mobility, because the all-important offices were tied to particular localities; against personal initiative, which the guilds systematically discouraged. As in Islamdom, development did take place, but as much despite the system as through it.

The immediacy of the individual human being vis-à-vis society as a whole thus made for important freedoms. But it exposed persons to certain dangers against which the rights of corporate bodies afforded a surer buffer in the Occident. Even in Islamdom, the individual adventurer, relatively free as he might be, was wise to associate himself with some recognized group – Sufis of some tariqa, ulama at some madrasah, merchants of some trade, or, at a less respectable but almost equally protected level, members of a futuwwah brotherhood, or beggars or thieves of some town quarter. In such groups membership was largely self-chosen and the discipline imposed might be very lax. But the strength of such groups against arbitrary interference by the amir was correspondingly less. And those who wished to undertake a new sort of enterprise – for instance, investment in a new type of project – could be hard put to it to find a place in any solidarity group which would resist a tyrant's hand. Such undertakings could and did get launched without being smothered by the jealous rigidity of guild regulations; but they could and did find themselves taxed out of existence or even plundered by short-sighted amirs so soon as they became sufficiently prosperous to attract notice.

Yet in Islamdom there remained wide personal liberty for a man to make his own choice within a reasonably predictable framework and in a range that was relatively broad, given agrarianate-level social conditions; and even to make choices differing greatly from those of most other men. Such freedom was essential for a further sort of freedom of action – freedom of historical action, freedom to initiate new ideas and teach them, to suggest and help carry through new policies and patterns in social life, more generally to set about consciously to modify the conditions within which life was being carried on. But for this, in addition to simple personal freedom, there must be appropriate channels for individual initiative on the social level. The nature of such channels differed, even more than on the purely personal level, according to the pattern of legitimation.

In the High Medieval Occident, one of the most intriguing scenes, from the viewpoint of the development of human self-awareness and self-determination, was that in which the pope solicited suggestions from all Western Christendom on what to do about the presence of Islam, when the Crusades seemed to be failing. Serious persons responded and among the conventional exhortations were some relatively far-sighted projects, including plans for reforming the church itself in the name of making action against Islam more effective. Relatively little came of most of these plans, yet they were intended and received seriously. For such an approach to historical problems was not an isolated occurrence but was grounded in the Occidental pattern. The great church councils, in which a hierarchically limited number of autonomous holders of episcopal office gathered to consider and vote on matters of dispute, formed a model of such consultation. But the spirit was more general. If each particular establishment had its own autonomous rules, they had once been shaped and could be reshaped anew; moreover, it was the office of bishops and popes, kings and emperors, to make sure that all was going well in their jurisdictions and concerned individuals might hope that good advice might find favor with them.

In China, the custom of private memorials offered on public problems was even more highly developed than in the Occident and more effective, in the context of the most powerful and the most rationally considered bureaucratic government in the world. In Islamdom, such channels for initiative and reform was not so available. After the collapse of the caliphate there was no central establishment from which reform might be expected to proceed, and to have permitted serious institutional initiative to the amirs would have been to disrupt the unitary pattern across Islamdom on which Muslim contractualism depended. When Malikshah asked for advice from his courtiers, what he wanted and received was not projects for solving particular institutional problems but general precepts to guide his conduct as an absolute monarch, which with little change would apply to any ruler. It would seem as if a primary intention of those who developed the self-contained sharia, which gave such little scope to initiative by a caliph, was to reduce the realm of free political action to a minimum – looking to the security of trade rather than to the adventures of an aristocracy of any sort. In any case, at courts where status was not ascriptively assured, but depended on personal relations with the ruler, serious reform movements, which always threaten vested interests, could not be mooted without the personal support of the ruler, who otherwise would be moved by rivals to eliminate the reformer without ado.

The social activism which nonetheless the Islamic spirit did call for was expressed, in the Middle Periods, above all through a repeated and many-faceted drive for sharia-minded reform. This ranged almost imperceptibly from the revivalist sermons of preachers who assailed the manners and morals of all classes, including, at their most daring, the amirs themselves, to the full-scale revolts of reformers who tried to implement the hope for a mahdi who would fill the earth with justice as it had been filled with injustice. The career of Ibn Tumart illustrates both extremes. Though such reform movements were not able to bring in the millennium, they cumulatively went far toward reinforcing the independence and effectiveness of the sharia and of the institutions under its protection. Reform projects of a more particularized sort became more important in Islamdom in subsequent centuries, but military venture with wholesale revolt continued to pose an ideal for reformers, to which the most zealous approximated as best they could, and which was realized again and again.

It is not easy to choose exactly comparable figures to point up the contrast between the two societies, since so often the career through which a man could arrive at a position of influence presupposed quite different steps in the two settings. But both Umar Suhravardi and Bernard of Clairvaux were men mystically inclined yet of conservative piety; and from their positions as spiritual advisers they were drawn into the major political ventures of the day, where they played an influential, if not always successful, role. Both were confronted with the long-standing injustice of agrarianate life and in particular with the license of innumerable military powers let loose by the disappearance of central bureaucratic authority. Both represented the response to such a situation by a monotheistic conscience. The truce of God, imposed in the Occident with elaborate regulations and special courts, was not Bernard's invention, but he helped make it effective; it may be compared to the attempted disciplining of the futuwwa men's clubs to which Suhravardi contributed, and the control of the amirs by the way of personal involvement therein. Each approach enlisted the highest motives of those concerned, yet in a form adapted to the social order and to the sense of form developed in the two societies. The truce of God invoked the hierarchy of the church in favor of specially protected days and civil statuses. The futuwwa reform invoked the sharia duties of Muslims by way of a network of personally assumed obligations. Each approach had some success, but did not prove an adequate solution.

Since here I have been comparing two societies on the level of high culture and of the most abstract possible patterning on that level, we must be reminded that such patterning is of limited relevance to the course of actual history. The fact that, for an artificially stilled cross-section of history, one can formulate phrases that indicate a wide formal presupposition seemingly underlying the various aspects of a given culture must not be construed too substantively. People's minds are not necessarily set differently. The congruence results from the fact that in each complex of cultural traditions, the several particular traditions must mesh, must gear. At any moment there must be at least a temporary equilibrium among various temperamental tendencies and cultural traditions such as those in art, science, or politics, developing autonomously but interdependently. This need for congruence, moreover, is concretized in the human ideal images that tend to prevail in key high-cultural circles; for each such image is necessarily one human whole. But this image and the equilibrium it may answer to need not be taken as a "casual" drive "underlying" the particular cultural and historical facts subsumed under it, though it may, in turn, help mold them.

Such pattern abstractions have their use, but they can lead to seeing historical developments as the logical outcome of a closed circle of concepts seemingly presupposed in the high-cultural thinking of a society. The civilization as a whole (on the high-cultural level) is thus made analogous to a particular ethnic group (with its folk culture) in having collective patterns of expectation which mold its social and historical possibilities; though the attempt to trace such patterns even on a simple ethnic level is generally premature. Such conceptualistic interpretations of civilized history have been congenial to certain philosophers and to many philologians, for it seems to allow them to see the whole process of history simply through deepening their perception of the texts at hand. But they fail to grasp the play of interests at all levels that undergirds the formulations as well as the historical process generally; and especially to allow for the difference between high-cultural formulations and the unarticulated springs of human action at all class levels. Hence they scarcely allow for the rapid cultural changes that so often ensue when new opportunities are opened up. In particular, they tempt people to read back artificially into the Occidental past various lauded traits of Modernity in the form of supposed seminal conceptual traits in law, science, esthetic form, etc.; in this way, some writers have produced an exaggerated notion of the Occidental genius, and falsified the relation of both the Occidental and the other heritages to the advent of Modernity.[6]

[6] The most brilliant interpretation of Islamicate culture as resulting from a closed circle of concepts is that of Gustave von Grunebaum, expounded in his many books and articles, all of which are worth reading. It is no accident that he exemplifies at its best what I call (Introduction, *Venture of Islam,* vol. I) the Westernistic commitment or outlook, which commonly envisages Western culture in just this way. In his "Parallelism, Convergence, and Influence in the relations of Arab and Byzantine Philosophy, Literature, and Piety," *Dumbarton Oaks Papers,* 18 (1964), 89–111, at the end especially, it becomes clear that in his analysis, the formative assumptions of Islamdom (and Byzantium) are derived at least in part negatively, by way of contrast (what Islam *lacks*), from certain contrary formative assumptions he ascribes (in the Westernistic manner) at once to the West and to Modernity. This method almost assures in advance that "Eastern" cultures, as lacking what he finds unique to the West, will turn out to be essentially alike, but will be separated from each other just by what they have in common – that is, in his view, by a dogmatic claim to completeness, which also has suppressed their occasional glimpses of a Western-type or (preferably) Western-inspired rationally open humanism. The formative assumptions he sees in the West, on the contrary, turn out to be central to what is most distinctly human. For instance, he refers to these assumptions as "the attitude toward the world

Islamicate influence on the Occident

Cultural exchange between Islamdom and the Occident in High Medieval times was drastically one-sided. In a limited number of cases, Muslims learned something from the Occidentals: for instance, in the art of fortification in Crusader Syria (though even in this same art, the Crusaders learned from the Muslims also). But by and large, Muslims found almost nothing that they thought learning from the Occident, though even from the more remote China they were already by the Earlier Middle Period adopting techniques and occasionally even more abstract ideas. In contrast, Occidentals were absorbing cultural practices and conceptions of many diverse sorts from Islamdom, and this absorption was of far-reaching importance to the growth of their culture. This was largely due, of course, to the superiority of Islamicate cultural competence, at least at the beginning of the period. The contrast was then exaggerated further by the pre-eminence of Islamdom in the Oikoumenic configuration. Contact with the Occident was peripheral for Islamdom, and no more important or even less important than contact with eastern Europe, Hindu India, or any other of the various regions with which Muslims were in close contact. For Occidentals, eastern Europe and Islamdom were the only alien societies accessible, and the western outposts of the Muslims in Sicily and Spain, of relatively minor import to Islamdom at large, loomed very close and large in the Occident.

The influence of the Muslim presence was twofold: as a source of ideas and as a challenging presence. First, it brought about more or less explicit adoption of given cultural practices. Sometimes this was direct, as when the works of Abu-Bakr al-Razi were translated into Latin and used in medical treatment. Sometimes this was more indirect, by way of what has been called "stimulus diffusion." It seems likely that descriptions of Islamicate windmills, introduced from further east into Mediterranean

into which man grew during the Renaissance"; here "man" cannot refer to the biological species type (as in "man has thirty-two teeth") nor even to mankind collectively (as in "the unity of man") but (as so often in Westernistic literature) makes grammatical sense only as referring to a long-lived mythical being, "Man," who has personally undergone a series of crucial experiences in successive historical periods, and who is identical with that primary figure of Westernistic myth, "Western Man," whose cultural traits as finally unfolded are held to be the highest and most human yet achieved.

All this assumes an organic fixity in each cultural tradition, represented in a personified ideal human image, which merely unfolds in time its inherent potentialities. On the limitations of such determinacy in the traditions, and the difficulty of comparing the development of the Occident and Islamdom on the basis of seminal culture traits, see the section on historical method in Chapter 5.

Islamdom by the beginning of the period, were the occasion for the appearance of windmills in the Occident by the end of the period. But since the arms of the mill were spread horizontally among the Muslims and vertically in the Occident, clearly what passed was the basic idea and not the complex practice of building windmills in its particulars. Much of the Islamicate influence on the Occident was in some degree of this indirect sort.

Indeed, the diffusion of cultural details was subject to diverse limitations. Items which could find no ready niche in the new society, however efficient and useful in the old, were not adopted. Camel transport, though very effective, was not adopted in the Occident partly because of climate, but also partly because even in the most southerly parts the ox sufficiently filled the relevant niche and a change would not have brought enough advantage to pay. What *was* adopted was likely to be transformed, even when contact was direct and the practice immediately imitated. Even technical details, when taken over, often had to be rethought and adjusted so as to fit into the technical context of the new society. If, as it appears, the Gothic arch was suggested by corresponding arches in Islamicate buildings, in any case the way it was used and hence also the details of its construction were very different in a cathedral from what they were in a mosque; the total effect and meaning of the arch were entirely new.

This high selection and rethinking was even more important when it came to the properly esthetic and intellectual levels. Here, for the most part, Occidental imitation and adaptation of Islamicate material was restricted to what was rooted in traditions already largely shared by the Occident, at least on a rudimentary level. Thus the romantic poetic tradition of the troubadours seems to have depended directly on the somewhat prior corresponding tradition of Islamicate Spain; but this went back ultimately to old Hellenistic traditions, long since partly echoed in Latin, and seems to have received its immediate forms from local Romance tendencies common to Spain and Gaul. Though some elements of the tradition are probably traceable to old Arabian motifs or at least to the local work of Arab Muslims, clearly a large part of it was congenial to moods and forms already found in the Occident.[7] It is this tendency for the culture to adopt from abroad only what was already half-known that has sometimes made it difficult to sort out Islamicate "influences" in the

7 S. M. Stern, *History and Culture in the Medieval Muslim World* (London: Variorum Reports, 1984), has shown that a specifically Arabic intervention in the process of developing Romance verse in both Spain and Gaul (whether among Muslims or Christians) is possible, perhaps even likely, but not yet demonstrated.

Occident from indigenous growths. (It has also contributed to the notion in the modern West that the Islamicate intellectual culture offered nothing but originally Greek ideas, perhaps slightly further developed.[8])

Perhaps as important as the actual number of technical methods, pieces of information, and books that the Occidentals learned from the Muslims (or from Jews of Islamicate culture), was the confrontation with Islamdom as a historical fact. Many of the books that the Occidentals got from Islamdom they could have gotten from the Greeks themselves – and later did; whereas the sort of insight that could not have been gotten from the Greek tradition was largely overlooked by the Occidentals anyway. What perhaps mattered most was the stirring of the imagination and the challenge to the ingenuity of Occidentals who, in the full flush of their increasing economic prosperity and the rising cultural level associated with it, found themselves looked down on and hemmed in by a society which shared none of their overt assumptions and yet was obviously, at least at first, culturally and politically superior. The Muslims posed a challenge to the Occident such as the Greeks of Byzantium, long respected but latterly overcome and almost despised, could not.

The distant contact in Syria as a result of the Crusades does not seem to have had much effect on the Occident in terms of direct borrowings; but the very fact of the Crusades' being undertaken shows the tremendous stimulus that the Muslim presence formed, and the very process of Crusading – their one great joint effort – taught the Occidentals more sophistication, perhaps, than they could ever have borrowed from their unwilling Syrian hosts. The political greatness of the papacy owed much to its leadership in those wars. In Sicily, where Occidentals ruled over subject Muslims and Greeks of high culture, much was learned on the factual level; but possibly the greatest impact on Occidental cultural and political life was made by the Latin rulers of the island, notably by Frederick II. The Latin rule there was unique in the Occident for its bureaucratic solidity – required because of the high-cultural level of the local population and their intimate relations with Muslims as well as Greeks; and this in turn made possible the unique role of Frederick II as disturber and ultimately inspirer of other Latin princes. The third locus of Muslim-Occidental relations was the Spanish peninsula, where imita-

[8] H. A. R. Gibb, in "The Influence of Islamic Culture on Medieval Europe," *Bulletin of the John Rylands Library*, 38 (1955), 82–98, offers a suggestive study of how a high-cultural tradition tended, in pre-Modern times, to maintain its own genius despite great influence from the outside. He is speaking only of diffusion and not considering the more contextual effects of the sheer presence of the alien culture and its challenge.

tion and adaptation of Islamicate ways was at its height, and whence they were most regularly spread over Europe. Here perhaps more than anywhere else it was the tremendous prestige of Muslim learning that persuaded Occidentals to study works in Arabic that they did not trouble to study in the original Greek, though by 1204 Latins were thoroughly at home in the Greek-speaking countries where the Greek books were to be found.

Though the most important influence of the Muslims on the Occident may have been the stretching of the imagination which they encouraged, yet the particular points of cultural adoption were crucial in Occidental growth as it in fact did take place. Even the Greeks were translating works from Arabic and Persian, for they were the most vital languages of the age this side of Chinese. Perhaps most important were technological borrowings. Crafts and manufacturing methods, commercial methods of organization and even political methods (in Sicily), and agricultural skills could be taken over fairly directly. By and large Islamdom, especially at the start of the Earlier Middle Period, was more advanced technically than most of the Occident; however, by the twelfth and thirteenth centuries the two societies were growing on roughly the same level and it is then sometimes hard to know in which society a new development came first. In some fields, such as the steady improvement in the uses of gunpowder, it may well be that corresponding inventions were made roughly simultaneously but independently, as the technical level came to be ready for it in both areas at once. As yet the history of the Occident is better documented in these matters and often new inventions can be attested slightly earlier there; this may be the case for certain complex kinds of stills and for the use of the compass. But in many other cases, such as the manufacture and application of the many items which, like alcohol, still bear among us names derived from Arabic, the priority is sufficiently clear. The wide range of Occidental dependence can be suggested by a random and very partial list of English words derived from Arabic (though many of these words came to Arabic in turn from Persian or Greek): orange, lemon, alfalfa, saffron, sugar, syrup, mask, muslin, alcove, guitar, lute, amalgam, alembic, alchemy, alkali, soda, algebra, almanac, zenith, nadir, tariff, admiral, check-mate.

In natural science, especially in mathematics, astronomy, medicine, and chemistry, but to a degree in all the fields then cultivated, the Occidentals frankly acknowledged their debt to Arabic books, which they eagerly translated throughout much of the High Medieval period. In the process, classical Greek texts took on an Arabic dress (the "Almagest" of

Ptolemy retains in Latin the Arabic article *al-*) and numerous Muslim writers, not only Ibn-Sina ("Avicenna") and al-Razi ("Rhazes") but many lesser men, became commonplace Latin authorities. Astronomical tables compiled at Muslim observatories were authoritative. (We still use the Arabic names of many stars.) Only those works that had been produced by the early twelfth century were translated, for by the time the translations into Latin ceased, the most recent writings were not yet well enough known to have come to the translators' attention. Discoveries made in Islamdom after about the date had to be remade independently in the Occident later.

This was not, of course, a matter of "bringing back to the West" its own heritage, meanwhile "preserved" by the Arabs: the Latin Occident had played almost no role in building up the Hellenic scientific corpus even at the height of Roman power, and the Occidentals can less properly be called its heirs than can the Muslims, in whose lands much of the scientific corpus originated. And when the scientific heritage was finally carried to the new territory in the northwest, it did not die out (as some Westerners have supposed) in its homelands in the eastern Mediterranean and between Nile and Oxus; at least at first, the scientific productivity of the Occident did not markedly improve on that of Islamdom, and after High Medieval times it may have declined again for a time to a level below that of Islamdom. Nevertheless, the Occidentals did prove apt scholars, able by the end of High Medieval times to continue the tradition on their own without further reference to the work being done in Arabic and Persian; and though for a time there was a partial lull in Latin scientific work, the tradition persisted and later led to the great scientific transformations of the seventeenth century.

The problems of Philosophical metaphysics received in the Occident, as in Islamdom, a more sustained and socially organized attention. Here too the most important texts came at first by way of Arabic; translations initiated a great Aristotelian revival. But both the Aristotelian and the Platonic traditions had been rooted with sufficient solidity in Latin in imperial days, though chiefly by way of secondary writings, so that the impetus that came from Arabic brought nothing radically new. The new writings were made to serve a dialogue that was arising before they were introduced. Thus the position of Ibn-Rushd (Averröes) in Islamdom had justified an accommodation of the private wisdom of the Faylasufs to the social supremacy of the sharia, at the expense of any properly theological speculation; in Christendom, his attitude, under the name of "Averroism," served rather to justify an accommodation between a radically rationalistic Philosophy and Christian theology itself. The most important consequence of the translations from Arabic was to raise Occidental thinking to a higher level of sophistication. Even here, then, despite the obvious transference of particular texts, the influence of the presence of Islamdom, great as it was in the form of cultural diffusion as such, was even greater in the form of the challenge to the imagination posed by the very existence at such close range of Islamicate sophistication. Provided the particular texts were not so alien as to be totally unintelligible – that is, given that the Islamicate heritage had much the same roots as the Occidental – it mattered perhaps relatively little which particular texts the Occidentals came upon, compared to the fact that they were exposed emotionally to a society in which texts of high sophistication prevailed at all.

In the fields of the Abrahamic tradition and of mysticism, at first sight there seems to have been no Islamic influence at all. Ghazali (called "Algazel") was known for his exposition of the Falsafah metaphysic rather than for his Islamic refutation of it. Probably religious experience as such was not shared. Rare was the Occidental who had a serious enough acquaintance with Islam for such influence to be imaginable; most Occidentals who wrote about Islam repeated the most grotesque misinformation, designed purely as encouragement for the faithful against a foe they should regard as despicably irrational. But on the level of metaphysics, among a few, contact was possible. It has been suggested that certain Christian mystics, notably Raymond Lull of Spain (1235–1315), who indeed was one of the rare souls that did know something of Islam, may have learned something from their Muslim counterparts, and so from Muslim metaphysics later than Ibn-Rushd; though they could scarcely acknowledge the fact, if they were themselves aware of it. Lull's thought was marked by a boldness and breadth of vision not without affinities to that of such men was Ibn al-Arabi, of whom he must have known; and especially by way of Giordano Bruno, Lull was one inspiration of the much later imaginative ebullience that ushered in Modern times.

In the field of esthetic culture, the penetration of Islamicate themes and methods is harder to trace than in the technical and intellectual fields. Some prose fiction was translated directly. But art, above all, transforms whatever it feeds upon. Specialists have traced the introduction of numerous lesser motifs at one point or another from Islamdom in architecture and in what in the Occident are called the "minor" arts. The elaboration of musical instruments was given a great impetus from Islamicate models, and even poetry, as we have seen, at its Medieval peak in the troubadours, probably made use of old Arabic traditions. But popular tales and pious legend, which formed the substratum of much of the best prose, were nourished in part from Islamicate sources. Some of Dante's materials have been shown to bear striking analogies with certain Islamicate materials – notably some points in a description of Muhammad's ascent to Paradise – which were available in Italy at the time on the basis of translations from Spain. But here again, the heart neither of Dante's poem nor of the Occidental esthetic culture generally was seriously touched by the alien details. Probably in this realm also the most important consequence of the Islamicate presence was its challenge to the imagination.

By the end of the Earlier Middle Period, the Occident had become a significant force in the life of Islamdom. The Occidental efforts at conquest in the east Mediterranean has been mostly turned back, and they had been limited in the west Mediterranean to a line somewhat north of the Straits of Gibraltar, efforts to cross the seas having failed. For two centuries the Occident was not to advance again. But Occidental culture had become independent of Islamicate resources and had pulled abreast of the Islamicate in sophistication. The Occidentals of Italy and Spain retained the dominance over the Mediterranean seaways and their commerce which they had gained in the Earlier Middle Period. Thus they blocked in the west Mediterranean that expansion which characterized Islamdom everywhere else, and which elsewhere expressed and probably reinforced the genius of its social order.[9]

[9] The most accessible study of Islamicate influence on the Occident is *The Legacy of Islam*, ed. Thomas Arnold and Arthur Guillaume (Oxford: Oxford University Press, 1931). The "legacy" in question is not that to modern Muslims but that to the Occident, rather prematurely conceived as the heir to a moribund Islamdom. Not all the chapters are relevant to this theme, but many are. The best is by H. A. R. Gibb, "Literature," pp. 180–209, who brilliantly traces what influence can be found in Occidental literature. The chapter on the visual arts, Thomas Arnold, "Islamic Art and Its Influence on Painting in Europe," pp. 151–54, is also useful, but less discriminating as to what "influence" really means. H. G. Farmer has a useful chapter, "Music," pp. 356–75. The studies on the natural sciences, e.g., Max Meyerhof, "Science and Medicine," pp. 311–55, all suffer from the misapprehension that what can be traced into the Latin was substantially the whole of Islamicate science; this means that they leave untouched some serious questions about Occidental selectivity, but they are good as far as they go.

9

The unity of later Islamic history

Islamic civilization as an object of study

In a "history of mankind," Islamic civilization should be studied not only in the several regions where it flourished, but also as a historical whole, as a major element in forming the destiny of all mankind.[1] The vast Islamic society certainly has been this. Not only in the first centuries, but also in the later periods the fate of Islam is of world-wide import. This is true above all because its conscious hopes for a godly world order represent one of the most remarkable undertakings in history and because its less self-conscious general cultural heritage is laden with human values. But later Islamic history is important also for understanding how the current world situation came about. At the moment when the new life in the West was transforming the planet, the circumstances in which Islam as a whole found itself conditioned the affairs of half mankind and hence the possibilities open to them of response to the new West. Hence much of the significance of regional

[1] One of the very few serious analyses of the development of later Islamic civilization as a whole is that of H. A. R. Gibb, in the latter ages of the opening chapter of his *Mohammedanism: A Historical Survey;* (Oxford, Oxford University Press, 1962) cf. also his "An Interpretation of Islamic History," *Cahiers d'histoire mondiale,* Vol. I, 30–62 (July, 1953), to which the present article is in effect a highly inadequate annex. I must explain that the approach here suggested has not been fully embodied, as of this writing (1957), in the paragraphs prepared for Volume Four, since they had to conform to a general outline which had unavoidably been drawn up from the perspective of local Western history. R. Brunschvig, pp. 56–59, in *Unity and Variety in Muslim Civilization,* ed. G. E. von Grunebaum (Chicago: University of Chicago Press, 1955), gives a recent statement of some of the problems involved here. I believe that if one thinks in terms of a historical complex rather than in terms of some single categorizing principle, as he seems to try to do, the problem of delimiting Islamic civilization becomes less serious. At this point it should also be pointed out that, as English usage of the terms "Islamic" and "Muslim" is increasingly recognizing by assigning different meanings to the two terms, "Islamic" *civilization* has included both followers of the "Muslim" *religion* and followers of other faiths.

Islamic societies, such as those in the Near East or in India, lay in the part they played in determining the course of Islam as a whole. Islamic civilization in its later periods is enormously complex and diverse. But our problem is not just to find the common characteristics underlying the diversity, though this is important. It is to trace the ways in which elements either of unity or of diversity have been relevant to the fortunes of the civilization in its role in world history.

In the early centuries of Islam it is not hard to study the civilization as a whole, but this becomes increasingly difficult in the later periods. Even in the more strictly "religious" sphere, that of *fiqh* and *tasawwuf,* the difference in detail is obvious, for instance, between the Indian and the Arab or Turkish centers of Muslim learning. In the sphere of general culture, of institutions and of arts and letters, the diversity is very marked. Yet a common cultural heritage and a common cultivation of the Arabic and (in most areas) Persian languages, as well as a common attitude to the relation between society and religion, assured at least a minimum of interaction and continuity among the various Islamic regions; in all of which, accordingly, developments can be seen which are sometimes alike, sometimes related by their very contrasts. Identification with Islam as a creed, in an ever larger part of the globe, continued to carry with it the more or less full adoption of a vast body of cultural practices, itself varying not only from area to area but from century to century, yet constituting in all its diversity a civilization with in some degree its own single story.

I believe that one of the obstacles to the envisagement of this civilization as a whole has been what can be called in Arabistic bias. This is the most unfortunate of a series of biases which hamper Islamic studies. Islamists have naturally always approached their studies in terms of one or another special perspective, and Islamic history has been conceived in radically different ways according to the vantage point chosen. Each vantage point has had its own limiting effect. Those who have approached it from the point of view of its relations with Western Europe have recalled the two waves of conquest launched in their own direction, and have tended to divide Islamic history into an Arab and a Turkish phase; or rather, as a closer acquaintance with Ottoman culture laid bare something of the internal development, into a sequence of Arab, Persian, and Ottoman phases. Such an approach informs the selection of data in Brockelmann's *Geschichte der islamischen Völker.* A Russian point of view is illustrated in Barthold's little volume on Islamic culture, which traces a sequence from Arabic and Persian to the Turkish not so much of the Ottomans as of Central Eurasia.[2] From a third vantage point, that of scholars in India, British or Muslim, the phases are more naturally Arabic, Persian, and Indo-Muslim. The Arabistic bias is analogous to that of these other three viewpoints. Arabs, and also Western scholars who as Semitists or for other reasons concentrate on the original centers of Islam, often stop short with only an Arab phase; they tend to see the whole civilization as suffering eclipse after a first few centuries of Arab glory, at least 'till the revival of Arab independence in modern times. Since one or another such partial viewpoint is implicit in practically every treatment of broad-gauge problems in Islamic studies, there has resulted a certain vicious circle: for want of a satisfactory general perspective, the historical position of Islam has been obscured, and want of a sense of the historical position has reinforced the tendency to narrow perspectives.

These different viewpoints are often so unconsciously taken for granted that they lead to curious misstatements. Thus I have read in an Indian work that after the Mongol conquests in Iran the last refuge of Islamic civilization, the one unconquered court to which the Muslim scholars flocked, was Delhi.[3] On the other hand, we often read in the work of Arabists that after the same conquest the only refuge was Egypt.[4]

Some degree of distortion is no doubt scarcely avoidable. But this latter Arabistic twist, which disregards the more easterly Muslims, is, I believe, unusually baneful. Examples of petty factual errors arising from it are unpleasantly numerous.[5] More important is the fact that it arises from

[2] V. Barthold, *Musulman Culture* (Tr. S. Suhrawardy, Calcutta: University of Calcutta, 1934), especially pp. 117 ff.

[3] A. B. M. Habibullah, *Foundation of Muslim Rule in India* (Lahore: Muhammad Ashraf, 1945), p. 155.

[4] E.g., *Unity and Variety in Muslim Civilization*, p. 153–154, "then [after the Mongol catastrophe] all orthodoxy flowed back into Egypt," the political structure of which is then described as representing the Muslim east, in contrast to "the Muslim west" after the Almohads. When study is restricted to these two exceptional cases, centralized Egypt and backward North Africa, it is not surprising that Islamic society after the Mongol invasion receives disappointingly little analysis. Cf. C. Brockelmann, *History of the Islamic Peoples*, tr. Carmichael and Perlmann (London: Routledge and Kegan Paul, 1949), p. 234, where some Arab countries are also ignored.

[5] The writer just cited in *Unity and Variety* allows himself to say – at least with a certain consistency – that the Saljuqs joined together "all of Muslim Asia with the exception of the corners of Arabia" – overlooking Ghazna and Sind and Multan (p. 152). Another writer in the same representative volume, typically considering the Arab west on a more detailed scale than the rest of Islam, says curiously that "neither Greek nor Pahlevi, nor Aramaic nor Coptic held out against [Arabic]. Only Berber and Latin [and in one sense Persian] persisted" – making one think immediately of Kurdish, Armenian, and other

certain deeply rooted attitudes and so is not readily self-corrective. As Westerners we have tended to admit Islam into "world history" only at the point where it impinges (with the Arabs in Frankish Gaul, and later in medieval Spain) most deeply upon the development of our own West. This initial preoccupation with the Arabs was joined to a natural interest in the "pure" Islam of the original Muslims, with the result that Islamists have tended to include as really Islamic at most developments of the first three or four glorious centuries, when Arabic was unchallenged as a language of culture. Hence there has arisen a usually unspoken equivalence between the terms "Arabic" and "Islamic," which is as unfair to Christian and Jewish Arabs as to the overwhelming majority of non-Arab Muslims. It is not uncommon for an article in the *Encyclopaedia of Islam* on a given institution, festival, or architectural form, or even for a book, say, on Islamic art, to be written as if the subject were practically limited to Arab countries even in the later Islamic centuries.[6] On the other hand, the millennia of pre-Islamic Arabian history are subsumed, by an accident of philology, under the banner of Islam. The cumulative distortion that results is unintentional but nonetheless effective.[7]

popular or learned tongues from Georgia to Sind, which deserve to rank at least with Berber! (p. 208).

[6] Cf. *E.I. on maristan, mawlid, madrasa, masdjid,* etc. To be sure, in many cases the writer gladly included any information from outside of Egypt or North Africa which came to his attention. Occasionally one finds evidence of an interesting attitude that might be called neo-Umayyad, implying that the name "Muslim" is merely a latter-day honorific of the Arabs, and that non-Arab Muslims are joining as clients and at the last minute a tradition which reaches unbrokenly back to the Sabaean kings – hence only Arabs are truly "Muslims," the others are "islamisés"; in the *E.I.* article on Malays, Arab influence is reckoned as Islamic *despite* the fact that it came in a Persian form! It is not surprising that some laymen will take from the shelf a "History of the *Arabs*" when they want to learn about *Islamic* history, perhaps in order to understand Pakistan! To be sure, in the reaction against Sufism and the Persian cultural tradition, many modern Muslims abet this attitude.

[7] A certain defense of ignoring Islam east of the Iranian highlands – though the majority of all Muslims now live in those eastern areas – is offered by Sauvaget, in his *Introduction à l'histoire de l'orient musulman* (Paris: Maisonneuve 1946), pp. 13–14; that the culture of the "outlying" territories (in which he includes India) has not been formed so exclusively by Islam; or that at least they have been merely passive, not actively creative. Such a position raises problems in the definition of a civilization as a proper object of historical study, and it might be suggested that not only few Islamic lands, but few ages (perhaps not even the earliest age of Islam) offer the cultural homogeneity combined with fresh creativity which Sauvaget demands. But in any case, his stated distinction does not make sense. Though the Malaysian countries, or even Bengal, might be excluded by his criteria, it is surely arbitrary to omit the Punjab or even the Gangetic plain, where so much distinctively Islamic thought and action has originated. Sauvaget reveals his actual reason for omitting most of the truly eastern territories of Islam when he makes an east-west division of Islam in which Egypt and Turkey appear as "eastern." Egypt can indeed be ranked among the eastern *Arabs,* though it lies west of Mecca. But only if Islam and the Arabs are identified can Egypt be ranked as "eastern" in *Islam.*

The expansion of Islam as a world-historical phenomenon

This Arabistic emphasis has contributed to one conception which has been peculiarly unfortunate from the standpoint of the problems of later Islamic history. The phrase "expansion of Islam" is commonly identified with the great expansion of the Arabs from the Arabian Peninsula, that is, with the establishment of the Arab empire in the seventh and early eighth centuries of our era. Here it designates the quite rapid conquest by the Arabs, under the aegis of incipient Islam, of territories most of which were then or had been previously already linked together under either the Roman or the Persian empire and were in some measure assimilated culturally to the two empires whose decline gave the Arabs their opportunity. From the point of view of the civilization, this is not so much an *expansion* of Islam as the carving out of its *initial domain.* Whatever may have been the case with Islam as a religion, there was certainly no question yet of the expansion of an Islamic civilization in the full sense. In the first years of the Arab empire the prevailing civilizations continued to be Hellenistic-Christian and Sassanian, while the pre-Islamic Arab culture of the ruling class was only gradually Islamized, either in Arabia or elsewhere. When within two or three generations the original frontiers of islam had been substantially fixed, there followed a period of three centuries of practically no expansion at all, during which the various peoples within the original limits were combining to build up the Muslim religion and the Islamic civilization of history. Islam now ceased to be the code of a ruling class and became the many-sided of whole populations and the core of a new and distinctive civilization.

But there did come a time when one can speak of the "expansion of Islam" as a full-fledged civilization. From about 1000 on, the territory of the Muslim faith and of its associated culture expanded unceasingly in almost every direction (and indeed the faith continues to do so, not only in the Old World but in the New). By the sixteenth century the area of Dar al-Islam had almost tripled. This is the most important single fact about the Islamic society as a whole in its later periods, at least from the point of view of its interaction in world history.[8]

[8] As can be seen from a map, alongside the main bloc of lands from Transoxania through Syria and Egypt can be set, as areas of roughly the same order in size, that to the northwest in Anatolia and Europe, and again that to the east and south in Turkestan and India; Spain and the Maghrib find their equivalent in eastern Africa and again in Malaysia; Arabia – in the Sahara and the Sudan. (The notion of *dar al-Islam* has been liberally interpreted, as by Muslims themselves, to include areas lately under Muslim rule and

This expansion, especially before 1800, had two major world-historical features. In the first place, from the eleventh until the nineteenth century Islam was par excellence the region to which the less civilized peoples of the Old World were converted as they were brought within the horizon of urban civilization, whether in sub-Saharan Africa, in Malaysia, in Central Eurasia, or even some backward borderlands of China and India. Only in relatively limited areas did Buddhism, Christianity, and in a measure Hinduism rival it. Indeed, so powerful was the Muslim appeal that, unlike the others, it was even able to make large-scale advances in territory where another major religion had prevailed. Its initial territory, of course, had been largely converted from Christianity, Judaism, and Zoroastrianism. But even later it advanced, for instance, into Europe among the Christians of Anatolia and the Balkans, into several regions in Hindu India, and among Buddhists and Hindus in Indonesia and even Indochina.[9] Among "primitive" peoples its preeminence was unrivalled 'till the advent of Christianity, especially in the nineteenth century, with unprecedented new cultural advantages; and even then Islam continued to be a formidable competitor for the allegiance of the uncommitted, whether in Siberia or Africa or Malaysia.

The second world-historical feature of the great Islamic expansion is that, despite its unexampled dispersion throughout the Eastern Hemisphere – in Europe, Africa, India, China, Central Eurasia, and the Far South East – Islam maintained not only religious but even some measure of social bonds among its scattered communities. In this way it came closer than any other medieval society to establishing a common world order of social and even cultural standards, such as was in fact accomplished in some respects after the advent of European world hegemony in the nineteenth century. And though it failed to establish such a hegemony in the world as a whole, it succeeded in some measure in a very crucial sector of the world – the whole basin of the Indian Ocean; including the Indian subcontinent, where large Hindu populations accepted Muslim rule and where even the Marathas, when they reestablished Hindu kingdoms, commonly continued to recognize the suzerainty of the Muslim

still carrying an Islamic coloring.) The map, designed to bring out the crucial world position of Islam, is of course on an equal-area projection; the sense of proportion is quite lost if the Mercator's projection is used – a projection practically tailor-made to reinforce Western prejudices and which unhappily still appears not only in many scholars' books but also, all too obviously, in their thinking.

9 It has come near obliterating Hinduism outside India; cf. on the fate of the ancient Hindu Cham people of Indochina, P. Rondot, "Notes sur les Chams Bani du Binh Thuan," *Revue des Etudes Islamiques*, 1949, p. 18.

Mongol emperors and the excellence of the Indo-Muslim culture which centered at the Mogul court.[10]

It was therefore above all with Islamic powers that the Europeans wrestled when they took over control of the "Indies trade" and eventually of the Old World generally; and the traces of this fact are visible, sometimes directly and sometimes in devious ways, all over the face of modern world politics. The delicate relations between the British and the Indian Muslims, whom they supplanted, account for much of the involved sequence which led to the foundation of Pakistan, for instance.[11] The unpredictable role of Islam in the Soviet empire, and the availability to Negro Africa of a longstanding alternative to the West as it seeks orientation in the wider world, are both cases in point. Above all there is the unique role of vague but potent pan-Islamic sentiments in the non-Western non-Communist zone, the African-Asian zone of the "neutralists" – just the area in which Islam once had near hegemony. Even India, the greatest non-Muslim state in the area, cannot but take into account the sentiments of its very considerable and well-placed Muslim minority.

The expansion of Islam was, then, of first-rate importance in the historical development of the whole hemisphere, and so deserves special consideration in any history of mankind. Also from the point of view of Islamic history as such, it was an immense performance and one with far-reaching ideological implications. Hence the study of the problems posed within Islam by the expansion and by the centrifugal tendencies it occasioned is one of the chief concerns which requires us to envisage Islamic history as a whole. As Gibb has pointed out,[12] the expansion had a great deal to do with the role of Sufism as an element of social structure and hence even in the integration of intellectual life. To a lesser degree it likewise affected the outcome of the Persian inspiration which was so prominent in the setting of esthetic and even to a certain point, political standards, but which could not in the end impose itself on all the far-flung centers of Islamic influence.

[10] The Muslim-Hindu symbiosis extended even to Vijayanagar. Cf., e.g. H. K. Sherwani, "Culture and Administrative Set-up Under Ibrahim Qutb-Shah," *Islamic Culture,* XXXI (1957), 127–141. As is suggested by the British use of the Persian language in India and by their designation of the period preceding themselves there as the "Mohammedan period" of its history, not only the lands of Muslim majorities but the whole area between Christian Europe and the Confucian Far East (that is, the greater part of the chief seats of history) tended to strike early Europeans as "Moorish" territory, for Muslims tended dominate the most significant spots: coasts and capitals. Hinduism and Theravada Buddhism functioned almost as enclaved religions for a time.

[11] This is brought out clearly, for instance, in Wilfred Cartwell Smith's *Modern Islam in India* (London: V. Gollancz, 1946).

[12] *Modern Trends in Islam* (Chicago, 1947), p. 25.

Contrasts between later and earlier periods in historical character

Before we go further into the characteristics of later Islamic civilization, we must venture a periodization which will help us to inventory the field and to recall the most important temporal contrasts in it. Taking as our cue the changes in the conditions faced by Islam in its expansion, we can make a break about 1000, when the expansion began; about 1250, at the Mongol crisis, when the central Islamic lands learned to bear non-Muslim rule; about 1500, when commercial control of the Indian Ocean passed from Muslim to Western hands; and about 1800, when Western world hegemony was established. Such a periodization, needless to say, is not meant to be exact; the breaks must all be read as plus or minus a generation or so. Nor has it any metaphysical status. Every analysis must in principle periodize for itself, taking into account not only shifts in relevant social and cultural patterns but also the character of the sources for study, such as the languages used or the type of document available. Nevertheless, the fact that all these breaks have world-historical implications make them peculiarly appropriate for purposes of general orientation.

In this sequence of periods, those after 1000 differ markedly from the earliest period as to the way in which Islam could be said to form a single civilization during the period and hence as to the sort of treatment the period requires for our purposes. This contrast must be clear if we are to conceive the historical unity of the later periods adequately.

It is of course futile to try to mark a particular moment when any new civilization appears – when, in this case, the new pattern of culture formed around the Muslim faith can first be set in unmistakable contrast to the major civilizations among which the Muslim religion was cradled; but in this case the time limits of that appearance are closely drawn. In nucleo, the new cultural pattern certainly existed no earlier than the day when Muhammad won his first convert, who entered into a novel form of relationship with him; or rather, perhaps, when a full-fledged political body, with its distinctive forms of behavior, was set up at the *hijra*. Even this date is too early. Within every civilization there are innumerable such local sub-cultures; to proclaim a new independent civilization, one prefers to wait till the recasting in Islamic terms of the leading aspects of Middle Eastern culture has clearly made a beginning. But this is already the case by the end of Umayyad times, and perhaps already in the generation of Abd al-Malik.[13] We can take, then, 700 CE as a round number (as always, plus or minus a generation!) for the start of the first major period of Islamic civilization.

One could, to be sure, construct a period of genesis, reaching far back, in retrospect, into both the Arabian and the general Middle Eastern pre-Islamic past; a period very important for some purposes. But it is the three centuries from about 700 to about 1000 which form the first period of full-fledged Islamic civilization, and which are to be contrasted to the later periods. It can be called the period of classical Abbasid civilization (though at its beginning and at its end, after 945, the Abbasids, were not ruling), since it is with the Abbasid capital that we associate its characteristic cultural life. This differed in two ways from that of all the later periods. In the first place, it was the culture of very nearly a single state, the Caliphate, with a single language of culture, Arabic, and was limited rather sharply geographically; that is, more or less to the Middle East, with certain extensions. It had a preeminent center of cultural formation, in Iraq, which was already at least as creative as Syria in Umayyad times, and which continued to be not only the cultural but the political center of gravity until well into the tenth century. In part because of this fact, the civilization was relatively homogeneous over all its area, and in particular possessed the sort of unity that makes for a straightforward narrative; the want of which is felt keenly in tracing the developments of later periods.

A second contrast is equally important in the opposite sense. The background of the classical Abbasid period is anything but single, and the most prominent cultural activity is that of weaving into a new whole diverse heritages: the Hellenistic and the Christian, the Jewish, the Iranian, and the Jahiliyya Arabian. It is a time of active integration and the study of each of the various strands in the cultural complex presupposes, as background, its own separate antecedents. In the later periods the main body of the heritage is already given as a whole, and cultural activity is a matter of multiplication and differentiation rather than of integration. The student must begin his studies with an acquaintance with a common background dating from classical Abbasid times and be prepared to work out its varying implications in different situations.

Perhaps a third, related contrast should be added, which is not a

[13] Cf. R. Blachère, "Regards sur l'acculturation des Arabo-Musulmans jusque vers 40/661," *Arabica*, III (1956), 247–265. Cf. Nabia Abbott, *Studies in Arabic Literary Papyri*, I, Chicago: University of Chicago Press, 1957, p. 20 ff.

matter of the historical texture of the periods so much as of their human significance, but which influences study. That is, the classical Abbasid period is rich in fresh thinking and cultural experimentation, whereas the great work of succeeding periods more often takes the form of a deepening of established traditions. It is as yet too soon to know how much the sense we have of decadence in these later periods is a product of our current tastes. But in any case we readily find brilliant times the most congenial to study, and neglect less brilliant times which may be equally significant in our destiny.

The period from the fall of Abbasid power in the tenth century to the establishment of Mongol power in the thirteenth corresponds roughly to what in Europe is called the High Middle Ages, and fully deserves the same name in Islam, as the age of Firdawsi, Ghazali, Saladin, Ibn al-Arabi, and Sadi. Its historical characteristics already contrast fully with those cited for the classical Abbasid period. During it the expansion of Islam is well launched – both into Byzantine territory and into northern India, as well as in less prominent areas such as across the Sahara. At the same time, creative cultural centers become numerous, including, notably, Spain and Khurasan. A second language of culture, the Persian, matured. It is already impossible to trace the story of Islam in terms of any one political or geographical center; even the Saljuq empire during its brief span of prominence, significant as was its role in the development of the pattern of relations between the military and the *ulama*, had limited significance for the farther east, for Egypt, and for the farther west. After 1100, the story in every aspect of culture is unmitigatedly many-centered. Moreover, the most important cultural developments presuppose a common matrix of living tradition. The rise of the Sufi *tariqas* for instance, revolutionary as it is for the whole spiritual outlook of the culture, presupposes the social cohesion guaranteed by the *sharia*. Likewise the development of Persian poetry builds on an esthetic basis common to all Islam. The sort of historical unity to be found – one of common heritage and of interrelated problems, rather than one of common activity based on diverse heritages – is already the reverse of that of Abbasid times.

This continues to be the case throughout the later Islamic periods. If 1000–1250 can be called the High Middle Ages, then 1250–1500 is properly the Late Middle Ages, as continuing in a less brilliant way most of the cultural trends developed in the preceding period. Then follows an age remarkably dissimilar, that of the three great empires, Ottoman, Safavid, and Mogul, roughly 1500–1800. It is these latter two periods which fall into the scope of Volume Four.[14] In both of these later periods, as in the case of the High Middle Ages, the Islamic developments presuppose an established cultural foundation upon which many centers are building in various ways, but interrelatedly and hence without a full break in the unity of the Islamic society. The later Islamic periods cannot be studied as one does the fresh emergence of a civilization, nor can they be reduced to a neat unilinear story. Yet, like other fields of large-scale history, they have aspects that can and must be appropriately studied in broad terms. (That is, of course, merely to say that Islamic history, in the greater part of its course, is typical of civilized history. Some should like to study only "integrated" societies. But the creation of a new civilization is a rare thing, and even more rare is the establishment of a relatively self-sufficient, self-perpetuating cultural pattern, such as that of ancient Egypt or that of post-classical China, as a fairly stable institution whole over a long period. The Islamic cultures were not isolated enough to achieve this, being in the midst of world history, as it were, which would not let them alone.)

The apolitical character of the Late Middle Ages

There are in particular two tendencies that can be traced from the point of view of the role of Islam in the world at large. On the one hand, a pattern was being built up which was leading to an international Islamic order over perhaps the greater part of the civilized world; a most important aspect of this process was the expansion of Islam. This tendency was clearly developing in the high medieval period and was predominant in the late medieval period, till at least 1500; and it continued to be effective after that date. On the other hand, many aspects of the Islamic cultures were becoming increasingly inconsistent, or so it would seem, with such a single international Islamic order; and this second tendency became the stronger of the two in the period of the three empires, after 1500.

[14] The periodization here ventured, it will be seen, is as follows:
before 700: period of genesis
700–1000: classical Abbasid period
1000–1250: high Middle Ages
1250–1500: late Middle Ages
1500–1800: period of the three empires
since 1800: modern period.
It is clear that such a periodization has rather different ends in view from a division say, into Medina period, Umayyad period, Abassid period, Mongol period.

The Late Middle Ages opened with vital parts of the Dar al-Islam under pagan rule. This fact symbolized the character the Dal al-Islam was to bear throughout the period. With the end even of the claim of the Baghdad Caliphate to general sovereignty, Islam was now frankly decentralized even in theory as it had long been in practice: what is more, the decentralized society could not depend on even local governments for its survival, but must make its own way.

In the High Middle Ages political powers – the reforming Almoravids and Almohads in the far west, the Sunna-supporting Saljuqs and Ayyubids, the early Delhi Sultanate whose Turkish and Islamic dignity is portrayed by Barani,[15] even the quixotic Muhammad Khwarazm-shah – commonly expressed some sort of Islamic political idea. The split between civil and military life had begun, indeed, but politics was not dead. Particularly in the older Islamic lands, this seems to be rarely the case in the Late Middle Ages except in some frontier states. Although the Mongols were soon converted, the prestige of their states continued to rest on a pagan past. Other dynasties could boast even less a political idea. The Marinids and Hafsids with whom Ibn-Khaldun had to do are politically soulless. The Mamluks of Egypt maintained a centralized state solely, it would appear, because the form of Egypt almost forced them to. The Turkomans of the Black Sheep and the Turkomans of the White Sheep offer the classic cases of nomads turned military rulers, and are served by no Nizam-al-Mulk.[16] Timur is the classical case of an irresponsible Muslim conqueror. Even India, after Tughluq and Bahmani times, is a congeries of independent provincial powers, few of which distinguish themselves. To be sure, the structure of many of these states (for instance, the Mamluks of Egypt and Syria) is of considerable interest. But as regards positive historical policy, the popular state of the Sarbadars of Sabzawar in Iran appears to be almost a unique exception. Characteristically, it was dominated by Shi'ite Sufi *shaykhs*. Almost everywhere political boundaries, never fundamental within the Dar al-Islam, were of even less importance in this period than ever before or after. Unless future research discloses unsuspected highlights, we must feel that precisely in the Late Middle Ages politics became as irrelevant as they ever have been in any civilized society. Such a state of affairs is reflected by the political thought of the period,

[15] Diya-al-Din Barani, *Tarikh-e Firuz shahi* (Lahore: Sind Sagor Academy, 1974), pp. 36–38, 43–45.

[16] Contrast the unpolitical role of Dawwani, author of the *Akhlaq-e Jalali*, in Walter Hinz, *Irans Aufstieg zum Nationalstaat* (Berlin, 1936), p. 115.

which apparently abandoned all hope of forming political life according to its norms.[17]

Yet as a social order, Islam continued to gain territory, as well as a more complete adherence within territory already gained. The faith, with its culture, was able to use the most diverse means. Sometimes the advance was by conversion of rulers: thus the Mongols of Iran and of Transoxania adopted the religion of the majority of their subjects, while the Mongols of the Golden Horde were converted although at best only a fraction of their subjects were Muslims. Sometimes it was by the expansion of strong frontier powers. From early in the fourteenth century, when most of India south of the Ganges was conquered by the Delhi Sultanate, the Deccan continued under Muslim rulers; at the same time the Balkans were conquered and held by the Ottomans: in each area converts were attracted by the prestige and privilege of the new faith. Sometimes the expansion was more through individual penetration of populations by merchants and mystics, or through the rise to power of Muslim adventurers, as in Kashmir, where the dynasty became Muslim before most of the people. In one way or another, Islam continued to advance in the Sudan, and spread both on the East African coast and in Malaysia, so that most of the Indian Ocean trade with the Middle East (and hence Europe) came to be in Muslim hands. It was evidently at this time that Islam gained its strong foothold in Yunnan and other parts of China. During the period, Muslim rule receded seriously only in the far south of India and at the western end of the Mediterranean; otherwise, Islamic power kept increasing till the end of the fifteenth century, when Islam was far the most widespread of the great religions. Moreover despite its wide extension it did not lose its social cohesion; a Muslim was accepted as fellow-citizen everywhere from Morocco to China, as Ibn Battuta's travels are always brought forward to show.

Whether conquered or conquering, and even in areas remote from the original Abbasid territories, Islam consistently improved its position during this apparently apolitical period. In northern Africa, in the Middle East, in south and southeast Eurasia, Islam showed itself the most dynamic social order even where non-Muslims were in the majority. We do not know why this was. It has been suggested, as by Professor Muham-

[17] It is precisely in this period that the most despairing doctrines of the *imamate* were formed. That these are to be thought of as a particular phase, rather than as an end-product even in the Arabic zone, is pointed out by H. A. R. Gibb and H. Bowen, *Islamic Society and the West* (Oxford: Oxford University Press, 1950), Vol. I, Part 1, p. 34.

mad Habib,[18] that at least in India this reflected the relative social mobility encouraged by Muslim principles. Certainly it reflects considerable social and cultural flexibility, appropriate to Medieval mercantile and political conditions. Almost without exception, the Islamization of new areas begins with the cities, among the more cosmopolitanly minded. Only gradually does it spread into the countryside.[19]

The Tariqa *as the pivotal late medieval institution*

In any case, religiously oriented orders independent of the official politics and culture – that is, above all Sufi *tariqas* or brotherhoods – played a major role in articulating the society. The *tariqas* had been forming before the Mongol assaults, but it is probably only in the Late Middle Ages that, as a normally adopted institutional form of religion, they came to the point of really dominating the religious scene. There is a long distance between Ghazali, pioneering for Sufi respectability before Sufi's had yet formed into the historic *tariqas* and Ibn-Taymiyya, whose anti-Sufi doctrine two centuries later was like a voice crying in the wilderness. To be sure, the *tariqas* were not everywhere triumphant. In Delhi in parts of the fourteenth century, for instance, even the main orders dared not raise their heads.[20] But even then they retained their power in the provinces. The vitality of such organizations is indicated by their role in the most effective political structure of the period, the Ottoman state being built in Byzantine Europe. The *ghazi* or *akhi* organizations which apparently provided much of the social base of the early Ottoman state, if they were not regular *tariqas*, had similar characteristics, as popular religious groups independent of state or *ulama* and with widespread affiliations of their own; in time they seem to have merged into the *tariqas*, as the more usual organizational form of the period. The Safawiyya *tariqa* in Azerbaijan seems to have had similar *ghazi* characteristics, which also, later, issued in a state.

Outwardly, to be sure, the vast Islamic society was held together by the common recognition of the sacred law, the *sharia*, on the basis of the

[18] Introduction to the new edition of Elliot and Dowson, *History of India*, Vol. II (Aligarh: Cosmopolitan Publishers, 1952).

[19] In the Sudan, for instance, a considerable degree of civilization – as in the pagan empire of Ghana – seems ordinarily to precede Islamization; and within an Islamized area, it is the rules and urban centers that first accept Islam. Cf. Likewise, on the role of the mixed city populations is the Islamization of Anatolia, C. Cahen, "Le problème ethnique en Anatolie," *Cahiers d'histoire mondiale*, Vol. II, No. 2 (1954), especially p. 355.

[20] This development has been studied by Sayyid Nurul-Hasan, unpublished thesis, "Chishti and Suhrawardi Movements in Medieval India," 1948.

provisions of which every Muslim had his assured status, and knew what to expect of others, both in point of law in the narrower sense, and in that wider range of social relations which includes etiquette. This system of law and ethics had been established in detail by the close of the classical Abbasid period and was regarded as universally binding on Muslims. It was self-perpetuating, its experts (the *ulama*) requiring no official appointment. The variations in its application by persistence of extra-*sharia* law and custom almost everywhere limited its effectiveness, yet it secured sufficient uniformity to allow a large degree of mobility and intercourse throughout the Dar al-Islam.

But bereft of the context of the Umayyad and Abbasid Caliphates, the *sharia* does not seem to have provided an adequate spiritual vision in itself for most men. It was Sufi as it was embodied in the *tariqas* that provided a common framework of personal piety. The mystically inclined, of course, found strength and guidance in the common discipline of the *khanaqah,* where followers of a given *tariqa* gathered under the leadership of a *shaykh* for spiritual exercises, or even lived as full-time devotees. Ascetics could find support in some *tariqas,* and those inclined to cosmological speculation found the name of a *tariqa* to be an almost sure defense against bigoted hostility. Those who sought God through powerful personalities revered a pious living *shaykh,* or adored the tomb of a famous dead one; for the *khanaqahs* were commonly associated with such tombs. Finally, the simple villager with only an occasional interest in religion found the way open to transfer his ancestral superstitious or devotional usages to a Muslim *shaykh* alive or dead.

The *tariqas* were adapted to every situation. In the cities they informed the social life of the artisans, and eventually guilds came to be associated with *tariqas* as naturally as with patron saints. For townsmen and peasants alike their tombs, as shrines, became centers for pilgrimage and marketing. Above all, it seems to have been the Sufis who were the most effective missionaries in areas newly opened up to Muslim influence.[21] In the late Middle Ages the *tariqa* form of Sufism offered a richly varied and broadly tolerant spiritual atmosphere which was as flexible in its organization as was the *sharia* itself, and an effective complement to it in holding together the far-flung Islamic society.

Accordingly, the great issues of the time are far removed from those of the classical Abbasid period. General acceptance of the end of *ijtihad* –

[21] Largely devoted to this thesis is the book that has done most to analyze the expansion of Islam, but in a piecemeal fashion, Thomas Arnold, *The Preaching of Islam* (London: Constable, 1913).

which implied that further schools of *sharia* law were not to be developed, and that the recognized schools were no longer subject to basic changes – hallowed the amicable truce that was by and large maintained among the different schools of the *ulama*. It became common to teach the several schools of law under a single roof, a practice only partially established in the High Middle Ages. This was the great age of the *madrasas*, whose standardized character reflects the relatively uncontroversial character of their teaching.

The distinction between Shi'ites and Sunnites was more important. The Shi'ites formed a minority almost everywhere, a majority only in a few limited localities. Yet Shi'ite ideas had entered widely into Sufi lore; several *tariqas*, for instance, significantly traced their origin to Ali. Moreover, explicitly Shi'ite groups found it expedient to appear in the form of *tariqas*, even though at least the Twelve Shi'ite *ulama* did not generally accept the validity of Sufism as did most Sunnite *ulama*. The Bektashi order, prominent in the Ottoman domains, is one case. The remains of the Ismaili Shi'ite movement, after the downfall of the Ismaili state as a result of the Mongol conquest, took the outward form of a Sufi *tariqa* to avoid persecution, with the *imam* in the guise of a *shaykh;* this was not merely an outward adaptation, but corresponded to an inner sympathy with late medieval Sufism.

The issues, then, became largely controversies within and among the *tariqas*. The *tariqas* were numerous and varied. The most important had already been established by the end of the thirteenth century; during all late medieval times the number of orders steadily increased, most often by the setting off of new branches rather than by the establishment of new independent *tariqas*. The orders differed greatly among themselves, often standing for quite diverse approaches to the problems of the time. There were not only differences between the "urban" and "rustic" orders, the former being more sophisticated and conforming more to the *sharia*, but among the "urban" orders themselves. Thus of the two great *tariqas* of India during this period, the Suhrawardiyya tended to stand for greater orthodoxy in handling the *sharia*, and for readier acceptance of government office than did the more ascetic Chishtiyya.[22] Some orders, notably the Bektashiyya, seem to have catered in their cult to the non-Islamic customs of peoples newly won to Islam; some catered to the popular desire for wonders, such as the Sadiyya in Egypt. They differed also in their hospitality to mystical speculation; and in their attitude to

[22] Yusuf Husain, *L'Inde mystique au moyen âge* (Paris, 1929), p. 147 ff., tries to show that the Chishtis worked especially for Hindu-Muslim rapprochement.

the way of life of the members, whether celibacy was recommended or not, whether the full-time devotees should be chiefly wandering or gathered into convents. Thus the Khalwatiyya of Turkey demanded of each member a long retreat by himself once a year. Some orthodox orders asserted their freedom from the whole *sharia* law. The Qalandars, who were recognized as a *tariqa,* were antinomian devotees who seem to have rejected for the most part the institutionalization even of Sufism. Most of the *tariqa* life was limited to men, but in this period there were some convents founded for women also.[23]

These *tariqas* must have offered a great deal of social flexibility to the expanding Islam. Most *tariqas* tended to be associated with one or another region – the Shadhiliyya belonged to western Africa and Egypt, the Rifaiyya was centered in Iraq and the east-Arab lands, and the Kubrawiyya in Iran. An order like the Ahmadiyya was still more localized, being restricted almost to Egypt, where it was, however, very important. But khanaqahs of any *tariqa* might be found far from home, and individuals tended to travel widely. A *tariqa* like the Naqshbandiyya was very widespread in Iranian and Turkish lands, and the Qadiriyya was most widespread of all, though remaining centered in Baghdad at its founder's tomb. Among them the *tariqas,* which by the end of the High Middle Ages had come to form a network covering all the Dar al-Islam, offered fellowship and hospitality to an enormous number of specialists in Islamic culture. Moreover, the notorious tolerance of other faiths by many Sufi's cannot but have eased the acceptance of Muslim rule among all groups.

It can be suggested that they offered more even than this toward the cohesion of the Islamic society. Islam is par excellence the social, even the political religion. Since the time of the Madina Caliphate it has been unable to fulfill its goal of a social order in which the religious and the political aspects shall be one. But the aspiration could not be laid aside by seriously pious Muslims. It might, however, be transformed. The *ulama* never ceased to think of the ideal unity of Islam in terms of a *khalifa,* a Caliph ruling a human empire. The Sufis made much of a very different sort of *khalifa,* the human being who as perfected microcosm is the final end of, and holds limitless sway over, the world of nature and men together. He is a Muslim, and exercises his power largely upon and through Muslims (the Abdal); but there is a recognized place under his care for the believers in every faith however crude, not only peoples of the Book as in the historical Caliphate, but outright pagans. The kings

[23] L. Massignon, article *tariqa* in *E.I.*

who come and go are but the servants of such a saint, as many beloved anecdotes make clear; no Caliph had such power over his governors as the Sufi *shaykhs*, and especially the supreme *shaykh*, the Qutb of any given time, had over the earth's rulers. (That no-one really knew who was the Qutb in his own days only served to make his power the more awesome.)

The notion of the Qutb who, with all the *shaykhs* his assistants, continuously kept order in the world, is more than a piece of popular superstition; it is also more than a deduction from a subtle cosmology. It has serious social implications. The stories told of Abd-al-Qadir – whose foot was on the neck of every other saint – are no doubt in part the result of the ardent loyalty to their *tariqa* of the Qadiriyya *shaykhs*. That the leader of the Suhrawardiyya in India should be called Makhdum-e Jahaniyan – "he whom all worldlings serve" – no doubt in part reflects the imperious personality of the man. When the mild and saintly Nizam-al-Din Awliya told the story of the saint who, flying over a greater saint's *khanaqah*, failed to show respect and so was thrown to the ground by that saint's power, he wanted in part to teach his listeners humility.[24] But the notion which all these stories embody, of the invisible hierarchy of the *shaykhs* of the *tariqas* and their invisible government of the world, is an inescapably political one. It is as if the Sufi *tariqas*, in an age when it was no longer feasible for a single conventional government to give unity to the whole of Islam, were able to offer not only a flexible element of social order, but also a correspondingly elastic sense of all-Islamic political unity.

The Arabic and Persian zones: Late medieval intellectual life

The social expansiveness of the Late Middle Ages was accompanied by a tendency to codification and conventionalization in most spheres of cultural life. Again we do not know why (It cannot be entirely blamed on the existence of *madrasas*, which after all could and often did provide a wide range of training.) But it does seem likely that this fact made it easier for the *tariqas* to perform such functions as they did perform in integrating the Islamic society. On the one hand, as Gibb has pointed out, a rigid maintenance of orthodoxy was required in the religious sphere to counterbalance the laxity of the Sufis and the animism of many of the new converts.[25] For after all the *tariqas* presupposed, and were

[24] *Fawaid al-Fuad*, lith. 1302 H., Lucknow, p. 3.
[25] Gibb, *Mohammedanism, a Historical Survey* p. 145.

supplementary to, the orthodox *sharia*. (It is scarcely possible to imagine even the antinomian Qalandars without a widespread common social context, and indeed without a literalistic *sharia* to rebel against.) Moreover, the relative drying up of some other channels of creativity meant that the Sufi orders could draw on the most effective and creative minds of the society.

In the High Middle Ages Islamic cultural life had come to be divided more or less sharply into two geographical zones, and this division became more marked after the Mongol conquests. In Arabia, the Fertile Crescent, Egypt, North Africa, and the Sudanese lands, Arabic continued to predominate as literary tongue even where it was not the spoken language. Cairo was the intellectual capital of this zone, though there were lesser centers, as in south Arabia or in Spain. From the Balkans east to Turkestan and China and south to southern India and into Malaysia, Persian became the standard literary language among Muslims, and with Persian came a whole tradition of literary and aristic taste. The seats of cultural life in this zone were legion, especially in Iran. This is the phenomenon that makes Toynbee distinguish, in the late medieval period, two Islamic "civilizations," an Iranic and an Arabic.[26] The division, however, was never very complete. In an area like Malaysia, for instance, there were both Arabic and Persian influences. Arabic was used for certain religious purposes throughout the Dar al-Islam, and in these matters the authors of one zone were read in the other. At the same time, the Persian zone undoubtedly contained the larger number of Muslims, and the tendency of Persian ways to affect Iraq, Egypt, and the rest of the Arabic zone was very old, and continued in the Late Middle Ages. The Islamic world presented by the *Thousand and One Nights* is one world.

The Persian zone was not only the more populous but also by and large the more culturally creative. But many lines of activity took the same turn in both. This period produced definitive compendia and textbooks of orthodox religious and legal scholarship; for instance, it was a Persian of the fourteenth century who composed the nearly definitive Arabic dictionary, the *Qamus*. Various secondary problems were traced out in the same fields – problems which had escaped the attention of earlier scholars – either in the form of little monographs or of commentaries on earlier writings. Natural science was even less significantly developed than orthodox religious scholarship. It continued especially in the Persian zone in the Arabized Hellenistic tradition as an intellectual

[26] *A Study of History*, Vol. I (Oxford: Oxford University Press, 1935), p. 70.

luxury. It still attracted creative minds in the generation of about 1300, the time of Qutb-al-Din al-Shirazi, who considered the possibility of the earth's rotation. But by this time Islamic science had already ceased to be an active fertilizing element abroad, either in China or the West, and likewise did not seek light itself from abroad. A scientific culture was maintained within the Islamic lands, but little was done to advance it. Thus the state of Islamic intellectual life at this time set the stage for the fateful isolatedness of the coming Western scientific outburst.

A marked feature of the period, consistent with the muting of intellectual creativity, was the tendency for literary prose, especially in the zone of Persian influence, to become increasingly afflicted with the cultivation of a resplendent but often inappropriate ornateness – a characteristic not readily cast aside later. In the field of history the masterfully fair-minded Rashid-al-Din Tabib, who set high standards of scholarly care and of direct composition at the start of the fourteenth century in a vast world history drawing on materials from Europe to China, was less imitated than the elegance of his contemporary, Wassaf, who gave much pertinent information smothered in skillfully florid verbiage. But history and biography were sedulously cultivated; as was also systematic ethics, in which the Aristotelian tradition (as interpreted by the Muslim Avicenna) received its definitive Islamic form in Iran by the end of the fifteenth century. Especially in Egypt relatively fresh work was done in systematizing the information and insight of the past on an encyclopedic level which could be in its own way seriously creative, in the hands of such men as Suyuti and Maqrizi; and head and shoulders above these stands the Tunisian Ibn-Khaldun at the end of the fourteenth century. In a long work which served as introduction to his valuable historical studies he made use of the encyclopedic approach – mobilizing the resources both of philosophy and of religious learning – to develop a trenchant analysis of the dynamics of history in general and in particular of Islamic history in his own times, which he saw as a time of decline. His new departure was not followed up.[27] Probably the most vital line of intellectual endeavor, as might be expected, was the development and the critique of Sufi theosophy. At the start of the period, the Syrian school of Ibn-Taymiyya was noted for its all-out opposition; most of the positive work was done in Iran, developing both the Ishraqi metaphysics of light and the cosmic monism associated with Ibn al-Arabi.

[27] The contrast between Ibn-Khaldun's approach and that of some of his predecessors is analyzed in Muhsin Mahdi's *Ibn Khaldun's Philosophy of History* (London: G. Allen and Unwin, 1957).

The preeminence of the Persian tradition: The arts

The most prominent presentation of mystical monism was the work of poets such as Jami in the fifteenth century, who wrote prose commentaries on mystical texts as well as embodying such ideas in his verse. Even Ibn al-Kari al-Jilili, the most systematic expositor of the school, thought of himself as a poet. For the indubitably greatest cultural medium of the age, if one excludes the visual arts, was poetry. Here the Arabic zone falls completely behind; Arabic poetry, though abundant, failed to achieve much novelty or distinction at least after the fourteenth century. But Persian poetry, which had seen a period of unsurpassed greatness in the High Middle Ages, continued to flourish in the Late Middle Ages, but its tradition was now internationalized in many parts of far-flung Islam. The fourteenth century in Iran is that of Hafiz of Shiraz, greatest of all Persian lyric poets; contemporary with him was a splendid constellation of satirists, lyricists, panegyrists, and mystics. At the same time Amir Khusraw of Delhi at the start of the fourteenth century was the fountainhead of a notable Indian school. The fifteenth century is that of Jami in Iran; and is marked by the rise to mastery of Turkish poetry, essentially modeled on the Persian. This was in three forms; most importantly the Chaghatai Turkish of Turkestan, with Nawai, but also the Turkish of Azerbaijan and that of the Ottomans.

Appropriately enough, this internationalization of the Persian poetic tradition was carried out under the aegis of Sufism. Almost universally a degree of mysticism pervaded every kind of poetry. Awhadi inculcated a mystical morality, while Ibn-i-Yamin produced ethico-philosophical didactic verse also mystically tinged. Credited with the cultivation of a finer nuancing in the poetic tradition is Khwaju, author of romantic-mystical epics. Katibi the panegyrist eventually retired as a Sufi; Maghribi wrote pure praises of unity in the Divine. Niamatullah, a Sufi *shaykh* himself, was famous for the apocalyptic prophecies which alternated with his more conventional mystical verse. A parodist adapted his mystical symbolism to the praise of foods. Above all, the *ghazals* of Hafiz, half ecstatic and half mundane, represent the saturation of the most worldly images with mystical overtones. One cannot look for a straight-forward poet like Firdawsi in an age which saw different levels of meaning in every gesture.

It is in the development of the visual arts that we are most impressively reminded that there are other highly creative elements in the late medieval culture than those associated with the expansion of Islam and the *tariqa-sharia* pattern of institutional and social flexibility. These arts, even more than poetry, were dependent on courts, such as there were;

for the visual arts required not only time for their practice, but costly materials. In any case, their development in the Late Middle Ages presages for us, in a way, the following period of the three empires. Though the art is still stamped with common Islamic veneer, and though there is still a wide circulation of artists through the Islamic lands, there is a wider variety of local styles than before.

The Arabic zone held its own architecture. There this period was the great age for building *madrasas,* theological schools, common in a cruciform pattern and associated with the mausoleum of the founder; a pattern broken up toward the end of the period as social needs changed.[28] This is the time of the delicately silhouetted Mamluk minarets of Cairo. Further west building in some degree was simpler, and the tradition of the solidly square minaret was maintained; but it is the time of the rich strength of the fourteenth-century palace, the Alhambra. But architecture was at least as effectively cultivated in the Persian zone, and with more variations. In Iran and Turkestan the Mongol rulers took readily to building in the old Islamic manner, with even increased magnificence; especially the tombs of rulers were built with a massive majesty, culminating usually in a high dome, as in the early fourteenth century tomb of Uljaytu at Sultaniyya, or the blue and gold mausoleum of Timur at Samarqand a century later. The domed tombs were popular in India also, but there the architecture both of Delhi and the provinces witnesses to a number of experiments in the adaptation of Hindu elements and technique which lend a special charm, for instance, to the ruins around the Qutb Minar. In Azerbaijan and in Ottoman Turkey a form of mosque was introduced, perhaps from Byzantine models, in which the main prayer room is under the dome, as in the Blue Mosque of Tabriz, instead of forming, as usually, and open court. (I mention, of course, only a few of the many sorts of great architectural achievements of the time.)

But in some ways the most interesting development was in the decorative arts and here the initiative and the highest development was limited to the Persian zone, though motifs spread into the Arabic zone. With the Mongols there came to Iran a strong Chinese influence, which was felt above all in the various decorative arts; and which led to its greatest results in mural and miniature painting. Painting had been in the High Middle Ages cultivated in both Arabic and Persian-speaking areas, but its late medieval transformation was largely a Persian achievement. In

[28] G. Marçais, *L'Art de l'Islam* (Paris: Larousse, 1946), p. 126; a work which is extremely useful yet, I maintain, misnamed; it concerns chiefly Arab art, illustrating perfectly the Arabistic bias.

the fourteenth century direct imitation of certain aspects and types of Chinese art was common; by the fifteenth century, in such centers of royal patronage as Samarqand and Herat, the Chinese impulse was being absorbed, and a series of distinctive styles emerged; till at the end of the fifteenth century the miniaturist Bihzad crowned the emergence of a fully independent art.

Renewed political orientation after 1500: The three empires

By now we are inevitably moving over into the period of the three empires. After 1500 the forces making for a single, decentralized, and essentially apolitical Islamic society – spread across the eastern hemisphere and held together by the *sharia* and the *tariqas* – were overbalanced by various contrary forces. To be sure, Islam continued, by and large, to expand, though not without significant setbacks. Moreover, to a degree it continued to form a single vast society. The common heritage was continuously reinforced by traveling Sufi's and merchants, and by the social and political interrelations of which an example is given in the various actions of Nadir Shah, ruler of Iran, who brought ruin to Delhi on the one hand and tried to reach a religious settlement with the Ottomans on the other. (Indeed, something of the historical unity of the Islamic peoples has survived or even been fostered by the European hegemony of the nineteenth century; thus one can find circulating in Oman a publication list of a Bombay publisher, covering a variety of religious and non-religious subjects, which is very like what we would find in Delhi except that there are listed fewer Lucknow reprints and more works by modern Egyptian lawyers.) Nevertheless, a number of forces combined to work against the sort of unity which was being developed in the Late Middle Ages. One such force was the advent of the West; but probably considerably more important were forces emerging from within the Islamic civilization: new cultural interests, illustrated in the development of art, which were not tied up with the international social order; and, above all, the relative cultural self-sufficiency of the new *political* units that now arose.

In the early sixteenth century there occurred a series of important political changes which restored the integral role of government in society, though in a form different from what Islam had known in the past. In most areas of Islam the ruling power now came to represent significant political ideas. In particular, the central lands of Islam were dominated by three great and relatively stable empires, each of which built up its own distinctive social life and each of which affirmed its cultural individuality to a degree and with a frankness never before known in Islam. At best these several societies maintained important fraternal relations with each other; at worst there was, as in the case of the Ottoman and Safavid societies, a sworn hostility which (as Nadir Shah was to discover) was a matter of the feelings of peoples and not mere dynastic quarrel. The larger Islamic society, instead of being a decentralized network of ever-varied but seamlessly interwoven Sufi fraternities and Muslim groupings under a common apolitical *sharia*, seemed tending to become a sort of federation of great, internally integrated blocs.

In the first place, the political changes seriously affected Islam's religious evolution. At least since the Mongol invasion, Islam as a religion had been the chief binding force for the many Muslim peoples, and the local military states that came and went might well be looked on as a necessary nuisance. The pious were urged to have as little to do with them as possible and the governments in turn interfered only sporadically and on a personal basis in the development of religion. In the period of the three empires, religions came to be again institutionally and even intellectually associated with the state and its fate. By the middle of the sixteenth century in the central lands the Muslim faith was moving on separate paths traced out by the great empires, while in the remoter areas it threatened to become culturally isolated.

Ismail, the head of the Shi'ite Safawiyya *tariqas* – which had the roots of its power in the decentralized ways of the late Middle Ages and which depended for its military strength on tribal Turks as was so characteristically the case at that time – seems to have precipitated many of the events. He set about conquering, at the star of the sixteenth century, as much of the Dar al-Islam as possible and forcing the Sunni populations to adopt Shi'ism. He failed to convert all Islam to the Shi'a, but he did carve out a lasting empire in Iran, the Safavid empire. There he insisted that everyone should publicly curse such heroes of early Islam as Umar and Abu-Bakr and follow the Shi'ite form of the *sharia*. The Sunni *tariqas* were suppressed and much blood spilled; Shi'ite books and teachers were brought in hastily from whatever corners of Islam – chiefly Arab – the Shi'a had been strong in,[29] and the autonomous body of Shi'ite *mujtahids* – authorized leading interpreters of the

[29] Such facts were pointed out already by E. G. Browne, *Literary History of Persia*, Vol. IV (Cambridge: Cambridge University Press, 1929) p. 360; one must stress the revolutionary implications for social life of the religious change in Iran, which would themselves, perhaps, be almost enough to account for the want of a great poetry in Safavid times which puzzled Browne, as Browne's correspondent points out (p. 24 ff.). Cf. also V. Minorsky, in G. von Grunebaum ed., *Unity and Variety in Muslim Civilization*, p. 196.

sharia gained an undisputed ascendancy. Though the original Shi'ism of the movement had been the rather esoteric faith of a Turkish *tariqa,* gradually the *mujtahids* were able to impose a Twelve Shi'ite orthodoxy, with an intense emotional life centered on the community mourning for the martyred *imams* rather than on Sufi rites, and sharply separated by the imperial boundaries from an unfriendly world beyond. Muhammad Baqir al-Majlisi, in the seventeenth century, was especially effective in putting the doctrine into definitive form with the aid of the political authorities. The areas incorporated in the Safavid empire, Persian, Turkish, or Arabic-speaking, have been insistently Shi'ite since; and the peoples incorporated in the modern Iranian monarchy (and with them most Iraqi's) were till recent times divided from their Sunni neighbors in the west, north, and east by an implacable wall of distrust – each side regarding the other as infidel.

The fortunes of the Shi'a everywhere were henceforth insistently related to the fact of the Shi'ite Safavid monarchy. In Ottoman territories the Shi'a paid for its Iranian triumph in great massacres which forced Shi'ite groups underground and left the official life overwhelmingly and self-consciously Sunnite. In India a number of Shi'ite monarchies, in the south and later even in the north, could draw inspiration and even help from Iran, which was after all the hearth of so much of the culture of the Persian zone, to which India belonged. The tension between Sunnism and Shi'ism became a plague of international politics.

From being a dynamic frontier state in the Balkans and Anatolia, the Ottomans, in the course of the wars launched by Ismail the Safavid, became a great Sunnite empire consciously opposed to the Shi'ite one, when they extended their rule to include most of the Arab lands. One of the most remarkable features of the Ottoman constitution was the manner of incorporating the *sharia* and its guardians the *ulama* into the political organism. The *sharia,* though as always supplemented or overreached by secular legislation, was given an effective place of honor in the state; and to assure the interdependence of the two, the *ulama* were to some degree hierarchically organized. *Muftis* became state officials of great importance, and the head of the *ulama* the *shaykh al-Islam,* came during the sixteenth century to have a constitutional position almost on a level with the Sultan by whom, however, he was appointed. The Sultan himself emphasized his character as head of the whole body of orthodox Muslims and their representative against the infidels; and the expansion of the Ottoman empire, and at the end of our period its reverses, were regarded as those of Islam itself.

In northern India arose a third great empire, the Mogul, which rivalled in splendor the Ottoman and the Safavid.[30] Building on the traditions of the Delhi sultanate to some extent, but developing an effective and enduring central administration, the Mogul empire fostered a society in which, under a Muslim lead, Muslims and Hindus shared in a common political and cultural life which in important sectors they carried out in common.[31] The emperor Akbar, the first to have an effectively long reign, tried to establish for the Islam of his empire a recognized independence, with himself at its head.[32] This attempt failed, in fact; but Indian Islam remained nonetheless a world to itself, in which – in contrast to the practice in the Ottoman empire, which also possessed large non-Muslim populations but rigorously excluded them (as such) from political privileges – non-Muslims did not even pay the legal poll-tax. Indian Islam was distinguished not only by its special relations to Hinduism (at all levels) but by its own emotional tone – especially illustrated in the Shi'ite-like festivals the Sunnites hold in honor of Hasan and Husayn. The attempt of the emperor Awrangzeb to change the character of Indo-Muslim society for one more orthodoxly Muslim contributed to the breakup of the Mogul empire.

All three empires, naturally, modified the social patterns of their areas, which then went through complex changes as the character of the empires changed. I shall note only two points, illustrating the pervasive effect of the empires' structures. In India the very presence of the Muslims as a bloc fluidly differentiated by class in direct contrast to the castes had its effect not only on the Hindus but on the Muslims. While many of the lower Hindu castes seem to have turned Muslim outright, and caste came to be found in Muslim villages, the upper ranges of the caste system became adjusted to the role of the Muslims as tolerant rulers and arbiters and to co-operation with them, as the almost Islamic character of the Kayastha Brahmins witnesses. The Muslim upper classes, needing to set themselves off from the flourishing indigenous tradition, came to claim rank according to alleged sacred or foreign extraction – as Shaykhs or Sayyids, as Moguls, Afghans, or Turks. As to the Ottoman empire, considering that its structure was able to last for six centuries, it is no surprise to find that it was unique in a number of ways socially and

[30] Though Babur's adventures are closely linked to those of Ismail the Safavid, the Mogul empire proper was not permanently launched till half a century later; but the Afghan interlude which followed the exile of Humayun was developing the same administrative tendencies and for our purposes can be reckoned a part of the same development.

[31] Cf. K. M. Panikkar, *Survey of Indian History* (Bombay: Asia Publishing House, 1954), in the chapters on medieval and Mogul times.

[32] This is clearly the sense of the so-called "Infallibility Decree," which is the most significant of his religious acts for the Islam of his empire.

politically. The whole society was divided into functionally differentiated socio-religious bodies, such as the guilds, whose activities were effectively controlled by the government. On the basis of carefully compiled statistics, population moves were systematically carried out from one part of the empire to another for economic or for political reasons,[33] and the control of the economy at the height of the empire was very efficient. Within such a pattern, the *devshirme* was merely the most curious feature – the elaborate system by which the best of the non-Muslim youth was drafted into military and administrative service (after semi-voluntary Islamization and a rigid training) to the exclusion of born Muslims. Eventually the Muslim upper classes learned to bypass this restriction, making their way into the civil service to the great detriment of the state.

Breakdown of the system of international unity

It is not clear why these great and relatively stable empires came to be established at this time, in such striking contrast to the immediately preceding period, but it is likely that the invention of gunpowder and its use in cannon, which had lately developed in China and was having important effects in Europe at this time, helped to produce them by giving a strong advantage to a central power with large resources as compared with lesser authorities. In any case, their existence had its repercussions in the rest of the Dar al-Islam. For one thing, all of these empires faced away from the Indian Ocean; independent Egypt, and subsequently, independent Gujarat, Muslim powers with a direct interest in the Indian Ocean trade, were absorbed by the Ottoman and Mogul empires not long after the Christians from the West, above all Portuguese, had arrived in the area. Whatever may have made possible the initial Portuguese triumph, it is likely that the dominance of what remained above all land empires helped assure their relatively easy persistence in control of the seas. The Ottoman government did make some efforts to retrieve the Muslim position, but nothing to match its successful efforts to control the Mediterranean, and it eventually withdrew. The Moguls did almost nothing.

Eventually, the south Arabians of Oman and Hadramawt were able to accomplish a great deal on their own account against the Portuguese,

[33] Omer Lutfi Barkan, "Les Déportations comme méthode de peuplement et decolonisation dans l'empire ottoman," *Revue de la Faculté des Sciences Économiques de l'Universite d'Istanbul*, 11th year, 1953.

but they could never reverse the cardinal fact that the long-haul oceanic trade had passed into Western control. In Arabia, in East Africa, in Malaysia, the Muslims were placed essentially on the defensive, even though in the Indonesian areas, apart from Portuguese seaports, they were increasing their power. At the same time, they had occasion to become spiritually more independent of the more central areas. Among both the eastern Arabs and the Persians, as well as in south India and Malaysia, the Shafi'ite school of *sharia* law had tended to be predominant. With the incorporation of the *sharia* tradition into the state organization in the Ottoman empire, the Hanafite school was given the supremacy throughout the empire over the historically preeminent Shafi'ites; while at the same time the Shafi'ites were suppressed in Shi'ite Iran. Though Cairo remained an important center, the center of gravity of the Shafi'ite tradition tended to shift to the Indian Ocean coasts.

The Muslims of the north suffered at the same time serious setbacks, and also became relatively isolated. Those of the Volga came under Russian rule (and eventually those of the Crimea also, though allied with Turkey); while Turkestan was divided between the long-pagan Kazaks and the culturally not much more stimulating Uzbek rulers, bitterly at war with Shi'ite Iran. The Muslims of the Central Eurasian highlands were eventually conquered by the Manchu empire and, like the Muslims of China itself, had little opportunity for contact with vital Muslim centers.

In the west the Ottoman power reached as far as Algeria; but Morocco, under a Sharifian dynasty claiming descent from Mohammed, which now replaced the insignificant Berber dynasties of the Late Middle Ages, maintained not only its political but its religious independence. The Sharif was honored as a holy personage, and adherence to him was almost the touchstone of the faith; by the end of the sixteenth century much of Muslim western Africa had accepted this allegiance, and parts of it have tended to look to Morocco as a religious model ever since, though in the western and central Sudan sultanates eventually rose which tried to emulate the Moroccan religious position of leadership. The earlier inclination to regard the rest of Islam as fallen away was only confirmed; the far west was almost self-sufficient. Culturally, Morocco stagnated. And though adherents for Islam continued to be won in the Sudan, the level which Timbuctu had already achieved before the Moroccan conquest seems to have been exceeded there.

In this dislocated society the *tariqas* continued to be found almost everywhere (though in the Safavid domain only in impoverished circumstances), and they played even an increasing part in local life; but they could not play the same international role. In Ottoman territories the *tariqas* favored by the Turks received something of an official position – even the Bektashiyya received this dubious privilege[34] – and enjoyed great pomp. The heads of the North African orders played at least as great a role, though on a somewhat different basis; their heads – like the Sharif – received an almost anthropolatrous devotion from the people. Foreign orders, such as the Qadiriyya, were introduced freely into India to supplement, and perhaps dilute, the traditional ones. Most of the great orders steadily increased their territorial range and one or another order was introduced into every corner of Islam – thus with the saint Abd-al-Rauf in the seventeenth century, the Shattariyya gave self-confidence to a strong mysticism in newly converted Malaysia.

But the orders came to show less originality; they were many of them wealthy and shot through with popular superstition. The most interesting of the new branches of *tariqas* now set up were those devoted to reform. Reform was sometimes carried out by orthodox *ulama* working within a Sufi framework, such as Ahmad Sirhindi at the beginning of the seventeenth century in India, whose main object was to correct in an orthodox sense the tolerance of free speculation which had been common in the *tariqas* of the late Middle Ages; but who accomplished this by claiming for himself more intensive mystical experiences than his rivals could boast.[35] Sometimes reform was the work of simple and pious mystics. But there also arose in Arabia in the eighteenth century a reform movement which was radically and frankly anti-Sufi, that of the Wahhabis, which was to have far-reaching effects in the following century.

Interrelated development of separate regional cultures

In the three great empires the visual arts were on a high level and magnificently productive, and they continued to be unmistakably Islamic in character. But their cultivation did not serve to maintain the international Islamic order as it had been developing. For that, art was a very secondary matter; a village mosque in Kerala has its own solemnity, but with its pitched roof it bears almost no resemblance to the mosques of the great tradition as represented in the Deccan or North India or

[34] The Bektashiyya retained an independent spirit, nevertheless, as J. K. Birge has shown, *The Bektashi Order of Dervishes* (Hartford: Hartford Seminary Press, 1937), p. 159.

[35] Cf. Burhan Ahmad Faruqi, *The Mujaddid's Conception of Tawhid* (Lahore: Shah Muhammad Ashraf, 1943), p. 18 f., 64 ff.; this modern study is one example of the influence of these thinkers on the promoters of Pakistan.

Turkey. Rather the arts served to set off and glorify the several great regional societies.

In the Safavid empire architecture was represented most perfectly in the magnificence of the imperial city of Isfahan with its garden boulevards and open, landscaped palaces and impressive use of columns. The floral type of decoration was enriched with every sort of form, including motifs borrowed ad hoc from Europe and China. A high level of elegance was maintained till the end of the seventeenth century, after which political catastrophes put an end to the great age of building, which was linked to the fate of the dynasty and the capital. In the Ottoman empire Iranian elements, such as the use of blue tiles, continued important; but in the sixteenth century in the cardinal field of mosque architecture the Turks perfected a fully new type. Already the domed prayer hall had been developed in west-Turkish lands; it was now perfected practically under the shadow of the Hagia Sophia (but with a totally different effect from the Byzantine – the sense of space is one of ordered extension rather than of monumental bulk). This development was led by the military engineer Sinan, who turned his hand to baths, palaces, fountains, tombs, and every sort of building as well as mosques, each time creating a masterpiece. The new type of mosque was built throughout the empire, in the Arab as well as in the Turkish-European areas, and the peculiar pointed minarets that usually went with it are like an emblem of the empire. Finally, in the Mogul empire of northern India the Indo-Muslim style of architecture was brought to fulfillment in the mighty works of Fatehpur-Sikri and the gleaming Taj Mahal, together with a host of other gems large and small.

Architecture has for Islam always been the supreme form of visual art, and it continued so everywhere in this period also. But painting, both mural and miniature, was cultivated in all three empires and very highly developed in the Safavi and Mogul empires. The important school of Tabriz, the first Safavi capital, followed the lead of Bihzad. Early in the seventeenth century the school of Isfahan, the later capital, found its most outstanding master in Riza Abbasi, who excelled in portraits and in genre scenes, in which he shows a subtle sense of humor. He was not without Western influence. In the Ottoman empire the miniaturists, though they attempted with much success to follow the Persian example, did not achieve quite such high distinction, perhaps because painting was frowned on by the *ulama* who played so important a role in the structure of the empire. In the Mogul empire, on the contrary, the art, at first imported from Iran, took on a vigorous independent form. Portraiture was very highly developed as well as the depiction of every sort of legendary and Indian theme. The art was cultivated not only by the Muslims but among the Hindus, particularly among the Rajputs.

It must be added that almost every fine art and craft was practiced with great skill in all the empires. Calligraphy was regarded – as before – as one of the highest arts, and its masters much esteemed. In northern India the Islamic tradition of vocal and instrumental music (and, of course, of dancing) was crossed with Hindu taste to give birth to the subtle northern school of all-Indian music, prized by Muslims and Hindus alike.

As Arnold has pointed out, the visual arts, and especially painting, were not only extremely sophisticated at this time, but had gradually come to be accorded unprecedented respect by such representatives of the public as historians and biographers.[36] The artist, or among the Ottomans, at least, the architect,[37] sometimes had, if not the standing of one of the *ulama*, at least something like that accorded to the poet and the singer. But these arts were courtly, or at least associated with great established houses. Outside the three empires, whether in the Arabic or in the Persian sphere of influence, they were far less cultivated.

Poetry also came to be an expression of the regional cultures at least as much as of an international Sufism. In Iran itself, though poets stately and sweet continued to produce profusely, nothing could match the giants of the past; some of the greatest of Persian poets were more appreciated in India and Turkey than at home (and indeed many of them went to live at the Mogul court). In northern India the main vehicle of Islamic verse long continued to be Persian; but in the Deccan there flourished, by the sixteenth century, a Sufi poetry in Urdu, the common language of Muslims in northern and central India; this poetry developed not only traditional Persian themes but also themes taken from the Hindu background. By the eighteenth century Urdu had come to be used in the north as well, and produced classical masters who were greatly appreciated by certain groups of Hindus as well as by Muslims. In the Ottoman empire it was Turkish that was most cultivated. For Arabic, though dialects of it were spoken in much of the empire, played a distinctly secondary role in cultivated life, being treated almost as a dead classical tongue. With the advent of the Uzbeks in Turkestan, the Chaghatai Turkish that had led the field in the time of Nevai tended to languish, though it was still used throughout the north. But Fuzuli of Baghdad in the sixteenth century, who also composed in Persian and

[36] Thomas Arnold, *Painting in Islam* (Oxford: Oxford University Press, 1928), 32–37, speaks especially of the recognition given from the times of Magrizi and Khwandamir on.

[37] Leo A. Mayer, *Islamic Architects and Their Works* (Geneva: A. Kundig, 1956), p. 28, notes the high status of at least some architects in the Ottoman empire after 1500.

Arabic, did his best work in the Turkish of Azerbaijan, and has been called the greatest Turkish poet of all times.[38] Finally, modeling itself on the master poet Baqi of the sixteenth century, the western or Ottoman literature became the most important of the three forms of Turkish. Each *tariqa* had its own poetic tradition, and the Turkish work is generally regarded as more valuable than the contemporary Persian poetry.

Outside the great empires new Islamic literary languages also sprang up. On the east African coast Swahili, which had been developed as the language of the Muslim Bantu, came to possess a sophisticated poetic tradition which could rival Arabic within the region. At the other end of the Indian Ocean a Malay literature grew up under the influence of Persian, and consisting in large part of renderings from Persian and from Urdu. It also took over much from the earlier Malaysian heritage, particularly in poetic forms, only partly Persianized. All of these regional literatures – Arabic, Persian, Turkish (in three forms), Urdu, Swahili, Malay – as well as some lesser Muslim languages which began to be cultivated in this period, used the Arabic alphabet, were infiltrated with Arabic and (in most cases) Persian words, and treated traditional Arabic and Persian themes in their poetry. But of the literature then being produced, it was Persian alone that had an audience among most of the other peoples; and even it was little read in the Arabic zone except so far as Turkish rule imported it.

The intellectual life of the three empires likewise built on a common heritage, but served to meet the special problems which arose in each empire. Throughout the Dar al-Islam history was written, usually of the local or regional Muslim community, its learned men and its rulers. The Turkish historians of Ottoman times are especially noteworthy, the most celebrated being Ali Chelebi of the late sixteenth century who, like many other scholars, could write prose without overaffectation despite the heritage of floridity from the Late Middle Ages. Travel literature and other sorts of descriptive prose were of course also at a high level.

Iran was an influential center of philosophical thought, which, however, developed themes broached before, particularly in Sufi circles. In the seventeenth century arose a school of mystical theologians, teachers and students of Mulla Sabra, in whose system monism was pushed to a subtle extreme in exploring the relation of personal consciousness to cosmic structure. The philosophical thought was often tied up with special Shi'ite problems – notably at last in the case of the Shaykhi – as was suitable in Shi'ite Iran. In fact, with the Shi'a a majority, the whole basis

[38] Cf. Mehmed Fuad Koprula-Zade in *E.I.*, "Turkish Literature."

of religious life had to be rethought in Shi'i terms. Gradually there emerged a corps of *mujtahids* which maintained a vigorous intellectual independence within the new orthodox limits.

Mogul India produced a series of thinkers who devoted themselves to the problems of coexistence with Hinduism, sometimes under a favorable impression of Hinduism, as in the case of prince Dara Shikoh; more often in an attempt to reassert, in historical or in psychological terms, the superior social value of a dominant Islam, as in the tradition leading up to Shah Wali-Allah. Among theme they helped to forge the cultural and intellectual tradition which bound Muslims together as an Islamic community in the Indic subcontinent; a tradition without which the geographical monstrosity of Pakistan would be incomprehensible, and the passionate advocacy by many Pakistani leaders of Urdu as a preeminently Muslim language would seem absurd.[39]

It must be added that natural science was for the most part a mere tradition, the effective standards of which probably declined everywhere. It is a rare example of escape from this tradition when Ottoman geographers, who in the fifteenth century had made use of Arab empirical studies of the Indian Ocean to improve their scholarly learning, in the sixteenth century made similar use of the Western explorations.

In all three empires scholarly life was many-sided and often very sound, if not usually highly creative. Outside of them Islamic intellectual life was sometimes rather rudimentary. In the Turkish north the excellent memoirs of Babur, who himself came south to found the Mogul empire, seem to have marked a high point in the prose tradition, though an orthodox Muslim learning was maintained. Within the Ottoman empire some Arab talent was drawn into the general Ottoman life: but neither within the Ottoman empire nor in the several Arab lands outside it was there more than routine achievement in the Arabic tradition. A figure like Sharani, a mystical thinker of the sixteenth century who brought a warm personal touch to the older patterns, was exceptional. In the countries of the Sudan the sacred law was taught, and history composed, in Arabic; no local language being able, during this period, to

[39] Since Urdu is, properly speaking, a mother-tongue chiefly in just those areas which remained in India, its use in Pakistan might seem to be an anomaly forced by the *U.P.-wallas* contrary to the trends of the time. Particularly in Bengal it is quite alien. But it was Urdu which was the final vehicle of that all-India Islamic culture to which the founders of Pakistan were looking back, more than to simply a vague all-Islamic sentiment. The chief flourishing centers of that all-India culture (except Lahore) were in Urdu-speaking territory in the north or the south of what is now India. To accept the vernaculars of the actual territory of Pakistan would be tantamount to admission that Pakistan as constituted cannot, after all, revive the old and glorious all-India Islamic society.

replace it. In Malaysia there were controversies, largely secondhand but applied to situations arising from local habits of mind, over the nature of Sufi monism. Though there were intellectual problems in the several regions common to all the participants in the Islamic tradition, there seem to have been no all-Islamic intellectual movements.

The decline after 1700

The two centuries from 1500 to 1700 were by and large a time of relatively strong institutions, of a confident intellectual life, and above all of imposing esthetic creation. By 1700 the social and institutional structure of each of the three empires was weakened, and soon after 1700 all were giving clear evidence of decline. The Ottoman empire came to be dependent for its territorial integrity on the disunity of its European enemies. The Safavi empire was destroyed in a rising of Afghan tribes, and only inadequately restored under less polished rulers. The Mogul empire was broken up entirely, and not only Muslim but Hindu powers fought for its fragments, even while recognizing the suzerainty of its titular head. It seems likely that the increasing activities of Western Europe in the eighteenth century, by upsetting the established patterns of interregional trade, helped to undermine the economy in some areas.[40] But the internal dialectic of Islam itself cannot be held blameless.

In this century of disaster, the trend to independent regional evolution became still more marked, while by and large the cultural vigor of all the Islamic peoples declined. It is at this time that Urdu effectively replaced Persian in India, and it is at this time that Ottoman Turkish broke away most effectively from the Persian tradition, in the Tulip Age; yet by the end of the century (or the early part of the next) both Turkish and Urdu poetry are conceded to have been at a low point. In Iran itself the whole century represented a literary trough. The Iranian art of the miniature also declined in the eighteenth century, and imitations of Western art as well as of Indo-Muslim art failed to revive it. Iranian architecture was not renewed after the taking of Isfahan by the Afghans; while in European and Anatolian Turkey an Italianate style, modeled without too much inspiration on the Western Renaissance architecture, came into favor for palaces

[40] Cf. Gibb and Bowen, *Islamic Society and the West*, Vol. I, Part 1, pp. 296, 307 ff. To a certain degree the unhealthy influence of the new West probably went back to the sixteenth century. Cf. also W. H. Moreland, *India at the Death of Akbar, an Economic Study* (London: Macmillan, 1920), who suggests that already under the cosmopolitan Mogul court at that time, with its delight in Japanese, Chinese, Persians, Arabs, and Europeans, and in their goods, native industry was suffering.

and homes. Despite some fine poetry, it was perhaps the least creative century in the history of Islam. It was then that the tendency to purist religious reform that had been apparent throughout the period took radical form among the Wahhabis in the center of Arabia.

Later Islamic society and the rise of the West

Islamic history in the period of the three empires was very nearly the same as world history; at least, it represents the more normal part of world history. In the northwest were the lands of Christian Europe, relatively restricted in area, to which we shall return; in the northeast were the relatively isolated Confucian empires; most of the highly populated or highly cultured lands between were at least within the orbit of Islam. Beyond, in southern Africa, in Australasia, in the Americas, in Arctic Siberia, were thinly populated lands as yet of little apparent importance. Islam, having absorbed so much territory, and seeming to be on the way to absorbing the rest (for this was its conscious program), might seem to be articulating itself in regional societies after a pattern which could be applied to the whole world, in which Muslim solidarity and a common heritage would make for mutual intelligibility without requiring closer association. In fact, whatever the Islamic societies might have in common, there was a tendency for their historical interrelations to be only to a degree closer with each other than with any other regions of the eastern hemisphere. Each empire used the Chinese invention of cannon, together with European or Turkish improvements thereon. The wealthy of Mogul India imported not only Persian luxuries, but European and Chinese specialties. A lagging Persian art turned both to India and to Europe for a like sort of shallow stimulus. The world of Islam – and with it the various lands of the Far East (and together these made up most of the human world) – was living at a historical tempo approximately as rapid as had prevailed in civilized history for five thousand years; and at this tempo civilization continued gradually adding to its cultural resources while building up sophisticated societies in loose interconnection with each other.

These interconnections were somewhat intensified at this time by the world-wide activities of European traders. In this period, however, the role of Europe was for the most part limited to ocean trade, though by the eighteenth century Europeans came to have more and more noticeable influence. The Western Europeans were long weak on land – till the eighteenth century – not only in the Indian Ocean area, where even the islands whose interior they controlled were few, but also in Europe, where the Ottomans continued on the offensive till the end of the seventeenth century. They played a minor and rather indirect role in the changes which make us contrast the world position of Islam in the Late Middle Ages on the one hand and on the other its dominant trends in the period of the three empires. These Islamic developments, on the contrary, did not play a major role in preparing the way for the Western expansion. The wide activity of Muslim merchants had played a major part, for instance, in opening up the trade-routes which the Europeans then took over ready made, and in weakening the traditional Hindu and Buddhist powers in such places as Sumatra and Java. Above all, it was the internal weakness of Islam which left a cultural and economic vacuum into which the West could pour.

For behind the seemingly unimportant activities of the Westerners lay all-important transformations going on within Europe itself, which immensely speeded up the pace of historic events there, and were preparing a momentous superiority in social and economic organization on the part of the West, which must reveal itself explosively sooner or later. In the generation about 1800 occurred the French Revolution and critical phases of the Industrial Revolution in England. In the same one generation the British seized hegemony in India (where late in the eighteenth century they still controlled only a province or so); the French landed in Egypt and awoke the Arabs; the British and Dutch reorganized Indonesia; the Turks learned to put through Westernizing reforms; and almost all Muslim peoples found they must adjust themselves to an economic, if not a political domination by a West which was no longer merely an unusually strong trading people, but was a carrier of unexplored but dynamic new ways of living.

In an essay ranging over the history of half humanity in periods at least as complex historically as most periods in history, I have been forced to leave out whole aspects of culture and do ridiculously scant justice to others. My excuse has been my attempt to place the later Islam in a world-historical setting. I have tried to suggest some lines along which to analyze the unfolding of Islamic civilization in its later periods as a dynamic cultural heritage, notably inquiring in what consists the unity of its history. At the same time I have tried to underline the important place the course of that civilization must hold in any history of mankind as a whole.

10

Modernity and the Islamic heritage

What can historical processes mean for the moral individual?[1] In particular, what are the moral implications of the acceleration of the pace of historical change in modern times? Here I shall tackle only a few aspects of such questions; I shall deal with the acceleration of history as it confronts concerned Muslims in particular. But I refer to Muslims and not just as believers in a given creed, but rather as participants in a great cultural heritage prevalent in a wide part of the modern world. What I have to say about the case of the Muslims, will, I think, have some relevance for all moral individuals in our times.

I am discussing the concerned individual – the person who consciously attempts to bring to bear high cultural ideas, not only in the private life but in the society he is a part of. History sometimes seems to proceed almost independently of the hopes and the anguish of such people. 'Yet they are, after all, the only ones worth discussing history seriously with; for they at least are paying attention to it in a morally responsible way. For that reason alone, their plight would be important to the historian. But in fact such people supply much of the flexibility of imagination and the richness of spirit which make possible such positive development as does come at points of challenge or of crisis, where otherwise there is too often mere blind floundering. Accordingly, their place in the historical process can be, on occasion, determinative. Their spiritual and cultural problems, their concern with the need for roots in a coherent heritage, their attempts to give ideal form to the diverse demands of their age, have palpable, sometimes tragic and sometimes magnificent effects on the actual course of events.

[1] This paper was delivered on 20th April, 1960, to a seminar of the Committee on Social Thought at The University of Chicago in a series devoted to "the meaning of the historical process for the moral individual." It has been somewhat revised for publication.

The Modern acceleration of history as a world-wide event

Before I enter into the moral problems raised, I shall have to sketch the nature of the modern acceleration of history as it appears on the world scale. For on the level of world history this acceleration, this speeding up of events which we are all so excitedly or so desperately aware of, is too commonly misinterpreted. Sometimes it is made merely a common stage in a sequence through which all peoples pass, each in its own time.[2] As we shall see, this is to oversimplify badly. Sometimes it is made merely a feature of Occidental history, having only secondary effects elsewhere.[3] This approach is often more sophisticated than the first and must therefore be paid special attention. But in the end it is, perhaps, even more misleading. For our purposes, it is important that the reader see how far the advent of the Modern historical impulse has been a single, unparallelable, world-wide event.

Unfortunately, the misconceptions I refer to are not restricted to Westerners, although they originated in the West. Modern Muslims have adopted both their geographical and their historical conceptual frameworks largely from Western writers; on the whole, they have modified the Western historical image only superficially, giving Islam, as far as possible, a share in the heroic role otherwise ascribed to the West. As the Western historical image is ethnocentric in its very categories and terminology, not just in its conclusions, the Muslims have not escaped its effects.[4]

When the acceleration of history is thought of from a strictly Occiden-

[2] We find variations of this approach from Condorcet through Marxism to Rostow, with his crucial "take-off stage," which allows only secondary modifications from land to land. How sound studies can be which nevertheless are subject to the weakness here cited is illustrated in the useful volumes edited by Bert F. Hoselitz, *The Progress of Under-developed Areas* (The University of Chicago Press, 1952), and *Agrarian Societies in Transition*, in *Annals: American Academy of Political and Social Science*, Vol. 305, 1956.

[3] An American example is Henry Adams; recent examples are exceedingly numerous, for instance, Daniel Halévy, *Essair sur l'accélération de l'histoire* (Paris: Iles d'or 1943); J. G. De Beus, *The Future of the West* (London: *Eyre and Spottiswoode*, 1953), or Christopher Dawson, *Dynamics of World History* (New York: Sheed and Ward, 1956), which is outstanding. The most famous recent writer to make the Modern acceleration a function of the peculiarity of Occidental culture is, of course, Toynbee. To be sure, the distinction here made between the two approaches is quite schematic. The better writers almost elude such classification; thus the remarkable work of Andre Varagnac, *De la préhistoire au monde moderne: essai d'une anthropodynamique*, (Paris: Plon, 1954) presents an attractive scheme of universal stages while remaining persuasively Europocentric in its concrete analysis.

[4] Cf. Marshall G. S. Hodgson, "In the Center of the Map," *Unesco Courier* (March or May 1956), for a brief suggestion of the way in which the Western Medieval worldview has persisted into Modern times in a scientific disguise. (The illustrations there are inconsistent with the text and have nothing to do with it).

tal point of view, the relative rapidity of historical change in our times is traced back, almost without intermission, to early Medieval times within Western Europe. It is noticed that almost from the time of Charlemagne on – from the very origins of a distinctively West-European society – the pace of cultural change, of innovation, and particularly of increase in technical and cognitive power, gradually became more and more rapid, till in recent centuries it has become ever more exhilarating – or frightening. In the nineteenth century, Europe saw more change than in a great many earlier centuries together, and in the twentieth century a single decade seems to see almost as much increase in the sheer bulk of technical knowledge as the whole of the nineteenth century. All this is seen as essentially characteristic of the West-European civilization down to the present. That is, it is thought of as a key feature which specially distinguishes the society which produced Charlemagne, Richard Lion-Heart, Charles V, Napoleon, and Churchill from all other societies, which are thought of as essentially unchanging. A British poet speaks of preferring "fifty years of Europe" to "a cycle of Cathay."

Accordingly, the problems the process poses – economic, social, and above all moral – are thought of as the problems of "Western Civilization," and the future many are troubled about is the future of "Western Civilization." The problems of other societies are thought of as essentially different, to be interpreted primarily in terms of their own past traditions, which would be more static or more spiritual, depending on the point of view. Or else, to the extent that they are adopting modern practices (called "Western" ways), the other societies are thought of as being at least superficially "Westernized," absorbed into the long heritage of the Occident; in this case, they are thought of as sharing in the problems posed by the acceleration of history essentially on the same terms as the Occident itself – with a time lag and perhaps minor local variations, and only to the extent that they do become effectively an extension of the Occident. Accepting such an analysis, but interpreting the special Western traits negatively rather than positively, some Muslims persuade themselves that if they can avoid both Westernization and Western control, they can escape the modern "Western" problems.

But this point of view generally rests on the conceptions of world history found in those Western high school texts which trace the whole human story primarily from Babylonia and Egypt, through classical Greece and then Rome, to Medieval Western Europe and thence to the Modern Occident, bringing in other areas only parenthetically and by way of contrast except as they touch Western Europe. It presupposes the traditional Western ethnocentric division of the civilized world into the

"West" (itself) and the "East" (all the other societies), in which the West may be smaller, but is considered at least the equivalent of all the rest together in importance. (It is an indication of how blindly some Muslims have accepted the Western conceptual framework, that they have accepted this dichotomy also.)

Seen in a wider setting, the historical career of the West-Europeans was eccentric but not remarkably outstanding until quite modern times. Above all, it was integral with the whole wider Afro-Eurasian historical life. There was a continual accumulation of technique and of knowledge, a continual expansion of the geographical limits of urban, literate society in most parts of the zone of Afro-Eurasian civilizations for some several millenniums.[5] This was not peculiar to Western Europe – in fact, until recently the main centers of this growth were elsewhere: in China, in India, in the Middle East, in Eastern Europe. Moreover, this cumulative growth was everywhere, on the whole, accelerating: in the later millenniums the rate of historical changes for the Afro-Eurasian civilized zone as a whole, in particular the rate of accumulation of technique and knowledge, was distinctly more rapid than in the earlier millenniums. It must be added that, partly as a result of continuous interchange and interaction, the level of growth remained approximately constant throughout the civilized zone. Give or take five hundred years, the various civilizations kept roughly abreast: the Medieval Chinese and the Medieval Byzantines were about equidistant from the ancient Sumerians. In these respects, Western Europe simply formed part of a wider historical complex and shared its most generalized characteristics.

There were two ways in which Western Europe, before about 1600, appears as atypical. Cultural and territorial growth was more rapid than in the more central areas; and notably in the Italian Renaissance, there were outbursts of high cultural creativity of an excellence unusual in Afro-Eurasian history. But on investigation it can be shown that these two traits do not, of themselves separate Western Europe from the main lines of historical development of the rest of the Afro-Eurasian historical complex. On the one hand, the relatively rapid growth was in large part that of a frontier – for Western Europe formed, in effect, one of the zones of frontier growth of the Afro-Eurasian complex. It can be compared in certain key points to the rapid growth of civilized culture in the Sudanic lands or in Malaysia in the same period; or, in even more interesting ways, to that in Korea and Japan. In each case there was a relatively late and relatively

[5] For a closer analysis of the wider setting of hemispheric history see my "Interrelations of Societies in History," to appear in *Comparative Studies in Society and History.*

rapid increase in urbanization, along with a rapid rise in the sophistication of cultural activity; in each case, the new cultural ideas were largely borrowed from earlier centers, and creativity was often a matter of adaptation to local conditions and assimilation with older local traditions, rather than a major contribution to human life as such. (It is unfortunately not within the scope of this paper to document all this at present; the degree in which Medieval West-European growth borrowed from Arabic and Greek centers, and even indirectly from so far afield as the Chinese, is one of the most intriguing fields of recent research[6]; less has been done with the cases of Sudan and Malaysia.)

On the other hand, though the bursts of cultural creativity of late Medieval and Renaissance Western Europe were unusual, they also were by no means unparalleled in Afro-Eurasian history. Even apart from the great classical flowerings of the ages of Confucius, Buddha, Isaiah, and Socrates, there appear other major cultural renovations from time to time, such as those of Gupta India, with its distant repercussions, and that of classical Islam, which ultimately transformed the face of half mankind. Even the sixteenth-century West-European domination of the ocean trade-routes, replacing in part an Islamic domination, was scarcely a more astonishing achievement than the late Medieval expansion of the Dar-al-Islam over half Europe and most of India and throughout the Southern Seas. In the sixteenth century the West-Europeans still dealt on essentially equal terms with the other peoples of the Afro-Eurasian historical complex. These atypical traits in West-European history do indeed bear closely on the fact that the great modern transformations occurred in precisely the West-European area. But, taken in themselves, they are insufficient grounds for making the pre-Modern acceleration of the pace of history a peculiarly West-European or Occidental trait. The acceleration within Western Europe was clearly a part of a much wider picture, and cannot soundly be understood except in that wider context.

It is in the seventeenth and eighteenth centuries – from about 1600 to about 1800 – that the transformation occurred in Western Europe which put the Occidental peoples on a fundamentally different historical basis from their neighbors with whom they had till then shared the broad, slow movements of Afro-Eurasian development. By 1800, the Europeans and their overseas settlers found themselves in a position to dominate, almost without question, the rest of the world. Only two hundred years before, they had dealt on equal terms – sometimes getting the worst of

[6] Joseph Needham's *Science and Civilization in China* (Cambridge: Cambridge University Press, 1954) is the most striking work, but not necessarily the most cautious.

the encounter, as often with Ottoman Turkey, sometimes getting the better, but with no greater differential in social power than already had long existed here and there among other Afro-Eurasian cultures. What had happened by 1800 to the West-Europeans can well be called the Great Modern Transformation. For it was something that at the same time had happened to the whole world, too, as we shall see. As soon as it was essentially completed within Europe, its effects were worldwide and began to be felt drastically not only in Europe but in all other civilized lands as well. The distinctly Modern acceleration of historical processes, in contrast to the gradual increase of speed which had been taking place already in pre-Modern times, has been one aspect of this great Modern Transformation. It has moreover, as we shall see, been a central and essential aspect of it, distinctive of it both within the Occident and throughout the world.

There is more truth than some non-Westerners, avid of progress, would like to admit in the case of those who make this Modern Transformation a function of a distinctive Occidental genius. But if we look at the Modern acceleration of history from the point of view of world history at large, rather than merely from that of local Occidental history, this crucial aspect of Modernity, at least, can no longer appear chiefly as the trait of one regional society among others. Whatever the shift of pace may have meant locally, it has also been, from the start, an interregional event. It could be no more localized than was the previous, slower acceleration of history. For at least three thousand years, Afro-Eurasian history had formed a single vast historical complex, in which all regions constantly interacted and shared common historical presuppositions were introduced. This disruption extended as widely as had the Afro-Eurasian historical life into which it burst. From a world point of view it is this total event which forms Modernity, and not merely the face it bore within Europe; nowhere is this clearer than precisely in the shift of historical pace itself.

The problems it poses must correspondingly be seen in a more comprehensive way than the pure Occidentalists have seen them. But it is not enough to see the acceleration as a universal "stage" all go through. First, we shall see that the Modern acceleration carries a different set of economic, social, and moral implications in other parts of the world from what it does within the Occident. But then, I believe, we must go further and recognize that it bears a world-wide aspect distinct from either the Occidental or any other local aspects; and that from this point of view, the problems posed by the historical acceleration are ultimately common to the Occident and to all others after all, but on a basis far wider than that of merely "Western" civilization. To see this we must study the whole Transformation more closely.

The nuclear, evolutional aspect of the Modern Transformation

The Transformation is sometimes regarded, by those who do not make it an inherent peculiarity of the Occidental genius, as a particular stage of social development which Western peoples had reached and in which all others might later be expected to follow them as their own development led them to the same stage. This hits closer home than the purely Occidentalist approach; but its exponents too often overlook on the one hand the peculiar role played by the Occidental background, and on the other hand the peculiarly historical character of the Transformation as a total world event. Such studies do, however, help to bring out one side of the Transformation, that which it displays where it formed institutions from within: where it introduced a distinctive new spirit, and not merely, as it often did, a new situation. Such an evolution within parts of Western Europe formed the nucleus of the whole event.

A key aspect of this Transformation was the institutionalizing of technical innovation. We may conveniently use this as an index of the presence of the Transformation on what may be called its "evolutional" side, marked by the presence of its distinctive spirit. This took many forms. It involved, for one thing, a new sense of quantitative measurement, as Professor Nef has pointed out,[7] men came to count the minutes of the hours in their daily intercourse, they calculated the rates of economic increase over spans of years, they computed infinitesimal increments in their scientific calculations. More generally, all the technical aspects in a wide range of thought and action were given an unprecedented primacy. All other considerations – esthetic, traditional, supernatural, personal – were relatively muted. This was above all a matter of attitude. Men expected each other to put technical calculations foremost in science – even at the expense of beautiful philosophical vision (the keynote was struck when ellipses replaced the cosmic circles as a result of appeal to minute instrumental measurements); to put technical calculations foremost in economic decisions – at the expense of traditional lore about markets or about craft standards; to put similar considerations first even

[7] John U. Nef, *Cultural Foundations of Industrial Civilization* (Cambridge: Cambridge University Press, 1958).

in social organization, at the expense of personal ties and traditional sanctions.

Moreover, the expectation that such technical calculations would lead to continuous change, at least to technical improvement, was given institutional form. During the seventeenth and eighteenth centuries, the idea became dominant that scholarship meant changing past ideas, and adding to them, more than it meant preserving them; the new learned societies were intended to embody precisely such constant innovation. Men learned to expect that wealth would depend more on inventing new machines or finding new markets than on cleverly exploiting old ones; they offered prizes for the best inventions and came to plan their investments on these assumptions. And in political life instances were to be found where the "laws" (as distinct for merely administrative measures), which had been regarded as the constituent and ideally permanent trait of a given people, were put into the hands of a continuing special institution, a legislature, to make and unmake according to current need.

By the time of the generation which flourished about 1800, in certain spots in Western Europe at least, and in certain aspects of science and economic production and (from 1789 especially) of social order, these new principles were already fully established. These nuclear, "evolutional" aspects of the Transformation, as embodying a new spirit, were then limited to Europeans. But they had unexpected effects forthwith in the whole world.

The Modern Transformation in its irruptive and interactive aspects

Another aspect can be called "interactive," resulting directly, both in Europe and elsewhere, from this evolution within Europe. In this aspect, it introduced a new situation into the course of interacting historical events, without necessarily carrying its distinctive spirit. (The new situations evoked changes of spirit of their own.) It is this aspect which first confronted the Islamic peoples. From the point of view of the relations of Western Europe with the other civilizations, three crucial innovations were in effect by the generation of 1800. To begin with, the new European societies had come to possess a much higher degree of social power than any others – those in control of a given social unit were in a position to control far more economic, military, or intellectual force. This had the effect of creating a radical, political, and social gulf between the

Europeans and all others, who were in effect at the mercy of any concerted effort the Europeans might make. (This gulf corresponded in some ways, in fact, to that between even the earliest urban societies and primitive tribes – in the introduction of civilization, likewise, there was an accompanying acceleration of the pace of history.)

Secondly, this gulf became the most important single fact of life for the non-European societies because of a natural trait of the great technical transformations: the exploitation of ever-new technical possibilities almost by definition drew no boundary lines – in the search for goods, resources and markets, the Europeans rapidly became intimately dependent upon conditions at the farthest corners of the globe. In consequence, the Europeans came to have a vital interest in affairs everywhere and, having both interest and power, moved, during the generation around 1800 (and almost unwillingly) into effective domination of the greater part of the civilized world – India and Malaysia being conquered outright (before then, Europeans had controlled chiefly port towns at most), and the rulers of the Middle East being forced to hinge all their policies on the presence and character of the new West. Soon, closing the gulf between the West and others became the preoccupying goal everywhere.

Finally, the new European societies were changing, and increasing this crucial social power, at an enormously faster rate than that at which the other societies of the Afro-Eurasian zone had been accustomed to change and were still changing. The gulf kept widening. This had the effect, for the world at large, of laying down sharp conditions under which alone the political gulf might possibly be closed. Development must no longer proceed at the old pace; that is, any independent local transformation of the kind, which might have been in the offing given another five hundred years, could not be awaited. The Transformation must be taken up in the form in which it had appeared in Europe, and it must, moreover, be taken up with far greater rapidity, and, therefore, in some drastically different manner, if the ever-increasing gulf in social power were to be closed. This was the initial meaning of the Modern acceleration of history for most of the world: a terrible pressure of time in the face of the transformed West.

While the interpretation of the Great Western Transformation, and with it of the Modern acceleration of history, as a natural stage for all peoples is in some ways an improvement over a purely Occidentalist interpretation, it is still radically deficient. One can think of the Transformation as a natural destiny, awaiting its proper time as the various peoples evolve into readiness for it, only if one limits it to its "evolutional" aspects. But in the historical reality – and not only for the non-Western parts of the world, but even for the West itself – it is possible to segregate out the "evolutional" and "interactive" aspects only very artificially in the actual historical impact, they are most inextricably interwoven. The "interactive" relationship of Bengal and Lancashire, for instance, was crucial for both from the start of the Industrial Revolution. The invention of a steam engine was an event not merely in certain industrial towns, but in London far to the south – and in the Scots highlands (which lost population) and in Denmark (whose agriculture was finally transformed) – and (at the same time) in Bengal or Egypt. The same continued to be the case with every major subsequent invention; in whatever town it was located, it was an event everywhere. The Great Transformation was not simply a stage but precisely an event (if one may use that term of something which took two centuries to happen), happening once for all, of which all the world felt the impact even if in some cases with some delay. And its effects were very different according to the historical relationship of a given society to the event.

Though the Transformation, particularly in the generation of 1800, wrought tremendous destruction in the West, this was eased at the time, and soon largely compensated for, by constructive results which were largely missing elsewhere at first. Whereas among the Occidental people the net effects of the Transformation were at least technically advantageous, the reverse was often its effect elsewhere. Whereas in the Occident there commonly resulted an increased degree of political freedom, the same events tended to produce an unprecedented despotism elsewhere, even when there was no direct military occupation from the West. Whereas in Europe the whole process often stimulated a fertile cultural creativity, elsewhere it was long, for the most part, simply culturally destructive, again whether there was Western conquest or not.

The world-wide character of the advent of Modernity (and of the shift of pace that came with it) about 1800 is illustrated in the fact that the Modern world "population explosion" reaches, in a great many non-Western areas, back approximately to that date. This is no doubt because in all other areas open to interregional trade – that is, all "civilized" areas – the control of warfare, pestilence, and later famine by Western direct or indirect intervention was beginning then. The population increase, moreover, began having serious effects very early; it seems to have helped rigidify the Hindu castes, for instance, and elsewhere to have made for intensification and diminishing flexibility in agriculture. And typically, where in the Occident the effects of population growth, absorbed into industry, were in many ways favorable, elsewhere they commonly were not.

I cannot document fully in this essay the implications of recognizing the radical character of the Transformation of 1600–1800, as a world-wide event contrasting with all previous Afro-Eurasian history. But some of the implications must be listed. When we see that the pace of Modernity is not simply a phase in Occidental life, we see that it is misleading to speak of "stagnation" as a primary trait of the latter-day non-Western societies before a recent "reawakening." Centuries of relatively slow, normal development or even of some degree of decadence were punctuated everywhere, in Western Europe also, with rarer bursts of outstanding creativity. It is the condition of the non-Western societies which was normal in early modern times; it was Western Europe which was departing from the common pattern of five millenniums. The appropriate question is not, "Why did the Muslims lag behind?" but "Why did the Occident suddenly become so different?"

But by the same token, the misfortunes of others cannot be laid to the colonialist malice of certain Western powers; it arose from a universal historical situation, in which the role of Western Governments was secondary and derivative, responding to needs which arose independently (and was perhaps often more constructive, in the circumstances, than we are inclined to admit). We are not dealing with difference among peoples as such, but between two historical conditions. The Modern Western expansion cannot be made analogous, except very partially, to earlier regional expansions – those of the Medieval Crusaders or of the ancient Greeks or those of the early Arabs or of the later Muslims. Those earlier movements took place within a common hemisphere-wide historical context; they represented temporary shifts of power, but the overall pace of historical change and the long-range level of social power were approximately the same on each side; fortune reversed itself readily enough. Indeed, it is even misleading to date the Modern Western position from the exploits of Columbus and Vasco da Gama, which could still be interpreted in terms simply of one people displacing another, at least within the Eastern Hemisphere. The first oceanic expansion was spectacular enough but did not in itself destroy the persisting Afro-Eurasian historical pattern; it was already showing signs of being reversed in the crucial Indian Ocean where the true Modern expansion began from northwestern Europe. Those who like to trace the rise and fall of Persians and Romans and Arabs and British and Americans and then perhaps Chinese are overlooking the crucial point.

Again, if the Transformation, or at least a key aspect of it, is regarded precisely as a departure from the patterns of Afro-Eurasian historical process in which Medieval Western Europe formed an integral part, the older Occidental tradition is unlikely to hold all or even most of all answers to the problems raised by Modernity. It is of enormous importance in understanding historically the precise course of events. But fundamentally, Modern historical conditions represent a sharp discontinuity with all pre-Modern historical forms, Western and non-Western alike. (It is one of the weaknesses of the orthodox Marxist analysis that it generalizes too freely from special Occidental experience.[8]) Accordingly, it is dangerous for non-Westerners to expect to model their hopes of development too closely on earlier stages of the Occidental development. It is dangerous to trace Modern capitalism too narrowly to the capitalist developments of the late Occidental Middle Ages, which in themselves were not really unprecedented in Afro-Eurasian history. Similarly, I would suggest that the common Muslim thought that Islam requires a Luther and a Reformation of its own is likely to be misleading unless it is taken only in the most rarefied allusive sense. Luther does not yet represent the Christian confrontation with Modernity in its essential features. The fifteenth- and sixteenth-century Protestant movements can well be compared, for the extent of their historical impact in their own time, to the fifteenth- and sixteenth-century Shi'i movements, which transformed the religious configuration of Iran. If the Protestant movement has more relevance to Modern conditions, this is in part through the accident of historical association; it cannot be said that Modernity arose less readily in Catholic lands. But both Protestant and Catholic Christianity have indeed (as have Judaism) passed through intense renovation under the impact of "evolutional" spirit of Modernity from the time of Pascal through that of Kierkegaard to that of Buber; if Muslims look for an analogy from the West, it is to such figures they must turn.[9]

[8] My "Hemispheric Interregional History as an Approach to World History" in *Journal of World History*, Vol. I, 1953–4, pp. 715–23, discusses the effect on most historical theories of the traditional Western distortion of world history.

[9] In my "A Comparison of Islam and Christianity as Frameworks for Religious Life," *Diogenes*, no. 32, winter, 1960, pp. 49–74, I try to point out the radically contrasting character of the two faiths, which must face quite different problems in responding to Modernity. If that analysis is right, Muslims must come to terms with the relation between legalism and mysticism, the relation between the demand for a just social order and a recognition of the validity of diverse faiths, and other such problems, which Modern Christians have not seriously had to face, and which are not so simple as they may appear. Please note that the article in *Diogenes* was abridged; moreover, some unfortunate errors crept into it; the full form, with corrections will be found in the reprint no. 10 in the series of the Committee on Southern Asian Studies of The University of Chicago.

Finally, it is too early to trace a single general course of development within Modern times, to be expected, with modifications, in all lands. Abd al-Hamidian despotism and British liberalism, modern democracy and totalitarianism, modern capitalism and socialism all have in common features which make any of them inconceivable in any previous age. All are responses to the great Transformation of 1600–1800 and we surely have not yet seen the ultimate response to the new pace of history. For the first couple of centuries, at least, the non-Western peoples, as we shall see, must face the event – all of it, not merely its latest chapters – in a different way from the West. But finally, even the West has been so radically altered by Modernity that the change it has faced has been on a like order with that of the other regions. Hence ultimately all regions, the West among the others, are facing the same order of problem together. The future is very much uncharted for all alike; it is open before us. It is concerned individuals who will make some of the most crucial decisions about it.

How the initial "interactive" effects of the Transformation limited the development of its "evolutional" effects

We must take up certain of these points in more detail. It is fashionable to speak of the current world crises in terms of a "revolution of rising expectations" which is dated by some as World War II or (in the U.S.A.) even blamed on latter-day American indiscreet activities in far places. The particular expectations referred to are real enough, and their current form is in some ways quite recent. But policies based on awareness of this alone would remain dangerously shallow. The difficulty arises when, as too often, Westerners set the current "revolution" against an imagined background of "traditional" or "dormant" centuries.

As we have noted, Western ethnocentrism has imagined a world history in which the Far-Western corner of civilized mankind has figured as half the whole, paired with a vast, vague "Orient," and as the "active" half to boot; the primary role of the West in the world can then readily be felt as something of long standing – dating in principle from at least the time of Caesar and in practice from around the time of Columbus. (Unfortunately, many Muslims also have accepted something of these presuppositions. Thus Muslim apologists have spent much breath proving how superior Medieval Islam was in this or that respect to the Medieval Occident, and then drawing the wholly unwarranted conclusion that thereby Islam was superior to all the world)! It is, then, hard to link in our minds the supposed beginning of Western world domination with its current phase – they seem separated by a long, quiet interval in which that mythical dragon, the "Orient," simply slumbered. In fact, however Western world domination, in the serious sense which is to be associated with the Modern acceleration of history, dates from not much longer ago than a century and a half; and the century and a half must have been extraordinarily active ones wherever it reached. The current so-called "revolution" is merely the latest phase of a process which began – in Egypt, in Turkey, in Gujarat, in Bengal, in Java – with the French Revolution itself.

The case of Egypt is both exemplary and relatively well-studied.[10] While for about three centuries before Napoleon's landing in 1798 it had not been one of the most culturally active of the Islamic lands – it was something of a backwater in that period compared to Turkey, Iran, and northern India – yet it was in its own way an important intellectual center, with a university which drew students from all over the Arab and African lands, and was possessed of a quietly productive economic life. Life there had perhaps been less disturbed than in the more active Islamic centers by the new Western economic, political, and intellectual activity, which had become increasingly obtrusive in the course of the eighteenth century. But in the climax of the eighteenth century, in the generation of the French and Industrial Revolutions, Egypt felt the impact of the new Western Modernity as keenly as any other land.

Napoleon stayed in Egypt only briefly (in contrast to a good many other conquering Western armies of those decades), but his very presence had destroyed the prestige of the old order, most notably of its military leaders, and had put the land into unresolved turmoil. In the confusion, an Albanian officer of the Ottoman army, Mehmet Ali, was enabled to seize power, destroy outright the old military ruling class, and set about building himself a state on the magnetic model of Napoleon's own mighty empire. But while the confusion resulting from the world-circling skirmishes of the new Western powers was sufficient to enable him to destroy much, he found that the background of two centuries of steady social and intellectual transformation, which Western Europe had known, was totally lacking, and this lack restricted his ability to build certain narrow limits – limits then unfamiliar, but which were to become commonplace.

He was able to destroy the old army and build a new one, formed of

[10] Relatively old, but remarkably well put, with essential bibliography, is Kohn's chapter on Egypt in his *Geschichte der Nationalen Bewegung im Orient* (Berlin: K. Vowinckel, 1928), translated by Margaret Green as *A History of Nationalism in the East* (New York: Harcourt Brace, 1929); but it deals only with the relatively brief period of full British rule.

local conscripts and equipped from Europe and trained by Europeans, which in fact allowed him to create a large "independent" empire in Arabia, in Syria, in the Sudan – until the Europeans agreed at a conference that he must withdraw, which he then had to do immediately. He was able to do something else, rather more basic: he destroyed the old rural economy, confiscating properties and replacing the traditional landlord relationships with direct interference from the state; and in the place of the old economy he put a large-scale dependence on the single crop of cotton to feed the new European factories. The new cotton crop made great incomes for some, except when financial panic in European capitals reached out and took away their profits, and also the livelihood of the transformed Egyptian peasantry. That is, Mehmet Ali was able to develop a military rule which, while it could not defy the West, could effectively break down all local traditions, reaching with its new efficiency into every humble home and tyrannizing there. And he was able to link the economy of his state to the European world market, reaping wealth for a new and rootless class which had ousted the older families from their privileges; but only as a dependent economy, a producer of raw materials, at the mercy of Western capital.

Mehmet Ali tried to do several other things as well. He tried to introduce mechanized industry, but (lacking any technical resources for this) was reducing to trying to run machines by the power of oxen, and soon gave up. Instead, the local market was soon overrun with Western machine-produced goods, which put the skilled craftsmen out of work, disrupted the social cohesive force of guild-life in the towns, and, for want of any constructive substitute, left chiefly both economic and social degradation.

This degradation was increased when, with his new-found tyrannical powers, he seized the old pious foundations, on which the amenities and even necessities of much of the social and intellectual life of the land depended. The schools were made directly dependent on the state and – as his schemes called for more resources – the curriculum of the great Azhar University was impoverished, restricted to the narrower theological interests which it retained during the nineteenth century.[11] He tried, indeed, to build a new intellectual life, modeled on the West; but here also his successes were at best ambiguous. He opened many schools, but the students who went there to study had been prepared in the methods of a medieval scholasticism and were at a loss when asked to

[11] Cf. J. Heyworth-Dunne, *An Introduction to the History of Education in Egypt* (London: Luzac, 1938)).

learn modern chemistry or engineering. Eventually these schools were consolidated, and after wasting much of the time and intellectual powers of a generation, the new schools began to produce men who at least could read modern works with some intelligence, though they were too busy trying to keep up to contribute anything yet of their own.

But this success, in turn, had its destructive aspect. The students of the new Western schools had no serious knowledge of the Islamic past of Egypt, and found little sympathy for – or from – the masses of their families. Yet the best students were drawn into the new schools; less active minds, on the whole, seem to have been reserved for the traditional schools, which lost both range and intellectual quality, though they alone were left to support the cultural continuity of the land. There resulted two educated classes: one group possessed of much modern book learning which alienated them from their own people and who knew almost nothing of the very religion they professed; another group, increasingly incompetent custodians of that religion, who knew nothing of the intellectual springs of modern life.

The contrast with what had happened when Napoleon invaded Germany is obvious. Historical change was no less rapid in Egypt than in Germany; but while in Germany it made for a more vigorous economic, social, and intellectual life, the same world-historical events had largely contrary results in Egypt. For in Germany the innovations in administrative technique, in machine production, and the rest, if not quite so far advanced as in France or in England, nevertheless had been prepared by the gradual training of generations of former medieval clerks and craftsmen in more and more technically-advanced ways – as had been the case in England and France themselves; for fundamentally Germany was part of the same general society as were England and France. In Egypt, on the contrary, the same events tended to destroy what craftsmen's skill and what intellectual soundness had in fact existed there in the eighteenth century.

When subsequently it was time to rebuild, to industrialize and democratize, in such lands as Egypt, the human resources were even less sufficient than what they might have been a century before. So those that had were given, and from those that had not was taken away even what they had. The Islamic peoples soon found it of supreme importance to try to develop the "evolutional" aspects of the Transformation. These, they found, were the prosperous aspects – even in point of sheer power. But it was not now a question of adopting them *de novo* – of sheer diffusion, in the anthropological sense. Modernity had already, in a real sense, arrived. The attempt had to be to alter a less advantageous outcome of Modernity, exchanging it for a more advantageous. This was a much harder task. It might even involve a change in the nature of Modernity itself within Europe, to the extent that European Modernity presupposed the division of the world between metropolitan and more or less (economically) colonial areas. At the least, it involved reversing one of the chief historical decisions of Modern times; worse, it involved changing a self-perpetuating relationship of power. Thus when the Egyptians, after two generations of experience, tried to control the extravagant tyranny of Mehmet Ali's dynasty through constitutional forms, the British landed gunboats and settled the problem in their own way – imposing foreign tutelage instead of a constitution, and curing extravagance by cutting down on education so as to maintain payments on foreign debts. But the case of other lands makes it dubious whether the British occupation was really needed to ensure such an outcome. Economic and intellectual force alone could have comparable results in, say, the Turkey of Abd al-Hamid.

The story of Egypt was repeated – usually rather less neatly, and in a wide variety of circumstances – among most of the lands of urban and literate civilization of the Eastern Hemisphere. "Colonial" rule was almost incidental to what was a historical development largely outside the control of any given Europeans themselves. Eastern Europe – that is, Russia, the Balkans, and Turkey – had in varying degrees been associated relatively closely with West-European culture, both in original institutions and in continuing intercourse; the process of adopting Modern ways began earlier there and often proceeded with less drastic discontinuity than in the rest of the world, where the cultural background was more decisively different. Japan, almost uniquely, deliberately insulated itself at the very beginning of the Western Transformation, (long before there was serious danger of direct conquest or interference); meanwhile it built within its own islands institutions – and intellectual awareness – which enabled it to escape some of the more destructive aspects of the impact when it had finally to give up its insulation. Elsewhere, the nineteenth century saw the humiliation and degradation of most of those societies which did not happen to share in the original cultural changes that launched Modern times after 1600.

A large proportion of those societies was more or less Islamic during the two crucial centuries of the Great Transformation. This fact contributed to magnify the humiliation still further. The original territory of Islam, as established in the Arab conquests of the seventh century, had been restricted to the Semitic-Iranian Middle East and some outlying lands, notably in the Western Mediterranean. But after about 1000, the Islamic society began a vast and enduring expansion which gradually carried into it large parts of Africa, of Eastern Europe, of Central Eurasia, of India, and of Malaysia, approximately tripling the area where Islam provided the dominant cultural stratum. This fact was not unobserved by Muslims, who traditionally took a keen interest in history. It was felt to be the divinely guided destiny of a community which saw itself as the historical embodiment of the Creator's will for all human society. For Islam interpreted the religious calling in a uniquely social and historical sense, considering men's role, as believers, to be to serve as viceregents of God in the Earth, ordering all life in justice. Islam was to be the final and most complete religion in a long series of more parochial faiths, and its mission was to create a universal godly society.

A major effect of the Great Transformation on Muslims was to contradict this historical conception and to undermine seriously the Muslim self-image. Not Muslims but the despised Christians of the far northwest, long since written off as too cold and fog-bound to produce anything more intelligent than the unpolished Crusaders that had already come from there, now suddenly had the mastery in the world's affairs. The Western world domination was even more shattering for Muslims than, say, for Hindus – who had been long used to semi-submersion in a Muslim-dominated world. Accordingly, the devastating effects of the Great Western Transmutation were compounded, in the case of the Muslims, by a sense of radical spiritual defeat, the exact obverse of the European historical self-confidence which characterized the nineteenth century.

It is obvious, then, that the problems posed to Muslims by the Modern acceleration of history must differ radically from those posed to the Western peoples. This is so in part precisely because the Transformation had from the first a world-wide aspect aand was not merely a phrase in an Occidental sequence; and because nevertheless it was not merely a "stage" parallel within all peoples but a single pervasive event. But before our consideration of the Muslim predicament, we must again deal with those problems in more general terms and with some special reference to the Western experience of them.

The individual in historical acceleration

Over my desk is a 1947 cartoon which shows a group of complacent turtles, one of whom delightedly exclaims, "Just think, we now are part of the speed-mad atomic age!" It is sometimes hard to believe that individuals can become in any way different just because historic events face them: we remain the same slow turtles. Yet there is an undeniable difference between an inhabitant of New York and an old Mayan villager, and some of the difference derives from a different relation to history. However small the difference in his actual ways of thinking and acting, in any case, for the concerned individual, the potential difference must be morally crucial.

Ultimately the meaning of any historical acceleration for the moral individual presumably lies in the changed relation of the individual's life-span to the pace of historical events. We may posit that human history is a matter of that action which alters the presuppositions of everyday life – whether in the political or any other sphere. At the beginning of urban civilization, history in this sense became effectively conscious. The then rapid increase in the pace of history lifted some individuals from an almost unhistorical existence into palpable historical life. The effect of an individual's actions in modifying the basic context of Primitive tribal decisions had been normally imperceptible – tribal history was scarcely distinguishable from family biography. In civilization, the basic social and cultural context changed more and more perceptibly each generation. In ancient and medieval times the social and cultural presuppositions of a later generation were fatefully altered by the actions of a philosopher, a conqueror, a prophet, even an inventor, so that the very type of decisions possible to human beings was changed. But only a few were in such a position, and the results of their acts were generally slow in being worked out. With the Great Modern Transformation, many more individuals, in an increasingly wide range of activities, have been in a position to make moves which will result in altering the context of normal decisions, that is, will "make history." And, on account of the continuing acceleration of history it has been not merely the presuppositions of a later generation that may be affected but those of one's own time. Increasingly, every twenty years, every decade, almost every year requires each concerned individual to re-evaluate his conceptions of the total situation within which serious decisions must be made, even as it increases the frequency with which he must make such fateful decisions.

The "evolutional" developments of the Great Transformation served to underline the role of the individual which the very pace of history gave such a potential importance to. It is not simply that the variety and even the richness of the careers and ways of life open to individual choice has greatly increased, though this fact is fundamental. The primacy of technical innovation in economic production made immediately for a wonderful diversity in specialities and in inventive imagination. But it could proceed very far only in terms of mass production for mass consumption. Accordingly, one feature of the transformation was mass involvement in the economic and eventually the social and intellectual process. The masses ceased to be illiterate peasants on the margin of the urban culture which was at the heart of the civilizations; increasingly the daily life of even the lowest classes came to be determined by an active and complex participation in the economic, political, and intellectual life of the cities, as consumers, producers, voters, school-goers, readers. The peasantry of the French Revolution already played a decisive role no *jacquerie* could have hoped for. This mass action is in some ways the enemy of individuality; yet it has of course enormously multiplied the numbers who find the wide range of Modern diversity open to them.

Combined with this participation of the masses in all aspects of cultural activity came a heightened level of expectations of the individual's performance, at least in certain directions. Initially, to be sure, the worker was required to learn a precision and a sedentary discipline which, though it differed in kind, scarcely differed in degree from what certain craftsmen, for instance, had already mastered. The individual must also achieve an adaptability to a constantly changing set of rules of the game of living which in some ways went beyond anything in earlier city life – and the difficulty of the process is witnessed to by the number of social work, legal aid, and other agencies which have latterly had to spring up to help individuals make sense of the times.

But with mass participation in culture came an increasing demand for a high level of social responsibility – for the democratic virtues. A man must not only learn a high level of abstract and rather impersonal honesty – and in some Western countries this has been remarkably well learned – he must become a paragon of egalitarian co-operatives and creativity. In marriage he must not domineer over his wife – who may get a divorce, but is expected more properly to join him "saving the marriage" by deepening the psychological awarenesses of both; nor must he settle his children's fate in advance, but must raise them to be capable of making their own wise decisions on marriage, moral standards, and even religion. He must learn to suppress his natural feeling of ethnic exclusiveness and be ready to "integrate" with all members of his society. And if he makes mistakes, he must not be let off with merely being punished for his sins but must try to "rehabilitate his personality." He must even cultivate the art of group decisions, of compromise and committee life, without recourse to an ultimate arbiter. He must, in the end, if all this is to succeed, do away with his neuroses and with all blockages to his perceptions and his objectivity, and emerge an intelligent, responsible citizen: to which goal the educators and psychiatrists of the most advanced lands have dedicated themselves. (The list would vary relatively little in principle as between the United States and the Soviet Union.) The whole of this, to be sure, is as yet far away; but enough of it has become a reality since the days of Rousseau and Pestalozzi to have altered the whole tone of moral discourse in the West.

The mass dimensions of life, with their inevitable stresses, and the demands for the democratic virtues, replacing the older codes, might be enough already. They have been aggravated by the sheer rapidity of change in the nature of the everyday questions of choice facing a man; the result is an acknowledged moral unsettlement of the individual. He can no longer have a self-image in terms of a fixed norm of social tradition in a given community. But for the concerned thinking man, this moral uncertainty is multiplied by the increased historical responsibility of the individual. An individual who chooses to act in any one of the many channels open to him has a historical leverage unheard of in earlier times. Where circumstances are changing faster year by year, the one thing sure is that old ways will not long persist – or not long by older standards; every new suggestion has a chance of being taken up. What is more, in the rush of innovation, viable new ways will beget a progeny of further changes in a short time merely by their presence. Before a scholar has put out the second edition of a pregnant work, his findings have become the basis for a spate of useful new articles by others. It was a handful of obscure young pacifists in Chicago a few years ago who launched the resistance techniques now being used by a whole generation of Southern Negroes in the United States.

This situation carries with it a number of implications for the nature of the responsible individual. With the number of intelligent and literate persons rapidly increasing, and with the number of historically significant acts of each one of them increasing if possible yet more rapidly, the notion of human greatness, for instance, is put in question. If greatness can be defined in terms of historically effective creativity, it may yet become, if not a commonplace then at least something divorced from our traditional associations with the notion. (Biologically, there seems no reason to rule out the possibility of every town of 50,000 being a fifth-century Athens; till now, it has been only historical reasons which have made this notion absurd.) Already every artist seems to think he must personally create a new departure in style if he is to rank as an artist at all. But more immediate to our present purpose is an implication with regard to the nature of morality. In certain extreme instances, indeed, a pressing sense of the actuality of history has led devoted men to conduct their whole lives on principles which were formerly associated only with the *raisons d'état* of princes and their ministers. But even persons who do not become dedicated revolutionaries may be sufficiently concerned with their role in determining the very pattern of the social order to find that morality, for them, is no longer a matter of purely interpersonal virtue, but is almost equally a matter of historical responsibility. The Christian concerned with the social gospel, the historically oriented Existentialist, the Gandhist of India – and the socially conscious Muslim, all quite as much as the Communist, come to test the moral adequacy of their lives very often almost as much by the degree to which they exercise a positive influence on their corner of the historical process as by the degree to which they carry out certain standards of person-to-person relationships or adhere to certain group loyalties.

Modern individuality in Islamic lands

The individual responsibility of the Muslim has been affected by the advent of Modernity in a specially complex way. As in all other aspects of Modern times, the first results have been those least constructive, and these have in turn stood in the way of the development of more constructive aspects of the Modern impact. As in the West, the individual lifespan came to embrace enormous, even shattering, historical changes, which a person had somehow to confront. But the changes did not at first carry with them the same richness and diversity of opportunity. The involvement of the masses in far-flung economic and political processes as peasants or as conscripts was for them largely simply destructive. Their old skills often became useless, their work became dependent on new unknown variables of the world market in addition to the old natural variables; but they did not receive a wide range of new skills or of new channels for rising in life. Their old moral relationships were gradually undermined. But an expectation of the more inward "democratic" virtues was one of the last and most difficult to develop.

This situation is reflected in the subtle barometer of literature. Before the time of Freud, at least, the new sense of interpersonal relations in the West was largely the work of the novelists, who taught their readers to perceive individuals not as black and white figures of one or another standard type, but as infinitely varied personalities with weaknesses rather than sins, strengths which were unique to each, and lives which were less strings of happy or unhappy events than growths in maturity, disintegrations, or the like. If this sort of presentation be regarded as the heart of the Modern novel as a moral force, the evolution of the novel in Islamic lands moves from the periphery inwards. It begins in the nineteenth century with historical novels, often melodramatic in psychological content, at any rate romantic; and then develops above all novels of social criticism and satire. Only later and with less force have come more intimate portrayals of personality.[12]

In short, the uprooting of the individual, putting into question his moral responsibility, came early with full force and in increasingly broad circles, while the correspondingly wide individual openings and moral sophistication were delayed and distorted. In the first phase, before the "evolutional" aspects of Modernity were far developed, effective historical responsibility was limited to much narrower circles than those which felt the impact of the new pace of change – to the few who found their way to top political power, for the most part. Their range of opportunities was still more limited, lying as it did largely in mere responses to the situations with which the West confronted them. Even in later phases, when a major emphasis came to be placed on developing locally "evolutional" aspects of the Transformation, the same frustration tended to rise out of the same juxtaposition of rapid historical change with limited historical opportunity. What was to be done was rarely a matter of creating something fresh and new in the world; too often all that could be hoped for was to maintain a still precarious military independence and a brave up-to-date front office. Instead of real creation there must be adaptation, even imitation. There was scarcely time for much personal novelty; unless in finding new ways to imitate more successfully; a chemist, for instance, typically was busy trying to introduce into his own culture, perhaps to translate, the continuing flood of information already known and to persuade bureaucrats of its relevance; he had no time for discovering new chemical principles.

The sense of personal responsibility that was developed was formed in this atmosphere to a large extent. To Westerners this sense of responsibility often appears on the one hand heroic and even grandiose; on the other hand impractical above all lacking in concreteness – the individual is dedicated to freedom and progress more often than to various special causes to which he could devote his particular talents.[13] It is under the aegis of this frustrated nationalism of the "intelligentsia" – overtrained and underemployed – that the long-delayed active involvement of the masses has finally come. The Modern sense of historical morality grows

[12] This comes out clearly in Hamilton A. R. Gibb, "Studies in Contemporary Arabic Literature," in *Bulletin of the School of Oriental Studies*, Vol. IV (1926–28), pp. 745–60; Vol. V (1928–30), pp. 311–22, 445–66; Vol. VII (1933–35), pp. 1–22.

[13] Gustave E. von Grunebaum analyzes numerous important sources of it in "(Das geistige Problem der Verwestlichung in der Selbstsicht der arabischen Welt)," *Saeculum* Vol. X, pp. 289–327.

as insistently among concerned Muslims as it has in the West. But among the Muslims the background is not the rational enthusiasm of the eighteenth century and the pious dreams of Horatio Alger success stories; it is rather a frustrating intensity of feeling to which the form Modernity first took there has inexorably led.

The dilemma of discontinuity between the Islamic heritage and Modernity

Now all this has obviously important implications for such fields as politics, religion, education, or art. But I must limit myself to one point, though that is a fairly large one: the relation of the individual to the cultural heritage of the classical civilization he is supposed to be heir to. This is especially relevant to the concerned individual, for it is the basis from which he must work. But the point is historically crucial also. If the Great Modern Transformation was a massive event, a change of historical pace and of the historical presuppositions of five thousand years, to which we are all still responding in our various ways, there is no reason to suppose that any pattern of response yet developed must be the final one. The future is still open. And crucial to any response must be its attitude to the pre-Modern heritages which the Transformation has put in question.

It is evident that the faster the pace of historical change, the more problematical the survival of any particular concrete heritage – it becomes increasingly dependent on school-curriculum planning, on conscious radio-planning, and the like. But the full potential scope of the problem has, I think, been masked in the West by the fact that technical Modernity grew up within Occidental cultural forms; there has never been any one given sharp break – not even, really, at the French Revolution; and indeed many forms which Modernity still takes reach back to the Medieval Western lifeways. When the problem is analyzed in the Muslim case, these modifications of it fall away, and it takes on a sharper air.

It has been questioned whether the Islamic heritage can survive at all, unless in the form of a certain local color – rudimentary sets of superstitions, children's games (the child's imagination seems to reproduce past points of his society's development anyway), and, at the least, special holiday gala to attract tourists. This is not to say that currently there is not still much that is distinctive of Islamic societies as such, even apart from religious ritual; in many areas the peasantry, while in some ways their lives have been sadly disarrayed by the economic advent of Modernity, have adopted little of the more positive, "evolutional" aspects of the Transformation save travel by bus and an interest in the movies. But these two things which they have adopted – even apart from the fact of the disruption of more satisfactory traditional patterns – are notoriously conducive to further change. Some films may stress the glories of the ancient Arabs or of the Moghul emperors, but at best they stress them in the same mood as does Hollywood in dealing with scenes from the Bible or the Crusades; inwardly they do little to preserve a genuine cultural continuity. Again, even where the older ways have disappeared, often there are newer ways – a part, undeniably, of the Modern spirit – which have grown up as distinctive of this or that Islamic people; the way Coca-Cola is served in an Egyptian office, for instance, is unmistakably both Modern and Egyptian. Yet these do not amount to a real continuity with the great Islamic civilizational heritage.

The real point in question for the concerned individual, is not whether significant national peculiarities will persist despite all the change of our times, but whether the "high cultural" tradition, that of fine arts, letters, religion, legal institutions, and the like, can survive: whether any form, however evolved, of the Islamic high culture, as it was built up before 1800, can survive as a genuinely creative force alongside other comparable cultural heritages in the world. It is said that all the world is being "Westernized," and that only the West-European heritage will in the end prove truly viable – if we, any of us, survive at all. Are the Muslims becoming Westerners, even if slightly second-hand ones? Is is true, at any rate, that the Islamic society is fatally wounded and is dying under the impact of Modernity? Or, to be more relevant, what sort of relationship with the Islamic past is possible and relevant for the realistic Muslim to cultivate? How can this compare with his relationship with the Western past? If history would stand still, or at least move no faster than in the Middle Ages, the answers would be simpler and more positive, for all the strangeness of modern technology. But in the heart of Modernity lies a principle of movement which in itself rejects any past except as it survives an ever-renewed scrutiny from a viewpoint in which technical efficiency is always a component.

The Muslim's break with his past has indeed been radical in a way that has not been true for the modern European. This is not merely a matter of the suddenness of the break with former institutions – a suddenness far greater than was necessary in Europe even in the French Revolution and the Umsturz; a suddenness; moreover, which must be repeated again and again, as Modernity itself moves on its way. (One recalls the classical case of the Turkish headgear: Mahmud at the start of the nineteenth century imposed the fez as a modern headgear to identify all Ottoman subjects regardless of creed, and met with bitter opposition; a century later, Ataturk raised even greater resistance when, to assure the triumph of a latter-day republicanism, he replaced the now-accustomed fez with the brimmed hat). It is further a matter of the cultural tendency of the new ways.

Often the change has meant not strictly Modernization, that is, change of the same sort as that which transformed the West itself, but actual Westernization in a regional-cultural sense. Superficially, this may enter as a matter of mere convenience, though it by no means always does. The adoption of Latin letters (rather than a reform of Arabic ones) as a means of streamlining the press, the use of the men's suit-coat – certainly no product of a time-and-motion-study mentality – as a means of toning down personal display, these things handily reflect Modern ways of operating; but they make use of old Western elements, which originally were only accidentally associated with primacy of technical considerations or any other aspect of Modernity proper. With care, such superficial Westernization can be avoided.

But even more subtly, an old-Western element enters into most basic efforts at Modernization, however zealously kept free of direct affiliation with Occidental communities. For, naturally enough, the main institutions of Modernity are colored deeply by the cultural forms of the society in which they were first produced. With an effort of the imagination, one can guess what the institutions of Modernity might have been like if it had developed, for instance, in Islamic society, say in the 23rd and 24th centuries, instead of in the West-European. For one thing, industrial society would probably not have been cast in the form of the nation-state. The nation-state, with its constitutionalism, its particularist charters of rights and responsibilities, stems from the corporate conceptions of Medieval Western society. From the very different legal conceptions of Medieval Islamic society, with their abstract egalitarian universalism, there might well have developed, instead of the nation-state, some international corps of super-*ulama*, regulating an industrial society on the basis of some super-sharia code. Such institutions, while demanding a break for Islam as radical as that which the West went through in modernizing, would yet have preserved some continuity of basic presuppositions. In fact, it has instead been the Western form of Modernity into which the Islamic peoples have had to enter, articulating themselves into nation-states which, however Modern, also inescapably do embody old Occidental attitudes. The presuppositions of an industrial nation-state, as against our imaginary industrial super-sharia order, reach deep into the Medieval Occident.

For the concerned individual, the Occidental component in Modernity has been made concrete in the demand that he assimilates at least the essential basic Modern thought of the West. It can be persuasively argued that to enter inwardly into Modernity, he must enter into the thinking of the great masters of the time of the Transformation itself – at least from Descartes and Kepler to Kant and Goethe. But to understand these, he must know the earlier Occidental background; indeed, he must be able to operate in terms of it. Though it may be maintained that in theory each cultural background should be expected to be producing its own masters in its transition to Modernity, in practice this is hardly clear. A truly comparable creativity has been almost ruled out by the conditions we have noted.

The attempt to develop the Islamic heritage in terms of Modernity

Nevertheless, most concerned Muslims are not ready to become Occidentals, to adopt the Latin masters for their classics, to accept West-European history as their history, to identify with Caesar and Cicero, Charlemagne and Columbus and Leonardo da Vinci as their heroes – still less to become Christians, Catholic or Protestant. During the middle of the nineteenth century, after the first shock of the new order had worn off, some forward-looking Muslims looked to a hearty collaboration with the West as the best road to a renewed and prosperous future. Such hopes became increasingly tenuous in many areas, particularly throughout the old Ottoman dominions, under the political disappointments of the last third of the century, and became positively unpopular with progressive minded men after the disillusionments at the time of the First World War. Since then, educated Muslims have been more and more intensely, even bitterly, aware of the threat of sheer Westernization and of their own passionate desire to avoid it.

Nationalism has been the most obvious ideological tool for breaking down parochial barriers and making possible that "evolutional" transformation of social life required for meeting the Modern challenges; the attempt to maintain or in many cases rather to revive their earlier, non-Occidental heritages is an important component of that nationalism. But it is not mere nationalism, but a search for more fundamental roots which persuades an Egyptian writers' club to have into their Cairo clubroom one of the lingering itinerant puppeteers to display for them his rather crude version of an art that once delighted all classes, but now has almost disappeared except in remoter areas where the radio and cinema are not yet common. They were not much interested by his offering, but some of them had hoped to tap something.

Accordingly, though continuity with the Islamic past is seriously disrupted, there are equally serious obstacles in the way of adopting the Occidental past. One of these is the matter of sheer bitterness, which in some cases must not be underestimated. The bitterness in the discontinuity with the Islamic past results from all the elements that make it so frustrating: that when the break is made, the results are more shattering than for Europeans; that even so, they are less satisfying, being at best so rarely a matter of getting ahead, but merely of avoiding falling too far behind. But in some ways still worse has been the necessity of chronic imitation. For it has meant imitating the enemy, imitating the unbelievers whom a Muslim of intense faith must feel are impious distorters of the godly order in the world, and in any case must feel are the source of the alien domination which it is precisely his aim to be rid of.

Even more basic than his bitterness is a persistent alienness in the Occidental tradition. For the Arab youth, say, to learn English and French – as keys to modern technique and modern literary form – is obviously useful. To learn Latin too, even the most concerned youth has no time, for he has his own classical Arabic to learn. He can see no advantage in preferring the puzzling Christian myth to the straightforward Muslim declarations of faith. It is always the most modern features of Western ways, not those of even a century since, that are to be adopted – not only in technology and science but in art and letters. And the most recent is with every decade removed further from the Occidental past, in both form and spirit. It is, after all, not the Occidental he wants, but Modernity. The pre-Modern Occident his ancestors had long ago learned to despise, and with some reason.

For this and other reasons, a major preoccupation of modern Muslim peoples has been the maintenance of their cultural roots. This has been attempted in diverse ways. Those ways which face the problems most probingly have naturally been those which attempted to revivify the Muslim religion in terms of modern life. Since Islam had always emphasized so strongly the ideals and even the details of social order, a seriously religious man must be concerned, more than in the case of many other faiths, with the institutional structure of the society. Hence a religious revival was almost bound to be more than a personal realignment and to come to grips with the whole range of changes produced by

Modernity. But each such attempt has proved, in facing the acceleration of history, to have its own difficulties, which so far have left the outcome unclear.

A sober and obvious solution was that represented by Muhammad Abduh of Egypt. He tried to introduce within the framework of Islamic orthodoxy an acceptance of modern science and all modern methods on the level of natural knowledge, as supportive of the faith – on the assumption that an enlightened and reorganized Islam could continue to be fundamentally the same Islam, but purer and stronger. He introduced important reforms, in this spirit, into the Azhar theological university against much resistance; his work has had great and permanent influence. But the rapidity of historical change did not merely require a constant effort of further adjustment. It upset the very balance of forces involved. Areas of life which had been important became secondary. With no new basic principle to introduce other than that of Modernity itself, Islam remained in effect a body of achieved points of view and practices. Increasingly it has seemed that with each change, many more were implied; till the host of the new far outweighed, in scope and perhaps in the fundamentality of their further implications, the old which was properly Islamic. It became harder and harder to see whether what had resulted from his work was not really just the rationalization, in terms of older formulas, of a new way of life. It seemed as if it were not the continuing, but reformed, Islam which served as framework for the new science, but the ways associated with the new science which allowed an increasingly limited place to a continuing, but reformed, Islam.[14]

Eventually, as the bulk of important questions shifted into the new, secular sphere, Muhammad Abduh's work, despite his intentions, might logically issue in a relegation of Islam to an essentially private nicety. It would be denatured as a form of social organization, and attenuated even in personal life to a general moral sanction supporting the virtues fostered by Modernity. This seems to be nearly the official form of Islam in Turkey, where it is said Christian missionaries can be consulted in reviewing the adequacy of ethical teachings in Muslim textbooks. Such an Islam is widely prevalent elsewhere, too. In Pakistan schools, I understand, Islam has been reduced, on occasion, to "brotherhood, tolerance, and justice." The phrase is an excellent one, but if misunderstood it could sanction utter vagueness. Not only does it not

[14] Something of the outcome is suggested in the very sober work of Muhammad Abduh's admirer, Taha Husayn, *Mustaqbal al-thaqafah fi Misr,* translated into English by Sidney Glazer as *The Future of Culture in Egypt* (Washington: American Council of Learned Societies, 1954).

set Islam off clearly from other faiths, it does not set it off from many purely secular philosophical aspirations.

Many persons may not care about the difference. For the culturally concerned, it can mean jettisoning any effective continuity with the heritage. It threatens to reduce him to a hand-to-mouth existence in the moral sphere which may effectively sterilize his efforts at understanding events in a long-range perspective. This is not to deprecate moral interpretations of a faith, or common understanding across religious lines. I intend only to point up a cultural dilemma.

Perhaps more profound, and certainly more radical in conception, than Muhammad Abduh's efforts were those of Muhammad Iqbal of Pakistan. Taking advantage of the researches of modern Islamists, he developed a theory of world history in which historical Islam had a pivotal role precisely from the point of view of the possible outcome of the Modern Transformation. He hoped that therefore the positive heritage of Islam could be worked into a dynamic Modern form which would discipline Modernity from within Modernity itself.[15]

He divided civilized history into two periods. One was that of the religious revelations, starting with very primitive mankind and becoming ever more sophisticated to the time of Jesus and Paul. Human thought in this period was gradually developed out of the realm of magic and symbol into the rationalism of Plato and Aristotle; but even in such rationalism, thought was not yet scientific in the modern sense; in its abstractness it was unable to control the concreteness of evolutionary and historical reality. Revelation was still needed to supplement rationalist thought and provide ultimate symbolic norms, adequate authority for actual social and practical life as it unfolded from stage to stage. To fill this need came the numerous irrationalist religions, each better than its predecessors, but still imperfect. After the peak of non-concrete, symbolical rationalism had been reached in Plato and Aristotle, however, the human mind was finally ready to make the great leap to a fully adequate, scientific way of thinking. But this it could not do in terms of its old rationalism as such; there had to come a new historical impetus – which must, in that time, still be a revelation. It came as the final revelation, that of Muhammad.

For in Muhammad's revelation, Iqbal thought, was introduced the very principle which dispensed with the limitations imposed by the old sort of rationalism; that is, the attitude of positive and open-ended yet

[15] In treating of Iqbal, I have perhaps somewhat extrapolated his thought at points to illustrate certain of its implications.

still logical and systematic observation which made possible inductive science. Hence the finality of his prophecy, for now the human mind was able to mature to the point where further revelation would no longer be necessary to help it along in its historical growth. Iqbal tried to show this partly in terms of the Quran itself, with its appeals to the observation of nature and its relative freedom from myth, ritual, and supernaturalism; but chiefly in terms of novel forms of thinking which he thought he saw in various Muslim philosophers and scientists, forms which would account for the marked difference in tone between the scientific thought of the ancient Greeks and that which the Latin West took over from the Muslim Arabs, and from which developed modern science. The scientific implications of the new principle inherent in Muhammad's revelation took time to be developed in human minds; hence the Muslims themselves came to see it only gradually. They had, however, worked out its essential features, on the level both of theology and of practical science, when the Occident, after its fertilization by translations from the Arabic, took over the task from them and moved ahead with spectacular rapidity. The whole of Modernity, with its sense of technical rationality, has been its fruit.

But it was no accident, Iqbal could maintain, that it was non-Muslims who most rapidly developed this germinal principle of Islam. For another aspect of Muhammad's revelation – which the Occident did not however, accept – had been equally important. This was the principle of historical continuity in the new divinely-founded and world-embracing community – a community which had not only produced the first intimations of modern science but had spread itself unprecedentedly over the eastern hemisphere, creating a trans-national network of social institutions founded on a strong sense of egalitarian justice. The finality of prophecy would itself endure as the permanent foundation, grounded in historical actuality, of all aspects of future human life. That is, Islam contained both a principle of movement – which, detached by the West, had produced Modern science – and also a principle of continuity; the two principles must ideally be in balance with each other. At one stage of the development of the principle of movement, it may have required a community less perfectly rooted in the divine ultimate to develop this one principle with full rapidity, unchecked by the other. Eventually, however, the community that is more truly divinely rooted must take over again and restore balance in the development. He could hope this would come just in time (he was writing after the First World War), before the one-sidedly materialistic and rootless West destroyed itself and the whole world too.

For Iqbal, then, Islam was not simply a code of ever-dwindling range of relevance, but the enduring resource of an evolving historical community, constantly to be worked out anew in detail, yet retaining its integrity in richly historical terms. This community must in the end, after the moral bankruptcy of the West, inherit the whole world, including the Modernity which it had initiated.

This was a beautiful and even persuasive theory, and no more false to history than the major theories which have inspired the broader-visioned historical actions of modern Western peoples. Yet it is after all false to history, as are so many Western theories. It is not merely that Iqbal, being western-trained, sees history (as do the Western theorists) chiefly in terms of the Mediterranean regions (though emphasizing the Middle East rather than Western Europe) and ignores the other major cultural centers and the broader historical processes that embrace them all. Decisive is the fact that his evaluation of the historical role of Islam (and therefore of its potentialities *vis-à-vis* the "rootlessness" of the West will not stand up under detailed factual criticism. He does not in fact show that Islam carries a more durable historical moral tradition than does the West.

In the Middle Ages, this need not have mattered overmuch. But a creative cultural revival cannot now be founded on intellectual speciousness. The very speed of historical change must make out of date the unexpressed conventions and barely balanced compromises on which any such scheme is based. Accordingly, Iqbal's attempted formulation of the solution falls before the too rapid surge of history by the same test as in the case of Muhammad Abduh. Despite themselves, his followers must end up, most of them, carving a niche for Islam within a world formed by Modernity, rather than integrating Modernity into a more fundamental Islam. In time, as more and more details associated with the Islamic tradition must give way, this threatens to again reduce Islam to a vague emblem of goodness.

Some groups have taken the approach outlined by Iqbal more seriously than is common, notably the followers of Mawdudi in India and Pakistan. They have tried to work out a system of modern industrial life as perhaps it might have been if informed by a Medieval Muslim morality rather than grounded in Medieval Occidental institutions. They wish to achieve capital investment without exploitative interest by taking as their point of departure the Medieval *waqf,* the pious foundation, or the Medieval partnership rules; they wish to take advantage of the intricacies of a modern legal structure without the biased pleading of hired lawyers, by taking as their point of departure the Medieval *mufti*, the impartial legal adviser to the judge.

It is the increased awareness of the individual's historical potentialities that encourages Mawdudi to propound his reforms in such radical terms. In Indian Islam he has a long line of predecessors, of whom he is fully conscious, who have worked to establish the Islamic social ideals in the place of a strikingly unideal reality. Ahmad Sirhindi for instance, was stirred especially by the spectacle of a Muslim monarch, Akbar, refusing to give even lip-service to the ideal of an Islamic state; but – like other Sufis (many of whom refused to be tainted by any dealings with any Muslim ruler) – his basic concern was with the drastic departure of all Muslim military rulers from the principles of equality and of humane justice which the Muslims' sharia inculcates. Shah Wali Allah, while concerned in particular at the decline of even outward signs of Muslim power in India at the end of the eighteenth century, was more fundamentally concerned to see established – by means of Muslim rule – the healthy social order which he felt Islam was ideally designed to bring about. In each case, their idea of perfect justice was extremely remote from the reality they saw around them – on the whole, perhaps as remote as in the time of Mawdudi.

But the concrete reforms they offered were in each case much less trenchant and less ambitious than Mawdudi's proposals. The most they could look to in practice was the restoration of the Muslim law in those aspects of life traditionally reserved for it, and a greater purity of the ruler's application of his still arbitrary power. Mawdudi's movement has called for a genuinely fundamental reappraisal of all the institutions of society, including the constitution of the state. For in Mawdudi's time the pace of history has put all these things vividly into question; the new entity of Pakistan has moved from basic law to basic law; the concerned individual has an obvious leverage in attempting to make even drastic changes. Because of the acceleration of history, Mawdudi can – and must – aim much higher than his predecessors.

Yet, at the same time, Mawdudi's concrete results have so far been still less adequate than what was accomplished by Ahmad Sirhindi and Shah Wali Allah. The very pressure of historical change which makes it relevant to propose a new sort of state constitution may make it futile to try to base it on Islam. Mawdudi and his friends – well trained in Islam as they are – have shown typically little sophisticated awareness of the actualities of the modern world. Perhaps their inventions might show some organic continuity with the Muslim law; but they have yet, I believe, to show how they may be developed in practice out of the world-wide network of Modern institutions. More precisely, one cannot picture an attempt to impose them seriously without inducing so drastic a revolution as to shatter (as would Communism) any historical continuity with older Islam, shattering it even more completely than continuity with what the modern West created. For the Medieval Islamic morality is not, in such matters, so fundamentally different from the Medieval Christian morality which was in fact explicitly rejected in the evolution of Modern institutions; how should it prove more viable than did the Christian morality? As yet, the most evident practical consequence of Mawdudi's efforts had appeared in riots against alleged heretics. This is surely not so much Mawdudi's fault as the fault of the same historical tensions which made possible his high aims.

The frustration of the concerned Muslim

Islam, meanwhile, without discovering a clearly viable basis for providing full spiritual roots for the rapidly evolving societies of the future, continues to remain vigorous as the one focus for imaginative self-identification in the perspective of the past. It is strong, even violently strong, as a principle of social allegiance and as rallying point of historical consciousness. It serves as a rationale for moral doctrine. And naturally at the same time it is a fertile source of controversies over such matters as sexual segregation, birth-control – or the status of infidels. "Islamic civilization" remains highly problematical, but at any rate Western civilization is not taking its place. In most Islamic lands, Islam and its associated cultural heritage must remain the point of departure for the concerned individual, if he has any such at all.

Yet the tensions between the Islamic heritage and the demands and hopes of Modernity remain unresolved. As compared with the West, the tension between cultural orientations (going back as far as the time of Mehmet Ali), between the older Islamic one often stagnant or fanatical in tendency, and the Modern one too often imitative and insecure, sometimes seems starkly unbearable and in any case not conducive to much hope. The more historical change presses (and such pressure is world-wide once it occurs at all), the more explosive the result – unless, perhaps, there may be evolving a new sort of cultural norm.

Sometimes, indeed, it seems as if the standard of expectations, the form of historical self-identification, that now serves will serve the concerned individual most readily is one without a heritage at all in the older sense. Such a standard would not be closely tied to any of the

Medieval civilizations and religions; instead, its watchword would be Progress, and for it the pace of technical innovation would provide its own norms. This may amount to the "Brave New World" – that appalling and all too possible vision of Aldous Huxley's; it may be fulfilled in the communist tendency to turn all civilizational background into valuable but lifeless museum pieces; or it may hold quite other premises, yet to be fully explored.

The acceleration of history, then, has had a double effect among consciously concerned Muslims. It has placed them in a historical situation at once highly demanding and diversely frustrating, where they have suffered an uprooting even more severe than that of concerned Westerners, but with far less of the compensating sense of historical experiment and achievement. This has underlined the need for them to reassert and reinterpret in modern terms the dignity of their Islamic heritage as a means of present self-identification without which they cannot creatively envisage a future. But the same historical situation has severely handicapped any such development of the Islamic heritage on a Modern basis. With its insistent primacy of technical considerations, the general tendency of Modernity continually to shift and blur the relevance of any given aspect of life tends to downgrade all bodies of tradition; but for the Muslims, the effort to counteract this tendency is frustrated by additional elements of discontinuity, resulting from the initially destructive impact of Modernity and from the continuing gulf between the West and themselves which the pace of events reinforces. The possibility of maintaining the values associated with deep nurture in a rich tradition seems slim.

The similarity between Islamic and Western problems in maintaining the heritage

Some still like to suppose that Modern life (or at least what is good in it) necessarily presupposes the long Occidental, even perhaps the Christian cultural heritage. They would like to see other peoples (and perhaps the Western Jews also) join in this. But from the world point of view, such a suggestion raises fundamental questions. It is not merely the alienness, the enemy-role of the West that has made so many Muslims consciously try to avoid any Westernization in a regional-cultural sense. At least as great a barrier has been the ambiguous relevance of the Occidental past to Modernity, even within the West. Actually, the cultural discontinuity in the West is in practical ways very like that in Islam. It becomes a question whether any of the older civilizations is showing signs of surviving as a living force (rather than merely as a part of the contributing background, like ancient Sumeria).[16] Many have felt that the repeatedly expressed concern with, above all, the "future of Western civilization" was arrogant, but it must be considered whether it is not, rather, delusive.

Here we cannot discuss such questions at any length, but they must be touched on, lest what has been said about the Muslims be left in a false light. Increasingly numerous are the concrete problems which show striking basic similarity in the Western and in the Islamic lands. This comes in part from the working out of the Great Transformation as a world-wide event, notably in the major threat to survival posed to all alike by the great gulf which it created. The more it is emphasized the more the non-Western lands succeed in adopting the more "evolutional," the more (at least seemingly) advantageous aspects of the Transformation.

In the schools, for instance, the problem becomes remarkably alike in Egypt and the United States: how can a serious heritage – the great Classics in either case, above all – be transmitted to a mass clientele with full responsibilities of citizenship, while at the same time meet the needs of a technical age? For even the technical need is not merely for enough mathematics and natural science; it is for an ability to assimilate ever-new information over a very wide range. It requires an ability to judge among claimants to authority in enormously varied fields, in addition to a knowledge of some one set of facts. Such education is likely to be essentially the same everywhere, and everywhere will strain the educator's resources. Everywhere, many educators find no room left in it for any set of ancient classics. In art, again, it is a question in each area how we are to retain the reality of a sense of style. The twentieth-century geometric and abstract styles bear almost equally little relation to each of the older traditions, and are used with equal facility as bases for "nationalistic" reminiscences everywhere. How should an American child learn to know as "his own" the Italian Renaissance prints and as "alien" the Japanese Tokugawa prints which have an equal place of honor on the living room wall?

In the churches, Christians wonder how to transcend a threatening polarization between religion as a technique for "peace of mind" in an age where all formulable dependabilities are undermined, and religion as a sectarian refuge from submersion in the anonymity of two billion television sets. But Islam faces much the same dilemma between those for whom it is a vaguely defined assurance of righteousness, and those

[16] Certain aspects of this question have been stated quickly by Dennis Wrong, reviewing Max Lerner's "America as a Civilization" in the *American Journal of Sociology,* March 1960.

for whom it is a tool of defense against the encroachments of Modernity and the West. It has been suggested for some time that the several religions should join force in "combating materialism and atheism." This might prove premature. Each of them has a more basic problem in learning how to make the inherited religious lore speak with greater creativity to modern men; even here to a degree, at least, they must all use like methods.

It can be questioned whether, in concretely facing these questions, concerned men of a West-European cultural background, Catholic, or Protestant, or Jewish, who hope to prevail over the relentless technical rationalizing which comes at an accelerating pace in all aspects of life, can claim to have found principles much more sound than those found by Muhammad Abduh or Iqbal in Islam. It is for this reason that it can be suggested that the relative ease of the transition, in the West, has masked our problem of continuity, making it relatively painless rather than eliminating it; and that Westerners can see their own problems mirrored in a clearer and starker and therefore somehow truer form when we look at the problem of continuity in Islam. The faster history moves, the more Westerners are likely to become aware of the problems themselves.

In the end we must no doubt recognize that the breach with our several pasts is a common problem not to be solved in isolation by any of the peoples – not even by the Western peoples. it is clear to us now that this is the case with the problem of armaments and of the risk they carry with them of undue militarization within each land. Some are suspecting it will prove to be the case with such questions also as juvenile delinquency and the problem of developing a sense of responsibility in a mass society; it may eventually prove to be equally the case on the level even of theology. If it is true that we must come to solve all such questions co-operatively, Europeans, Muslim, Hindus, Chinese together, then concerned Westerners will have to learn to see the problem of the great gulf created by the Modern Transformation as its own problem too, and learn somehow to reach across it, envisaging our common problems in terms that allow for the divergent effects of Modernity on both sides of it. And the concerned representatives of other traditions likewise will have to forgive the West its guilt and accept it as a partner in solving the common dilemmas. For Modernity is neither the outcome of purely Occidental traits nor a stage through which each land can pass in its own way. It is an event in our common world history which we must face together.

III

The discipline of world history

11

The objectivity of large-scale historical inquiry

Its peculiar limits and requirements

To this point, we have been analyzing various relatively particular historical movements from a world-historical point of view. But this sort of search has led us repeatedly into problems touching the nature of historical inquiry generally. It is not, in fact, surprising that the introduction of a genuinely world-historical viewpoint is likely to have repercussions in almost all aspects of historical thinking. In this final section we shall see that interregional history does indeed require its own types of historical thinking; but we shall go further. We shall suggest that the types of thinking required for it are not merely a special case of historical research. They are central to the historical disciplines as an autonomous field of public inquiry. From one important point of view, world history, interpreted as interregional history, must form the core of the intellectual organization of the historical profession.

Despite the enormous amount of research already accomplished, our historical knowledge is still far from meeting the demands we make on it as we try to form and criticize our vision of mankind. It is already a large order, that we want to know our own immediate background and how it has formed us, and to know the past of greatly differing peoples so as to expand our sympathies. These piecemeal interests already carry us round the world and back; and it has so far taxed historical ingenuity and imagination, how to provide insight which is at once so wide-ranging in scope and yet humanly meaningful in detail – as against the typical textbook or survey. In addition, every alert individual, and above all, every socially active group, religious or political, tries to have its own sense of history as a whole, giving its own orientation a perspective in depth across space and time. To understand or criticize these senses of history as a whole, we must look to substantial historical study; for the function of such study is precisely to discipline our ideas of the course of history – at the least so as to reduce the number of errors we will entertain. But much of the groundwork for this, both factual and theoretical, is not yet laid. The inadequacy of our knowledge becomes increasingly painful year by year in our present world where peoples of traditionally different historical backgrounds – Europeans and Indians, Muslims and Chinese – must live together and forge a sense of common humanity. We scarcely know one another, and must hope that historical scholarship will be able increasingly to do its part in giving us the necessary perspective on ourselves and our neighbors.

It is a commonplace, therefore, that the study of history is still in its infancy; we cannot expect to complete the work of scholarship merely by a slight extension of past methods. The responsibility upon historians is far-reaching and is not to be met without exploring a great many broad and refractory subjects and working out the tools for dealing soundly with them. Such tasks are admittedly not easy, but they must be undertaken.

The universal relevance of historical inquiry

In a sense, some conception, however vague, of world history as a whole has always formed the core of historical science, at least implicitly. Recognition that *Universalgeschichte* must somehow or other be tackled if historical research were to hang together as an intellectual whole has been persistent among such historians as Ranke. Certainly, at least the common Western image has underlain and oriented most of the routine modern Occidental historical work, so far as it was at all independent and wide-ranging – not a matter of refinements on someone else's work. Without such a world image, in its various interpretations, historians might have possessed a series of curious questions, but could not have related them to one another even so well as has been the case.

But the centrality of *Universalgeschichte* has been eagerly attacked; and, in fact, it has never become an accepted and well-articulated basis of historical scholarship. Some attacks upon it have been essentially negative. The type of "philosophy of history" symbolized by Hegel has led many to a healthy distrust of anything going close to the "big questions." They have rightly wanted to avoid fanciful constructs into which actual data have had to be tortured to form a system of overall historical development.

Along this line, some have insisted that there can be no universal history because mankind has not formed a whole except biologically; there must be no *Weltgeschichte,* but only *Weltengeschichte* – the Occident is one world, India another, and so on. This approach is sometimes in fact a result of a recognition of the importance of other regions than the Western. It is a rebellion against a world history that was a history only of the "Western world"; and, for want of more positive orientation, it has taken a negative form. But, as we have seen, there are no such closed worlds, at least within the Oikoumene; an attempt to construct a series of separate historical fields in such terms leaves too many and too crucial loose ends. The answer is not to erect a series of "world histories" on the model of our earlier Western one, but to reject that model, and its very methods, altogether, to construct a new sort of world history on new lines. If Oikoumenic history begins to be rightly understood, and also the place of the Oikoumene in world history at large, it is evidently possible to develop world history which shall be genuinely worldwide, but yet free of the *a priori* system-formation associated with the improper sort of "philosophy of history."

A second line of attack on *Universalgeschichte* has arisen from the demand for historians to develop general rules about the dynamics of historical processes. What causes – not this or that revolution, but – revolutions in general? What causes the rise and fall of dynasties, states, cultures, religions, not just in given cases, but as such? What causes the expansion of a people, the contraction of an economy, the florescence of an art or a literature? It has been felt that for history to be scientific, it must not merely (as has been the orthodox position since the nineteenth century) use exactingly objective methods in determining particular facts; it must produce generalities as universal and undated as those of physics. It must be a "social science" – like sociology and anthropology, but with a different starting point, if an almost equally universal final domain. For those who have been consistent in this concern, "philosophy of history" in the Hegelian sense has been as much anathema as for the more orthodox detail-historians; though perhaps for a different reason. Though a man like Toynbee seems to combine the two approaches, scientism and *a priori* universal pattern building, this is chiefly because of his utter lack of methodological clarity. Actually, the traditional "philosophy of history" has always been sufficiently historically-minded to look for the uniqueness in historical developments, and for a unique way in which they combine into a whole – it has not produced general laws, in fact, but the analysis of a single unrepeatable sequence. (Even the more consistent cyclists, from Vico on, for all their admission of a sort of repetition of type, offer little to those who want a host of general rules; for they, far from abstracting various types of historical dynamics from the particular context of a given total historical development, anchor their whole analysis more undetachably than ever to such overall developments.)

This interest in historical dynamics as such is a worthy concern. It is obvious that, moreover, without a proper interregional historical background, as we have been developing it, it cannot be adequately worked through. That is, a genuine world history should be as much an aid to such concerns as a false type of world-historical theorizing, based on a false historical image of the world, has been a handicap. However, an abstractive study of historical dynamics, important as it is, is not history in the proper sense. Interregional history must establish itself as history proper before it can serve the interest of the study of historical dynamics. And it is in history proper that it is one of the – if not the chief of – the keystones. Its lack – or rather, the presence of inadequate and only semi-articulated substitutes in the form of unconsciously assumed world images – has had a pernicious effect on all historical research, and has gone far to give reason for the innumerable complaints against historians for not becoming "a science," as it is somewhat naively put.

What is wanted is not best expressed, perhaps, by the term "a science." To divide scholarly inquiry into mutually exclusive "sciences" can carry overtones of denying the unity of knowledge – the ultimate interdependence of questions about all kinds of existence. Yet it is true that we expect from historians, as from any other recognized scientific discipline, a body of knowledge which is a permanent and cumulative public possession – not merely an exacting but transitory melange of points of local interest. In this sense, no amount of detailed "scientific" objectivity can give to history the dignity that has been associated with the term science.

As contrasted to mere private antiquarianism, historical scholarship, as an activity appropriate to general support by the human public over the generations, must be concerned with answering questions of a universal human relevance. Historical study does indeed consider its data in their aspect as particular events. It is concerned with "who" not "what sort." That is, whatever its level of abstraction – one man's execution on a given day, or the disruption of a whole life pattern in a movement lasting over centuries – it is concerned with its subject for itself, and not as an example of some wider generality. (We shall come back shortly to this fundamental and persistent but sometimes rather elusive distinction between the attitudes of a historian and a social scientist.) But questions about particular events may take on a universal relevance. All men have reason to be as seriously interested in that unique sequence of events wherein the human species was differentiated out from its animal background, as in the general rule that water, wherever found, is always compounded of hydrogen and oxygen. Though the first is a unique event, irreversible, and the second an ever-recurrent type, each bears universal human significance.

History is a *public* discipline then in virtue of the questions it studies possessing a permanent public interest. But how shall such an interest be determined? In contrast to a limited realm of disciplines wherein the criterion of public interest can be cast in the form of a seemingly absolute distinction, the criterion in the historical field must be discovered through historical study itself. In pure physics and chemistry, most clearly, but also in one aspect of all physical, biological, and even social studies, a distinction may be made between rules that may be formulated to hold regardless of particular moment or place; and generalizations valid only in a given context of time and space, and hence not really absolutely general. A generalization defines future potentialities, at least within the context where it holds. Future potentialities are certainly of relevance to all faced with choices. A generalization of unlimited context (it is philosophically discussible whether, in the ultimate evolution of the universe, there really can be such; for practical purpose certainly there are) of necessity defines future potentialities for (in principle) every man. Hence such generalizations are commonly held to be of universal relevance *ipso facto*. This incontrovertible point of assurance has helped give such disciplines as can afford to restrict themselves to such questions (in my wide-ranging sense, only those disciplines subsumed under physics and chemistry) a popular and even a philosophical prestige which other scholars, and even historians, have sometimes been tempted to envy.

The criterion for legitimate public interest in the historical field (to leave other cases aside) is not so simple – and, in fact, has been little agreed upon (though in practice sometimes it seems as if the human demand for such a criterion had implicitly settled on "the affairs of church and state"). That is, there is no sharp line between antiquarianism and history; just as the exact line, in the geological and astronomical field of physical sciences, is unclear between a matter like enumerating the pebbles on a particular beach (clearly at best of private interest, in itself) and enumerating the mountains on the moon (granted as of public interest). As the old criteria of the successions of church and state becomes less convincing, it might be left up to the not entirely unjustified rule of thumb, which however is philosophically not adequate, that any questions a given reading public happens in fact to be interested in, or that will bear on such questions, are to be pursued in the profession as being of legitimate enduring public interest.

But to the extent that historians do concern themselves with distinguishing what is genuinely of public interest, of legitimate relevance to the profession, it is this properly in close association with that which makes history a single public *discipline*. It is this in virtue of the questions it studies being interdependent – the answer to any one cannot be well elucidated without the answers to others – so that fully developing one corner of the historical field involves other neighboring corners – which in turn involve further corners – of decreasingly direct, but of sustainedly indirect, relevance to the first. This is, of course, what gives any intellectual discipline its coherence. "A science is an organized body of knowledge" does not mean knowledge organized administratively by departmental subspecialties. Dynamically formulated, it means precisely that any discipline of intellectual inquiry is the pursuit of a body of interrelated questions, such that a success in one question carries implications for the group as a whole. To be sure, all serious inquiry is so related in some degree; all definable fields are ultimately merely specialties and subspecialties, and sub-sub-specialties; but it does help to distinguish out significant levels where the grouping of questions is at least relatively self-sufficient. Human social history is such a recognizable field, even though when Western historians have tried to delineate their recognition of it, they have commonly been betrayed by a false world-image into conceiving it in terms of the Westward distortion.

It may be necessary, in some quarters, to point out that to make the nature of the historical field depend only upon "common methods" of inquiry is misleading. Those who make the "scientific" character of historical study to reside in its detailed objectivity often correspondingly make its unity as a field lie in its distinctive method. But, just as chemical methods can be used for particular applied tasks which form no part of chemical science as an ongoing human inquiry, so historical methods can be used quite meticulously in antiquarian pursuits. Historians need each other not to share new methods, but because of the substantive interrelations of the fields they are exploring. It is this that makes them a profession still, even though the original expectation that one man should know all of history has yielded to proliferating subdivisions as in all other disciplines. It is the interrelation of the questions pursued that makes the discipline. To vest it in the nature of the methods involved – as is done more often unconsciously than consciously, I think – is, however, not merely misleading. It is, in effect, to give up the search for a legitimate basis as a public discipline, for methods in themselves are but tools and can give no particular assurance of the interest or significance of their results.

Human social history (to which we give the title "history" par excellence) is to be distinguished from other disciplines studying human society, not fundamentally by its methods (historians have learned much from the methods of others, in fact), but by the sort of questions asked. (Human) history and the several (human) social sciences study much the same phenomena. Empirically, they are set apart indeed by different methods and by different traditional viewpoints as well. Historians have worked out from chronicles of official acts, and prize the documents of public archives; sociologists began with theories about stages of modern progress, and exalt statistics; anthropologists started wanting to know what the original nature of men was and their hallmark remains studies of kinship patterns. Yet all three groups, in their own ways, have come to claim a universal domain over human society, and use whatever methods seem most appropriate to a given theme. What gives the historians, at least, a distinct common interest is a special attitude which is unmistakable when recognized. A sociologist will study a revolution in Mexico as a sample of a type – revolutions anywhere. A historian will study that same revolution as a particular combination of human achievement and failure at a given point in time and space. Even if both the sociologist and the historian happen to be studying a given man's career as a sample of a type of career important in that revolution, to elucidate the latter, the difference of aim persists. All historical statements, even about individuals, are in a sense generalizations from a range of particulars. But the generalization the historian is looking for about the revolution, is sought not for its generality as such but for its immediacy to the particular revolution. And the thorough historian will soon find himself interested in the individual for his own self, and distinguishing out so far as possible the unique and irreplaceable, as well as the typical, in his contribution to the revolution as a whole; something which, *ex hypothesi*, is not supposed to interest the sociologist save as it may subserve other, complementary generalizations about the course of revolutions generally. The historian will study the American Revolution for its meaning in defining the nature of the American soul, or at least its tradition; he will study the Crucifixion for its unique place in Christian experience.

The questions historians study are certainly closely related to those studied in the various social sciences; in a sense, the whole field of human society is an indivisible field of inquiry, and any distinction among the several disciplines within it is likely to form a barrier to full understanding. A distinction between social "science" on the one hand and history on the other, particularly, is likely to be untoward. Yet human history will continue to have its own autonomy, at any rate, because the type of questions it pursues will continue to be interdependent in their own terms. This is partly a matter of the ultimately moral character of historical judgments; and this point we shall have occasion to pursue further later. It is also a matter of the immediate interrelation of the actions which may be called historical.

Again, just as the field of history overlaps in data, but is distinguished in type of question asked, from the non-historical aspects of the social sciences; so it overlaps in its data, but is distinguished in the type of question it asks, from the non-historical aspect of the "humanities," that is from the systematic and the critical aspects. To be sure, there can be a difference in approach as between a general historian dealing with the history of an economic institution, and an economist delving into economic history; and a corresponding difference between a general historian discussing the art of the Renaissance, and the work of an art critic turned art historian. But these differences are those of special qualifications and backgrounds; art history and economic history remain history (and may also remain, presumably, economics and art criticism). There remains another sphere, as in the social studies, so in the humanities, which stands apart from the specifically historical approach, and whose questions are less directly the concern of the historian as such.

The historical sphere in turn – in all its ramifications, humanistic or sociologistic – has its own unity. This is based in the fact that historians study first of all great deeds as such. Herodotus touched the true note from the start, but we must drastically redefine such greatness. The historical dimension of human life, that in which human actions can take on a historical significance, is that in which men, no longer limited by nature in the immediate sense, can by their action alter the conditions of their routine life – alter the natural framework (both of physical and of social nature) within which they live. Perhaps each man, in his highest spiritual potentialities, can do this for himself. Human social history studies men's doing this socially, for their groups, ultimately perhaps for their whole species. This is not to judge the historical relevance of any action only by its outcome in the end – least of all, in our own time. Genuine historical action may well change the conditions of life of a community which subsequently dies out, without directly affecting any other. It retains its moral validity as historical action nonetheless. But it has been true that human history has been sufficiently interrelated so that, in fact, most significant historical action has had a significant part of its significance in terms of even relatively remote consequences; changing the local conditions of routine life has had its repercussions throughout the Oikoumene; and in terms of the historic role of the Oikoumene, in the world at large, as we have seen. It is precisely in terms of the effect of changes in one place and time upon changes elsewhere, that historical questions became so fatefully interrelated, and it becomes impossible to answer adequately any one historical question without answering all.

Basic position of large-scale questions

Accordingly, we come to the fact that at the heart of what makes history a public discipline, what must distinguish the legitimacy of its research under public sponsorship, in contrast to mere antiquarianism, are the large-scale questions. These questions are often such as historians are hesitant of facing. They cannot necessarily be answered with a completely firsthand control of all the documents involved. Yet they are the questions for whose sakes the historical profession exists.

Large-scale questions deal with the characteristics of ethnic bodies, of states, of religions, of nations, of civilizations; with the characteristics of periods and epochs; with questions of progress and of decadence; with questions of the significance and mutual indebtedness of art schools, religious movements, scientific discoveries, economic systems; with what is Modern, Western, Oriental, Medieval, Classical, backward, conservative, liberal . . . with the "Oriental conception of monarchy," with the "modern attitude to business," with "Christian morality," with "Western traditions of art."

All these involve comparison of many diverse particulars in very broad contexts. All, accordingly, require appreciation of the many-faceted historical context of given events, particularly from the point of view of awareness of where comparisons are legitimate and where not. Almost always they involve, at a relatively small remove, men's conceptions of history as a whole – of underlying concepts like Europe, Asia, Africa, ancient, medieval, modern – that is, implicit world images.

They are, in a sense, impossible questions; yet they are the most important sorts of questions to which a sense of history is commonly applied. Without sound large-scale historical concepts, such questions are left without responsible professional disciplining. It is the implicit task of historians to discuss and rediscuss them with ever-renewed critical sifting.

Hence historians must come to some way of weighing the propriety and relevance of various total ways of looking at the historical scene: what parts are to be seen in what connections on what levels. For such pictures of historical development determine the very questions asked in basic research, as well as the way questions and concepts will be framed in current discussion. We know that the question determines the answer: what questions we ask set the range within which we can even look for data, and – in just that degree to which the question is univalent – sets the answer that objective and persistent inquiry will come to. The difference between most serious historical studies of what seems to be the same subject matter lies in the different questions posed. But sometimes it is forgotten that the categories used have a great deal to do with what questions will be asked. If our category is sovereign states, we will come to quite different pictures of inter-area commerce, because we will be asking different questions, than if we use climatic regions as our categories. If we are studying the history of the United States, Great Plains political movements take on a very different curve, and seem to bear a very different relation to educational and economic factors, than if we are studying the history of North America, including the Canadian Prairie provinces.

The problem of the (too often unconsciously adopted) presumptive categories is important enough in detailed history. On a large scale it becomes a most pressing problem, if only because traditional units of thought are even less adequately developed in the common language (which historians tend to take as final in such matters). Large-scale history cannot be discussed in terms always even of states or of inter-state institutions. In its more fundamental reaches, it is commonly handled in terms of regional cultural traditions or of civilizations. Even this, as we have seen in our study of the Oikoumene, is not enough. Large-scale history must be handled in a variety of sorts of historical complexes, including all these.

I use the term "historical complex" advisedly, as neutral and flexible, not tied to any given type of historical interpretation. Anthropologists may be relatively at home in this way of thinking; historians by trade may object to speaking of "historical complexes" – as too far from the concrete event. Yet, for placing the event properly, they are unavoidable. If we are not to be limited to a few types, standardized in common languages, we must be conceptually prepared to seek a variety of types perhaps previously unnamed. Whenever we find sequences of historical events interrelated in such a way that significant questions of substance (not, normally, abstract comparisons of categories) in regard to one of the sequences involve answers about all of them, we may regard what we have as a historical complex, whether it is a region with diverse cultural elements which closely interact (for instance, Buddhist-Hindu-Muslim Southeast Eurasia), or a single cultural tradition spread widely (for instance, Islamic culture From Java to the Niger), or a set of developments in a single tradition across many culture lines (for instance, The Greek-Arabic-Sanskrit-Chinese-Latin mathematical tradition). It may be a religious whole, a period with its own *Zeitgeist*, a trade network. The term certainly is not inappropriate for less extensive complexes of events: the discussion of slavery in the United States implies discussion of the Frontier, of oceans, of industrialization, of Canadian freedom, of Quakers, etc. – indicating that North American history forms one historical complex on one level; and this in turn is composed of lesser, and enters into wider, such complexes. We need the term to be wide enough to cover not only persisting cultural patterns, but persisting interrelations among historical elements even when the cultural content of those interrelations changes drastically – as is the case of the Oikoumene itself. This allows us to see the diversity of form which large-scale historical processes can take – and in terms of which we must be prepared to integrate our studies.

Once we come to see the crucial character of large-scale conceptualizations in its own terms, it is evident how crucial these are to all historical study. The study of any given historical complex is important in two ways. On the one hand, it is important to understand the nature of the given historical complex as a whole, on its own level – for only in terms of it do the full consequences, conscious and unconscious, of human acts come alive. On the other hand, study of the wider complex is essential for proper placement and interpretation of more special developments within it – thus a full sense of the Oikoumenic configuration allows us to see the later periods of Islamic history in their unity and variety; and allows us to correct basic distortions which falsified Occidental history. But it must be kept in mind that any given event or set of events is not either a matter of interregional, large-complex significance or of local; it is more often a question of distinguishing in what respects a given event is relevant to more or less broad-gauge historical complexes of events. Thus such a locally technologically significant advance as the development of mold-board plows in Northwest Europe does not have its significance as a technological advance as such (as we have seen), but rather only as it helps give, ultimately, the Europeans a different role in the Oikoumene as a whole. It is essential to put all inquiries about originality, all searches for filiations, in such perspectives; so that these inquiries, with their overt or tacit presuppositions of certain attitudes to race, to national culture, to *Zeitgeist*, can be sifted, and what is valid be properly *dégagé*.

Disciplinability of large-scale questions and of the categories they presuppose

But how valid can the answers to any large-scale historical inquiry be? However crucial they are, they will not serve to construct a learned discipline unless they can be answered objectively. That is, they must be subject to serious intellectual discipline which will overcome any tendency to subjective speculation in matters of such obvious personal relevance to all.

The attempt to study large-scale history is plagued with many problems, but we can set aside at least some that have been supposed to plague a universal history. We need not be deterred, of course, by the sheer quantity of past events in so wide an area. We are not concerned, after all, with each of the events that have happened in each nation, but only with those which have involved major segments of mankind, and so set a framework to all our historical experience. Those, while very important, can be presumed to be relatively few. For purposes of perspective (these need not be the only purposes of large-scale history, but surely they are important), a slim volume may be of more value than a fat one.

Further, we can at least postpone the insuperable problem of finding a universal scheme into which all history will fit – whether in terms of progress or of cycles, of a master-race or of a revelation. History is so rich that almost at the first touch it yields an overabundance of suggestions of pattern. We will find this true even for so broad a zone as we are concerned with. The historian need not fix upon a pattern for his whole field of inquiry before beginning his detailed work of criticism and exploration.

If a world history is philosophically possible, it will in any case be subject to two important limitations. It will not only be unlikely to deal with all or even most of the events that have troubled mankind from the beginning; further, it is unlikely to bear the type of human meaning which a sensitive history of a particular community can have. For it will deal with only such themes as are too broad in their ramifications to be conveniently handled within the limits of nations and cultural regions. Such themes are unavoidably somewhat impersonal.

Even with this much acknowledged, large-scale history retains its pivotal character; and this fact poses a crucial dilemma for the whole profession. We have noted above that, however unsatisfactory the pursuit of large-scale questions in wide historical complexes may be, it is inescapable for the serious historian. The scholar in any field must at the very least do whatever is necessary to eliminate as many errors as possible. But the whole point of historical thinking, for ordinary persons, lies precisely in the big questions. As a human being, unwilling to confine his moral horizon to the present moment as perhaps he pragmatically ought to, the ordinary person willy-nilly has his historical outlook; the historian must discipline it.

History, and all science and scholarship, is a matter of disciplining men's thinking – not of finding ultimate systems, but of improving point by point upon what the human public is crudely thinking at. Even if we cannot answer all the questions men pose – e.g., on universal history – we can and must show whatever can be demonstrated that is relevant to these questions. This much we cannot shirk. But if history itself is to maintain its worthy place among the scholarly disciplines, it must weave its very organization out of these larger questions, which remain its *raison-d'être,* or else grant the claims of some non-historically minded philosophers that it is at best but a secondary instrument of criticism, being essentially subjective where it counts. It is not by being scientific in details – demonstrating conclusively any number of points of minute documentation – that history can become a "science" – any more than the solution of any given private murder mystery is a "science" in the intended sense, no matter how "scientific" is the sleuth. But I believe it will indeed be found to be susceptible of such disciplined integration, and in a sense not basically different from any other type of study.

There is a line crossing through all types of historians, dividing those who will be concerned for such discipline from those who will not, cutting across all other types. It may be granted that what is important in Europe, as compared with China, is vast matters like Christianity, technical rationality, and the origin of our current world problems. But those who believe they can be answered only conjecturally or by inspiration and are not a serious scholarly concern, cannot well care for what "subjective" perspective is put into a "world" or "Western" history so long as the facts which happen to be in it are in detail correct; the title is rather an ornament than anything else. They cannot well care what periodization is used, or what the terms of any interregional comparisons they may happen to make by way of adornment; a fair comparison giving justice morally to each party will seem quite outside the pale of historical concern as such. Neither evaluative judgments, nor even the remoter sources of general conditions, so far as they do not enter into detail studied *ad hoc,* will seem relevant. Certainly, they will feel that all discussion about the Oikoumenic configuration is fanciful and cannot bear upon actual work they are doing. Among those humanistically inclined, they may concentrate on the exploits of individuals, but they will hesitate to admit the glories of nations as determinable by scholarship, let alone venture beyond the range compassed by explicit historical consciousness in their subjects. Among those scientifically inclined, they will be concerned with points immediately present to their problems, but leave broader perspectives to "philosophers of history." This orientation against the Big Problems is explicitly expressed only among those of a particular temperament, but no means universal, though found in all types of studies. Yet the tendency is so prevalent that the ordinary historical study often appears as negligent of such perspectives as if there were an explicit rejection of them.

But once the necessity of dealing with the large-scale questions is accepted, it will be found that they are subject to disciplinability in a scholarly sense; it is not necessary to have recourse to "philosophy of history" in the less respectable sense.

It has long since been established in what lies the disciplinability of historical detail. Just as the chemical experiment is a cumulation of evidence – in repeated experiments of various sorts – regarding the objects of study, themselves inaccessible (in this case, the abstract "laws"), to the point where further doubt must presume an untenable degree of coincidence – so historical study at best works with evidence (not, of course, the events themselves – which are as inaccessible as the chemical "laws," though for a different reason), to a like point of cumulative indubitableness, independent of the work of any one observer. Coincidences of various sorts in the evidence must accumulate to the point that, though any one of them might be due to chance, together they point to a single hypothesis that any independent investigator must accept. The recognition of these matters, indeed, may involve a wide knowledge of the habits of an age, of details of dating and language, of the remotest circumstances of a train of events. Much must depend upon points seemingly incidental to the matter at issue, which enter into the accumulated chain of coincidences.

It is in regard to the objectivity of larger historical treatments that a more serious question arises. Here the complexity of the inquiry, the breadth of the questions it asks, is such that it can no longer be a question of marshaling all evidence bearing upon a single occasion, but of selecting and arranging the evidence bearing on the wider questions at issue. In these more elaborate interpretations, accordingly, historians must vary according to their principles of arrangement and selection;

and appear willful and capricious. Nevertheless, the principles of objectivity applicable to the details still apply to the syntheses, only on a more subtle basis. In particular, any one elaboration can yield answers only to those questions which it poses – not only to those general questions it starts out with, but to those particular questions in terms of which it is built up; that is, its range of relevance is limited by its particular structure. Since any one inquiry must have a determinate structure, as we shall see, any one inquiry is limited in the account it can give of the general field it treats with. Accordingly, a large number of complementary studies is necessary to a balanced view of a given age or time, or even a given personality; yet each of them can be criticized with regard to its objectivity within the framework it has adopted – so that though there may be an indefinite number of different but complementary objective studies in a particular field, there may be an infinitely larger number of unsatisfactory studies in the same field that must be excluded.

Besides selection and ordering, categorizing also limits one's possibilities: periodization, grouping of people, or lines of activity – the choice of landmarks, the subordination of events, the coordination of conditions for purposes of comparison – the very grouping of materials into concepts, and the weighting of these concepts in ordering one's interpretation – all can vary, yet remain valid for one or another purpose. A study which averages out the reactions of peasants and artisans as "the lower classes" will read differently – answering different questions – from one which makes the distinction at the expense of clarity with regard to their common responses; a study arranging political events by reigns will legitimately read differently from one ordering them by cycles of prosperity.

It is thus unlikely that any one elaboration can even at best represent all viewpoints, assuming that would be desirable. Accordingly, historical writings will vary not only through the error and exploratory unsoundness at the frontiers of research, but in the most established areas, where many works must complement each other. As the perfect roundness of a circle can only be approximated to, in our measuring, by the infinite sides of a polygon, so in history – and perhaps in other fields as well, as they become more complex – a balanced view of a field will only be multiply achieved. Bury's notes, superseding details of Gibbon's *Rome,* corrects errors in view of better research, but it is otherwise with the difference between a modern historian who sees in Byzantium the effort to create a Medieval Christian society of a new sort, and on the other hand Gibbon's triumph of barbarism and religion – an orientation which continues to have its own validity.

This situation imposes on historians, however, the obligation not only of looking to the accuracy of their details, but of recognizing the limitations on the relevance of their treatments imposed by the limitations of their particular formulations. This is an obligation reviewers seem to have to point out too often, for too often a historian writes as if his particular presentation were a total and ultimate one, and makes false deductions as a result, at points where his work is inherently not relevant. Of sound works, it is said that one treatment supplements another; only in textbooks, where not so much an insight as a sort of commentary on hoped-for future reading is often desired, is there an attempt at least to mention all the major points of view in a field of inquiry, as throwing diverse but equally valid light on the matter.

Relevance of what is historically negative to the perspective required in large-scale objectivity

It is clear that a wide and subtle sense of perspective is a crucial intellectual virtue in the study of large-scale questions. This has a somewhat dangerous corollary: we must be as closely aware of "stagnant" cultural life as of florescent; we must study decline equally with progress. If we are aware of the spiritual danger in what is done, this need not be harmful. But there is sufficient tendency to do just that without such awareness to occasion a *caveat*.

Our historical consciousness, formed by Renaissance standards, has divided civilization (with increasing hesitancy) into classical ages and dark ages. The dichotomy was extended when we came to study not only Europe but Islam, India, China; we concentrated on the formative florescences, on the great and glorious innovators. That we now are running after all sorts of exotic growths, in art or in history either one, may well reflect a faltering of our taste – which indeed will have first appeared as early as the time when the Romantics discovered the European Middle Ages. This predisposition, to be sure, is very convenient for a study of Oikoumenic history, requiring as it does attention to the details of every sort of age. Nevertheless, the study has its justification, even for the understanding of the "classical ages" itself, and for the purest taste.

The historical significance of an unconscious whole

But large-scale history, however important, has its theoretical obstacles even when its validity on the level of inquiry has been granted. If history is to be regarded as the study of human action in the historical dimension, is not the study of much that must go to make up large-scale history a matter not of history, but of social science, or even of biology – to be drawn upon by the historian – ad hoc, when it comes to his attention, but forming no essential part of his work? In large-scale historical processes, three levels of movement are at work, all of which ought at best to be taken into account in evaluating what happens. In most of these areas, we are grossly ignorant, even for the best-studied regions. Even so, without holding such movements in mind, we can scarcely hope to pose appropriately the problem presented by such phenomena as florescences, declines, and the like. Aware of them, we can at least see the dimensions of the problems.

On the first level are what may be called extra-historical events – matters purely of climate, of disease mutations, of mutations among hominids, and the like. On a semi-historical level, unforeseen and unseen results of human actions, are such matters as changes in climate and resources resulting from human activity; diseases whose course is changed by human adjustments and wanderings; the demographic results of long-term migrations; effects on popular attitudes of drug uses among large sections of some populations; effects on health of food patterns resulting from economic organization; family (and hence educational) patterns; and of course the cumulation of technological invention. On a more strictly historical level, in that it is a question of conscious human action even though the results are here also commonly unforeseen, may be placed political activity and the creation of types of economic or social institutions; intellectual and spiritual openings and unfoldings of new implications; economic expansions and alterations in types of activity, at least where this is a local matter.

Now all of these sorts of development are partly blind, many of them quite unconscious; and no lines can very strictly be drawn among them. They all contribute to the development of history; no large-scale development can be properly understood without them. Certainly, if our history is to be centered on human achievement and failure, all these movements must be analyzed in connection with the primary questions which stir the historian: with the questions, who are we, we men, and what have we done. But in pursuing these questions, all these less immediate problems will be found to be strictly interdependent on the historical level.

A human historical act is, after all, not merely the conscious aspects thereof. It is the whole of the act, including the dumb matter acted upon and the conditions which make the act turn to something so different from what was intended – even when it seems to be most under control.

It is, then, in the perspective of interregional historical studies that the historical discipline can find its principles of integration. And the central feature of interregional history is the Oikoumenic configuration; for there is no real stopping point between essentially parochial studies and the Oikoumene itself.

A pure presentation of the development of the interregional configuration would not be, in the best sense, properly a history, though it might possess the dramatic interest of a panorama. It is rather a tool for historical investigation, making possible certain sorts of perspective. (A young economic geographer was lately complaining of the difficulty of escaping national limitations even in presenting European history, and cited in support the results of a demographic study of the Ruhr-Belgian-North French coal belt in the nineteenth century which brought out interesting material unavailable on the basis of conventional division by nations. Means of insuring international perspective are required for European history still, despite the presence there of a common set of institutions, and the existence of many "European" histories; how much more difficult, and wanting, are means for insuring interregional perspective!) There is needed a palpable basis for interregional outlook and orientation, a concrete picture to which a scholar can turn; this the study of the Oikoumenic interregional configuration can provide. Even though the Oikoumene as such does not form a regular historical specialty in the sense that the study of a particular linguistically marked complex of higher culture forms a full-fledged historical field, it is a distinct subject, the elaboration of which must require the special attention of interested scholars.

Awareness of such an interregional configuration will offer in any historical study – whether locally regional, or quite general – both direct and indirect advantages. On the one hand it will allow evaluation of the effect of the total interregional situation in limiting and in evoking local possibilities of development. This applies especially in the case of events and developments – e.g., in military, commercial, and even scientific and other cases, of a directly interregional character (for instance, the Mongol conquests). On the other hand it will also provide some guidance as to the interregional ramifications of a particular development, and generally its interregional character as ramification of developments elsewhere – e.g., in the study of the causes and conditions (both *why's* and *why not's*) of interregional "influences" (supplementing the study of the conditions of those influences found within the affected cultures themselves).

When it comes to this second type of advantage, it is not necessarily obvious that the separate working out in many areas of a common historical impulse, and even the contrasting responses or lack of them to a common historical situation, have serious historical meaningfulness; that it is important to be aware of the ramifications and unconscious convergences of particular developments outside a specified social framework. The tracing of the Hellenistic (via Buddhist) impulse in Chinese are, for instance, seems to have little organic relation any more to the Hellenistic culture itself, and it may seem futile to treat all the ramifications of that art as a single "interregional development." But to understand the *meaning* of the great visions which are properly the heart of history – the point at which the human spirit enters into its processes – in the unfolding historical dimensions of life, one must seek out the relevance and fate of these visions in the concrete historical development in which they were involved. One of the beauties of history, more than in biography proper, is that it illuminates the *condition humaine* by bringing out the priorly unknowable implications of a purpose which result from its being worked out on the same stage with contrasting purposes – to the effect that each vision means something other in its full historical context at last from what it could mean taken biographically. In history played on an interregional stage, these long-range unknowns enter in to humble even the largest of social visions – thus, what Islam has ultimately meant humanly, in its vast career, is very different, above all in Oikoumenic perspective, from what its most far-sighted creators expected. The importance of this sort of significance to ordinary historians is evident in the little "onlies" and "remarkables" with which historians sprinkle their judgments of the matters that come under their pen, and which so often look parochial from a wider viewpoint. And surely a philosophic historian may be glad for information which helps him to trace the unfolding of an idea, the essence of a situation, beyond the limits imposed by the consciousness of contemporary actors.

The history of Western Europe ought especially to profit from an interregional perspective, not only in the direct sense, in that the Oikoumeneic interregional situation as a whole has constantly had its effect on what was possible in Europe; not only in the sense that Western history as such has been particularly distorted in its sequence and character through the Westward distortion described in chapter one of this book, but more generally, because the peculiarly eccentric character of the West – it was so long a dependent frontier, so suddenly a center of world transformation, but almost never developed in and for itself alone – has meant that the human significance of Western history is more than usually tied in with a wider setting. Though for want of an adequate sense of the effective disposition of that wider world the need has never been met in terms much more concrete than Hegel's, one would suppose a primary interest in a history of the West would be precisely to trace our weird role in the world at large.

12

Conditions of historical comparison among ages and regions

The limitations of their validity

Large-scale history must find a great deal of its moral significance, in contrast to a sociological study of historical dynamics, in disciplining moral comparisons. As we have seen, it is in large measure the human need to make comparisons that make historical study of the big questions – which are directly or indirectly commonly matters of comparison – inescapable. This is not necessarily a matter of invidious comparisons. All moral evaluation, positive or negative, is a tissue of comparisons; we build our very self-identity upon comparison with what is not ourselves. To deal with the individual is to deal with the individual in a moral sense – individuality has ultimately no inherent significance save on that level – and this is to deal with the individual in terms of norms of some sort; and comparison with norms is but one aspect of a wider process of mutual comparison of diverse individuals. We know Leonardo is great by comparing his work with that of other painters. It has not been a false instinct, but the very mission of history, which has led historians to regard moral judgment of their heroes as a primary duty; and though the old-style explicit summing-up be no longer in vogue, the implicit judgment in terms of which our modern narratives are constructed is – as is the case with the novel, from which our new way was learned (not from natural science!) – more, and not less, rich in its moral analysis, if done well at all.

Accordingly, one of the major tasks of large-scale history is to develop the grounds for criticizing historical comparisons. It must criticize above all the units valid for various sorts of historical comparison, and the contexts in terms of which comparison can be relevant. But – for comparison always implies some sort of common context – this in turn implies discovering such valid elements of unity in history as may exist. In what ways does the historical field form a legitimate common context for the purposes of wide-ranging comparisons?

The unity of history as ground of comparisons

In my experiences teaching Islamic civilization to non-specialist students, I tried to get them to appreciate the cultural monuments of all kinds (literature, art, institutions, etc.) – a major object of historical study; but what they had to depend on as guides in approaching new material were such generalizations as they came across (for they *could not* remember many detailed facts long). To be sure, they remembered the simplest and most in accord with the prejudices of the environment; yet there were so *many* of these amateurish generalizations in what I had to have them read! It is precisely the "asides" (from the viewpoint of a detail-historian), the *comparisons* – that were crucial in the course: e.g., Meyerhof, "Arabian science like moon and stars between two [European] days" – but these presuppose a false structure to carry their meaning.

Scholars dare not leave such matters – the whole point of their work – to undisciplined "asides" based on uncriticized world images. Proper comparison is the foundation of historical judgment. The very selection of historically significant subjects is a matter of comparisons, of course – it is pointless to spend labor ascertaining the circumstances surrounding Michelangelo's various works unless we are assured he is a greater painter than Aunt Suzie. More relevantly to our present purposes, it is essential to compare the right sort of units; that they be on a single scale. For most purposes, it would be misleading to compare on the one hand the painting of the high Renaissance in Italy, and on the other hand every kind of French visual art, in all periods from the medieval to the modern. Moreover, even when one has the right units of comparison, their treatment, the framing of questions about them, is equally a matter of sound comparison. In a discussion of Michelangelo in Italian Renaissance art, the fact that he concentrates on the human form does not in itself call for much comment, for in this point he does not differ from other Renaissance artists. On the other hand, if more recent painters are involved in the discussion, his stress on the human form becomes more important, Here soundness of comparison calls for more than a sense of proportion in the items immediately under discussion; it calls for an understanding of a wider context. One must not compare Michelangelo with some modern seascape painter, say, simply in point of their choice of the human and natural forms without being aware that their choices were shared with others in their respective times, lest the comparison be irrelevant to any significant questions about the two painters themselves. The process of comparison must be disciplined so that by choice of comparable units of comparison and by awareness of relevant context we can know what are the significant questions – what is and what is not a problem.

So soon as one or both of the members of a comparison are involved in or influenced by such a historical configuration as the Oikoumenic, this fact must be taken into account. In a comparison, for instance, between Viking and Polynesian explorations, the much closer association of the Vikings with the technology, trade, and even politics of the wider Oikoumenic zone cannot be ignored in evaluating both the naval problems involved and the final results. Being part of the Oikoumenic zone meant initially a constant contact with a wider society of relatively rapidly changing cultural level: during the centuries of exploration, home conditions changed significantly. The rise of kingdoms in the Scandinavian states, and their Christianization, affected both the motives for expansion, and the types of relationship retained with the original centers. Norse trade with the Middle East and with Europe provided a changing basis for alternative estimation of the gains of exploration. And finally, the Viking colonies were either absorbed into their corner of the Oikoumene or lost; that there was no dispersal into persisting isolated communities was partly the result of geography, but partly the result of the high degree of far-flung interdependence that Viking life was involved in.

The connection with the Oikoumeneic configuration can be of several degrees. A comparison between West-Europeans and Mexicans at the time of Columbus which left out of account the wide non-European background of Europe would be obviously unfair if used, as it has been used, to deprecate the native abilities of the Mexicans. In the case of peoples only marginally associated with the Oikoumene, where one is more closely involved than another, there may be equal unfairness involved in a straight comparison, or unsoundness in evaluating influences, potentialities, or courses of development. In any such case, it may be necessary to recognize the particular conditions of the Oikoumenic configuration at the time of the comparison, and how they relate to the member that is more closely linked to the Oikoumene: whether interregional trade by literate peoples is a serious factor or not, whether an atmosphere of receptivity for a universal religion is to be expected or not etc. Thus a comparison of some remoter people with the pagan Arabians in Hellenistic times – when under unusual circumstances they might produce a Zenobia, and the civic magnificence of Petra or Palmyra – cannot be the same as a comparison with the likewise pagan Arabians in Christian times, when under unusual circumstances they might produce Muhammad and the other prophets of his time; for quite apart from any internal differences in the Arabians' life at the two times, the all-Oikoumeneic influences they were subjected to differed, and differed in decisive ways.

To be sure, in such cases one can take into account the broader historical environment piecemeal, noting the European environment of the Vikings, or the Middle Eastern environment of the Arabians. The Vikings to be sure were in some touch directly with the Middle East, and the Arabians with India. But such further contacts can be likewise taken into account *ad hoc*, without any attention being paid to the Oikoumene as a whole. The reasons for bearing in mind the Oikoumenic configuration at large are in part to assure a full view of possibly relevant elements, and in part to assure a proper sense of proportion. These reasons are especially weighty in the case of comparisons between situations both fully within the Oikoumenic historical complex.

The unity of history is above all interdependence, in ages and regions, in terms of the problems posed (ultimately, indeed, the problems posed *to* the historian as inquirer – though this depends in part on problems posed to the men in the past), rather than of the human action taken to solve them – the materialist historian's unity from below rather than the idealist's unity from above (a higher unity); but ultimately the two unities are two faces of one coin, since the problems are problems only by virtue of their being the objects of action; while action from above has a moral obligation to follow the unity of its problems even when this is not fulfilled – even where it is not fulfilled in our own times. It is the awareness of irreversible progression in nature and history that has made the question of the unity of history a matter no longer of negative relevance – the ruling out of something elsewhere of importance prior to that of what one is here involved in – but a matter of inescapable positive implications both moral and structural.

Structural unity: Its effects on the bases of comparison

I have sketched the ways in which the Westward distortion, as one effect of the want of interregional perspective, has distorted our several received interpretations of history. It will be suggestive to classify five types of interregional motif, considering briefly some of the problems arising in using them.

There are, in the first place, common events. The Indo-European migrations of the "Renovation" and "Subversion" periods, the Mongol Empire, the Black Plague are obvious examples of this type of motif, and here the interregional effects, and often the interregional causes, of the events are clear. Inevitably in such cases even regional histories delve into broader fields. In connection with such motifs, however, it is useful to include "accidental" material – that is, events outside the pattern of that motif itself, though of course it may share common causes with it in common circumstances. Such are the Turkish conquests in the Middle East previously to, and in India concurrently with, the Mongol Conquests, as are in the same way the Crusades. Each movement has a bearing on all the others, in this case in terms of strength of various states; moreover, in any common results of the main event, they will have modifying and supplementing effects – Turks did for India what Tungus started in China and Mongols finished; and both Turks and Tungus can then usefully be associated with the Mongol conquest, though in themselves not events common to many regions. This kind of accidental relation among otherwise local motifs only serves to bring out that any one motif is an abstraction from a far more complicated network; that some elements in the network must be treated as relatively accidental is purely a matter of convenience. It is to be noted further that many things can be treated from the point of view of being a common event. The Near Eastern Imperial Tradition, for instance, from Sargon to Alexander, both as a developer of administrative methods, and as a recurrent center of cultural mixing, serves as an interregional event, or a series of them, impinging on the whole Indo-Mediterranean area. In a different way the development of the pseudo-sciences, alchemy, geomancy, astrology, can, to the extent that they share ideas interregionally, be considered under the form of a common event, detrimental perhaps to the pure sciences, and in their progressive development having a distinct impact on the cultures. In these latter cases, however, it would be only as an incidental way of throwing light on them that they might be considered as common interregional events; they will be more easily handled as other types of motif.

Another evident type of interregional motif is that of paralled developments: the flowering of individual thought in the "Liberation Period," the evolution of scriptural religions, the development of supra-governmental law. Cases of simple comparison come in here, as that of India and China in the "Liberation Period": we can compare Ch'in with the Punjab, Ch'u with Magadha both in point of philosophy and political role, and then compare the victory of Ch'in with the contrasting Magadhan leadership in India, and the comparative vitality of the resultant empires. But such amusing speculations are not the gist of interregional study under this head. If we compare the intellectual traditions of Greek, Sanskrit, and presumably Magian peoples in the "Consolidation Period," for instance, there is probably a common Indo-European background, and almost certainly an interrelated local background against which to compare them. Here we have presumably common conditions and circumstances involved; treating the events as parallel and comparable is simply the easiest way to get at a difficult problem, when the common conditions are hard to study by themselves. It is probably ineffective to consider such parallel developments in terms of a predetermined stage that cultures must go through, which will be arrived at independently at a fixed time.

Clearly, for instance, there is not an inherent urge which sets off the development of supragovernmental law at a certain point – Roman law, the laws of Mani grow perhaps roughly at the same centuries, but only roughly; Muslim, Christian, and developed Hindu codes that persist from government to government mature perhaps again roughly together in the middle of the first millennium; but there is no fixed point at which they do so, or any fixed manner. However, the development of scriptural religion and of the large-scale state, of critical philosophy and of economic modes is similar among them all, and, especially in economic matters, more or less constantly interacting and forced to a mutual accommodation, it is to be expected that in such can be found grounds for a roughly contemporaneous development of stable law. Such mutual accommodation over a long period of time does not make for immediate and personal relations among participants in a movement, and so for strict contemporaneity of generation, any more than it does for an originally harmonized pattern. Yet it is likely to be of fundamental importance in determining the course of any broadly significant movements. It is unlikely that any major type of development in one area will fail eventually to be felt among its neighbors in some form or other, and to be accommodated to at last throughout the interlinking Oikoumeneic Zone; the frequency of parallel developments which we have noticed supports such a supposition.

A consequence of this, incidentally, is that in studying interregional comparabilities it is not necessarily the outstanding galaxies in each culture that must be compared, but to gain a true picture often lesser but comparable figures in one with greater in another. If science is at certain times of special preeminence in Persia, and less so in the Punjab – or if mysticism develops greater names in the Punjab than in Persia – nevertheless in each case Punjabi science and Persian mysticism will be fruitfully studied to discover interregional relationships here at work.

A third classification of interregional motifs can be called supraregional: they are those developments which by affecting the conditions of the whole affect incidentally each region. The most obvious instance of such a supra-regional motif is the expansion of the Oikoumeneic civilizations. As civilizations gradually extended their sway, they brought about changes in the "balance of power" between barbarism and the cities, so that by neither a common event, nor by direct interrelations, a common effect was produced through the affecting of common conditions. The days of Attila differ from those of Genghis Khan in that in the latter's day Central Asia was swamped with civilization: an added feeling of nomadic vengeance combined with an immediate use of the full techniques of civilization to make the Mongol conquest quite different from the Hunnic, and productive of entirely different subsequent results. Chinese, Europeans, and Iranians, even Indian Buddhists, had combined quite unconsciously to make the whole continent a changed place, with changed results. Similarly, by the time the Western Metamorphosis was under way it was only the more isolated regions of the Hemisphere that had not been explored by Arabs or Chinese or Indians, and to which the basic trade routes and means of exploitation had been already opened up; one might hazard the guess that only in the second half of the Second Millennium, when this was done, was the European world conquest possible.

Similarly possessed of a supraregional quality is the cumulative progress that continues through thick and thin. In such times as the "Revision Period," in the early Byzantine Mediterranean Basin, there seems to be little of a spectacular nature, yet the introduction of silk, the Diophantine mathematics, and the continuous itemic improvements in law, medicine, and administration, religion and art, add up at last to the body of material, possessed ultimately interregionally, on which such a movement as the Islamic florescence, or the Western Metamorphosis, appear. Indeed, many developments have an aspect that could be looked at in this way. The rise of coinage throughout the zone in the first millennium B.C., apparently in independence, changes the conditions of interregional trade to a degree, at least indirectly, by its affects on internal trade, at last directly; again, the problem of centralization faced and met by so many separate governments at different times has its bearing on the total course at last of interregional movements.

A convenient fourth type of motif is the activity motif; cases where a particular activity involves interregional relationships. Good examples here are the course of science, and the development of monastic ideals insofar as the friars and dervishes, bikhus and fakirs impinged on one another (even their pious emulation had its interfaith aspects): whether monasticism begins in India or not, it is an activity common to many areas, with its particular and often intermingling carriers. Especially interesting as an interregional activity is the commercial exploitation of the Indian Ocean basin. From Zanzibar to Malacca, religious, commercial, and philosophical strains from many cultures and areas interweave to form by the "Reconstruction Period" an area quite distinctive and almost unified in respect simply to these interregional activities.

As a fifth type of interregional motif I suggest the regional focus. Very frequently a region serves a particular interregional role, its very position and inner condition becoming a continuing motif of more general history. Thus Gupta India, in "Revision" times, gathers into it impulses from around it, and retransmits them in all directions, a focus for many trends, as well as productive of its own. In comparatively recent times Africa beyond the Sahara has served as a meeting ground for Muslim and Christian missionaries, traders, and military, and its position and its exploitable condition have played an interregional role. On the contrary, the gradual civilization of Central Asia made it the more powerful as a center of conquest of surrounding areas, perhaps; at any rate, its position and military quality have made it a conquering center since earliest times, and as a region it has that interregional role. An eccentric case of a region playing a role as such in interregional history is that of the early Occident, which through Rome became the seat of the Mediterranean Empire, and influenced the Middle East and indirectly farther parts of the Oikoumenic Zone in its *nouveau-riche* manner. Indeed, every new region has an interregional role of some importance, like that of Russia as it gradually developed to the point of quite transforming the fronter problems of both the Latins and the Byzantines; or that of the Far South East, with its focal role in commerce. Throughout Oikoumenic times the geographical position of the Middle East, at the very least, made it a central focus for the whole Zone, between Europe on the northwest and India on the southeast, the sea routes to the Indies and the land routes to the Far East, Africa on the south and Russia and Central Asia on the north. Even Buddhism seems to have spread from India to China first through Iran, so that it was Parthians who first translated from Sanskrit to Chinese. The place of developments in the Middle East, and of the Middle East in developments, is a theme carrying consistently through Oikoumenic history; that region is not only literally a Mecca of civilization.

These five types of motif, of course, are anything but mutually exclusive or categorically exhaustive. They are rather alternative ways of considering interregional phenomena. They serve to point out, at any rate, the variety and complexity of interregional factors. Thus, a specific interregional history will want to give in general each region and each period its due. It will inevitably emphasize perspective and context, rather than the specific origin of institutions, perhaps best left to more local histories. For the interpretation of mankind, it is the perspective which interregional history can give which will determine the treatment of motifs.

Whatever one's general orientation to world history, however, the monographic problems will be similar. These world-historical problems require treatment independently, over and beyond the treatment they may incidentally receive by specialists in this or that region. Interregional history deserves attention upon its own merits. There must be more studies of "influences," of course, and generally of relationships among cultures. But these will not fully serve the purpose so long as they are limited in outlook to only one region – e.g., how has India influenced *Europe?* Yet, regarded from a world viewpoint, even these limited studies will have a place among the innumerable studies of every sort that must arise in tracing interregional affairs. For many of all these will be pursued within a very local field; only the purpose which informs the inquiry will be world-historical. What matters is that this purpose emerge with clarity. To this end, scholarship in interregional history must become more aware of its special problems and outlook.

Not only do historical movements distinctly overlap the regional cultures, but within a region cultural elements are frequently too intermingled to allow of treatment solely in terms of mutually exclusive regions. It will limit our view of the time to treat the various aspects of Gupta India as intelligible only within the limits of that society, or as matters of incidental impingement of that society on others; for India in Gupta times is a center of cultural activity whose full meaning and results can be seen only in connection with the condition of the rest of the world at the time. A study of Hellenistic art will cut right across Gupta India, linking it on the one hand with earlier times to the west, and on the other hand with its own times to the northeast and southeast, which it is influencing. The same could be said of Hellenistic science, and here the influences leading out of Gupta India and of the succeeding centuries are westward as well as northward and southward. For commerce the India of early centuries A.D. was center for influences out of the Indies, which the Tamils were colonizing, west and north. The Buddhist and Hindu religions came out of India itself, Hinduism spreading particularly east, and Buddhism in Gupta times especially north and west. Colonization and commercial development from south India influenced the Indies and Indochina even more than their trade influenced lands further west and north. In many instances, as in the case of the colonization and of the intense Buddhist activity of north India, the effects were ultimately felt much more in other areas, the Far East and the far South East, than in India itself. In short, India in Gupta times acted as a focusing and redistributing center for many trends and movements, almost like a hub of the whole Oikoumenic Zone for a time. To deal with India in that period as essentially a self-contained cultural region would be to miss a wealth of significance in what was going on.

A different type of circumstance, though even more obvious, in which a regional approach is insufficient, is that of the "marginal" regions which, while having an inevitable continuity within themselves of time and space, also exhibit a bewildering confusion of regional cultures within themselves. The interaction of cultural elements from the Far East, from India, from the Middle East, and from the modern West, combined with distinctive developments of its own, have made the far South East a remarkable region to challenge handling in terms of the exclusive culture patterns. As in the case of its growth into an imperial preserve of modern seapowers, so in most other ways the development of Indochina and Malaysia can be viewed only in terms of the interactions of many cultures, themselves not behaving in fully distinct ways. The various religions that have passed over the area are recalled by Hindu Bali, last remnant of the earliest doctrine; the Hinayana Buddhist mainland; Mahayana Buddhist sculptures in the islands it once so painfully won from Hinduism only to lose again; the Loyal Islam of the archipelago; and the Christianity of the Philippines, which were imperfectly covered by the older faiths, and left for the late comer. In literature, art, and science Chinese and Sanskrit influence have combined to make well deserved the name Indo-China; while under it all Toynbee at least can see an independent Hinayana culture surviving through the ages. It seems absurd to try to reduce the kaleidoscopic changes in the most characteristic elements of culture to incidental relations of larger regions; for it is evident that a continuity of cultural development is forced on the area by time and space. Java and Sumatra, when fighting for and against Buddhism, were not in completely different circles of intelligibility; and when Java adopted the Sumatran faith, Javanese culture did not change its basic position in the world overnight. Malacca and Singapore have long been crossroads of mankind, whatever their faith or tongue, and can be understood only in terms of Oikoumenic and now global development.

A composite region like that – another example is Central Asia, where

Buddhism, Christianity, and Islam have all prevailed, and many regions have been joined with politically and socially – will manifestly present a minimum of advantage to a regional study, and a maximum of light will be thrown on it in the course of studying interregional problems. An ambiguous case like Russia requires interregional light in a different manner. Russian history does not fit into the categories for the most part of the Latin West, but in recent centuries has been so bound up with it as to be inseparable, in certain respects, at least between the times of Peter the Great and Lenin. On the other hand, Russia had not been intelligible simply as an outpost of Byzantium. Yet it can never be divorced intelligibly either, from South or from West. As in the case of the far South East, the only solution is to develop a more general framework within which Russia can find a place; but, whereas in Indonesia interregional trade and other such interactions will be of major importance as factors in terms of which the region develops its particular forms, in Russia, no doubt, greater scope can be allowed for internal cultural development, and interregional relations in the form of geographic balance or of common events and developments impinging on Russia will be instead a fundamental frame of reference.

However, there is more to the problem of relative spheres of a regional approach and of an interregional approach in understanding the relations of the various regions. It is sometimes suggested that whatever may be said of the objective correlations and regularities, the "causal" development of cultures, their human significance is to be sought, if anywhere, only within a particular culture, whose forms are to be interpreted as a common whole; that any relations among these, while they may have profound causal effect on the various cultures, have no significance except in terms of the particular worlds of meaning identified exclusively with each culture. This point must be accorded due respect, as it is an important part of a general recognition among us that without immediate value, the indirect knowledge of science is dead; that no *consensus gentium pragmaticorum*, no evaluation by a congress of general semantics is adequate in human affairs. Nevertheless, the ordinary formulation of it in terms of exclusive cultures leaves much of human history in the lurch – the Far South East, say, as well as those recognized periods within a culture which are not highly "integrated" in Sorokin's sense. It concentrates on finding meaning for men only in the general cultural configurations, noting only in passing that of course life has meaning for people in all sorts of connections, whether their individual personalities or their cultural backgrounds are highly integrated or not.

The units of historical comparison

Several sorts of historical complexes

The historical complexes peculiarly relevant to *world* history are the largest units of historical activity isolable short of the world taken as a whole (world history defined as those historical processes which involve so much the greater part of mankind that their study from the perspective of any localized area, such as Europe or the Far East, must remain fragmentary). Some examples of the several sorts of concepts of historical complex follow, with appropriate roles of each. (a) The Oikoumene – the civilized zone of Eurasia and northern Africa, which gradually expands during the millennia from ca. 3000 B.C. to recently – is a major historical complex; but for good historical handling of world history, certain component units within the Oikoumene must be dealt with: (b) A "civilization" is the commonest unit generally used – a matter of common backgrounds and current interrelation, a common social-cultural context in which art is created, institutions modified, and so forth, cultural matters outside of which are not *as such* much present to the consciousness. (Two common limiting features are: common religion or common classical and/or polite language[s].) "Civilizations" are appropriate units to use from the point of view of internal spiritual and intellectual evolution and its dialectic – art, institutional economy, religion, philosophy, even in this respect science. (c) A "region" is a geographical area (in which historical considerations determine its delimitations) of common interactions, relatively free of major physical barriers to communication or interactions – which may include strongly contrasting cultures in juxtaposition (e.g., Indochina-Malaysia or the coexistence of Chinese and the Yunnan Thais). "Regions," including the Oikoumene, are useful units from the point of view of external interrelations of power dynamics, of finding *constants* relatively external to the cultural development proper. (d) A "cultural area," for "area-studies," has less historical than cross-sectional considerations delimiting it, including those of physical geography and geology perhaps (e.g., the geographers' Middle East). A "culture-area" is useful for coordination of various disciplines, especially for *planning*. (e) A "civilized tradition" is a matter of common basic background in culture and history, without necessarily constant contact among different parts (e.g., Japan and China); two: "India-Middle East-Europe" and "Far East"; for four, Far East, India, Middle East, Europe. This concept may be useful from the point of view of underlying institutions and their transformations, anthropology, comparative studies, and so forth.

Regionality

Every cultural complex of wide enough scope to be reckoned a "civilization" is prevalent over what may be called a "region." But there are many other regions that cannot readily be defined in terms of a given civilization. For instance, much can be said about the Middle East which is true of both pre-Islamic and Islamic times; and if one can, indeed, speak of "Middle Eastern civilization" (for instance, in the seventh century when civilization in that area is being transformed into what will then be called Islamic), it is because we are aware of the region first, as an area of identifiable cultural traditions; and so can be led to refer to a "civilization" characteristic of that region at any given time, though from first to last such a civilization may vary enormously. Again, India is a clear region which can be discussed in Indo-Muslim times despite that fact that it is only a part of the "Hindu civilization" – indeed, the very question, "is there a common and distinctive civilization in India then?" presupposes that there is a common historical complex – a region of historical interactions.

For a region in our particular discussion is merely an area of historical interrelations and interactions, closely-knit enough so that many questions can be dealt with in its terms without spreading out to a still wider region – that is, in practice, to the Oikoumene. Hence a hodge-podge like the Far South East still forms a region, because Hindus, Buddhists, Muslims, and Confucians, and finally even Christians, lived out their history so much in each others' hair that however different their cultural patterns they formed a common region. The proto-Thai of Yunnan, though not Chinese, formed for a while a part of the region of China, not because they participated in its culture, but because they were drawn into its history.

The Oikoumene is the largest region. But smaller regions than it are what one is referring to when one says "interregional" – and, so far as this is contrasted to "local," the regions are the largest complexes usually isolable before one comes to the level of the Oikoumene, or at least of, say, the Indo-Mediterranean historical complex. Regions are more flexible to deal with than "cultures" because, while including them, they allow for many other sorts of cases.

In designating usable regions for the purposes of interregional history, there is not always the same traditional difficulty as in the case of the West. However, there is a problem, indicated for one thing by a lack of regional terminology. The only standard regional method we have in use now goes by continents, the only concession to cultural regionalism being to divide off Europe from the rest of Eurasia. This results in a concept, "Asia," the miscellaneous remainder, which has no geographical, ethnographical, or political function, except to exalt the status of Europe as homologous to its vast self, and to confuse well-meaning professors who talk hopefully about wedding the "ideals of Asia" to the "skills of Europe."[1] But these "continents," not even useful for geological purposes, are hopeless for studying man. At least four-fifths of humankind live on the one continent Eurasia; and to divide Eurasia into two as we have does not solve the problem, for though "Europe" is almost a reasonable region, the lumping all the rest together as "Asia" merely encourages the Westward distortion. To meet the need we have evolved terms like "Near East," "Middle East," "Far East," which are the best available yet; but they are not clear even so, for all these terms have different meanings attached to them by different people. While for some the Near East is the area of the old Ottoman Empire, for others it is restricted to the Balkan Peninsula, and for others it expands to include Iran, since Iranian history is inevitably bound in with the general course of the Ottoman area. It is probably in this latter sense that it refers to an area most frequently useful for interregional purposes, though each of its meanings of courses has its uses. In this same expanded sense "Middle East" is now used by the British military, a term usually restricted in America to lands well east of the Mediterranean, and often extended even to include India. The Far East as a term is equally difficult, sometimes referring to the old Chinese and Japanese empires, sometimes extending southward as far as Malaysia, and sometimes expanding to include, with India, half the human race, and so to become completely unwieldy.

The term "West" is of course similarly ambiguous, being sometimes used in the sense of the nations of old Latin heritage, being sometimes expanded to include Russia and the Balkans, and sometimes contracted to refer to Britain, France, and Germany as against the "Central" German powers. But besides their ambiguity it is the common fault of these terms to preserve, in their form, the old division into "West" and "East," for "Near East" and "Far East" inevitably suggest a correspondence to similar divisions within the "West."

The inadequacy of terms, of course, merely cloaks an inadequate regional equipment for use in interregional study. If interregional his-

[1] Much the same ambiguities adhere to the term "Asia" as to the "Orient." An amusing example of the use of the word is found in Michelet: "Long had those two sisters, those two halves of humanity, Europe and Asia, the Christian religion and the Mussulman, lost sight of each other. . . ." What would the Hindu Mahasabha say to that!

tory is the study of those phenomena too wide to fit conveniently into any particular region, it is necessary for economy's sake to know what regions hang well enough together to be dealt with on the regional level. Within the Oikoumenic Zone, moreover, distinguishing regions, like the Far East and the Latin West, which form relatively constant parts of the Oikoumenic Configuration, are of particular use in orienting ourselves in the infinitely complex network of relations across the Zone. Perhaps the most significant of such regions are the Confucian Far East, the peninsula and island of the far South East, India and nearby areas, and vast reaches of Central Asia, the Middle East from the Nile and the Aegean through Iran, the Russian area, and the Occident. Certainly in addition to these are likely to be helpful at various times overlapping regions, the Sudan, the Mediterranean Basin, the Levant, for instance; and for relatively many purposes certain subdivisions can be noted – within Western Europe, the south around the Mediterranean, and the north on the Atlantic; within India, the Deccan and the north; within China, again, the south and the north, the Hoang-Ho Valley.

It is still necessary to an understanding of the role of Oikoumenic conditions in interregional history, to examine the role of the Oikoumenic regions in regard to each other. One can hardly, of course, think of the various regions as fixed entities; nevertheless it is helpful to abstract fairly constant regions within the Oikoumenic Zone, within which regions there is a degree of cultural integration – a common religion, during much of the time, a common literary heritage, and a common political framework. To a large extent the Zone divides itself up very conveniently into such regions, and there is a regular configuration which they form over many centuries, which while constantly growing and changing remains recognizable from the time of its formation in the first millennium B.C. till the Western Metamorphosis upsets it. For instance, the Confucian Far East forms from Chou times a distinct region in such a sense – as it expands, new countries like Japan are not always incorporated directly under the imperial rule, but, recognizing common political standards, and often enough having a common reverence for Chinese imperial authority, Japan and China, as well as the lesser nations in their vicinity, form a common diplomatic region as well as a literary and religious one. Moreover, in the Oikoumenic Configuration this Far Eastern region has for millennia the same general relations with other regions: overland immediately with Central Asia, and beyond the Middle East; by several routes, but also by religious ties, with India; by sea with the far South East, and thence with other seafaring regions.

For use in an interregional study in such a sense, it is likewise useful to define a region in the far west that is also fairly constant in these senses; and in the Latin-using area such a region is ready waiting for us. In origin the term Occident applied to the western half of the Roman Empire, essentially Italy, Africa, Spain, and Gaul. The Greeks never considered themselves Westerners; for them Delphi was the center of the world; but the consciousness of cultural dependence drove the Latins to count themselves as west of center.[2] In this western Mediterranean area with its hinterland to the north we have for the duration afterwards of the Oikoumenic Zone a region consistent enough to be studied as a cultural whole; for in the main there has been a continuous Latin tradition over it all, except Punic Africa, though its center of gravity shifted northward as it grew. From the time when the various naval colonists, Phoenicians, Etruscans, or Greeks, were brought into the Latin empire, through the time when "Romania" of the west was divided into Germanic Christian kingdoms, through the rise of Carolingian and Papal power which brought uncertain hegemonies to the area, up till the time when the Concert of Europe was still recognized, the area maintained its cultural and to some degree or other its political unity against the rest of the world, be it Orthodox, Muslim, or further afield.

To be sure, just what shall be considered regions for purposes of interregionality will be largely a matter of convenience. A study of the relations between northern Italy and southern France is likely to be considered a matter of general European interest, while the relations between northern Italy and southern are classed as an Italian affair; so arbitrarily could the relations between the Latins and the Byzantines be considered either as local or as interregional. Conceivably a region inclusive of Africa and Europe could be set off from other regions, and its students study the several matters that such a region would have in common; but this would probably not be convenient, and such study would probably be more fruitful if it were associated with other interregional study, as the lines of connection it would trace are scarcely more close than those among any other great areas. The regions themselves, and consequently the interregional field, are fairly well marked

[2] Some historians have been misled by their own feelings of the Latin West as essentially the world into an emphasis too great on the "universalism" of Latin Medieval political theory. Truly universalist was Chinese political theory of the time, even with so brilliant a man as Wang Anshih, picturing China as the world; but the Latins were *then* a bit more modest; the Emperor of the Respublica Christiana was admittedly emperor of only the West, and functioned as general in chief solely (as in the Crusades) when the Respublica was fighting foreigners, beyond its local jurisdiction.

out by the regional studies already done. Moreover, variable as the regions are, their function for the purposes of study persists. One cannot assign Tibet to either the Far East or India or Central Asia at all times, or for all purposes at any one time. Nevertheless it is as part of one or another of such regions that we study Tibet when it enters into the broad movements that have covered the hemisphere. As being next to India, it learns to use the Syrian alphabet, along with Italy and with Bengal; as part of the Far East it is covered with Buddhist missionaries along with Parthia and with Japan; as part of Central Asia it fights for control of the trade routes along with the Huns and with the Arabs.

Periodization

The different sorts of historical complexes bear different relations to time and periodization. "Regions" would have minimal time-delimitation (though they are meaningless apart from human settlement patterns). "Culture-areas" would be present-oriented. "Civilized traditions" would be seen as persistent through the period of civilization, at least provisionally. "Civilizations" are the briefest and most fractionable sorts of world-scale historical complexes; they, above all, can be regarded as having limits in space as well as in time (points of relative discontinuity with regard to central features in terms of which the cultural context must be defined), e.g., Islamic civilization, despite its continuity with the Sassanid, definitely is new in the 8th century; or, to take a smaller unit than is perhaps relevant to world-history, one can fractionize down to a "civilization of the Renaissance in Italy and environs."

Just as the Oikoumenic Configuration needs to be clarified spatially, in the finding of suitable regions in terms of which to study it, it also must be clarified in time, so that a usable periodization is available to deal with its development as a whole. Of course, any overall periodization will have to be arbitrary, particularly in earlier periods, while the Configuration was only in process of formation. However, the only general periodizations at present in use are the Ancient-Medieval-Modern ages, and the centuries. The former slice off periods too big for use, even were they possessed of any natural significance for interregional affairs. The latter do not take advantage of what integration there is in the development of the Configuration, and so fail to be either suggestive or useful in marking off units that can be satisfactorily dealt with. The value of periodization consists in its abstracting lengths of time during which it is useful to deal with comparable development or common events as groups. For instance, the time of the flowering of individual thought, before referred to, covered several centuries usefully compared together; the same is true of the expansive and nationalistic movements of early modern times. Another useful element in periodization would be to have ages fairly uniform in length, even if not in creative content; there is an advantage in recognizing a barren period as such (if it be barren really), as we inevitably do, for instance, in a century periodization; for barrenness needs to be explained and evaluated, too.

Historical complexes in modern history

For characterizing modern history, consciously appropriate kinds of historical complex must be selected according to the problem dealt with; old categories are often misleading. Among those problems about the nature of modern culture history in which *choice of sorts of historical complexes* is relevant are the following: (A) those involving the selection of units of comparison, when modern phenomena are involved; thus the comparison of "Western" and "Islamic" patterns, or "modern" and "medieval" (within the West), or (better) modern (in the West or elsewhere) and medieval (Western or, e.g., Islamic); (B) those involving the envisaging of contexts of inquiry; thus the interpretation of modern art within West-European art since the Italian Renaissance, or within European art since the Archaic Greeks, or within the world-wide setting (and various backgrounds) of the modern transformation, since the 18th century; and (C) hence in particular, problems of the explanation of what is distinctive in modern society, which involve defining what is modern, and defining what other units are comparable thereto and involve at the same time the setting of the context, intra-European or otherwise.

Such problems can commonly not be envisaged in terms of the historical complexes generally used, since these commonly do not offer proper comparability with the modern situation: the Oikoumene itself has in effect ceased to exist as a continuing historical complex – but it is useful for comparisons across time. "Regions" have come to have, under modern conditions, a quite different significance, communication having been transformed; they are more local in importance – having been replaced in effect by "culture-areas," of limited usefulness in analyzing the past, as noted. "Civilized traditions" institutional study and comparison is adequately relevant only within a period (between the advent of civilization and the modern transformations) when the type of institution they presented had basic continuity; hence not in the modern setting except in a limited degree. As to "civilizations," for most such purposes it will be necessary to regard the several historical civilizations (including the West) as having come to an end with the advent of the great "Western" or "Modern" transformations. They have been superseded by a new type of historical complex, world-wide, and not necessarily comparable with any of the old civilizations – which must be compared as a historical complex with any that are of use, according to the requirements of a particular question – with the Oikoumene, or with *any* of the pre-modern civilizations.

Orators' preoccupations with "Western Man," etc., are accordingly for the most part dangerously misformulated!

Creativity and decadence

Cultural creativity and cultural decadence both happen all the time, but are usually neither of them predominant – for cultural conservatism is. (We must distinguish between decline of creativity from an efflorescence and actual regression. This is especially easy in science and scholarship generally, but also holds in art and perhaps even in politics.) The question is, when does one or the other, by exception, become predominant, in an epoch of flowering (which is afterwards looked on as classical), or in an epoch of decay (as distinct from epigonism? Either flowering or decay may take place in individual fields; the civilization as such is characterizable so only when key fields (key for that civilization or for purposes of a specific inquiry) decay or flower, and the civilization as a whole reflects this – and here decay may happen with or without a corresponding flowering of something new. A civilization may be defined as the cultural pattern formed in and conserved after a period when cultural creativity is predominant – hence such flowering periods are of special importance; but also, a civilization may be defined in societal terms, in which case the above becomes merely a special case – but an important one, and perhaps a type-case.

The cultural creativity of modern times is a special case – only partly matched by the Classical flowerings (and lesser ones throughout Oikoumenic history) or even by the original settings up of civilizations – in that to a greater degree than before cultural creativity has become institutionalized – measuring cultural creativity and regression by level of taste, knowledge, and skill, and by the structure of institutions supporting these (including for these purposes justice as one cultural activity measurable in these terms).

Cultural florescence (with special rules in addition for art and science) will happen when the *persistent forces of disruption* become strong enough to overcome the powers of authority without being so overwhelming as to suppress in their turn the equally *persistent forces of creation,* while cultural decadence is of two main types. The first is decadence which occurs by the internal logic of a state structure or art form or whatever, by the law of Exhaustion – the stalemate whereby one would have to descend to a lower level (anarchy, of government or art) to break a deadlock created by an overworked form (of taste, of authority, etc.). This is so alike in point of (a) art forms like the baroque where art cannot persist in the classic form because new generations' taste demands something fresh, but cannot be crude as would be demanded by a truly fresh start on a line for which taste is not yet developed; and in (b) point of politics, where a constitution has become out-of-date but so entrenched that its modification without recourse to crude political forms is impossible – e.g., the alienation of lands for monks and lay lords in late Byzantium; or even (c) in science, where a theoretical structure is more readily heavily and at last stranglingly amended rather than dangerously overthrown – e.g., the Ptolemaic system, for which neither heliocentrism nor spiral orbits nor others could offer help. Exhaustion can mean mere conservatism, or can contribute to actual regression, e.g., by barring the path of better minds and turning them elsewhere.

The second type is decadence which occurs by a persistently effective dominance of the forces either of disruption or, in certain cases at least, of cultural suppression, e.g., puritanism. (Decadence and creativity in *science* is a special case; for science is especially dangerous to the *status quo;* hence most intellectual orientations, whether religious or [as in the case of Confucianism] esthetic, are anti-scientific. Hence science can flourish only when the power of the intellectual *status quo* is somehow in abeyance. *Art* also is a special case from the point of view of flourishing and decline, for [apart from iconoclasms which hit only certain media] it is always in demand and hence has a way of chronically being at high levels, subject only to internal developments of particular tastes coming gradually to climax and then becoming overripe. Hence to judge general decadence or flowering by *either* science *or* art is very dangerous.)

Where growth is not functioning at best is decadence; where growth does not make up for loss is decline. What is called decadent includes: (a) in art and religion, the corruption of taste by accustomment to specialized highly developed standards, features whereof will be falsely exaggerated to produce a seeming freshness; (b) in political institutions, corruption of judgment by dependence on established patterns of power rather than the inherent sources of it; (c) in economic life, decline of enterprise in favor of security, but on an enterprise level (as versus primitive); (d) in intellectual life, dependence on past masters rather than on one's own initiative. Decadence is the normal state of affairs in human culture once a high level has been reached – correlated on the subjective side with a systematization of the universal feeling that the younger generation is going to the dogs. The question is always: what makes a culture escape this in one or more aspects? To what degree are different aspects of culture separable in this respect? What sorts of correlations are there between decadence as defined above (which almost equals conservatism) and decline in a more absolute sense (e.g., actual loss of knowledge), other than the fact that since loss is continuous, then if it is not balanced by growth it causes outright decline.

13

Interregional studies as integrating the historical disciplines

The practical implications of an interregional orientation for scholars and for the public

It will have become evident in the course of this whole study that an interregional historical outlook is long overdue and must have far-reaching effects. If it is true that interregional history lies at the heart of the mission of the historical profession as a whole, its pursuit will be important not only for itself, but for all branches of historical study. In any case, a better orientation in it has implications for a still wider circle – that of the lay public (for whom in any case historians labor). It will not be amiss to stress certain aspects of the practical implications of the Western world image which have only partially been brought out hitherto, and then to suggest means of introducing a truer interregional perspective into the profession and thence to the public at large.

The want of an adequate basis for interregional perspective cannot be completely filled through tracing the development of the Oikoumenic configuration. Nevertheless, this can contribute to making it easier to gain that perspective in general, and so to an improvement in all the many cases where that want makes itself felt. I hope that the sheer massing of examples in which such a perspective is wanting will have underlined its urgency – examples both old and new, for though some of the blatancy of the old is no longer in fashion, it serves to remind us of the attitudes underlying much thinking that we still take for granted, and which must be consciously uprooted if it is not to continue subtly affecting us. The task must be done ever again till it sticks.

Further, various false approaches to an interregional perspective must be avoided. In regard to Western distortion of history, for example, it is clearly not a sufficient disposition of the matter, simply to decide to give the Orient a still larger share in our histories than it now receives; for to decide so is to leave in our minds the conception of "East and West" – and indeed unconsciously to exalt the West as ever. For to gather all the other civilizations under one heading is to correlate them as a complementary entity with our West, as a grouping of nations complementary with the groupings of our little Western nations, and so quite to distort their significance while exalting our own. Under such circumstances, where commerce between India and China is treated as if comparable to that between Italy and Germany, a sane interregional history is out of the question. If only because the "East" is so overwhelmingly important, this would be true: up till the last several centuries the West has figured so little in the Oikoumenic Zone at large that a history of "the Orient" of all the Zone except the Latin West, would amount very nearly to a history of civilization by itself. However, even more fatal to interregional history is the distortion of conditions in the Zone as a whole. There is a pair of maps in Shepherd's Historical Atlas, on "Medieval Commerce in Europe" and "Medieval Commerce in Asia." They are designed to present commerce in homologous halves of the hemisphere; but actually while the former is a purely regional study, the latter is a study of interregional trade routes: for instance, trade in Europe is indicated just as fully on it as is trade in India. 'Asia," for practical purposes, here included Europe as much as it does India, or any other area. But unfortunately we do not have here an interregional study under a regional name; for only the routes of interest to Europeans are indicated – the significant route, for instance, between Yunnan and Burma is ignored, as are even the most important across India. What we have instead is only the usual extension of Western history. By lumping the rest of the Oikoumenic Zone together as "Asia" or the "Orient" such an anomaly is disguised, and interregional history put quite out of the question.

One sort of apparent "cosmopolitanism" – which might be mistaken for actually reflecting an interregional perspective – in fact falls into the trap of regarding the past development of others as being of significance only as it has entered into the Western Metamorphosis; that is, others' pasts must be evaluated only in terms of their effect upon Western history. Such a view delights to show how great was the contribution of the present Arabic-speaking countries to world progress – before 500 B.C. It traces broadmindedly the contributions of Sanskrit thought to Schopenhauer and Emerson; it points out that paper and gunpowder came from China. But no matter how justly expanded such tracings might be, even if they came to include all the vast and more recent contributions of other lands to the peripheral West, still their fundamental fault would remain: they assume that the modern West is the only significant end-point of progress; that developments leading to present conditions in other lands have no meaning. Thus to judge all cultures by the criteria only of our own is clearly an irresponsible action, and cannot hide under the fact that the great modern Metamorphosis centered in the West.

That Metamorphosis has had a profound effect; but it has of course had as profound an effect on the West as on anywhere else. Therefore insofar as earlier conditions in the West are still of importance, so will earlier conditions of other lands also be of importance. Neo-Thomists in our universities will be quick to point out that Medieval scholasticism has not ceased to have importance in Western countries. But in the centuries after 800 A.D. the same type of scholasticism was flowering everywhere, and Sankara, al-Ghazali, and Chu Hsi are equally living forces with St. Thomas. The scriptural religions had all about the same time everywhere to come to terms with the earlier philosophies of individual wisdom; it was – considering the similar imperial and philosophical backgrounds, as well as the direct interrelations which we know were a factor influencing at least the Western scholasticism – a development in itself of interregional significance, and continuing in its effects into the present without regard to its effect on Europe alone.

We must force ourselves to realize what it means to say that the West is not the modern world, gradually assimilating backward areas to itself; but is rather a catalyst, creating new conditions for other forces to work under (though in this case, to be sure, the West itself is also thoroughly transformed).

The feasibility of the problems set in interregional perspective

The work is ready to our hand, though it is clear that as yet interregional history is not highly developed. We have information, we have the beginnings of a criticism of it in detail, and we have a number of systems in terms of which to begin the analysis. Simple lack of information may in itself seem a hopeless obstacle, for a moment. We are ignorant; but rather through a lack of consideration of the materials available, than through the lack of materials. Confucian lands are at least as excellently documented for more than 2000 years as Mediterranean and European lands. Since the arrival of Islam all the Middle East and more recently India have been well covered. Less favored areas and earlier times are by no means out of reach, either through occasional literature or through archeology. We spare no pains at ferreting out material on the darkest corners of European history, and there is no real reason why the same cannot be done at all the points of significance to interregional studies.

To be sure, with the multiplication of languages an individual student will find it harder to get at the source material, even where the actual material needing to be covered might be less than within a regional history. Even where adequate editing has been done, this remains a problem. It is possible that a significant development in interregional history must wait upon the working out of more successful methods of cooperative scholarship. Indeed, it might seem that interregional history was in this respect in the same boat with all the other sciences, integration among which is so longingly called for by those who realize the meaninglessness of extreme specialization. However, in this case the least we can do is to cease calling our extended Western history, world history; and to take care not to make broad interpretations of history on its basis. Meanwhile, any monographic material that can be achieved will be of potentially great significance; and indeed much has already been done – particularly in relations between the West and other areas, especially the Middle East; and to a degree in other relationships, as between Iran and China.

Already, however, there seems to be enough material extant to support flourishing hypotheses more or less in the interregional field. There are a number of types of approaches to interregional history or its periphery already developed. In particular there are various one-factor analyses; the group of analyses that have followed Spengler more or less distantly; and the anthropologists.

The anthropological tradition cannot be expected to suffice for the handling of interregional history in the Oikoumenic Configuration and still less in the present. Intercultural diffusion among "primitives" has only the broadest relation to interregional relations in the Oikoumenic Zone. It can be suggestive and very helpful for archeological times, but historians must develop civilized interregional history in terms of its own problems. Using the aid of the three approaches being made to the problem, we must consciously develop it for its own sake and in its own terms.

It would seem that, in spite of the considerable theorizing already done and the several monographs in various aspects of interregional problems that are already available, the field still really awaits recognition and a clarification of its scope and problems.

The suggestions here made, of course, are not intended to present a theory of history, except as some idea of what has happened is minimally necessary to an effort to go about finding more. The "Oikoumenic Zone" is not suggested as an entity to be characterized, but as a methodological conception linking together a group of civilizations which, being in contact with each other, involve special problems of study. Similarly, with the distinction among three forms of interregional history, or five types of interregional motif, or indeed the conception of a region at all – they are of heuristic value or none. This can perhaps be taken for granted, as we have learned long since to base discussion on problem solving, to be clear to what our symbols refer, and to be conscious of abstracting, as it is put by different people. However, it seems to be still necessary to point out the fact, in full view of the difficulty with which we apply it in practice. These suggestions, therefore, are designed not to present a picture of what happened, but to bring out some of the problems involved in studying interregional history; not to supplant whatever has been done, but to guide more adequate interpretation of it.

In summary, the needs for interregional history can be grouped under three heads. First, we must recognize the field, distinguishing it on the one hand from extended Western history, which at present is commonly meant by the term "world history"; and on the other hand from a series of regional histories, however much value they may have in themselves. Monographs on particular problems and theories at least related to the subject are already available, but until the field is recognized as such can hardly help the study along decisively.

Second, we must, negatively, free ourselves from various older ways of thinking of broader problems of history, which interfere with an interregional approach. We must recognize the limited role in history of our West, as one region among others, during much of its development distinctly peripheral; and even in modern times, as not the substance of the age, into which other lands are merging insofar as they are significant at all, but instead as the center of important events affecting both the West and other lands, and significant from an interregional point of view in their interregional, rather than their local aspect. As a corollary of this placing of the West, we must leave behind the Westward pattern of history and the "East and West" dichotomy in studying the development of the Oikoumenic Configuration; and we must free our theorizing of the turns of thought which arise from assuming the Westward pattern.

Third, postively, we must go on to developing means of organizing the various types of interregional history, particularly within literate times, finding the scope and value as organizing elements of various types of interregional motifs, and studying from a consciously interregional point of view various circumstances of significance. At the same time we must look toward synthesizing hypotheses, making use of all the contributions already under way in the field, each for its particular aspect of the problem involved.

We cannot know in advance what significance further exploration in the interregional field may possess; but it seems likely that it will provide a reorientation for many aspects of regional history, as well as provide in itself a body of material of basic significance for understanding the total development of mankind.

Interregional study as integrating the historical field in itself and relating it to other fields

The reason for disciplining a field of inquiry is to ensure, not that either writers or readers will become more profound – this is ultimately a moral, or "psychological" problem – but that the results of educated shallowness be less misleading. (For scholarly inquiry only incidentally results in increase in positive truth; in the first instance, it means keeping error within bounds.) Disciplining a field of inquiry first requires delimitation of it: not in an exclusive sense, that there should be no overlapping, even as to the formal disciplining of a field (part of the disciplining of the historical "field" lies in the recognition of manifold and reciprocal interrelations with generalizing cultural studies); nor in the sense of particular subject matter; but in that a field consists in a particular type of question, the answers to questions of which type are in some way interdependent; and the discipline consists in recognition of what requires to be taken into account to assure minimal error and maximal relevance in answering that type of questions in view of their particular interdependence; while all or some of the questions involved may also be subject to other disciplines at the same time.

Historical inquiry concerns questions about *human commitments;* e.g., about standards of appreciation of excellence and about group loyalties; *hence* it deals with the dated-and-placed so far as it is *exceptional,* rather than the timeless so far as it is *typical* (as do the natural sciences, and even the generalizing-cultural inquiries – which can be called generalizing not as if historical statements did not generalize in a relevant sense, but in that, of any two statements related to each other as general and particular, the relatively general statement is the end-concern of the generalizing inquiries, while the reverse is true of historical inquiry). It may be that history and philosophy represent the two sorts of immediate questions humans must answer: historians, the *exceptionalizing* ones about *who* we are, i.e., what commitments we have (not what we are, the manipulabilities we have); and philosophers, the *normativizing* ones about where we are, i.e., not the *typicalizing* ones of the natural sciences, for which every individual becomes an example of a type, but the immediate questions which are yet not about what is exceptional in each in his biographic-historical commitments. History and philosophy would then be the two immediate moral-cognitive disciplines, cognitive in a sense that art is not, though it too is immediate, so that artists form a third non-typicalizing inquiry, but quite different because esthetic rather than moral in immediate form.

In what way are questions about the exceptional interdependent; how do they form a field? (a) As to method, of course; a few useful caveats may be said about all such questions; but on this level, only, not enough to provide much far-reaching discipline of historical questions as such; if historical questions had only this in common, they ought better be integrated with other types ad hoc, for purposes of serious disciplining. (b) On the moral level: the reasons for making inquiries about human commitments are moral; rest ultimately on the proposition that maximal human responsiveness requires respect of others; that respect of others requires respect of what they hold precious; and that such respect requires understanding of it in a context common to oneself and the others (since there is no understanding except in context); hence the moral requirement of inquiry into, at once, one's own and others' commitments: into the human heritages. On this level, all the great commitments are morally related, not in the sense of being all morally equivalent (respect does not involve admiration as such), but of involving moral commensurateness; the meaning of one moral commitment is modified by the coexistence of other moral commitments and by the possibility of mutual interaction among them. (c) On the substantive level of interactive events: history is a single field so far as the human commitments have in fact been interrelated through common contexts and commonly acting events (not, of course, necessarily events with common outcomes!), interrelated both negatively and positively.

For the context, the typical, must be understood if the exceptional is to be understood. (Hence the intimate involvement of historical with generalizing-cultural questions; even though to inverse ends, they deal, at least potentially, with the same questions). So far as both the moral and the substantive contexts of the exceptional, i.e., of the great human commitments, are one, the historical field is one, and will require disciplining in respect of the way in which its questions are interrelated on those levels.

Hence, to hierarchize and interrelate the value of questions, so that any particular question will be most likely to be studied in terms of its fullest potential meanings in any given direction, we need sophistication in the recognition of points of *relevance;* i.e., of the terms on which *comparisons* (the heart of all inquiry), implicit or explicit, can be most revealing.

One of the most symptomatic indices of this will be terminology: the way in which categories of comparison are ordered. Not that any particular set of terms, however multiple, is to be required in historical studies (though we could use a much more adequately differentiated number of stock terms), but that a sophisticated handling of them be expected. E.g., to take a most obvious case, geography. The first step is to avoid using geographical terms, and hence units, defined by political boundaries at the time of writing. But to accept terms defined politically as of the time written about has also its limitations from the viewpoint of long-term comparisons: one needs to have terms for various regions of various orders of complexity (and size), which will allow comparison not only in one area over time, but among different areas with some degree of true comparability. Finally, one needs to develop a way of handling terms which will maximize awareness of their implications: hence the advantage of phrases like "from Nile to Oxus," even though intentionally left vague, and perhaps even if eventually stereotyped into Nilo-Oxian, over black terms like "Middle East," however exactly defined in the given work, so far as the former phrase exacts awareness of just what all is covered, so that if a comment applies only to a part of the whole, the part will be mentioned rather than the whole unless there is a specific reason for mentioning the whole. Other terminological niceties of the same order: learning to differentiate between what pertains to a dynasty as such, and what pertains to a general culture under the dynasty's rule; between government and state and society; and so forth, including differentiating between a subject matter as practically used, and its theoretical studies. (All Islamic studies and in particular art history in the Islamic field are rich with bad examples; but, with less radical obviousness, so also are Westernist studies.)

For the choice of terms determines what categories one uses; the categories determine the form and limits of the questions posed; and the questions posed determine the answers that can be expected. But since comparison must be over the whole field, categorization must form a complete system: perceiving the relations and discontinuities over all mankind in time and space. That is (and the more so, the more substantive interrelations can be shown to prevail; but even without them), world history is the only adequate foundation for the proper interrelation of historical questions.

All kinds of world history will be of help as serving as foundation for the disciplining of historical inquiry; but some elements will be of more import than others. The commonest approach to interregional questions has been a diffusionist approach. But doubtless a contextualist approach is more fruitful; precisely insofar as the *exceptional*, and the points of commitment to be more exact, resides rather in creation against a background, than in borrowing on a level.

Functions of world history books and criteria for evaluating them

There are a number of different functions a book of world history can perform. In each case the book must be designed with its particular function or combination of functions in mind, and the role of the Oikoumentic configuration in the narrative will vary accordingly. In all cases the Oikoumenic pattern should at least be made clear, for awareness of it is an essential element even in regional history. But in some cases the Oikoumenic configuration will at best provide merely essential background, more or less referred to in the book's structure; in some cases it can provide one of the main principles of organization; and only in particular circumstances can it logically provide the only major principle of organization.

The first and most immediately essential function of a world history book is to provide overall perspective and an understanding of wide interrelationships when a reasonable knowledge of more local history is presupposed. Speaking of this function, Bossuet likened such a history to a world-map, in which all the countries can be seen at once and the place of each in relation to the others becomes clear. Such a history must almost necessarily be fairly brief, its treatment of any given subject being highly condensed; otherwise the reader cannot keep the whole canvas in mind at once, but gets lost in the detail. Since it must stress relationships among different parts of the world, rather than the local history which is presumed known through special treatises, interregional history and particularly the development of the Oikoumenic configuration should determine the outline and even a good deal of the substance of the book. In a book having exclusively this function there should be no more place for concentration on favored times and places than there should be in a world map. It is unfortunate that just as our traditional world-maps, those on Mercator's projection, have violated this basic rule, so our traditional world histories, even when claiming to fulfill the function of affording perspective, have violated the same rule in the same way.

Writers of world histories, however, unlike makers of world maps, can appeal to the fact that affording perspective and showing interrelationships are not necessarily the exclusive functions of a world history. A perfectly respectable function, if function limited in philosophic scope, is to bring together in one place a certain minimum of information about all the various fields of history in which the reader may be interested. Such a work is like a world atlas – in contrast to a world map, it can legitimately show any given area in as much detail as required, provided that all areas are covered in some degree or other. Such a work may be a one-volume school text, where it is desired to be done with "history" in only two courses, one on the national history and one on all the rest. In a textbook for the second course it is presumably necessary to make up for the lack of a course in regional history by giving special emphasis to those parts of the world with which the national history has been specially connected. Or such a work may be a many-volume collection designed for the customer who wants to have the world on one shelf. In this case the salesman will have an easier time – and rightly so – if the fields about which the customer has the most prior knowledge, and will have the most curiosity about details in, are covered with special thoroughness. These catch-all works may of necessity, then, be badly out of porportion from the point of view of fulfilling the first function, that of affording overall orientation.

The disproportion in such works has often been far more extreme than necessary; but some disproportion is bound to remain. Often in such works there is no internal organizing principle to make up for the effects of a catch-all type of selection; but presumably, if the history of the Oikoumenic configuration could serve as a guide in arranging the works, the worst results of their disproportion could be avoided. The reader could at least be made aware of the proportions of the whole as a result of the very plan of the work, as well as through repeated references to the wider background against which local developments are taking place. Subtitles, if not the main headings themselves, could remind him of the point he had reached in the overall story. Then subsections could be multiplied almost indefinitely for favored areas and times, yet the reader would at least realize that these areas were being favored, and that the scale of their treatment was enlarged. Reference to Oikoumenic history in such compilations, then, has potentially a peculiarly significant role to play, in spite of their apparent resistance to its outlook.

A more scholarly function for a many-volume world-history is to provide an up-to-date compendium of the current results of research in all historical fields. Such a history is likewise of the "world atlas" type, and its organizing principles will not be basically different, usually, from those of the "catch-all" popular world histories. At least to a degree, in addition, it must give most space to those fields which have been most thoroughly studied. It is this highly honorable but still not philosophic function which the scholar most frequently has in mind when he contributes to a "cooperative" world history; and often the editor is hard put to it to preserve any semblance of guiding ideas. Here, obviously, interregional studies should find their place like any other studies, and the Oikoumenic configuration through them.

It is possible, however, for a world history to be written neither on the model of a world-map, designed for orientation, nor on the model of a world-atlas, with encyclopedic purposes, whther popular or scholarly. It may be essentially an interpretive essay, with an insight into the nature of mankind to expound. Such books must necessarily be organized in terms of the insights being expounded. For some it can be supposed that Oikoumenic history will take on supreme importance; for others it will become a dry and external matter. For all the development of the Oikoumenic configuration must have the place at least of an essential limiting condition in their speculations and interpretations.

It is certainly desirable that our world histories designed for educational purposes find a reasonable balance among these functions. They should certainly provide overall historical orientation – a truly proportional world-map. They should also, if possible, bring forward at least a modest degree of insight into the historical side of human life, taken as a whole, and their organization must depend somewhat on the particular insights they happen to be stressing. And they need not refuse to meet the interests of teacher and student half-way, at least to the extent of dwelling upon developments of unusual human significance. In their "world-atlas" aspect, they dare not dwell only on the familiar, nearby scenes; but selection there can be.

There are, of course, many ways in which some such balance can be achieved (and it is to be hoped that all of them will be fully explored as soon as possible). It would be good to have a book which would go out of its way to counterbalance conventional preoccupation with our Western regional background by centering the whole story on interregional relationships, and tracing our Western rise – as well as the path of other regions – in terms of these relationships. Or it is an attractive thought, to emphasize the growth of science and scholarship and the widening of esthetic and perhaps even religious sensitivity, as far as possible on an all-human level, with social and political elements in the story strictly subordinated; the refinements of art and to a lesser degree of scholarship are in principle of a universal appeal. In each such approach the

Oikoumenic configuration would provide an essential backbone, safeguarding the first from oversimplification or irrelevant proliferation by defining levels of significance in interregional relations, and the second from an unchecked diffuseness of appreciation by suggesting lines of interrelation.

A third such blended approach to an educational world history book would be to concentrate on the major regional cultures at key periods, thus widening and balancing out the cultural horizon and yet keeping a limited number of fields in focus. If a limited, but judiciously selected number of regions are seen at their best, the human value will be obvious, and the teachers will sense a vitality of subject matter; and though always it is to be hoped that a world history course need not double for a Western history course, yet if it must do so then at least some portions of the book can give a coherent picture of the West in itself. In such a book, an Oikoumenic orientation is essential to prevent its degenerating into a group of unrelated vignettes. The orientation would show up less by constant reference than by the very selection and juxtaposition of the civilizations studies, as well as by the context into which they would be set.

Conclusion: Islamic history as world history

Marshall G. S. Hodgson and *The Venture of Islam*

Edmund Burke, III

At a time when orientalism is under attack both from within and without the profession, the publication of Marshall G. S. Hodgson's three-volume work, *The Venture of Islam: Conscience and History in a World Civilization*,[1] is an event of major importance. So rich is its subject, so complex and ambitious its analytic scheme and serious its moral purpose that it is difficult in brief compass to give an idea of the book. In the following pages, I discuss those aspects of the work that seem to me most important for an understanding of its achievement and significance. In the end, I shall argue, *The Venture of Islam* must be seen as the most ambitious and successful effort to salvage the orientalist tradition to date.

Having said this, I should add that *The Venture of Islam* is also a controversial work, one likely to generate continuing debate both on points of detail and on its overall vision of the history of Islamic civilization.[2] Already, it has been criticized as a highly personal and partisan account. Such charges, it must be said, are true, but they are also beside the point. Indeed, the very greatness of the book stems from Hodgson's own personality, his cranky obsession with terminology and presuppositions, his insistence on seeing Islamic civilization in a world historical context, and his stubborn Quaker moral conscience. The rest is scholarly monographs. There is much about Hodgson's spirit that recalls the youthful impatience with mediocrity which so marked the writings of Marc Bloch and Lucien Febvre, the founders of the *Annales* school.[3] Perhaps it is not

[1] Marshall G. S. Hodgson, *The Venture of Islam: Conscience and History in a World Civilization* (3 vols.; Chicago: The University of Chicago Press, 1974), Vol I., *The Classical Age of Islam;* Vol. 2, *The Expansion of Islam in the Middle Periods;* and Vols. 3, *The Gunpowder Empires and Modern Times*.

[2] Hodgson's footnotes are one of the delights of the work and are not to be overlooked. They collectively provide a systematic settling of accounts with the field, and a fertile list of topics for future research.

[3] I am thinking especially of Lucien Febvre's *Combats pour l'histoire* (Paris, 1953), portions of which have been published in English as *A New Kind of History* (New York, 1973). Hodg-

too much to hope that a new generation of scholars, nourished by the example of Hodgson, will follow in the path that he has traced out.

The Venture of Islam is both an original scholarly synthesis and a major new textbook for undergraduate survey courses on Islamic civilization. Toward the end of this essay, I shall have more to say on the difficulties of trying to read it both ways at once. Here, I should like to stress that the work is first and foremost a textbook, whose purpose is to seek an understanding of the human achievement of Islamic civilization on its own terms. At its most general, by tracing the history of Islamic civilization, it seeks to inform the reader about the nature of civilization. It examines Islamic civilization as a part of the human heritage and seeks to demonstrate its importance in world history. More specifically, through the study of societies and cultures that provided the context for the actions of concerned Muslims, Hodgson seeks to explain why they behaved as they did.

Islam in the mirror of Marshall G. S. Hodgson

By all accounts, Marshall Hodgson was an unusual person. Even in the rather Bohemian atmosphere of The University of Chicago in the late 1950s, he stood out for his ascetic temperament, militant vegetarianism, and leftish political beliefs. His prickly obsession with details, his vaulting ambition, and his inability to suffer fools made him often a difficult colleague. One senses from accounts like the rather uncharitable one of Saul Bellow[4] that he was an elusive figure – fascinating, frequently insufferable, always brilliant. No doubt his personality had much to do with the fact that he left few followers and no school to carry on his work. His death in 1968, at the age of 47, left *The Venture of Islam* (on which he had been working for over a decade) two-thirds finished. In the end, *The Venture of Islam* became as much his personal venture as Islam's. A very great debt is owed to Reuben Smith, for many years his closest collaborator, who selflessly saw the manuscript through to publication.[5]

son's effort differs from that of the *Annales* historians, of course, in that he focused upon the study of civilizations (understood chiefly in terms of the high cultural artifacts of the major literary traditions), while they emphasized social and economic history. It is in the spirit of the two, and the concern with methodology, that they resemble one another.

4 Saul Bellow, *To Jerusalem and Back: A Personal Account* (New York: Macmillan, 1976), pp. 105–9.

5 See the Preface by Smith for an account of the state of the manuscript on Hodgson's death, and the nature of his editorial assistance. In general, Smith was scrupulous to avoid changes that went beyond the stylistic. The published version of the work is thus substantially as Hodgson left it.

The Venture of Islam is as much the product of a particular time and place as it is of a particular man. Its pages are suffused with the atmosphere of The University of Chicago in the late 1950s and early 1960s during the latter phase of the remarkable Hutchins experiment. In particular, the book owes much to its origins as the text for the undergraduate survey of Islamic civilization, a course taught by Marshall Hodgson from its inception in 1958. The book went through several early editions, and was accompanied by a three-volume *Introduction of Islamic Civilization*, a series of selected readings from the Islamic classics in English translation.[6] A notable part of the undergraduate program at The University of Chicago was the study of world civilizations through their classical writings. Originally, the program had been limited to the study of Western civilization, but was broadened in the late 1950s to include surveys of the civilizations of India, China, and Islam. Inevitably, Hodgson's approach to Islamic civilization was greatly colored by the "Great Books" orientation of the college curriculum. It was also influenced by the conception of *civilization* developed by the younger Robert Redfield and Milton Singer, which provided the overarching framework for the sequence of courses. In still other ways, *The Venture of Islam* owes much to Hodgson's membership on the Committee on Social Thought, in the 1950s and early 1960s a unique interdisciplinary graduate program of broad and eclectic scope. (At the time of his death, Hodgson was chairman of the committee.) Here, the influence of John U. Nef and Mircea Eliade seems to have been most important, together with that of Edward Shils. The book also reveals the influence of Hodgson's colleagues in Islamic studies: Gustave von Grunebaum (to whom it is jointly dedicated with John U. Nef), Muhsin Mahdi, Robert McC. Adams, Wilfred Madelung, Clifford Geertz, Lloyd Fallers, and of course Reuben Smith. Finally, mention must be made of William McNeill, whose *Rise of the West*[7] played a significant role both as model and as foil in the working out of Hodgson's framework of world history. Simply to list the names reminds one of how remarkable an intellectual environment The University of Chicago was in those days. As Albert Hourani has said, it is difficult to imagine *The Venture of Islam* having been written anywhere else.[8]

[6] The reader was a companion to a *History of Islamic Civilization* published in 1958 in an offset edition. This gave way to a first edition of *The Venture of Islam* (in two volumes) in 1961, also in offset, intended for students at The University of Chicago.
[7] William McNeill, *The Rise of the West: A History of the Human Community* (Chicago: The University of Chicago Press, 1964).
[8] See his review of *The Venture of Islam*, in *Journal of Near Eastern Studies* 37, I (1978), 53–62.

I have argued that I consider *The Venture of Islam* to be as much Hodgson's venture as Islam's. To an extraordinary degree, the work is shaped and informed by the personal beliefs and ethical concerns of its author. In just what ways is this the case? One way to approach this subject is through the two persons who seem most to be the touchstones to Hodgson's thought: Louis Massignon and John Woolman. Their spirit suffuses virtually every page of the work. From a consideration of these men and their meaning for Marshall Hodgson, it is possible to derive the chief characteristics of the work.

A striking feature of *The Venture of Islam* is the tone of empathy and respect which it adopts toward Islam. This characteristic serves to distinguish the book from the majority of more "objective" studies. Hodgson has taken pains "to remove his shoes before entering the mosque" (in the words of Mahmoud Ayyub), and in the process he encourages his reader to enter fully into the spirit of the civilization. Here the talisman is the work of Louis Massignon (especially articles like his "Salman Pak et les prémices spirituelles de l'Islam iranien")[9] and the latter's efforts to achieve an understanding of Islam from within. From Massignon, Hodgson has borrowed the psychosociological "science of compassion." It is the constant effort of the scholar to "never be satisfied to cease asking 'but why?' " until he had driven his understanding to the point where he has an immediate grasp of what a given position meant, such that every nuance of the data is accounted for and withal, given a total of presuppositions and circumstances, he could feel himself doing the same."[10]

Ultimately, it is to Wilhelm Dilthey and Carl Jung that Hodgson looks for the justification of this application of the principle of *verstehen*. Characteristically, where with Massignon this method often resulted in a murky mysticism, Hodgson makes of it a controlled effort of the historical imagination.

John Woolman, an eighteenth-century American Quaker, is the other major guide to understanding Hodgson's intent. Scarcely known today outside of the Society of Friends, Woolman in his own time was a pacifist, an opponent of slavery, and a sharp critic of the mercantile values of colonial Pennsylvania. His *Journal* has continued to exert an enormous influence among Quakers.[11] It is with an epigram from Woolman that the work begins: "To consider mankind otherwise than brethren, to

[9] Louis Massignon, "Salman Pak et les premices spirituelles de l'Islam iranien," *Societe des Etudes Iraniens* 7 (1934).
[10] *The Venture of Islam*, I, 379, n. 6.
[11] John Woolman, *The Journal, and Other Writings* (New York and London, 1952).

think favors are peculiar to one nation and to exclude others, plainly supposes a darkness in the understanding." The citation is clearly intended as an implicit judgment upon the smug Eurocentrism that has informed most of the writing on Islam by Western scholars. With this device emblazoned on his escutcheon, Hodgson sets forth to combat the many errors and presuppositions of previous studies. A central purpose of *The Venture of Islam* is to demonstrate the possibilities of a new kind of Islamic history, methodologically self-conscious and guided by a more adequate framework of world history. Hodgson argues his case at length in the text and in the numerous footnotes sprinkled throughout the work. It is for this reason that the work begins with a lengthy methodological section entitled "Introduction to the Study of Islamic Civilization." In this syllabus of errors, we see Hodgson at his most polemical, as well as his most teacherly. The central concepts and epistemological assumptions of orientalism and of civilizational studies are submitted to scathing examination. Nothing is exempt, not even the venerable Mercator projection map, which Hodgson argues is a "Jim-Crow projection" that has seriously warped our image of the world.

In a more general sense, the citation of Woolman serves to focus attention on Hodgson's Quaker beliefs. In ways both great and small, *The Venture of Islam* is marked by the impress of Hodgson's Quaker conscience. It is axiomatic for Hodgson that "the individual sensibility, focused in a point of conscience, is one of the ultimate roots of history." A major theme of the three volumes is the capacity of the Quranic message repeatedly to inspire men of conscience to confront the dilemmas of their age in response to the challenge of its ideals. Thus the work proceeds by a series of meditations on the styles of piety of selected Muslim moral epigones: Hasan al-Basri, Ahmad Ibn Hanbal, Abu Hamid al-Ghazali, Jalaluddin Rumi, and Mughal sultan Akbar, and the modernists Muhammad Abduh and Muhammad Iqbal. What interests Hodgson about these men is their effort to work out anew the implications of the act of Islam in their own age. In such an approach to Islamic history, it is almost as if Hodgson had somehow reinvented the Muslim biographical dictionary, albeit one in Quaker disguise. This represents a sharp break with the conventional political/dynastic way of presenting Islamic history in which the heroes are the great generals, statesmen, and builders of empires. It also constitutes one of the most effective means of encouraging the reader to momentarily suspend disbelief and enter into the mental universe of particular Muslims.

Hodgson's Quakerism manifests itself in still other ways. One is his scandalized response to the fact that the initial spread of Islam owed much to the sword. But his pacifism is outraged when it comes to a consideration of terror tactics employed by the Mongols in their advance into the lands of Islam. Hodgson exhibits an almost morbid fascination with the towers of human skulls erected by the Mongols to demonstrate the folly of resistance. His attitude toward caliphal absolutism is similarly tinged with an abiding suspicion of the state which I take to be Quaker (although it may also represent the influence of Leo Strauss, a Chicago colleague). It is perhaps for this reason that Hodgson prefers the flexible international political order of the mid-tenth to mid-thirteenth centuries, which he claims was characterized by a relatively open social structure and relative individual liberty.

Hodgson's moral stance is most evident in the epilogue, "The Islamic Heritage and the Modern Conscience." In it he reveals his belief in the moral unity of mankind in the modern age, and asks what meaning the Islamic religious heritage can have for modern human beings. He gives a number of answers: one is that we are all (including the West) in the same boat, as a consequence of the unsettling of all moral heritages in the modern world. Thus the study of the fate of the Islamic heritage can instruct us about our own and become part of the common patrimony of mankind. More revealingly, however, Hodgson invokes the Quaker example when he hopes that the Islamic community, as a place where concerned individuals can jointly give witness to their beliefs, may share in shaping the course of humanity as a whole. By some subtle alchemy of the spirit, in Hodgson's hands the history of Islamic civilization comes to resemble in the operation of its ideals through time a history of the Society of Friends.

Islamic history as world history

One's first impressions of *The Venture of Islam* are rather overwhelming. It is painted on so vast a canvas, so thickly populated with historical figures drawn from so many ages and climes, and so rich in new ideas and concepts, that the reader may miss the fact that it is built upon an explicit framework of world history and a theory of civilizational studies. This section treats Hodgson's attempt to situate Islamic history in a world historical context – a necessary preliminary to which is a searching examination of the methodological presuppositions of the orientalist tradition. The following section treats Hodgson's theory of civilizational studies.

Marshall Hodgson was not only a person of humanistic conscience and eclectic, far-ranging curiosity – he was also a systematic thinker who delighted in the search for patterns in world history. Long before the current impasse of the orientalist tradition had become glaringly evident, Hodgson was already convinced of the need for a radical reorientation of our historical and geographical attitudes toward the rest of the world. In my opinion, the effort to write a history of Islamic civilization informed by the multiple awarenesses that derive from such an undertaking constitutes Hodgson's most important achievement. One may dispute his views of particular features of the civilization which he calls Islamic; nonetheless, he has accomplished a feat of enormous significance in enabling us to see, for the first time, that civilization whole and entire in its unfolding through time and in its relations with its neighbors.

It is crucial to an understanding of *The Venture of Islam* to recognize that it is based upon an explicit framework of world history, and that its author was at once profoundly immersed in the classics of Islamic civilization and a world historian. Hodgson left several hundred pages of an uncompleted world history at his death. What that finished work would have looked like, we cannot say, but its general outlines are clear from his previous work. Among Hodgson's earliest publications is an article which appeared in the *Journal of World History* in 1954 called "Hemispheric Interregional History as an Approach to World History."[12] Here in brilliant but highly schematic outline are to be found the central themes that subsequent works would but fill out in greater detail.[13] In this article Hodgson argues that a necessary preliminary to a new framework of world history is a systematic criticism of the basic presuppositions of Western historiography. Only with a radical reorientation of our historical and geographical attitudes about the world is it possible to undertake this task. Accordingly an important segment of Hodgson's energies is focused in this article upon the methodology of world history. Only with this accomplished does he go on to present his own framework.

Hodgson's critique of the Western tradition of world history centers on such issues as the problem of perspective (in world historical terms, Europe is a fringe area of the Afro-Eurasian zone of agrarianate citied life, and it does not emerge on the center of the world stage until 1800), the problem of terminology (the use of such truncating terms as "the Orient" and "Asia" as opposed to "the Occident" and "the West" to refer

[12] Marshall Hodgson, "Hemispheric Inter-regional History as an Approach to World History," *Journal of World History* I, 3 (1954), 715–23.

[13] See also Hodgson's "The Inter-relations of Societies in History," *Comparative Studies in Society and History* 5 (1963), 227–50; and "The Great Western Transmutation," *Chicago Today*, n.v. (1967), 40–50.

to the rest of human literate society), and the unconscious racism of the Mercator projection map (with its Eurocentric distortion of the southern hemisphere). The lines of argument developed by Hodgson in this article provide the basis of his criticisms of the orientalist tradition in the "Introduction to the Study of Islamic Civilization," which opens the first volume of *The Venture of Islam*. A brief digression to consider these criticisms should make clear the radical nature of Hodgson's conception of his task.

Hodgson's attack on the orientalist tradition of scholarship is noteworthy for several reasons. One is that it comes from someone whose training, and in many ways professional self-image, were those of an orientalist. Among the most successful passages in *The Venture of Islam* are those in which Hodgson works his way through a text, guiding the reader to a richer and more complete understanding of the resonance it must have had in its own time and place. Yet Hodgson was profoundly discontented with the results of the philological approach to civilizations. He was in search of a more complex vision, one less the prisoner of a narrow textualism and more open to the interplay of cultures across linguistic barriers. He was opposed to the epistemological assumptions that inform the orientalist tradition. Finally, he insisted that discussions of Islamic culture be securely rooted in a historically specific context. Hodgson's critique of orientalism is therefore one that comes, in a sense, from within the tradition. But it is also, revealingly, one that is based upon a radically different conception of the nature of the historian's task.

Most recent attacks upon orientalism have emerged within the context of the anticolonial struggle.[14] Insofar as orientalism served as a cover and justification for Western dominance, this was no doubt inevitable and even (despite certain excesses) justifiable. While by no means indifferent to the political uses to which orientalism has been put, Hodgson situates the problem at a more general level of discourse.[15] Thus he distinguishes five frameworks within which students of Islamic studies have tended to operate: Christianity, Judaism, Islam, Marxism, and what he calls "Westernism," each with its own characteristic set of epistemological assumptions and complementary patterns of distortion. Yet the absence of

[14] Among others, see A. L. Tibawi, "English Speaking Orientalists: A Critique of Their Approach to Islam and to Arab Nationalism," *Muslim World* 53, 3–4 (1963), 185–204, 298–313; Anouar Abdel-Malek, "L'Orientalisme en crise," *Diogene* 24 (1963), 109–42; Abdullah Laroui, *L'Ideologie arabe contemporaine* (Paris, 1967) and *La crise des intellectuels arabes: traditionalisme ou historicisme?* (Paris, 1974). See also Albert Hourani, "Islam and the Philosophers of History," *Middle Eastern Studies* 3 (1967), 206–68, and Edward Said, *Orientalism* (New York: Atheneum, 1978).

[15] *The Venture of Islam*, I, 26–30.

explicit commitment to one of these traditions, Hodgson points out, provides no assurance of objectivity. Indeed, he says, it may simply disguise an unanalyzed, piecemeal commitment to partisan viewpoints. Similarly, "it is no guarantee of balanced insight to be a Muslim, nor of impartiality, to be a non-Muslim."[16] A degree of objectivity can be attained only through constant methodological self-consciousness, and by embracing the tensions between one's own "great tradition" and that of Islam. In the effort to write history from a world historical perspective, not only Christians and Westernists are guilty of biases deriving from their ultimate orientations, but also Marxists and cultural nationalists of all stripes. Hodgson's critique of orientalism is accordingly rooted in quite a different set of premises as the recent attacks on that tradition, even while there is much in their denunciations with which he would sympathize. I shall return to Hodgson's critique of the orientalist tradition in the section that follows.

What is Hodgson's framework of world history? A more truly adequate world history, he argues, would have to begin with the proposition that the history of human literate society must be the history of Asia and its outliers, and that Europe has no privileged role in such a story. Here we touch the heart of Hodgson's quarrel with such writers as William McNeill, whose *Rise of the West,* while a major advance over previous attempts at a world history, is flawed in its basic conception. A world history worthy of the name must focus upon interdependent interregional developments on a hemisphere-wide basis. One implication of this approach is an emphasis upon literate societies (especially the four great core areas in which civilization developed), at the expense of central Asian pastoralists and Burmese hill folk. What fascinated Hodgson was the possibility of telling the tale of humanity as a whole, but this time from the perspective of global history, and not in a skewed, Western, self-justificatory version. His history would be one that concerned itself especially with those phenomena which cross regional boundaries: the spread of Hellenistic art, the development of mathematics, the diffusion of Indian forms of monasticism, the establishment of the Mongol empire. For Hodgson, it was axiomatic that the constant acquisition of new techniques (cultural and otherwise) and discoveries all over the world cumulatively led to changes in the possibilities of future development everywhere. The spread of gunpowder weapons is but a particularly dramatic example of the operation of this principle. In his emphasis upon the interconnections between civilizations and upon

[16] Ibid., p. 27.

the cumulative development of the common stock of human techniques and cultural resources, Hodgson's Quaker convictions appear with clarity: all men are brothers, and in the eye of history, Islam is but one venture among others.

Hodgson utilizes a number of different periodizations of history in his presentation. One is a twofold division between the Agrarian age (to 1800 C.E.) and Modern times, which serves to frame his discussion of the Great Western Transmutation (on which more in a moment). From the perspective of the history of civilizations, however, a periodization composed of four major divisions is utilized: (1) the early civilizations (to 800 B.C.), (2) the Axial age (800 to 200 B.C.), (3) the post-Axial age (200 B.C. to 1800 C.E.), and (4) the Modern age (since 1800 C.E.). The term "Axial age" Hodgson borrows from Karl Jasper's to refer to the great period of cultural florescence which was formative of Chinese, Indian, Mediterranean, and Irano-Semitic civilizations. Islamic civilization emerges in the post-Axial period of agrarianate citied life. With the emergence of Islamic civilization, the Nile to Oxus zone, which had hitherto been divided into warring camps, reasserts its primacy within the ecumene. While preceding centuries had witnessed the gradual development of a tendency toward religious communalism within the region, with separate literary languages carrying different strands of a common cultural tradition, the coming of Islam reversed this trend, and witnessed the unfolding of a cosmopolitan civilization carried by first one, then several Islamic languages. In world historical terms, Islamic civilization represented an attempt to establish a total civilization on a hemisphere-wide basis, embracing most of the ecumene. The Islamic venture underwent a series of transformations over time. Not until the onset of modernity did the persisting regional configurations within the ecumene reassert themselves, and unifying forces gradually weaken. The way was left open for European domination, followed by the rise of nationalism in the Islamic world.

Central to Hodgson's method of doing world history is his use of ideal types to inform and orient his analysis. This gives his study of Islamic civilization an analytical power lacking in other parallel efforts. While critical of aspects of the work of Max Weber, Hodgson has evidently learned much from it. But it is the method of Weber, and not so much his conclusions, which Hodgson has adopted. Thus, for example, his use of the twin concepts of agrarianate citied life and technicalism underpins his efforts at explaining what it is which sets off the pre-modern era (to *c.* 1800 C.E.) from the Modern age. As we shall see shortly, Hodgson has derived a series of ideal types which he associates with each of the major phases of Islamic civilization, based upon their social, economic, and cultural characteristics. The pyramiding of these ideal types thus provides *The Venture of Islam* with an architectonic structure of extraordinary richness and complexity. (Those who have misread Hodgson's intent as merely descriptive should look again.)

An examination of the ideal types developed by Hodgson to replace the tradition/modernity dichotomy, that of Agrarian age and Technicalism, may serve to illustrate his overall method. The first concept of this couplet, the Agrarian age, refers to all of human history from the rise of civilizations until roughly 1800. It is developed in the opening section of Volume 1 in considerable detail. Civilizations of the premodern era, Hodgson posits, were ultimately based upon their ability to extract land rents of some sort, with other sources of wealth playing a distinctly secondary role. The surplus generated by the agrarian economy was thus limited by the possibilities of agricultural production. Neither commerce nor industrial production (still less pastoralism) could provide sufficient revenue to supplant the primary dependence of the privileged classes upon agriculture. Since literacy was a virtual monopoly of the privileged, the cultural production of a given society was in turn dependent upon agrarianate revenues. Intensive investment of this necessarily limited surplus could under favorable conditions produce a cultural florescence. But all such florescences were limited in duration and extent. Inevitably, less favorable conditions would reassert themselves, and the civilization would conform once again to more normal agrarianate standards of expectation. (The same built-in ceiling determined the careers of political and economic florescences.) By this analysis, Hodgson argues that great breakthroughs, of the sort that gave birth to Modernity, were impossible under agrarianate conditions. This is to say that while innovation and change could and did exist in the Agrarian age, no such set of changes could proceed to the point where they began to transform the very nature of the relationship between man and the environment.

The rise of the West, or what Hodgson calls the Great Western Transmutation, presents a sharp contrast with the Agrarian age, and thus with the course of human history.[17] Beginning about 1600, Western society experienced a series of unprecedented changes that intersected an built upon one another in ways that soon altered the very context of historical action by freeing cultural change from its agrarian base. Hitherto, within the Afro-Eurasian historical complex the overall rise in the level of social

[17] Ibid., III, 176–200. Cf. also his "The Great Western Transmutation."

power – which had cumulatively been quite marked – had occurred on a basis of rough parity. Any really basic new developments had been gradually adopted everywhere within the space of four or five centuries. Thus the superiority of the Arabs over the Portuguese in the eighth and ninth centuries and of the Portuguese over the Arabs in the sixteenth were both relatively ephemeral developments, soon balanced by appropriate adjustments over time. The Western Transmutation broke down the historical presuppositions by which such gradual diffusions had maintained a rough parity between the regions of the Afro-Eurasian ecumene. Western society experienced a cumulative and interdependent set of changes in key sectors whose decisive effects made themselves felt everywhere from the beginning, in a steadily increasing but discontinuous fashion. The very bases of agrarian life found themselves progressively undermined, though initially at least old lifeways seemed to continue unchanged. Henceforth even routine acts acquired a new significance. A new historical age was born, the age of Technicalism.

What is notable about Hodgson's discussion of the onset of Modernity is less his analysis of the overall process of change (called "technicalization"), than the insertion of it into a world historical context. Several important consequences flow from this. One is that by situating the Western Transmutation in the history of citied life throughout the hemisphere, he establishes its connections to all that had come before. "Without the cumulative history of the whole Afro-Eurasian Oikoumene, of which the Occident had been an integral part, the Western Transmutation would be almost unthinkable."[18] A host of inventions and discoveries originating in other regions (among them gunpowder, the compass, and printing) played a major role in the Western breakthrough. So too did the existence of a vast world market, itself largely the work of Muslim merchants and traders. The rise of the West, when viewed in this fashion, no longer seems quite the inevitable development it has widely been assumed to have been, nor does Western civilization appear to have been unique. The line that runs from the Greeks to the Renaissance to the Industrial Revolution is finally an optical illusion, the product of a highly selective historical imagination. From the vantage point of world history, the Western Transmutation is the cumulation of processes of cultural change going on throughout the ecumene for more than a millennium.

A second consequence of viewing the rise of the West as a world historical phenomenon is that it enables Hodgson to address the issue of what he calls "the development gap." If the concept is old-fashioned, the insight is

[18] *The Venture of Islam*, III, 198.

contemporary. Once under way, Hodgson argues, the Western Transmutation "could neither be parallelled independently nor be borrowed wholesale."[19] It could also not be escaped. The unprecedented level of social power of the West enabled it to intervene in other societies in countless ways and almost from the beginning to set the terms of its relationship with them. The social basis of civilized life was transformed. For the rest of the ecumene, "what was significant and creative in cultural activity was keyed not to the problems of an urban elite in an agrarian society but to those of non-technicalized elites in a technicalistic world."[20] The decisive altering of the context of historical action meant that for non-Western peoples "the same forces that built up the economies and cultures in the advanced lands broke down theirs, and they became the 'underdeveloped' lands, those with relatively low investment levels."[21] In his efforts to conceive of the processes of modernization as occurring from their inception on a world scale, Hodgson's work parallels that of neo-Marxist "dependency" theorists such as Andre Gunder Frank, Samir Amin, and Immanuel Wallerstein.[22] Like them, he is interested in the pattern of relations between "core" and "periphery" of the world market. He has a number of prescient observations to make on the significance of the industrial and democratic revolutions for non-Western societies. While finally his understanding of the Western Transmutation is much more in tune with the theorists of modernization than with the neo-Marxists, by situating it in a world historical context, Hodgson took a decisive step toward breaking with the modernization paradigm. Had he lived to revise the final sections of *The Venture of Islam*, it is likely he would have gone on to develop a more comprehensive theory of his own. Regardless, it is significant that Hodgson was under no illusions as to the possibility of Western-style development occurring outside the West.

What is it that distinguishes modern times from the agrarian age? Hodgson's answer is *technicalization*, a concept he defines as "a condition of calculative (and hence innovative) technical specialization, in which the several specialities are interdependent on a large enough scale to determine patterns of expectation in key sectors of the society."[23] The brilliance of this conception may at first escape notice, and Hodgson's

[19] Ibid., p. 200.
[20] Ibid., p. 202.
[21] Ibid., p. 203.
[22] Andre Gunder Frank, *Capitalism and Underdevelopment in Latin America* (New York, 1969); Samir Anim, *Le developpement inegal* (Paris, 1973); and Immanuel Wallerstein, *The Modern World System*, Vol. I., *Capitalist Agriculture and the Origins of the European Economy in the Sixteenth Century* (New York and London, 1974).
[23] *The Venture of Islam*, III, 186.

clotted prose style does not help matters. Yet in the concept of technicalism, Hodgson shows himself to have been an important, if unconventional, social thinker. Concepts such as industrialization and capitalism privilege certain aspects of the process by which the transformation took place, but they leave unexplained its astonishing capacity to effect far-reaching changes in even the noneconomic sectors. They are neither sufficiently precise, nor sufficiently general. For Hodgson, the very essence of the process was a cultural one: the transformation of one's way of looking at the world according to calculative rational principles. Here one senses the influence of the Weber of *The Protestant Ethic*. Indeed the concept of technicalism may be seen as an extended gloss on Weber's *rationalization* (though Hodgson argues that Weber's term drastically overstates the extent to which rationality is uniquely characteristic of the modern age). Technicalism finally is associated with certain moral qualities, most notably vastly greater efficiency and technical precision, and a certain kind of person, the autonomous individual of humane and cooperative spirit. As an intellectual construct, technicalism goes far toward illuminating the cultural aspects of the complex process by which the modern age has come into being.[24]

World history has a reputation of being the playground of dilettantes, full of airy generalities and poor metaphysics. Hodgson's secure grounding in the culture of a particular civilization, and his methodological self-consciousness (which in another person might have induced a severe case of intellectual paralysis), enabled him to bring an unaccustomed rigor to the study of world history. *The Venture of Islam*, for all its faults and quirky inconsistencies, reveals the many benefits that may derive from the attempt to place the history of Islamic civilization in a world historical context. Its lessons, therefore, go beyond the provincial confines of Islamic studies.

The Venture of Islam *and civilizational studies*

Few scholars today feel comfortable working with a concept as broad as *civilization*. Ours is a time of careful monographs, not of universal his-

[24] That is, the concept of technicalism is keyed to the requirements of a cultural history. It is largely congruent with classical modernization theory of the early 1960s in Hodgson's usage, and indeed the later term for him denotes the political and economic aspects of the Western Transmutation. While a form of "modernizationism," Hodgson's efforts to situate the process in a world context and in terms of the relationship between Europe and the rest of the world make him an interesting trasitional figure. Had he lived to complete the revisions of Book Six, I suspect that his ambivalences toward modernization theory would have become even more manifest.

tory. When assessing Hodgson's contribution to civilizational studies, however, one must remember that the study of civilizations had an honored place at The University of Chicago during the period he was writing *The Venture of Islam.* Although Hodgson struggles valiantly to rehabilitate the concept of civilization, I find this level of his analysis the most difficult to accept. Yet even here, the great care which he has taken to make himself understood makes a dialogue possible. Grant him his initial premises, and he can make a powerful case for himself. What is Hodgson's approach to civilizational studies? How does it inform his understanding of Islamic civilization?

Those who would utilize the concept of civilization must deal with the extensive criticisms that have been made of it.[25] A major difficulty facing those who have employed it has been the tendency to view civilizations as timeless essences whose fate is predetermined at the moment of inception by their constituent elements. Islamic civilization has frequently been viewed in this way. A second difficulty has been in distinguishing between *civilizations* and *cultures.* (How large a unit is the term "civilization" to include? A city-state? A literate tradition? An empire?) A third and related problem is that of determining where one civilization leaves off and another begins. (Viewed in one way, Christian Byzantium is a part of Greek civilization; viewed in another, it is a part of Christendom.) A final criticism is the culturalist bias of civilizational studies. What connections are to be made between the level of elite lettered culture (on which the study of civilizations necessarily operates), and the historically specific social and economic contexts in which the civilization is rooted, across regional and class lines? It is a merit of Hodgson's approach that he recognizes the cogency of these criticisms, and he seeks to provide answers to them.

Central to Hodgson's approach is the notion that cultures and civilizations are dynamic rather than static, and that they are characterized by internal differentiation and continuing dialogue with their formative ideals such that certain ideals may dominate at one point, only to recede later. Civilizations, then, are not determined once and for all by their intellectual traits (let alone essences), and they are not the prisoners of the dead hand of the past. A civilization, for Hodgson, is a compound culture, "a relatively extensive grouping of interrelated cultures insofar as they have shared in cumulative traditions in the form of high culture,

[25] See Robert McC. Adams, *The Evolution of Urban Society* (Chicago, 1966), and Ruth Tringham, "The Concept of 'Civilization' in European Archeology," in Jeremy A. Sabloff and C. C. Lamberg-Karlovsky, eds., *The Rise and Fall of Civilizations* (Menlo Park, 1974), for recent discussions of the use of the term.

on the urban, literate level."[26] As for the difficulty of deciding to which civilization a particular cultural entity belongs, Hodgson sensibly points out that such questions cannot be conclusively resolved. For some purposes, Islamic civilization may be viewed as continuous with the Irano-Semitic tradition, and for others it is radically discontinuous. Hodgson is careful to define civilizations in an open-ended way, without reference to supposed life cycles: his discussions are exempt from hypostasizing so-called innate traits in particular civilizations.

What is Islamic about Islamic civilization? Hodgson's response reveals his general approach to civilizational studies. It is the presence of Islamic ideals, he argues, that marks off Islamic civilization from those that preceded it. These ideals provide the central standards of legitimation of the society. The dialogue of successive generations of Muslims with these ideals, that is, with the Quranic message as revealed to Muhammad, constitutes (in a sense constructs) the civilization of Islam. In this dialogue, there have been two major variants: the Sunni tradition and the Shi'a tradition. The main bearers of these ideals at any one time were not numerous, certainly never as extensive as the literate population. Rather, their numbers were limited to the small group of individuals who in every age have taken for themselves the task of seeking to realize these ideals. This group Hodgson calls the "piety-minded" (or later, the sharia-minded). The civilization produced by them can be considered in two dimensions. Most narrowly, it can be considered as religious, and the ensuing dialogue as a religious one. But it can also be considered in its wider, civilizational, aspects (including Christians, Jews, and other non-Muslims insofar as they participated in the dialogue). To clearly distinguish the latter from the former, Hodgson has coined the term *Islamicate* (on the model of Italianate).

The enormous extent of Islamic civilization also poses a problem for Hodgson. How is it possible to speak meaningfully about a civilization which spanned the Afro-Eurasian ecumene from Morocco to China, and which has endured from the seventh century until the present? The crticisms of those interested in tracing the social and economic history of specific parts of the Islamic world acquire pertinence at this point. Hodgson agrees that a civilizational history cannot address the diverse experiences of Muslims (especially nonelite ones) living in a variety of historically specific times and places. There is thus an important range of problems about which Hodgson concedes that he can say little. But, he argues, if one is interested in the unity, rather than the diversity, of the

[26] *The Venture of Islam*, I, 91.

historical experience of Muslims, then the concept of civilization acquires congency, and social and economic historians can have little to contribute at this level of analysis. There is a unity to Islamic civilization, at least until modern times, because Muslims (unlike Christians and Buddhists) remained in contact with one another and with the formative ideals of their civilization. There is an integrality to their dialogue down through the ages which makes Islamic civilization susceptible to being studied historically. Muslims shared a common point of departure, a common vocabulary, and (until relatively late) several common languages for discussing a range of important topics.[27]

Hodgson's approach to civilizational studies has some important advantages. The notion of a dialogue with the formative ideals permits him to conceive of an Islamic civilization that is sufficiently generously defined so as to admit all manner of subdialogues, parallel (often competing) cultural traditions, and regional variations. There is less chance of succumbing to the tendency to hypostasize with such a point of departure. Most importantly, this approach enables him to make room for a full treatment of the Shi'a variant of Islamic civilization in ways that neatly avoid having to refer to a putative Sunni "orthodox" interpretation. By thus escaping from the sterile and shortsighted debate over what "real" Islam might be, Hodgson has performed a major service. Similarly, his insistence on situating the origins of Islamic civilization in the context of the citied tradition of the Nile-to-Oxus, or what he calls (following Toynbee) "Irano-Semitic" civilization, makes clear the extent to which the rise of Islam represents a logical development of historic trends in the region and in the ecumene, as well as a sharp break with them. It also reduces the dangers of implicitly assimilating the destiny of Islamic civilization to that of the Arabs, who were its first carriers. Hodgson comes to this conclusion not out of some unacknowledged philo-Iranism, or an anti-Arab bias, but as a consequence of his efforts to study Islamic civilization in a world historical context.

An important aspect of Hodgson's method of civilizational studies is the contention that the cultural dialectic is a twofold process: the dialogue of the piety-minded with the formative ideals of the civilization, on the one hand, and the less direct relationship between the material bases of the society and its cultural products (in short, its civilization), on the other. As we have seen, Hodgson posits that under agrarian conditions, all civilizations ("Western" as well as "oriental") were much more

[27] See Hodgson's essay, "The Unity of Later Islamic History," *Journal of World History*, 5 (1960), 879–914, for a discussion of the problem of unity.

directly constrained by their material surroundings than we are. Thus cultural florescences, whatever their duration and brilliance, could proceed only so far before they reached an impasse. On the surface, this seems to smack of either a shallow Marxism (prosperity = cultural greatness; depression = cultural decadence) or a crude organicism (civilizations have life cycles). Hodgson's argument is rather different. If all Agrarian-age civilizations (Western included) were limited in their capacity to generate continual innovation, then it follows that all were essentially conservative in their evaluation of prospective innovations. Consequently, in considering them, we must shed our modern biases which tend to equate success with change. The function of education in the Agrarian age, Hodgson contends, was less to teach students how to think than to teach them how to act, less to study observable facts than to inculcate cultural norms. In pursuing this line of reasoning, he arrives at a major reevaluation of the civilization of the middle periods of Islamic history (945–1500 C.E.), which had commonly been regarded as a period of decline. I shall have more to say about this aspect of his work in the next section. Finally, questions of decadence, or some supposed law of civilizations whereby decay and disintegration are inevitable, are ruled invalid when approached from such a perspective. Did the Middle East decline, or did the West rise? The most that Hodgson will allow is that "a society may encourage investment in one sort of opportunity so heavily that it cannot quickly marshal its resources in other directions when new circumstances make other sorts of investment more profitable." Thus "the very excellence with which Islamicate culture had met the needs of the Agrarian age may have impeded its advance beyond it."[28]

Hodgson's theory of civilizational studies suggests than an inherently conservative culture will be offset by the periodic interventions of the men and women of conscience in each era, whose insights forge new strands in the ongoing cultural dialogue. This approach is successful as a pedagogical device. The reader is encouraged to take seriously the historical context in which these figures lived, and not merely to content himself with the putative contributions of each to Islamic history. Without this method, the tendency of Hodgson's mind toward abstract thinking would totally overwhelm, and his argument would be less convincing. Yet there are serious objections which can be raised against a theory of civilizations which places such weight upon the experiences of a few quite atypical individuals. Not only is Hodgson's theory too much the affair of Weberian virtuosos; in addition, we are not informed of the

[28] *The Venture of Islam*, III, 204.

criteria by which they have been selected. Hodgson's piety-minded individuals appear larger than life, while ordinary Muslim men and women, who had no such exalted notions of the faith of a culture in which they were embedded, are largely unrecognized, their concerns unvoiced, their connections with the great tradition (and other lesser traditions) largely unexamined.

Hodgson's approach to civilization is vulnerable on other grounds as well. A major conceptual problem lies in his idea that civilizations can be characterized by their formative ideals. But, we may inquire, how does one select which of the numerous ideals that can be extracted from the Quran and other authoritative Muslim writings is to be regarded as formative? While the problem of deciding what constitutes "real Islam" is put out by the door (by admitting a plurality of dialogues), it returns by the window. Hodgson's personal moral stance was so bound up with his sense of what Islamic civilization was all about that his views about what constituted its formative ideals cannot help but be influenced. By emphasizing the personal moral responsibility of the individual Muslim before God, and even more so by advancing an interpretation of the principles of the *sharia,* which emphasizes the rights of individuals against the collectivity (especially the state), Hodgson has boldly challenged the less moralistic interpretations of Gibb, von Grunebaum, and others. He has also laid himself open to the same charge of hypostasizing which he levels at others. Thus while Hodgson's intensely personal and obsessively systematic approach to civilizational studies has much to commend it, it is by no means exempt from criticism. In the search for a more adequate approach to civilizational studies, the idealist assumptions on which it is constructed (despite the sophistication of their presentation) continue to be, for this reader at least, unacceptable. The important question remains: is it possible to write meaningfully about civilizations without making such assumptions? What seems needed is an approach to culture which makes of it neither a mere reflection of material conditions nor the unfolding of an ideal essence through time. For all its Eurocentrism, the more open, less systematic approach of McNeill seems preferable.

The patterns of Islamic history

The Venture of Islam has a kind of architectonic structure, the complex patterning of whose major components is traced on a variety of different levels of abstraction. It also invokes a rather different periodization of Islamic history, or rather a whole series of them. What sort of Islamic history does this produce? How does Hodgson's version of that history jibe with the standard accounts? What, finally, are the chief advantages of his effort to insert Islamic history into a world historical context? In addressing these questions, I shall necessarily leave aside the numerous points of detail where Hodgson has erred, or where recent developments in the field have passed him by, since in a work of this scope there must inevitably be many. First, we look at Hodgson's interpretation of Islamic history.

On the most general level of abstraction, it is Hodgson's thesis that Islamic civilization served chiefly to institutionalize the more egalitarian and cosmopolitan tendencies in Irano-Semitic culture, giving a key role to the urban and communal expectations associated with the prominence of mercantile interests in the Nile-to-Oxus region. In a posthumous article, he argued that the development of these egalitarian and cosmopolitan features within the region has been the chief role of Islam in world history.[29]

On another level of abstraction, the history of Islamic civilization can be divided into three parts, the Formative Period, the Middle Periods, and the period of the Gunpowder Empires and Modern Times. One volume of *The Venture of Islam* is devoted to each. In the Formative Period (*c.* 600–945 C.E.), the chief developments are the replacement of Syriac and Pahlavi as the main vehicles of culture by Arabic, the emergence of a single comprehensive Muslim community in place of the earlier communal divisions of the region, and the failure of efforts to reestablish an absolutist agrarian empire, resulting in the development of a new, more flexible kind of social order. The Middle Periods (945–1503 C.E.) are marked by the emergence of an international society based upon the separation between state and society, the diffusion of Sufism, the development of Persian as a second major language of Islamic high culture, and the coming to maturity of the dialogue between the intellectual traditions. The Middle Periods were for Hodgson the high point of Islamic civilization, in which a cosmopolitan high culture coexisted with a society of great flexibility. The third phase of Islamic history, that of the Gunpowder Empires and Modern Times, is characterized by the reassertion of old communal and regional divisions within the ecumene. New regional empires were formed: the Mughal, the Safavi, and the Ottoman, but they only partly compensated for the political weakness of post-Mongol regimes. Cultural conservatism now worked to close off

[29] Marshall G. S. Hodgson, "The Role of Islam in World History," *International Journal of Middle East Studies*, I, I (1970), 99–123.

opportunities for innovation. Neither the revived Shi'ism of the Safavis, nor the Falsafized Sunnism of the Mughals and Ottomans proved adequate to the task of renewal. Simultaneously, the world historical context was altered by the rise of the West and the onset of the age of Technicalism. This sealed the fate of Islamic civilization – together with all other civilizations based upon major religious heritages.

Still a third level of analysis can be distinguished. *The Venture of Islam* is divided into six books, corresponding to the six phases in the development of the civilization: the period of Genesis (to 692 C.E.), the High Caliphate (to 945), the International Civilization (to 1258), the Age of Mongol Prestige (to 1503), the era of the Gunpowder Empires (to *c.* 1800) and Modern Times. This periodization of Islamic history contrasts revealingly with the standard dynastic chronological framework. It stresses continuities across dynastic lines and is keyed to the main phases in the evolution of civilization. The six periods are anchored, as we shall see, by a set of social and cultural features (themselves forming ideal types) which enable Hodgson to set off one from another. The unity of Islamic history is above all dependent upon the integrality of the dialogue down through history.

Alongside these periodizations of Islamic history, Hodgson offers a number of specialized chronologies which focus on more specific developments. For example, there are tables that contrast significant developments in Islamic civilization with contemporary events in China, India, and Europe. There are also charts of Muslim philosophic schools, Sufi brotherhoods, Shi'a geneologies, belletrists, and the like. As the canvas on which he works becomes larger, Hodgson adds tables that show events across the Islamic world, region by region. In this way, he gets the reader to develop an eye for tracing particular strands of Islamic culture, while simultaneously keeping the civilization itself in world historical context. We have definitely left behind the world of linear political time, to enter a realm in which broad historical patterns are orchestrated in ways that contrast with and reinforce one another in a variety of rhythms and tempi over the period of a millennium. In itself, this constitutes an enormous enrichment of our understanding of the unfolding of the civilization of Islam through time.

As a cultural history, *The Venture of Islam* traces the evolution of the intellectual traditions of the Nile-to-Oxus region from their inception to their final undermining in the modern world. Hodgson distinguishes three main intellectual traditions that have operated in the region in the post-Axial age: prophetic monotheism, Greek natural science and philosophy, and the Persian imperial tradition. With the coming of Islam, these traditions did not die out but were reformulated along Islamicate lines. The first and most important was the development of the Islamic religious sciences: Quranic exegesis, *hadith* criticism, and the study of *fiqh*. Hodgson was concerned with showing how Islam refashioned and continued preexisting themes in the Irano-Semitic tradition of prophetic monotheism. The touchstone of his analysis is his emphasis upon the formative effect of the assertion of *shari* concepts of legal and social relations upon the social and political organization of the community of believers. The second major intellectual tradition which gradually became folded into the emerging Islamic cultural dialogue was the Persian tradition of absolutist rule. Hodgson shows how the development of the courtly culture of *adab* built upon, yet also transformed, this tradition as it came into dialogue with the other emerging Islamic intellectual traditions. The tradition of Greek natural science and philosophy (essentially the legacy of Hellenism) is the third major avenue along which Islamic thought tended to develop. Like the *adab* tradition, initially at odds with the concerns of the piety-minded, the tradition of *falsafah* gradually became incorporated into the Islamic dialogue, as a result especially of the work of al-Farabi and Ibn Sina. By the end of the High Caliphate, the intellectual traditions had achieved fully Islamic form. From then onward, their mutual interpenetration and interaction helped to shape the fabric of Islamic culture. By the sixteenth century, while the capacity for self-renewal of the civilizational dialogue had not totally disappeared, increasingly the natural tendencies toward cultural conservatism of the Agrarian age had reasserted themselves. Accordingly, the Safavi, no less than the Ottoman and the Mughal, efforts at a cultural renewal were unsuccessful. In modern times the Islamic heritage has had diminished relevance to Muslims, as under the impact of technicalism, it no less than the other principal religious heritages had had to contend with a radically altered context for historic action. This, in highly schematic form, is the structure of the history of Islamic culture as it is presented by Hodgson.

Corresponding to each of Hodgson's six phases of Islamic history is a political formation, presented in the guise of an ideal type: Arab rule, caliphal absolutism, the *ayan/amir* system, the military patronage stage, the gunpowder empires, modern nation-states. During the first phase of Islamic history, society was organized around the principle of the primacy of the Arabs. Political legitimacy was based upon the notion of *jama'a* – the necessity of unity among the ruling caste of Arab Muslims.

During the phase of caliphal absolutism, which began in late Marwanid times and continued till 945 C.E., the old tradition of Persian kingship powerfully influenced the organization of the state around a centralized imperial bureaucracy and army. Although many of the piety-minded opposed caliphal absolutism, for several centuries it constitued a potent principle of social and political organization. Ultimately, however, the forces of cosmopolitanism and egalitarianism in the region most clearly identified with mercantile interests found themselves overly constrained by such a system.

As a result, Hodgson argues, a decentralized and flexible new international society emerged in the Early Middle Period, with its own implicit balance of social forces. This society, which Hodgson characterizes as the *ayan/amir* system, showed a remarkable openness and malleability. Several important formative elements helped to secure this trend. One was the militarization of agrarian authority, a process that began during the phase of caliphal absolutism. Through the evolution of the institution of *iqta,* a new group of largely Turkish military rulers, the amirs, came into existence. The political structure of the state and the extraction of agrarian revenues were decentralized into many autonomous and quasi-autonomous units. The caliphate itself lapsed into political irrelevance. Meanwhile, over and against the amirs another powerful social force was emerging: the mercantile interests in the cities and the newly prominent *ulama,* or more generally, the ayan. Their strength derived from the legitimacy that the ulama incarnated as the chief interpreters of the sharia (whose dictates served to focus and organize the activities of the community) as well as from the medial economic position of the merchants. During this highly cosmopolitan phase of Islamic history, the cultural dialogue reached its widest extent, and the interaction among the various strands that composed it reached its greatest intensity. A final formative movement in this period was the granting of *droit de cité* to the exponents of *tariqa* Sufism, and the crystallization of the various *turuq.* This greatly increased the penetration of the faith into lower social orders and aided the process of its diffusion abroad.

The Mongol catastrophe put an end to the international society of the Early Middle Period and inauguarated a new phase of Islamic history: the age of Mongol prestige. The Islamic successor states that emerged in the wake of the Mongol conquest were powerfully influenced by the dynastic prestige of the conquerors. Hodgson develops the concept of the military/patronage state as a means of highlighting its characteristic social formation. The predominantly Turkish elites who held sway during this period conceived of the state administration and the army as extensions of the royal household. Following the Mongol example, they were great benefactors of culture, founders of cities, and builders of architectural masterpieces. The influence of steppe institutions upon the social and political life in the Nile-to-Oxus region reached its apex during this period.

As the sixteenth century began these states gave way to the more stable gunpowder empires of early modern times, among which the Mughal, Safavi, and Ottoman empires were the most important. The reassertion of the absolutist tradition in the region, together with the continuance and further development of many of the basic characteristics of the military patronage states, produced a new age of Muslim greatness both political (where their achievements are evident) and intellectual; although clearly marked by the conservative spirit, Hodgson argues that these regimes were far from stagnant culturally, and that some sectors experience significant innovation.

Of course, the forces of change were already flowing in another direction. With the advent of the age of Technicalism, human history entered a decisive phase. In this section of the work, Hodgson focuses first on the origins of the Western Transmutation, and then on its impact around the globe. European economic and political dominance over the lands of Islam is followed in our own century by the rise of nationalism and the emergence of nation states. While the idea of technicalism constitutes a potent conceptual tool, the literature upon which Hodgson draws in his treatment of the modern period is at least a generation out of date. Given the meager theoretical and empirical literature upon which he draws, it is remarkable how well he does.[30] Book 6 existed only in draft form at Hodgson's death, and has been published substantially as it was. This is unfortunate, as the weaknesses of Book 6 mar one's overall impressions of *The Venture of Islam*, and certainly lessen its suitability as an undergraduate text. There is a deeper cause for dissatisfaction with Book 6 to which Hodgson himself is sensitive: by the modern period, the concept of Islamic civilization has lost whatever utility it may once have had. The continuous cultural dialogue on which he bases the concept was profoundly disrupted by the reassertion of regional languages and tradi-

[30] For example, virtually all of the literature on the social and economic history of Turkey, Iran, and the Arab East has appeared since Book Six was written. While the bibliography includes such classics as Albert Hourani's *Ababic Thought in the Liberal Age* and Bernard Lewis's *The Emergence of Modern Turkey*, it is unclear from reading the text that Hodgson was able to make much use even of these works. Of theoretical literature, such works as Barrington Moore, Jr.'s *Social Origins of Dictatorship and Democracy* and Eric Wolf's *Peasant Wars of the Twentieth Century*, not to speak of the entire critical literature on modernization theories, have appeared since Book Six was written. There are worlds of thought and experience which separate the early 1960s, when this section was being written, from our own.

tions within the ecumene. Whatever international elite culture may once have existed was seriously undermined by 1800, such that (for example) Moroccan Muslims could communicate only with difficulty with their African or Indonesian coreligionists. In some ways it might have been a neater conclusion to end the work with the dawning of the age of Technicalism. But one can see why Hodgson was tempted to carry it up to the contemporary period. This makes it all the more regrettable that he did not live to revise the final sections of his manuscript.

For Hodgson, the unity of Islamic history was a function of the ongoing dialogue of successive generations of Muslims with the formative ideals of the civilization. Concretely, this meant a preoccupation with the elaboration of Islamic doctrine and piety by the *ulama,* the corps of religious specialists charged with maintaining the integrity and vitality of the faith. In this study the concept of the sharia looms as particularly important, since it provides the foundation for Hodgson's interpretation. It shapes his treatment of the Formative Period, provides the basic explanation of the operation of the *ayan/amir* system of the Middle Periods (where it reaches a kind of apotheosis), and constitutes (with the concept of Sufism, on which more in a moment) the guiding concept in explaining the unity of the later periods.

From the first pages of *The Venture of Islam* it is apparent that the term *sharia* has a special importance for Hodgson: it serves to designate not only Islamic law, but the core of the civilization. The origins of the religious impulses that gave rise to Islam, Hodgson traces to the ethical concerns of Irano-Semitic prophetic monotheism. The working out of the egalitarian and populistic implications of the original Quranic message provides the motive force of Islamic history. By the end of the Formative Period, a religious law binding on all Muslims had crystallized in response to the egalitarian and populistic concerns of the piety-minded. The sharia provided Muslims with a focus for self-realization: its social and legal patterns gradually penetrated virtually all aspects of life, determining the organization of the community and carving out an autonomous arena where the ulama were supreme, over and against the courtly culture of the Abbasids and their successors. The chapter in Book 2 on the Islamic vision of the sharia is a brilliant presentation of the process by which Islamic law came into being. There and in the following chapter on Muslim personal piety, Hodgson emphasizes the potency of the Quran and of the image of the early Islamic community in providing an authoritative model of the just society and a focal point for worship.

However convincingly presented, this analysis contains the seeds of those same essentialist difficulties that Hodgson has rightly deplored in the work of others. By the time that we reach the chapter "Cultural Patterning in Islamdom and the Occident," where he presents an extended contrast between the two civilizations in the thirteenth century, Hodgson presents the sharia as nothing less than the organizing principle of Islamic society. In a comparison between Christianity and Islam as frameworks of religious life, he underscores the contrast between a religion whose central theme is the demand for personal responsiveness to redemptive love in a corrupted world with one whose theme is the demand for personal responsibility for the moral ordering of the natural world. He then traces the practical implications of each for the organization of the social order and the elaboration of culture. Thus he emphasizes the contractualism of Muslim civilization (the primacy of the rights of the individual over the collective) against what he calls the hierarchical corporativism of the medieval Occident: the *ayan/amir* system contrasted with medieval feudalism, the arabesque contrasted with the Gothic cathedral. Hodgson's argument is a tour de force, but ultimately the level of abstraction at which it is pitched renders it unconvincing.

Sufism is the other major concept in Hodgson's discussion of the unity of the Islamic civilizational dialogue. Taken together, the sections of Sufism are one of the best concise presentations of the development of Islamic mysticism, a splendidly sensitive introduction to a complex and sprawling phenomenon. But as contrasted with his careful distinctions in presenting the concept of the sharia, Hodgson's discussion on Sufism is informed by no such analytical power. He defines Sufism as mysticism, but neither is ever adequately explained. Polymorphous and often profane, the variety of Sufism and its resistance to intellectualizing elude Hodgson's categories. Only on the level of high love mysticism (the Sufism of Bistami, Rumi, and al-Ghazali) can Hodgson bring to bear his elaborate conceptual schemes and his "science of compassion" in ways that inform and enlighten. Brief sections on how to read Sufi texts, and a sustained meditation on a passage from Rumi's *Masnavi,* demonstrate the appeal and cogency of this method. Against the Sufism of the popular turuq, saint cults, and curing practices, Hodgson is powerless. At this point, the limits of his cultural elitism come out most sharply. In his scandalized attitude toward the corruption and degeneracy of the popular brotherhoods, Hodgson brings to mind the puritanical moralism of the reforming ulama who are the chief heroes of *The Ventures of Islam.* Those who seek a sociological, rather than a merely logical, presentation of the role of Sufism in shaping the fabric of Islamic societies should look elsewhere.

Conclusion

As should be evident from the foregoing, I regard *The Venture of Islam* as a remarkably impressive achievement. It has a richness and complexity beside which all other accounts of Islamic civilization seem pale. In many ways, its appearance represents a culmination of the Western tradition of Islamic studies. Necessarily, such an undertaking must be a highly personal one, and this *The Venture of Islam* is to an unusual degree. Yet Hodgson was also unusually self-conscious of the epistemological assumptions of the tradition in which he had been trained, and has consistently sought to place Islamic civilization in a world historical context. It is this feature of the work, in my opinion, which gives it lasting importance. Otherwise the cranky personal obsessions that frequently threaten to distract the reader could not be kept successfully at bay. Because *The Venture of Islam* is both so personal and so relentlessly impersonal a work, it is a very great feat of the historical imagination.

Hodgson's most important achievement, and the place where he had the most to teach us all (non-Islamics scholars included), lies in his effort to devise a new framework for the writing of world history. After reading him, even those of us who never attempt a hemispheric interregional approach to world history will become aware of the pitfalls of any less inclusive approach; his *Venture* points to the necessity for a thoroughgoing reappraisal of many of our central assumptions about the historical process. By continually seeking to insert the story of Islamic civilization into the history of human literate society, Hodgson has broken sharply with the old paradigms and taken a major step toward a new kind of history. His use of ideal types and his careful definition of key concepts provide a refreshing change from the smug assumptions that have guided past efforts at a history of Islamic civilization. The attempt to situate the rise of the West in a world historical context, in particular, merits the serious attention of all those concerned to understand the great transmutation which separates us from the world we have lost.

Hodgson's attempt to rehabilitate civilization as a useful concept in historical studies (and hence in the orientalist tradition) is more problematical. As I have endeavored to show, the attempt rests, in the final analysis, on Hodgson's use of the concept of sharia. Despite a serious effort to divest the study of civilizations from racialist assumptions, hypostatizing, and other errors, the idealist assumptions which lie behind the concept of sharia push him irrevocably toward cultural essentialism and thereby vitiate much of his achievement. While denying that he is engaged in a search for the "real Islam," Hodgson's venture is one that ultimately seeks to identify Islam with its formative ideals, and thus transposes the search from the level of sect (e.g., Sunni vs. Shi'a) to that of the religion as a whole. To the extent that it is possible to write a history of a civilization without falling victim to the old mistakes, one can applaud Hodgson's effort. But to the extent that historians are increasingly concerning themselves with the social and economic history of Muslims, rather than with their "civilization," Hodgson's venture appears a splendid anachronism.

The Venture of Islam is both an original synthetic account of the civilization of Islam whole and entire and a textbook for university undergraduates. It has the virtues of both sorts of works: it is very teacherly in places (it offers advice on how to understand Persian miniatures, Sufi writings, the forms of Muslim piety, and the work of specific writers like Tabari, Rumi, and Ibn Khaldun among others), and very scholarly and stimulating in others. By seeking to cover the entire range of Islamic history, and to do so within a single narrative framework, it has made a unique and important contribution to historical scholarship. But there are some important defects in trying to do both things at once. Thus, for example, *The Venture of Islam* is written on so abstract a level that it is difficult to teach to undergraduates. It also presumes far too much of students (or even colleagues) in the way of background. It utilizes a complex and eccentric language which is often distracting, such that Hodgson's thought often seems overly dense and impenetrable. If in the end the work is successful both as text and as scholarly synthesis (on balance I believe that it is), this is due to the high level of the author's personal engagement, which tends to call forth a correspondingly high-level engagement on the part of the reader.

The Venture of Islam challenges the reader on a variety of levels at once in the manner of a Sufi tale. It is mentally and morally stretching both for rank beginners (who miss the esoteric, abstract discussions) and more experienced readers (who will find it full of stimulating insights, often wrongheaded *obiter dicta,* and methodological encomia). I have found it endlessly fascinating and provocative; despite its many difficulties, *The Venture of Islam* deserves the widest possible audience.